THE LAW OF TRADING

INCLUDING MARKETS
&
FAIRS

Barry Hough

ii

Published by Earlsgate Press

© Barry Hough

First published 1994

British Library Cataloguing in Publication Data

A catalogue record for this book is available from the British Library

ISBN 1-873439-01-6

Printed in Great Britain by
The Book Factory, 35-37 Queensland Road, London N7 7AH.

To Mary, Bradley and Robert.

PREFACE

As street trading has generated considerable interest and not a little controversy of late, a book devoted to a study of this subject seemed overdue. The aim of this book is to describe and evaluate the Law of England and Wales regulating street trading and markets and fairs. A book of this scope cannot provide an encyclopedic survey of the subject; instead it focuses upon the principal controls, whether derived from public or private law, to which traders become subject when trading on the street and in markets and fairs. The book also offers an introduction to the general principles of Administrative Law which, by virtue of their profound impact on the exercise of local authority powers, are an essential component in any evaluation of this subject.

The essential focus of the book is upon the relationship between the trader and regulatory authorities and not that which exists between the trader and customer. It also examines the powers and duties of market owners and their legal relationship with market traders.

Accordingly, some important issues affecting the rights of the buyers in markets, such as the law of market overt, have been omitted along with the subject of prostitution. I have, however, included a note of the obligations on street traders selling food to register their premises as well as a brief survey of the food hygiene standards by which they may be bound.

I have received unstinting kindness and assistance from a large number of individuals in the preparation of this book. In particular, I owe a debt of gratitude to my colleagues including Christopher Harding, for his assistance in matters relating to European Community Law, and to Professor Arrowsmith who read part of the manuscript. Lillian Stevenson and Meirion Derrick have also given generously of their time in helping me locate materials in the law library at the University of Wales, Aberystwyth. I would like to express my thanks to Mr Barry Hudson, for bringing to my attention several important matters affecting pedlars; also to my wife, Mary, for her devoted support, and to Sandra Whitcomb of Earlsgate Press for her work on the book.

The manuscript was substantially completed in early November 1993 but, by virtue of the generosity of the publishers, I have been able to introduce some later material and, in particular, to note the Government's proposals affecting Sunday trading and franchise rights in relation to local authority markets.

Barry Hough
Aberystwyth, December, 1993.

CONTENTS

TABLE OF CASES

xii   *The Law of Street Trading*

xx   *The Law of Street Trading*

TABLE OF STATUTES

BILLS BEFORE PARLIAMENT

SECONDARY LEGISLATION

REGULATIONS

EEC

PART I

GENERAL CONTROLS ON STREET TRADING

CHAPTER 1

CONTROLS ON THE PLACE OF TRADING

Whilst "street trading", as the name implies, most often refers to trading on the highway, it also includes trading which takes place in other places to which the public has access, and sometimes even on private land. [1] Trading in such areas may be subject to the provisions of one of the various licensing schemes which are considered later in this book. But the general law governing trading on the highway and other public places has an enduring significance, not least because many important forms of street trading fall outside the scope of the licensing schemes. Moreover, even licensed trading is not always immunised from the effects of the general law. It is therefore appropriate to examine the general controls on the places in which trading may occur.

The principle underlying all the following instances is that each area of land is vested in a legal person having either common law or statutory powers of ownership and control. English law essentially follows a private model of land ownership.

(i) Recreation Grounds

Royal parks are placed under the control of the Secretary of State for the Environment. [2] Statute [3] confers a power to make regulations

---

[1] For the purposes of the street trading code, para. 1 (1) of Schedule 4 of the Local Government (Miscellaneous Provisions) Act 1982 defines "street" so as to include "any road, footway, beach or other area to which the public have access without payment". Thus "street" can include such places as markets held on private land.
[2] Originally the Commissioner of Works whose powers were ultimately vested in the Secretary of State by virtue of SI 1970/1681.

for the management of the parks. These are currently contained in the Royal and Other Parks and Gardens Regulations, 1977 of which reg 4 (5) prohibits trading in a park for which the written permission of the Secretary of State has not been obtained. Accordingly, a photographer taking photographs of passers-by could be convicted of an offence under the Regulations when trading in The Mall, which is part of St. James's Park, London. [4]

Other parks and recreation grounds are usually vested in the local authority and are often subject to by-laws made under a variety of different statutory powers, such as those conferred by the Public Health Act 1875, s. 164, the Open Spaces Act 1906, s.15 and the Local Government Act 1972, s. 235. [5] The latter power is a broad one enabling local authorities to make by-laws for the good rule and government of their area, and for the suppression of nuisances. Street trading is most likely to be controlled under by-laws made in accordance with these powers.

(ii) Village and Town Greens

A village or town green is land which has either been set aside under statute for the exercise or recreation of the inhabitants of a locality, or land over which such inhabitants have a customary right to indulge in lawful sports and past times. [6] Any such area had to be registered under the Commons Registration Act 1965. If its owner could not be ascertained, it vested in the local authority for the area.

By-laws enacted for the prevention of nuisances and preservation of order enable local authorities to control trading activities on village and town greens. [7]

---

[3] The Parks Regulation Act 1872, amended by the Parks Regulation (Amendment) Act 1926.
[4] *Burgess v. McCracken* (1986) 150 JP 529, distinguishing *Newman v. Lipman* [1950] 2 All ER 832)
[5] See *infra* Chapter 3.
[6] Commons Registration Act 1965, s.22.
[7] Enacted under the Commons Act 1899.

In the absence of lawful authority, such as an immemorial custom, [8] it is a public nuisance to place any "thing" on a village green if it interrupts the use or enjoyment of the green. [9] This is sufficiently wide to prevent the setting up of stalls and may also prevent a trader from placing his goods upon the ground if the use or enjoyment of the green is interrupted. [10]

A stall holder may also commit a public nuisance if he or she encroaches onto a green. [11] Trading from a fixed position without a stall may also constitute a public nuisance since there is an "occupation of the soil". [12]

(iii) Foreshore [13]

The foreshore is property owned by the Crown subject to any grant. Although many activities are tolerated upon the foreshore, strictly, the public has no general right of passage along it, unless there is a lawfully dedicated right of way. [14] More extensive rights can be acquired by prescription or custom, and these an be enforced if sufficiently proved in evidence. In *Mercer v. Denne*, [15] for example, fisherman were able to establish a customary right to dry nets upon the beach at Walmer.

---

[8] See e.g., *Elwood v. Bullock* (1844) 6 QB 383.

[9] By the Commons Act 1876, s. 29 "an encroachment on or inclosure of a town or village green, also any erection thereon or disturbance or interference with or occupation of the soil thereof which is made otherwise than with a view to the better enjoyment of (the green)" is deemed to be a public nuisance.

[10] Much will, of course, turn on what constitutes "interruption". A strict interpretation may be possible by analogy with *Wolverton UDC v. Willis* [1962] 1 All ER 243.

[11] Commons Act 1876, s.12

[12] *Ibid.*

[13] This is the land laying between the high water mark of medium high tide between spring and neap tides and low water mark: Limitation Act 1980 Sch 1 para 11 (3); *A G v. Chambers* (1854) 4 De G M & G 206. The meaning of "low water mark" depends upon the context, but it should normally be understood to mean the line which is low water mark from time to time: *Anderson v. Alnwick DC* [1993] 3 All ER 613. Note that trading on the foreshore may also be street trading: *supra* n. (1).

[14] *Blundell v. Catterall* (1821) 5 B & Ad 268; *Llandudno Urban Council v. Woods* [1899] 2 Ch. 705. The public, however, has a right of access for the purposes of navigation or fishing.

[15] [1905] 2 Ch 538.

In the absence of customary rights, or the consent of the owner of the foreshore, trading activities will normally constitute a trespass. Trading (including the placing of stalls on the seashore) may also be regulated by by-laws made under the provisions of s. 82 of the Public Health Acts (Amendment) Act 1907. [16]

(iv) Private Land

A trader normally commits a trespass where he goes onto private land to trade without the consent of the occupier. Trespass consists in an interference with another's right of possession of land. To maintain an action it need only be shown that the plaintiff has a right of possession in the land trespassed upon.

A trespass may be committed where, for example, a door to door salesman enters upon land belonging to another without consent, or where a trader, lacking permission, places a stall in a field in which an informal market is conducted, or where trading occurs partly on a public highway and partly on private land and permission has not been obtained. [17] Unless the trader has the consent of the person in possession of the land for any of these activities he or she will be a trespasser. With consent, the trader becomes a "licensee". Express permission, or an express licence, is unnecessary if it can be implied from the circumstances. It has been held that an implied right to call at someone's house arises where access to the property is by way of an unlocked gate. [18] A trespass would occur, however, if the garden gate were locked, or if a notice were displayed refusing admittance.

The occupier of land is normally free to revoke the implied licence at any time by requesting the person on his land to leave it. Such a person becomes a trespasser only after a reasonable time has elapsed sufficient to enable him to leave the premises. [19]

---

[16] Eg, *Anderson v. Alnwick DC, supra* n. (13).

[17] *Pugh v. Pigden & Powley* (1987) JP 664.

[18] *Robson v. Hallett* [1967] 2 QB 939.

[19] *Robson v. Hallett, ibid.* A comprehensive study of licences is beyond object of this book but reference can be made, for example, to Megarry & Thompson, *Megarry's Manual of Real Property*, 7th edit (1993) Ch. 12.

As we shall see, because a highway is normally dedicated only for free passage, activities such as trading from a pitch or stall on the highway will normally fall outside the dedication and so amount to a trespass.

(v) Highways: the Right of the Public at Common Law

Highways, along which supplies and customers must travel, have been described as the life-blood of many businesses. [20] This applies with even greater force to the street trader for whom the highway often provides the place of business. It is essential to understand the legal rules governing the use of the highway because they go to the heart of the regulation of street trading.

What Constitutes a Highway?

At common law, a highway is a way over which there exists a public right of passage. This right is one which allows "all of Her Majesty's subjects at all seasons of the year freely and at their will to pass and repass without let or hindrance. [21] Whilst the highway may be dedicated subject to certain conditions, (for example, as to the class of traffic which may use it) a way cannot be a highway unless the public has a right to use it.

This definition is wide enough to include footpaths, [22] lay-bys, [23] "service roads", [24] a pedestrian precinct, [25] bridleways [26] and grass verges.

For the purposes of the Highways Act 1980, s.328 and unless the context otherwise requires, the meaning of "highway" is extended to mean the whole or part of a highway other than a ferry or waterway. Where a highway passes over a bridge or through a

---

[20] Orlik (1992) 136 Sol. Jo. 891-3.

[21] *Ex p. Lewis* (1888) 2 QBD 191,197, Wills J .

[22] *Wolverton UDC v. Willis* [1962] 1 All ER 243.

[23] *Nagy v. Weston* [1965] 1 WLR 280.

[24] *Redbridge London Borough Council v. Jaques* [1970] 1 WLR 1604.

[25] *Hirst and Agu v. Chief Constable of West Yorkshire* (1986) 85 Cr App Rep 143 ; *Waite v. Taylor* (1985) 149 JP 551.

[26] Highways Act 1980, s. 329.

tunnel these are also taken, for the purposes of the Act, to be a part of the highway.

The Right of the Public in Relation to the Highway

It is often mistakenly thought that the ownership of the highway is vested in the public. This is not so. The sub-soil beneath the highway belongs *prima facie* to the owner of the land adjoining it. If the land on either side of the highway is vested in different owners, each is the owner of the sub-soil as far as the centre of the highway. If the highway is maintained at the public expense, the sub-soil is vested in the highway authority. In effect, however, it is still "private" land.

Principles of private law underpin the traditional approach to determining the public's rights in relation to the highway. These rights are narrowly defined. This is clearly illustrated in the leading case of *Harrison v. Duke of Rutland* [27] where a highway ran across a grousemoor owned by the defendant. The plaintiff had gone onto the highway to disrupt a grouse shoot, but was removed from the area by the defendant's men. He brought an action for damages for false imprisonment and assault; the defendant counter-claimed that the plaintiff was a trespasser on the highway.

It was held that the ownership of the sub-soil remained with the defendant even though a public highway ran over the land. The public highway was merely an "easement" or a permission for the public to pass over the land. Since the plaintiff had not intended to pass and repass along the highway, his purpose fell outside those for which the highway was dedicated. It was thus unlawful and constituted a trespass.

The highway is thus dedicated for *limited* purposes. This approach permits at least two levels of control. First the courts examine the kind of activity in question. At this stage the court may decide that the activity is not of a *permissible kind*. [28] If, however, the activity is one which is normally lawful-such as passing and repassing along the highway-the court can still restrain it by applying a second level of controls which examines

---

[27] [1893] 1 QB 142.

[28] E.g., trading from a stationary van: *Pitcher v. Lockett* [1966] Crim L.R. 283.

the *purpose* for which the activity is carried out. Policy issues inform both stages of this analysis.

(i) The Kinds of Lawful User
Even in *Harrison* there is confusion concerning what activities are permissible on the highway. Lord Esher MR was careful to stress that the public's easement over the highway was not limited to passing and repassing:

"Highways are, no doubt, dedicated *prima facie* for the purpose of passage; but things are done upon them by everybody which are recognised as being rightly done, and so constituting a reasonable and usual mode of using a highway as such. If a person on a highway does not transgress such reasonable and usual mode of using it, I do not think that he will be a trespasser." [29]

Both Kay and and Lopes LJJ, however, thought that the public's right of passage was legally absolute. Any other use would be a trespass against the owner of the sub-soil. Nevertheless, Kay LJ, accepted [30] that the highway is regularly used for other purposes, but he insisted that such uses would be a trespass against the owner of the sub-soil. Most instances, would, in his opinion, be too trivial to justify legal proceedings.

For the majority in *Harrison* the highway is dedicated solely for free passage. This means that stationary forms of street trading fall outside the scope of the dedication.[30a]

Some liberalisation of these rules benefits uses reasonably incidental to a right of passage. These are lawful uses of the highway provided that they are exercised in a reasonable manner. As Forbes J. observed in *Hubbard v. Pitt*, [31] this means that the tired pedestrian may rest upon the highway, a motorist may attempt a minor repair, and theatre goers may queue for tickets upon the pavement, provided these uses last only for a "reasonable" duration. And even these "incidental" uses may become unlawful if

---

[29] *Harrison v. The Duke of Rutland, supra* n. (27) at p. 146-7.
[30] *Ibid.* p 152.
[30a] Although they may become lawful if licensed under one of the relevant schemes: See *infra* p.15.
[31] [1976] QB 142.

they are so unreasonable in extent as to go beyond what the court understands to be the purpose of dedication of the highway. It was made clear in *Iveagh v. Martin* [32] that these principles do not benefit static forms of street trading:

"On a highway.... I may stoop to tie up my shoe lace, but I may not occupy a pitch and invite people to come upon it and have their hair cut. I may let my van stand long enough to deliver and load goods, but I must not turn my van into a permanent stall." [33]

In sum, these principles have far-reaching implications for street trading. They suggest that a distinction could be drawn between stationary and peripatetic forms of trading. Whilst the former are *prima facie* unlawful, the latter, such as pedlars, would *prima facie* seem to enjoy more extensive rights. They do pass and re-pass upon the highway and so their activities would seem to fall within the categories of permitted user. Nevertheless, the courts have not surrendered a jurisdiction to control even these kinds of trader since their purpose is not connected with the right of passage. Their journey is incidental to their trade. [34]

Highway Dedicated Subject to Street Trading

Exceptionally, a highway may be dedicated- or may be presumed to have been dedicated- subject to the rights of street traders. The right of the public to pass freely along the highway is then subject to the rights of the traders to operate on the highway. An example of this occurred where a street was laid out *after* a grant of an express right of market applying to the same site. [35] The rights of the public to use the highway were subject to the right of the market owner to conduct his market.

The preservation of customary street trading has sometimes demanded a generous interpretation of principle, which the courts have been willing to undertake as a recognition that it can sometimes have an important social utility. This was so where an ancient custom of placing "booths" on a highway during an ancient

---

[32] [1961] 1 QB 232, 273 Paull J.
[33] See also *Hickman v. Maisey* [1900] 1 QB 752, per A L Smith L.J. at 755.
[34] See *infra* pp. 11-12.
[35] *A G v. Horner* (1886) 11 App Cas 66.

fair would have been unlawful if the courts had not been prepared to presume a conditional dedication of the highway in question. The decision is a generous one because of the absence of any evidence that the highway was laid out after the fair was established. [36] Such cases remind us that it is unrealistic to regard the right of passage as absolute and show also how the straining of legal principle is sometimes necesssary to produce satisfactory results.

(ii) The Purpose of Lawful User
Although a use may be of such a kind that it *prima facie* falls within the scope of the dedication, it may nevertheless be unlawful because of the purpose for which it is undertaken. This is capable of having far-reaching effects for street traders because the law *may*, at least in some circumstances, regard the commercial exploitation of the highway as illegitimate. For example, even if a person passes up and down upon the highway - an activity which may appear to be within the dedication - it does not necessarily follow that his actions are lawful. It depends upon the purposes for which that person is on the highway. In *R v. Pratt,* [37] merely walking upon the highway for an illegal purpose constituted a trespass. In this case the defendant travelled along a public highway armed with a gun and accompanied by a dog. The dog was sent onto private land to send up pheasants which Pratt then shot.

Similarly, in the well known case of *Hickman v. Maisey,* [38] the defendant, a "racing tout", walked up and down a 15 yard stretch of the public highway watching horses in training upon the plaintiff's land. It was held that he was a trespasser since his purpose was not to exercise his right of passage but to act in connection with his business.

Some objections may be raised to this approach. At a fundamental level, it is uncertain what the inquiry into purpose is designed to test. Presumably it is only where the purpose of the user is the exercise of the right of passage that the purpose is lawful. Yet few use the highway with this as their ultimate purpose. They have other goals in view. Use of the highway is a means to an end. So the inquiry seems to test the end results of the user. This seems to

---

[36] *Elwood v. Bullock* (1844) 6 Q B 383.
[37] 4 E & B 860.
[38] [1900] 1 QB 752.

be unworkeable because it invites value judgments about which goals are socially acceptable. For example, the racing tout's purpose was held to make his passing and repassing unlawful. Had he been, for example, a person pacing up and down whilst waiting for a bus, the activity would have been lawful. In each case the actual use of the highway would have been similar. Is it desirable to distinguish them? It is suggested that a use which is *prima facie* within the dedication should not become unlawful merely because of the ultimate objective of the use.

Finally, *Hickman* attacks commercial user. The inference is that passing and repassing with a view to profit is unlawful. This suggests that even the peripatetic trader's legal position may be a precarious one. If pressed rigourously this may have surprising consequences. Proprietors of mobile shops and ice cream vans may all find that they are trespassing on the highway since they are conducting their business there in much the same way as the defendant in *Hickman v. Maisey*. Such results are arguably unacceptable.

Statutory Controls on Highway Use

Highway authorities are under a statutory duty both to assert and to protect the rights of the public over a highway for which they are the highway authority. Local authorities also have a discretion to protect public rights over highways in their area for which they are not the highway authority. [39] In addition, highway authorities have a common law power to remove obstructions from the highway [40] and this power survives the enactment of the Highways Act 1980. [41] There may be circumstances in which it is under a duty to exercise this power. [42] A highway authority which does not take action to remove street trading which is an obstruction of the highway may not fulfil its statutory and common law duties.

---

[39] S.130 (1) and (2) of the Highways Act 1980. On the nature and scope of this duty see *Re Guyer's Application* [1980] 2 All ER 520.

[40] *Bagshaw v. Buxton Local Board of Health* (1875) 1 Ch.D. 220.

[41] Highways Act 1980, s.333.

[42] *Associated Picture Houses v. Wednesbury Corporation* [1948] 1 KB 223.

Obstruction of the Highway

Statutory and other rules serve, in effect, to make some forms of street trading *prima facie* a criminal offence. Of these the most important in practice is the offence of obstruction of the highway. The common law offence of public nuisance, [43] which is founded on essentially similar principles to the offence of obstruction, is also available, but its practical importance is diminished following the introduction of the statutory offence. Before considering the statutory offence, it should be noted that the street trading code provides an alternative means of preventing obstruction of the highway. For instance, a licence may be refused where undue interference to traffic is likely to be caused. [44] Further, the licence will normally include a "principal" term governing the place in which trading is permitted [45] Under para 10 (c) of the code, a person who contravenes such a term will be guilty of an offence. [46]

The offence of obstruction is created by s.137 of the Highways Act 1980. This provides:

"If a person without lawful authority or excuse, in any way wilfully obstructs the free passage along a highway he shall be guilty of an offence and shall be liable to a fine not exceeding level 3 on the standard scale." [47]
Obstruction of the highway may lead to arrest. [48]

---

[43] A public nuisance is also a tort.

[44] Para. 3 (6) of Schedule 4 of the Local Government (Miscellaneous Provisions) Act 1982. The provisions of the code are considered in Ch. 10.

[45] *Ibid.* Para 4 (1) & (2).

[46] Certain forms of street trading are normally exempted from the licensing regimes (see para 1(2) of the code) and here it may be more difficult to establish "lawful authority".

[47] By s.17 of the Criminal Justice Act 1991, the new scale maxima are as follows: Level 1 £200; Level 2 £500; Level 3 £1000; Level 4 £2,500; Level 5 £5,000. Section 18 of the Criminal Justice Act 1991 (as substituted by s. 65 of the Criminal Justice Act 1993) requires the Magistrates' Courts, before fixing the amount of a fine, to inquire into the financial circumstances of the offender. The fine must reflect the seriousness of the offence, and the circumstances of the case as well as the offender's financial circumstances..

[48] Police and Criminal Evidence Act 1984, s.25 (3) (d) (v).

What Constitutes an Obstruction?

It is possible to interpret s.137 so that an obstruction occurs only where free passage along the highway is prevented or seriously impeded. This focuses upon the *consequences* of the encroachment and would impose a criminal penalty only where the encroachment has significant adverse consequences for other highway users.

An alternative construction would favour the view that any encroachment onto the highway is an obstruction *per se*. It would not matter that the encroachment was of a minor character, nor that highway users were not substantially inconvenienced. This approach would seriously curtail the activities of the stationary street trader operating, for example, from a barrow or stall, as well as those of the itinerant trader who stopped to make sale in one place but who remained there for an unreasonable period.

Although purporting to chart something of a middle course between these two extremes, in practice the courts have steered nearer to the second and more restrictive. Lord Parker C.J. emphasised the orthodox approach in *Redbridge London BC v. Jaques*:

"..any erection of a structure which for a period and not merely temporarily prevents free passage of the public or vehicles to *every* part of the road is an obstruction." [49].

The decision is one which imposes controls upon the activity of the trader regardless of whether the public is actually inconvenienced. The encroachment is sufficient by itself because it denies the public access to part of the highway. The severity of this approach can be seen in *Pitcher v. Lockett* . [50] Here a trader was guilty of obstruction where he parked his hot dog van in a line of other parked vehicles. It was these vehicles and not the van which caused traffic to deviate, yet the van was nevertheless held to be an obstruction:

"As soon as the van turned itself into a shop it ceased to make a reasonable use of the road."

---

[49] [1970] 1 WLR 1604 at p. 1606 emphasis supplied. See also *A G v. Wilcox* (1938) 36 LGR 593.
[50] [1966] Crim. LR 283.

It makes no difference that, despite the encroachment on the highway, the public can still pass substantially unimpeded. [51] Accordingly, it is not necessary to allege or call evidence to show that any particular person is in fact obstructed. [52]

"Wilful"

An obstruction is said to be "wilful" if it is "purposely" and "deliberately " placed on the highway. [53] There is no further requirement of *mens rea*. It only has to be shown that the defendant's action had the effect of obstructing the highway. [54]

"Lawful Authority or Excuse"

(i) Burden of Proof
There is some confusion as to whether it is for the defendant or the prosecution to show that the activity took place without lawful authority or excuse. In *Nagy v. Weston* [55] and *Hirst & Agu v. Chief Constable of West Yorkshire* [56] the court held that the burden lay on the prosecution. This appears to conflict, however, with s.101 of the Magistrates' Courts Act 1980 which appears to place the burden of proving lawful excuse onto the defendant.

(ii) Lawful authority
An obstruction may occur with lawful authority, if, for example, it is authorised by statute, [57] or under the authority of a local authority's licence or consent, or a pedlar's certificate. [58]

Informally Acquired Rights

As we have seen, a trader who has the benefit of a street trading licence will normally have a defence if prosecuted for obstruction of

---

[51] *Homer v. Cadman* (1886) 16 Cox CC 51.
[52] *Wolverton Urban District Council v. Willis* [1962] 1 All ER 243.
[53] *Nagy v. Weston* [1965] 1 All ER 78; *Hirst and Agu v. Chief Constable of West Yorkshire* (1986) 151 JP 304, at 311.
[54] *Arrowsmith v. Jenkins* [1963] 2 QB 561, 567 per Lord Parker C.J.
[55] [1965] 1 All ER 78.
[56] *Supra* n. (53).
[57] As in the case of a statutory market.
[58] *Hirst and Agu's case, supra* n (53) at p 310.

the highway. He has the benefit of an express grant of authority. One question is whether a trader can *informally* acquire a right to trade, in other words, whether a "lawful excuse" for a *prima facie* obstruction can be acquired independently of a valid licence or consent. This has arisen in particular where local authorities have been aware of the trading and taken no action (sometimes over a period of many years) to restrain it; in some cases they have even received rates from the stall-holder! In these circumstances stall-holders naturally feel a sense of grievance when a prosecution is brought against them.

An example of this occurred in the *Redbridge* case, [59] but the argument that a right had been acquired informally was emphatically rejected. A similar fate met the trader in *Cambridgeshire and Isle of Ely County Council v. Rust* [60] in which he made extensive enquiries of the district and county council as well as the Ministry of Transport before deciding to trade in the lay-by. At no stage was he told that he could not trade; indeed a police officer advised, after investigation, that he was not committing a criminal offence. It was nevertheless held that Rust's mistake as to his legal position did not provide him with a defence since none of the bodies he had asked had a power to licence his activities. The decision was subsequently criticised for placing a harsh interpretation on the words "lawful authority or excuse" in what is now s.148 of the Highways Act 1980. [61]

A similarly rigorous attitude can be seen in *Pugh v. Pigden & Powley*, [62] where it was held that the payment of rates on a stall did not confer "lawful authority" for any obstruction it might cause.

These decisions are consistent with the principle that a public authority cannot be estopped from performing its public duty [63] but may be subject to the *caveat* that general principles of administrative law concerning inconsistent dealings are developing at a rapid pace and the point may be reached where the above principles may require review.

---

[59] *Redbridge London Borough Council v. Jacques* [1970] 1 WLR 1604.

[60] [1972] QB 426.

[61] See A J Ashworth [1974] Crim L. R. 652; ATH Smith (1985) 14 Anglo- Am L.R. 3.

[62] (1986) 151 JP 664.

[63] *Western Fish Products v. Penwith DC* [1978] 2 All ER 204.

(iii) Lawful Excuse: Reasonable User

If an obstruction occurs without lawful authority in the sense outlined above, no offence occurs if it is done with a lawful "excuse". In practice this provision is particularly relevant to traders who are not required to seek licences under the code and other regimes, for example, newsvendors. [64] Without a licence, it is more difficult to establish "lawful authority" and so whether they have "lawful excuse" will often determine their position under the general law.[65]

"Lawful excuse" is often treated as synonymous with reasonableness. [66] If the activity in which the defendant was engaged was a reasonable use of the highway, and was not otherwise unlawful, no offence is committed. [67]

When giving meaning to "reasonableness" the courts are often engaged in value judgments about the purposes highways serve. Whilst some courts seem prepared to tolerate a wide range of socially beneficial activities as lawful, others adhere closely to the narrow orthodoxy which holds that the only right acquired by the public is the right of passage and rights ancillary thereto. Under this approach, any encroachment onto the highway is unreasonable because an encroachment is not an exercise of the right of passage. [68] As an illustration of how narrowly the courts can define the limits of lawful user, it has been held that an obstruction occurred where food was sold from a mobile vehicle parked in a lay-by off the carriageway where picnic tables and lavatories had been supplied by the local authority. The court asserted the orthodox view that the public is entitled to access to all parts of the highway, [69] but, as Barker suggests, [70] the decision

---

[64] *Infra* pp. 188-189, 225, 250-251.

[65] Pedlars need not obtain a street trading licence under the code but must obtain a pedlar's certificate issued under the Pedlar's Act 1871.

[66] See, eg, Lord Parker CJ in *Nagy v. Weston* [1965] 1 All ER 78, 80.

[67] See, eg, *Hirst and Agu v. Chief Constable of West Yorkshire, supra* n. (53) esp at 310-11 per Glidewell L.J.

[68] *Pitcher v. Lockett* [1966] Crim LR 283; *Devon CC v. Gateway Foodmarkets Ltd.* [1990] C.O.D. 324; also *Hertfordshire CC v. Bolden* (1987) 151 JP 252 where the justices found that any actual or potential obstruction of the public was so unlikely that it could be disregarded, but the Divisional Court held that these even so the facts were sufficient to disclose an offence under s.137. A further decision of interest is *Cornwall CC v. James* (Unreported) April 30th 1986.

[69] *Cornwall CC v. James* (Unreported) April 30th 1986.

shows little regard for what many would be regard as a more valuable public interest in ensuring opportunities for drivers to rest and take refreshments so as to avoid accidents.

Whilst decisions of this kind take a narrow approach to permissible uses of the highway, there is authority that the courts should adopt a more flexible approach to the question of reasonableness. This was made clear in the leading case of *Nagy v. Weston* [71] although just how far this will benefit street traders can be seen in the courts actual decision.

In *Nagy*, the Divisional Court recognised that unreasonableness is a question of fact and must be judged according to all the circumstances of the case. Relevant factors are the length of time the obstruction continues, the place where it occurs, the purpose for which it is done, and whether an actual as opposed to a potential obstruction is caused. [72] Further, in *Hirst and Agu* Glidewell L.J. suggested that some uses may be done with "lawful excuse" and so be lawful even if not reasonable in the sense outlined in *Nagy*. [73] This may mean that the factors indicative of reasonableness identified in *Nagy* may not be exhaustive.

The principles enunciated in *Nagy* would place transient obstructions perceived as having a "legitimate" purpose outside the scope of the criminal law. This may serve to de-criminalize such activities as queuing for a bus but, as applied to street traders, their effect is less certain. In *Nagy v. Weston* the defendant was properly convicted of obstruction after trading in hot dogs for five minutes from a bus lay-by adjacent to a busy highway; and even trading away from a main thoroughfare, for example in a "service road" would seem to be "unreasonable" in law. [74]

But it must not be forgotten that some trading may be preserved as a reasonable use of the highway where the public derive a benefit from it. Lord Denman C.J. emphasised this point which has resonance in modern times:

---

[70] [1989] JPL 410.
[71] *Supra* n. 66.
[72] See also *Cooper v. Metropolitan Police Commissioner* (1986) 82 Crim App Rep 238.
[73] *Supra*, n. 53.
[74] *Redbridge London Borough Council v. Jacques, supra* n. 59.

"(The trading in question) is not a general and total obstruction of (the highway) but a partial and limited one both as to extent and duration, *the public deriving...a benefit which may well be considered as equivalent."* [75].

Other more modern decisions also allow weight to be given to the social utility of the obstruction although there have been recent signs that the courts will not allow this development to be over-extended. An important decision in which a more liberal approach found favour was *Hirst and Agu v. Chief Constable of West Yorkshire .* [76] Here the Divisional Court accepted that the highways serve a multiplicity of purposes going beyond simply providing the means of passing to and fro. They are part of a social fabric and due recognition must be given to this. [77]

Thus the court seemed to signal that the public's right to unimpeded passage is, in effect, theoretical since society would wish to tolerate all kinds of infringements of it. The court emphasised that a balancing exercise is necessary in which the social utility of the defendant's action is weighed against harm caused. The right of passage is only one factor in this exercise.

The roots of this more tolerant approach do not, however, appear to be firmly established, particularly in the street trading context. Recently, in *Devon County Council v. Gateway Foodmarkets Ltd,* [78] the Divisional Court warned against giving "too much emphasis" to the social utility of the obstruction. Here the court re-asserted the narrow view that any encroachment upon the highway -unless transient or *de minimis* - is an obstruction because it denies the public access to a part of the highway. This means that the right of passage is again perceived as almost absolute. And even an obstruction lasting "a minute or two" may not in all circumstances be "transient". [79]

---

[75] *Elwood v. Bullock* (1844) 6 QB 383, 411.

[76] (1986) 85 Cr. App. Rep 143; [1987] Crim L.R. 330 noted and discussed by Bailey [1987] PL 495.

[77] This approach was followed in the street trading context in *Pugh v. Pigden and Powley* (1987) 151 JP 664.

[78] [1990] C.O.D 324.

[79] *Cooper v. Metropolitan Police Commissioner* (1986) 82 Crim App Rep 238.

This suggests that the courts are not prepared to embark upon a significant development of "reasonableness" based on considerations of social utility- the development which *Hirst and Agu* seemed to signal- in a way which will significantly advantage street traders. Static forms of street trading in particular-and some peripatetic ones [80] remain *prima facie* vulnerable to the more traditional tendency to equate any encroachment as an unreasonable and obstruction *per se*. [81] Even if the trader is mobile there remains some intolerance of his commercial activities. Certainly there are signs that the courts are still willing to treat commercial encroachments more harshly than those concerned with the exercise of civil liberties. [82] This suggests that the ghosts of *Redbridge* [83] and similar decisions are not laid. The trader should therefore seek to rely on "lawful authority", that is, a local authority licence rather than on the principles of reasonableness to provide him with a defence. [84]

Miscellaneous Offences

Obstruction of the highway is merely one of the weapons available to those wishing to control street trading. Others are also available, some of which overlap substantially with s.137 of the Highways Act 1980.

(i) Pitching a Stall or Placing Goods upon the Highway

Section 148 of the Highways Act 1980 (as amended) provides: "If without lawful authority or excuse - (c) a person deposits anything whatsoever on the highway to the interruption of any user of the highway, or (d) a hawker or itinerant trader pitches a booth, stall

---

[80] After *Cooper ibid.*

[81] Unless the trader has a street trading licence or consent.

[82] See eg *Hirst & Agu v. Chief Constable of West Yorkshire, supra* n. (53).

[83] *Supra* n. (59).

[84] Where a licensing regime such as that under the street trading code has been adopted this will also be important in order to to avoid prosecution under the code: See Ch.10.

or stand, or encamps on a highway" he or she shall be guilty of an offence.

As in the case of s.137, the fine shall not exceed level 3 on the standard scale (see above).

The section creates two distinct offences. Under paragraph (c) any person may be convicted provided that the object deposited on the highway actually interrupts passage. The paragraph (c) offence would not seem to be committed merely by the placing of an object, such as a barrow or stall, on the highway; there must be adverse consequences for highway users. [85] Paragraph (c) is thus primarily concerned with the *effects* of encroachment.[86]

It may be noted here that the Metropolitan Streets Act 1867 is to similar effect. It prohibits the placing of goods or articles on any part of street to the obstruction or inconvenience of other highway users unless for the purpose of loading or unloading and only then for no longer than is absolutely necessary. This provision has effect within a six miles radius of Charing Cross. [87]

Paragraph (d), of s 148, with its focus on "hawkers" and "itinerant traders" may have an archaic air but is still of service. Its predecessor (s.127 of the 1959 Act) was employed in the famous street trading case of *Cambridgeshire & Isle of Ely County Council v. Rust*.[88]

The offence under paragraph (d) is committed regardless of whether any adverse consequences occur at all. It is enough that the stall etc is placed on the highway provided that it is a hawker or itinerant trader who places it there.

It has been held that a trader selling ice cream from a motorised van was not "pitching a stall" subject to the *caveat* that a motor vehicle could become a "stall" if it were stationary for long periods. [89] But a snack bar detached from a towing vehicle has been found to be "stall". [90]

---

[85] Cf *Wolverton UDC v. Willis* [1962] 1 All ER 243.

[86] It may be used against street traders, such as pedlars, who place their goods upon the ground.

[87] Costermongers are excepted: Metropolitan Streets Act Amendment Act 1867.

[88] [1972] 2 QB 426.

[89] *Divito v. Stickings* [1948] 1 All ER 207.

[90] *Waltham Forest London BC v. Mills*. [1980] Crim LR 243.

A "Hawker or Itinerant Trader"

The Highways Act 1980 does not furnish a definition of either "hawker" or "itinerant trader". However, itinerant traders trading from a vehicle are probably included since these may be "hawkers"; [91] and pedlars who necessarily "travel and trade and foot" are probably also "itinerant traders" within the meaning of the Act.

Lawful Excuse

As in the case of obstruction under s.137 of the Highways Act 1980, the possession of a street trading licence or consent or pedlar's certificate will normally constitute "lawful authority or excuse" and thus a defence to a prosecution. Pedlars may be liable to prosecution under the paragraph (c) offence if they allow their goods to rest upon the ground for an unreasonable period.

(ii) Control of Roadside Sales

(a) A Control Order

Two statutory provisions relate to road-side sales. The first, s.7 of the Local Government (Miscellaneous Provisions) Act 1976, is adoptive. Section 147A of the Highways Act 1980[92] is of general effect. Even if a "control order" has not been promulgated, the street trader may fall foul of the 1980 Act. It is proposed to consider first the scope of s.7 of the 1976 Act.

This section empowers the local highway authority to make a control order prohibiting any person from trading on a highway. The placing of any stall within fifteen metres of the highway may also be prohibited.

The power is a discretionary one and may be exercised where the highway authority considers it appropriate to make the order to avoid danger to traffic or to facilitate the passage of traffic over the highway. It would be unlawful to purport to make an order for any other purpose. Certain forms of trading are exempt from the scope of such orders, and these include trading in lawful markets, mobile shops and facilities in lay-bys for road users.

---

[91] *Waltham Forest London BC v. Mills.* [1980] Crim LR 243.

[92] Added by s.23 of the Local Government (Miscellaneous Provisions) Act 1982, and further amended by the Criminal Justice Act 1982, s.46.

If a trader contravenes a control order, the highway authority may require him by notice to cease trading by a date specified in the notice. This should not be less than seven days after the service of the notice on the trader concerned. If trading continues after the expiration of the notice period the trader commits an offence punishable by fine not exceeding level 3 on the standard scale.

If, after seven days following conviction, the trader continues to trade he or she can be fined £10 for each day trading continues.

Unlike the related offence under s.147A (below), the trader does not have a defence of due diligence.

(b) Road-side Sales

Even if a control order is not made, the trader may encounter problems in trading on the highway by virtue of the provisions of the Highways Act 1980. (as amended)

S.147A of the 1980 Act prohibits any person from using any stall or similar structure, or any container or vehicle for the purpose of offering anything for sale on the verge of a trunk road or principal road, a lay-by on such a road, or unenclosed land within 15 metres of any part of such road.

The offence is only committed, however, where the trading activity causes or is likely to cause danger or to interrupt any user of the road. By this means the section seems not to prohibit trading *per se* but only in cases in which the *consequences* of trading fall within the meaning of the section. In another statutory context, it has been held, however, that any encroachment upon the highway necessarily "incommodes" highway users.[93] If applicable in this context such an interpretation would significantly widen the scope of s 147A.

A trader has a defence if he can show that he took all reasonable precautions and exercised due diligence to avoid commission of the offence.

"Due diligence" is not defined in the Act. Where similar words appeared in the Hague Rules, Willmer J in *Riverstone Meat Co. Pty v. Lancashire Shipping Co. Ltd* [94] held that, "An obligation to

---

[93] *Wolverton UDC v. Willis* [1962] 1 All ER 243.

[94] [1960] 1 QB 536 at 581 (reversed on other grounds [1961] AC 807).

exercise due diligence is to my mind indistinguishable from an obligation to exercise reasonable care...." [95]

If applicable in this context , it seems that a trader would have a defence if he could show that, having taken all reasonable precautions to avoid a danger or interruption to traffic, he or she could not reasonably foresee that such a danger or interruption would be likely to arise.

Conviction of the offence carries a fine not exceeding level 3 on the standard scale.

The section does not apply to mobile shops and other vehicles which are used to trade with the occupiers of premises; neither does it apply to the sale of newspapers, nor to trading conducted in a market for which tolls stallages or rents are payable. Street traders having a licence or consent granted either under Schedule 4 of the Local Government (Miscellaneous Provisions) Act 1982 or any local enactment regulating street trading are also excluded from the scope of this provision.

Inter-Relationship of the 1976 and 1980 Acts.
One difficulty for the would-be trader is that s.7 of the 1976 Act is not co-extensive with s147A of the 1980 Act and their inter-relationship is not altogether clear. An example of the problem concerns the sale of agricultural produce by the occupier of land on which it was produced. Even if a control order is made, s.7 exempts such a trader from control under the 1976 Act. He may, however, be liable under the 1980 Act since this lacks a similar exemption.

(iii) Miscellaneous Offences under the Town Police Clauses Act 1847

The venerable Town Police Clauses Act 1847, s.28 creates many different offences of which those considered below are the most relevant to street traders.

The Act was originally adoptive, but sections 21-36 were applied generally throughout England and Wales (but not London

---

[95] This definition was followed and applied by the Divisional Court in *J H Dewhurst Ltd v. Coventry Corporation* [1970] 1 QB 20.

and the metropolis[96]) by virtue of s171 of the Public Health Act 1875.

s.28 states that every person who in any street, to the obstruction, annoyance, or danger, of the residents or passengers, commits any of the enumerated offences shall be liable to a penalty not exceeding level 3 on the standard scale for each offence, or may be committed to prison for a period not exceeding 14 days. The most important in the present context prohibit the causing of any wilful obstruction to any footway or thoroughfare by means of a barrow; the placing of goods or any stall upon a footway; and exposing goods for sale on the footway beyond the line of any house or shop. The offer for sale or distribution of any profane, indecent, or obscene book, paper, drawing, painting or representation is also prohibited. There is no express saving for encroachments made with "lawful authority or excuse". Interpreted strictly, s.28 of the 1847 Act seems to be wider than s.137 of the Highways Act 1980. In theory, this may cause some difficulties because those traders having "lawful authority (i.e. a licence) may nevertheless in a literal sense "annoy" or "obstruct" other highway users. Arguably the words "annoy" and "obstruct" should be interpreted so as to protect traders having lawful authority for their activities.

Street nuisances in the metropolis are liable to be controlled under the Metropolitan Police Act, 1839 s.54 which (*inter alia*) creates an offence where a cart or barrow constitutes a "wilful" obstruction.

Removal of Obstructions

A local authority has a common law power to remove obstructions from the highway.[97] There is no duty to issue a notice or to take proceedings prior to removing the obstruction because the council has the same right to remove an obstruction as a private individual has to remove one from his own property. [98] This means that a

---

[96] For offences in London see Metropolitan Police Act 1839, s.54, and City of London Police Act 1839.

[97] *Bagshaw v. Buxton* (1875) 1 ChD 220; *Reynolds v. Presteigne* UDC [1896] 1 QB 604. See also S. 130 of the Highways Act 1980.

[98] *Per* Lord Russell of Killowen in *Reynolds, ibid,* at 609.

barrow or stall or anything of that nature   which causes an obstruction can be removed summarily from the highway.

Further powers are conferred by statute although these are normally to be exercised only after certain notification requirements have been observed.   Under s.143 of the Highways Act 1980 a "competent authority" [99]   may issue a notice requiring anyone having control or possession of a "structure" obstructing the highway to remove it within the time specified in the notice. Stalls, vans, trailers and similar objects left upon the highway for the purposes of trading may all fall within the scope of this provision. [100] If the trader fails to comply with the notice, the authority may itself remove the "structure" and recover any reasonable cost of so doing. They cannot act, however, within one month from the date of service of the notice. [101]

A similar power is conferred by s.149 which enables the highway authority to serve a notice requiring a person who deposits any "thing" upon the highway to remove it. If the individual responsible fails to comply, the authority can apply to the magistrates for an order empowering them to remove the obstruction. No such order is necessary, however, if the authority has reasonable grounds to believe that the obstruction constitutes a danger to highway users and ought to be removed immediately. The costs of removal may be imposed upon the owner of the obstruction [102] Alternatively, the authority may obtain a magistrates' order enabling it to dispose of the obstruction or to sell it and retain the proceeds of sale.[103]

---

[99] Below n. 101.

[100] S. 143 (4).

[101] If the highway is maintained by the district council, the competent authorities are the district council and the highway authority. If the highway is not maintained by the district council, the competent authority is the highway authority.

[102] Section 149 (3).

[103] Section 149 (4).

CHAPTER 2

CONTROLS ON THE MANNER OF TRADING

(i) Common Law

In the previous chapter we were concerned with the general legal controls governing the sites in which trading may take place. In this chapter we are concerned with controls upon the manner in which street trading is conducted. This is subject to the caveat that the distinction is a useful but somewhat artificial one because, as we have seen, certain street trading which is reasonably conducted may not necessarily constitute an obstruction; in other words it may be a lawful activity on the highway because of the reasonable manner in which it is conducted. Nevertheless, it is useful to treat separately the means of controlling what might be described as the nuisance effects of street trading. This will involve both a survey of enforcement mechanisms available to public authorities and those available to the individual. Such an individual may be an owner of adjacent land, a rival trader or perhaps someone suffering the adverse effects caused by some forms of street trading.

Nuisance

Nuisance is a particularly advantageous form of action because it allows for the recovery of purely economic loss. This is not normally possible under any other principle of tortious liability. For example, if the defendant's unlawful obstruction of the highway causes adjacent businesses to suffer a decline in profits, that loss may be recoverable as "particular damage" in nuisance. [1] The tort is

---

[1] Eg *Benjamin v. Storr* (1874) LR 9 CP 400.

also useful for "respond(ing) to the extent of the harm done, not, as in negligence, to the culpability of the harmer." [2]

A nuisance may be either private or public. It is public where the act or omission in question materially affects the reasonable comfort or convenience of the life of a class of Her Majesty's subjects.[3] Whether a sufficient number of individuals are affected as to constitute such a class is a question of fact.

The distinction between public and private nuisance is a fundamental one because, in the case of public nuisance, there are restrictions on who may be a competent plaintiff. This is considered elsewhere. [4] But it is sufficient to note here that a plaintiff who is sufficiently affected by the public nuisance may take civil proceedings to restrain it. And even if he does not wish personally to start proceedings, he may complain to the local authority which may itself do so. [5]

What is a Nuisance?
Fleming has commented that nuisance has become a "catch-all for a multitude of ill-assorted sins, linking offensive smells, crowing roosters, obstruction of rights of way, defective cellar flaps, street queues, lotteries, houses of ill-fame and a host of other rag ends of the law." [6]

Thus, apart from possible obstructions to the highway caused by street trading, nuisance may control litter, noise, smoke or fumes arising from it.

The Classes of Nuisance
For present purposes, a nuisance may arise in any of three different ways. In the first, the act or omission giving rise to liability may cause actual physical damage to property. [7] Street trading will only rarely result in such damage. In the second, liability may arise where the act or omission interferes with the reasonable enjoyment

---

[2] Gearty "The Place of Private Nuisance in the Modern Law of Torts (1989) 48 CLJ 214, 216)

[3] *A-G v. PYA Quarries Ltd.* [1957] 2 QB 169, 184.

[4] *Infra.* p. 371 *et seq.*

[5] Section 222 of the Local Government Act 1972, discussed *infra* p. 356 *et seq.*

[6] *The Law of Torts*, 6th edit, 1983, p. 378.

[7] *Halsey v. Esso Petroleum Co.* [1961] 1 WLR 683.

by the occupier of his property. Smoke, dust, smell, fumes or noise which emanate from the defendant's trading which materially affect the plaintiff's neighbouring property may all constitute actionable nuisance. Finally, a public nuisance also arises where there is an unreasonable interference with the public's right of free passage along a highway. Placing a stall upon the highway could thus constitute nuisance. Liability is imposed because, such a user is not a reasonable one. The law closely resembles that which has already been surveyed in chapter one. In this context we are more particularly concerned with liability for queues and crowds which cause a public nuisance by their encroachment upon the highway.

The Standard of Reasonableness
Fundamental to the law of nuisance is the idea of reasonableness. Not every act or omission which interferes with neighbouring property will be actionable. Liability arises if the defendant's use of land is unreasonable, and this requires an examination of its nature, extent, duration and the place in which it occurs.

The test to be applied, however, differs according to the kind of nuisance which is alleged to have been caused. Nuisances which injure property are subject to a more stringent standard than those which create a material interference with the enjoyment of land. As Veale J. held in *Halsey v. Esso Petroleum Co.*,[8] liability in nuisance for harmful deposits could be established upon proof that those deposits caused damage to the plaintiff's property provided that the damage was not trivial in character. The "locality" standard, by which standards of reasonable activity are judged according to the nature of the locality in which they occur, which is so important in the case of nuisances producing "sensible personal discomfort", has no application in cases of this kind.[9] The effect is that, even if conducted in a suitable area, trading activity which causes injury to property is nevertheless an actionable nuisance.[10]

---

[8] *Ibid.*
[9] See *St. Helens Smelting Company v. Tipping* (1865) 1 HLC 642.
[10] It is not clear whether the locality principle is relevant where economic rather than physical loss is at issue. (See Silvester [1986] JPL 570, 573-4) It seems, however, likely that Lord Westbury's rejection of the locality standard in *St. Helen's* should be confined to cases where the economic loss is consequent upon physical damage.

"Sensible Personal Discomfort".
Since the essence of nuisance is unreasonableness, an important
question is: what standard of comfort or enjoyment of property will
the law protect? Stated otherwise: what degree of intrusion must
an occupier endure?

Individuals in society must expect to encounter some degree of
inconvenience either for the sake of some important public benefit
or simply by virtue of living in a crowded urban environment. [11] The
law only imposes liability "...in those cases where the harm or risk
to one is greater than he ought to be required to bear under the
circumstances." [12] Knight- Bruce V-C expressed the rule this way:

"Ought this inconvenience to be considered in fact as more than
fanciful, more than one of mere delicacy or fastidiousness, as an
inconvenience materially interfering with the ordinary comfort
physically of human existence, not merely according to elegant or
dainty modes and habits of living, but according to plain and sober
and simple notions among the English people?" [13]

Reasonableness thus lies at the heart of the principle.

The "Locality" Principle
Where what is alleged is an interference with personal comfort,
much weight is given to the locality in which the defendant's act
or omission occurs. All law students are familiar with the Thesiger
LJ's *dictum* : "What would be nuisance in Belgrave Square would not
necessarily be so in Bermondsey." [14] Lord Loreburn L.C. once stated:
"A dweller in town cannot expect to have as pure air, as free from
smoke, smell and noise as if he lived in the country, and distant
from other dwellings, and yet an excess of smoke, smell and noise
may give a cause of action, but in each such case it becomes a
question of degree ...." [15] The law is the law of "give and take". [16]

---

[11] See eg *Harper v. GN Haden & Sons Ltd* [1933] 1 Ch. 298, 303 and *Andreae v. Selfridge
& Co. Ltd* [1938] Ch. 1.
[12] *Bamford v. Turnley* (1862) 3 B & S 66, 79.
[13] *Walter v. Selfe* (1851) De G & Sm. 315, 322.
[14] *Sturgess v. Bridgman* (1879) 11 Ch.D. 852, 865.
[15] Also *Polsue & Alfieri Ltd v. Rushmer* [1907] AC 121, 123.
[16] Per Romer L.J. *Harper v. G N Haden & Sons Ltd* [1933] 1 Ch 298, 320.

The Planning Context
The planning context may be of central importance in determining what is reasonable in the relevant neighbourhood. A grant of planning permission may, by permitting certain development of the land, fundamentally change the character of the use of that land. What is reasonable is then to be judged in the light of the new planning context. [17] This seems to be a sensible result: it would be bizarre if, having taken into account the interests of the community as a whole and having granted planning permission, the local planning authority could find its planning objectives frustrated by an action in public nuisance. If, however , the new use can occur without serious interference with neighbouring property, it may constitute a nuisance notwithstanding the grant of planning permission because the inference can then be drawn that the developer is acting unreasonably.

This means that, for example, if a grant of planning permission for a market or fair necessarily entails some noise and some inconvenience for local residents and others, provided that this is no more than is reasonable, it will not amount to a nuisance.[18]

Undue Sensitivity
Since, as we have seen, the guiding principle is one of reasonableness, it follows that a plaintiff who is unduly sensitive may not complain. [19]

Nuisance and Street Trading
The above principles mean that a trader who causes physical damage to property or who allows smoke, litter, fumes or noise to pollute the area may be liable at common law for nuisance if his activities go beyond what is judged to be reasonable. In addition, a number of statutory measures buttress these provisions of the general law. These are considered below. Before doing so, however, it is appropriate to examine liability for public nuisance where a trader obstructs the highway.

---

[17] *Gillingham BC v. Medway (Chatham) Dock Co. Ltd* (1993) 91 LGR 160.
[18] This is consistent with *Polsue & Alfieri Ltd v. Rushmer, supra.*
[19] *Robinson v. Kilvert* (1889) 41 Ch.D. 88 NB The principle does not, however apply to "sensitive" buildings: *Hoare v. McAlpine* [1923] 1 Ch. 167.

Public Nuisance and Obstruction of the Highway
The law of public nuisance may provide a means of preventing
street trading taking place where this is an unreasonable
encroachment onto the highway. Whether a public nuisance occurs
is ultimately a question of the reasonableness of the user in
question. Accordingly, many of the principles governing the law of
obstruction under s.137 of the Highways Act 1980 are derived from
the law of public nuisance and do not require re-statement here. In
this context we are more particularly concerned with manner in
which street trading is conducted and how public nuisance may
provide a means of imposing civil liability for the obstruction of
premises and for queues and crowds which form on the highway as
a result of the trading in question.

Obstruction of Premises
Obstruction of premises may arise in various circumstances, for
example, by virtue of the trader's stall or van. It may also occur if
crowds gather at the stall and obstruct access.
     The obstruction of the access to private premises can amount to a
nuisance if it is unreasonable or excessive. [20] Street trading which
obstructs light entering at windows may also be actionable. [21] The
principle has, however, been refined where what is at issue is an
obstruction caused by a crowd or queue.
     There is no rule that a street trader will be liable in nuisance
for every crowd or queue which, having formed at his stall,
obstructs neighbouring premises. On the other hand, it is clear that
such liability can arise. Much will depend upon the reasonableness
of the trader's conduct in causing the crowd to gather, the extent of
the crowd and its duration. There is, however, considerable
indeterminacy in this matter because "reasonableness" in this
context is not self-executing.
     An early example of liability for queues occurred in *R v.
Carlile*[22] in which the defendant was convicted of the common law
offence of nuisance after displaying effigies in his shop window
which caused a large crowd to gather. In his summing up Park J
formulated a "necessity" principle which has subsequently given

---

[20] *Hubbard v. Pitt* [1976] QB 142.
[21] *Benjamin v. Storr* (1874) LR 9 CP 400.
[22] (1834) 6 C & P 636.

rise to some difficulties. He stated that had the defendant's actions been necessary in the *bona fide* carrying on of his trade, "the law would do what it could to protect him." [23] The defendant had admitted, however, that the display had actually damaged his business. He was liable in nuisance for having done something "unnecessary".

There are two cases in which queues forming outside a theatre were held to constitute a nuisance. In *Barber v. Penley* [24] North J held that the plaintiff was justified in bringing an action against a theatre owner in nuisance where queues gathering outside a theatre congregated up to two hours before the doors were opened obstructing access to her premises for that period.

Barber was followed and approved by a majority in *Lyons, Sons & Co. v. Gulliver*, [25] but the court emphasised that there was no rule that a queue or crowd would be an actionable nuisance per se and that much depended on the circumstances. [26] In a strong dissent, Phillimore L.J. stated that, since the queue in *Lyons* was "very nearly as inoffensive a queue as can be seen" [27], he felt that the court's insistence that not all queues would be unlawful was somewhat hollow.

However, no liability occurred in *Dwyer v. Mansfield* [28] where, during war time rationing, queues formed outside the defendant's shop which the plaintiffs alleged interfered with their businesses.   Atkinson J. decided that if a nuisance had occurred, the defendant was not responsible for it. Liability could only be imposed where the defendant had done something which was "unnecessary" for his business in order to create demand. "Normal" trading was not sufficient. In this case the crowds gathered because the rationed goods sold by the plaintiff were in short supply. Atkinson J. distinguished the theatre cases on the ground that the theatre company "did that which created the

---

[23] *Ibid.* at p. 649.
[24] [1893] 2 Ch. 447.
[25] [1914] 1 Ch. 631.
[26] *Ibid* at pp. 639, 644-5.
[27] *Ibid.* at p. 652.
[28] [1946] KB 437.

demand" [29] and, somewhat puzzlingly stated that this was not "necessary"

The "necessity" principle was also applied in *Fabbri v. Morris* [30] to make a shop keeper liable for a queue which gathered to buy ice cream at a shop window. Liability was imposed because it was "unnecessary" for the shop keeper to trade in this way; she could have avoided creating a queue had she traded from inside her shop.

Thus much turns on the interpretation of "necessity" . If it means no more than "unavoidable", acceptable results are produced. In *Fabbri*, for example, the obstruction was not "necessary" because it could easily have been avoided. But where the courts hold that a trader who creates demand does something which is "unnecessary" the courts enter the realm of sophistry. Such an application of "necessity" would penalise a trader dealing in a entirely new product for which *ex hypothesi* there was no existing demand. Demand could only be created by advertising and yet to stimulate demand in this way would seem to fall foul of *Lyons* if an extensive crowd gathers.

In substance *Dwyer* and the theatre cases share a fundamental similarity: in each case a queue formed because of a shortage of supply. Any purported distinction between these cases based on "necessity" disguises the real balancing of interests which is inevitably inherent in nuisance cases. The question is one of reasonableness: does the purpose for which the queue gathers, outweigh the inconvenience which it causes?

There are other decisions in which this has been recognised and in which no attempt has been made to invoke the "necessity" principle. An old example of this occurred in *Ball v. Ward* [31] where, an obstruction caused by a crowd gathering on the highway (on the edge of a market place) was held to be reasonable because the defendant was lawfully trading from a pitch in the market place. The conviction for obstruction was quashed on appeal because the court clearly regarded his actions as reasonable: the

---

[29] *Ibid.* at 440.
[30] [1947] 1 All ER 315.
[31] (1875) 33 LT 170.

detriment of the encroachment was outweighed by the importance of market trading. [32]

Thus the most satisfactory approach would be to subject the cases on obstruction caused by queues to the ordinary principles and to abandon distinctions based on the "necessity" principle.

In addition to the common law of nuisance a number of statutory provisions create criminal offences as a means of restraining various kinds of nuisance.

(ii) Other Controls on the Nuisance Effects of Street Trading

By-Laws

District councils and London borough councils have power to make by-laws for the prevention and suppression of nuisances. [33] The power enables local authorities to control nuisances and this includes a power to regulate street trading. By-laws may, for example, be enacted to regulate the playing of musical instruments in the street, [34] but cannot impose an absolute prohibition on such activities. [35] By laws are considered in the following chapter.

Litter

The Environmental Protection Act 1990, s.87 makes it a criminal offence punishable by a fine up to £1,000 to leave litter. The offence is committed where litter is left in "any public open space" (which means a place in the open air to which the public have access without payment) as well as any covered place open to the air on at least one side provided it is available for public use. In addition to protecting "public open spaces" the Act also seeks to protect highways [36] and this will be of particular relevance to the activities of street traders.

---

[32] See more recently *Pugh v. Pigden & Powley* (1987) 151 JP 664.

[33] Local Government Act 1972, s. 235, considered in the following chapter.

[34] See, e.g. *R v. Powell* (1884) 48 JP 740.

[35] *Johnson v. Croydon Corpn.*(1886) 1 QB 290.

[36] Section 87 (3).

To mitigate the effects of s.87, there is provision for an authorised officer of a litter authority to issue a fixed penalty notice. [37] This means that by paying the fixed penalty of £10 within 14 days the offender can avoid conviction of a litter offence. The Act designates, amongst other bodies, county councils, district councils and London borough councils, as "principal litter authorities" in England & Wales.[38]

The local authority has a duty to keep highways clear of litter so far as it is practicable to do so.[39] In addition, any person aggrieved may complain to the magistrate about litter on the highway or other places designated in the Act. [40] Who is a "person aggrieved" is a matter of some controversy and is considered below. [41] The complaint is brought against the body having the duty to keep the land free of litter, and the magistrates are empowered to make a "litter abatement order" requiring the litter to be removed. [42] In the case of most highways likely to be the subject to street trading the responsible authority is the local authority for that area.

Street litter control notices may also be issued [43] to prevent the accumulation of litter where this is a recurrent problem. The notice may require the occupier or owner of the premises to keep the frontage of their premises and any area of open land adjoining or in the vicinity of the frontage to their premises free of litter. Under the Street Litter Control Notices Order 1991 [44] a street litter control notice can be issued in respect (*inter alia*) of commercial and retail premises where food or drink is sold for consumption off the premises. Provided that they fall within the definition of "premises" [45] the activities of hot dog vans and similar may

---

[37] Section 88.
[38] Section 86.
[39] Section 89.
[40] Section 91.
[41] Expressly excluded is a "principal litter authority": s. 91(3).
[42] Section 91 (6).
[43] Section 93.
[44] SI 1991 No 1324.
[45] "Premises" is defined to include land: s. 127 Environmental Protection Act 1990. See *infra* for a discussion of the meaning of "premises".

become the subject of these rules since they have a reputation for causing persistent litter problems.

It should not be forgotten that control of litter in street trading is also possible under the street trading licensing schemes. Action may be taken against the trader responsible under the terms of the street trader's licence. [46] Breach may lead to revocation of the licence.

Where the licensing authority disposes of the refuse arising from street trading they may impose the cost of doing so on the street traders. [47] Failure to pay these costs can also lead to revocation of the licence.

Statutory Nuisances

The Environmental Protection Act 1990 Part III buttresses common law nuisance with specific types of statutory nuisance. For the latter specific enforcement mechanisms are also established. Although there may be difficulties in applying the controls to at least some kinds of street trading, it is likely that some of the nuisance effects of certain trading could be restrained under these provisions.

By s.79 the following are statutory nuisances :

(a) Any premises in such a state as to be prejudicial to health or a nuisance;

(b) smoke emitted from premises so as to be prejudicial to health or a nuisance;

(c) fumes or gases emitted from premises so as to be prejudicial to health or a nuisance;

(d) any dust, steam, smell or other effluvia arising on industrial, trade or business premises and being prejudicial to health or a nuisance;

---

[46] See *infra* the street trading code para 4 (6).
[47] Para 9(6) of the code.

(e)   any accumulation or deposit which is prejudicial to health or a nuisance;

(f)   any animal kept in such a place or manner as to be prejudicial to health or a nuisance;

(g)   noise emitted from premises so as to be prejudicial to health or a nuisance.

(ga)   noise that is prejudicial to health or a nuisance and is emitted from or caused by a vehicle, machinery or equipment in a street: [47a] and

(h)   any other matter declared by any enactment to be a statutory nuisance.

The Scope of the Controls
It is not clear how far these provisions extend to the various kinds of street trading. The difficulty turns on the meaning of the word "premises". Section 79 (7) defines premises so as to include land and (with an exception for one kind of vessel) any vessel.

The word "premises" has been subject to varying interpretations in a range of contexts. It has a number of meanings, one of which is "a building of some description". [48] In *Andrews v. Andrews*, for the purposes of the Workmen's Compensation Act 1906, "premises" was held to include "some definite place with metes and bounds, say land, or land with buildings on it" [49] and also a vessel or "anything of that kind". [50] It did not include a street.

In *Tower Hamlets Borough Council v. Manzoni and Walder* [51] demonstrators who protested in the street could not be subject to a noise nuisance notice because they were not situated on "premises" within the meaning of the legislation. [52]   This difficulty has now

---

[47a] Inserted by the Noise and Statutory Nuisance Act 1993, s.2.

[48] *Thanet DC v. Ninedrive Ltd.* [1978] 1 All ER 703, 710. Walton J.

[49] Per Buckley L.J., [1908] 2 KB 567, 570.

[50] *Ibid.* at p. 571.

[51] (1984) 148 JP 123.

[52] Interestingly, premises included "land". The demonstrators were not held to occupy "land" and did not fall within the Act. Note the definition of premises in s79

been addressed by the insertion of paragraph (ga) which is discussed further below. This suggests that , at the very least, noise caused by street traders such as pedlars who do not operate from a stall cannot be the subject of a noise nuisance abatement notice.

Further difficulty in employing the statutory controls against street trading appears in *Thanet District Council v. Ninedrive* [53] in which the Shops Act was considered. The Act defines "shop" to include any premises where any retail trade or business is carried on. Walton J. held that in this context "premises" did not include the land on which market stalls were operating. However, this was subject to the important *caveat* that each individual stall might be a "shop" for certain purposes (and presumably therefore, "premises") within the meaning of the Act. If this is correct and has a general application it means that noise pollution emanating from individual stalls might fall within the controls of the 1990 Act. The insertion of para. (ga), to which reference has already been made, patly overcomes the present difficulty of interpretation avoiding a reference to "premises". It extends to noise caused by any vehicle, machinery or equipment (including a musical instrument) in the street.

Vehicles

The position of a trader operating from a mobile vehicle is also uncertain. It might tentatively be argued that a van could constitute "premises" under *Andrews v. Andrews* where premises was held to include a "vessel or anything of that kind." "Vessel" would embrace most marine craft, so the additional words "anything of that kind" may refer to non-marine vehicles such as a motor van.

Judicial policy seems to favour a liberal construction of the legislation in order to control the effects of noise pollution which are now widely regarded as one of the most serious and commonly encountered forms of pollution. This is a powerful argument for not excluding from a regulatory structure designed to be an integrated system of pollution control street activities which are a nuisance or likely to be prejudicial to health.

---

(7) similarly includes "land", but this would not seem to embrace those trading on foot if the *Tower Hamlets* case is good law.

[53] [1978] 1 All ER 703.

Burden of Proof

Since the effect of the legislation is penal in character a criminal burden of proof applies [54]

"Prejudicial to Health or a Nuisance

"Prejudicial to health" is defined to mean "injurious, or likely to cause injury to health." [55] The Act offers no definition of nuisance. It is clear that the formulation "prejudicial to health or a nuisance" is disjunctive in effect, so that a trader who causes a nuisance which is not prejudicial to health may be guilty of a statutory nuisance. [56]

Nuisance

Notwithstanding earlier authority to the contrary, [57] it is now settled that the nuisance means either a public or private nuisance at common law. [58] Not all public or private nuisances are included, however. It has been held that "to be within the spirit of the Act a nuisance...has to be one interfering materially with the personal comfort of the residents, in the sense that it materially affected their well being although it might not be prejudicial to health." [59] Dust or other substances falling on a car would not, under this view, be a statutory nuisance; but dust falling into hair or eyes would be indictable since these would interfere with personal comfort.

The act or omission complained of must affect neighbouring property if a nuisance is to be established. If only the premises on which the act or omission takes place are affected, a statutory nuisance can only arise if the act or omission is prejudicial to the health of the occupants. In the street trading context this unlikely to cause difficulties.

Since common law principles remain relevant, the interference with neighbouring property must be unreasonable. Relevant to this question is the time at which the trading took place and its frequency. The latter is particularly important because, at least for

---

[54] *R v. Newham Justices ex p Hunt* [1976] 1 All ER 839.

[55] Section 79(7).

[56] *Bishop Aukland Local Board v. Bishop Aukland Iron Co.* (1882) 10 QBD 138.

[57] *Betts v. Penge UDC* [1942] 2 KB 154.

[58] *National Coal Board v. Neath Borough Council* [1976] 2 All ER 478.

[59] *Wivenhoe Port Ltd. v. Colchester BC* [1985] JPL 175, 178.

the purposes of private nuisance, the interference must be for a "substantial length of time". [60]

Inert objects which are visually offensive are not statutory nuisances. [61] so that a pile of, builders rubble, tarmacadam and old tin cans could not be controlled under the Act.

"Prejudicial to Health"
"Prejudicial to health", means "injurious or likely to cause injury to health". Narrowly interpreted by the courts, it embraces only disease and not personal injury: "a threat of disease, vermin or the like". [62] Accordingly, the pile of builders rubble, and old tin cans in the *Coventry case* not a statutory nuisance. It was held not to pose a risk to the health of those entering the site; it did not threaten disease. It might have been different if rats were found to nest in the rubble. [63]

The distinction between accumulations which may wound and those which may infect with disease seems a highly unattractive one. It might be asked whether a wound which became infected would make the pile of rubbish a statutory nuisance? Even if it did, not many of those living near the site would probably have taken the view that safety to limb is as much a matter of "health" as freedom from disease.

A statutory nuisance may be committed even though there has been no complaint from a member of the public. The evidence of police officers is sufficient. [64]

The Categories of Statutory Nuisance
The common elements of the statutory tort having been considered the detailed provisions may now be examined.

---

[60] *National Coal Board v. Neath Borough Council* [1976] 2 All ER 478, at p481, *per* Watkin J., with whom the others agreed.
[61] *Coventry City Council v. Cartwright* [1975] 2 All ER 99.
[62] *Ibid. per* Lord Widgery C.J. at p.102.
[63] If rats do enter land in numbers the local authority may be under a duty to take action under the Prevention of Damage by Pests Act 1949. The occupier of the land infested is also under a duty to notify the local authority if rats and mice are present in substantial numbers.
[64] *Wellingborough DC v. Gordon* [1990] The Times, Nov. 9th.

(a)   any premises in such a state as to be prejudicial to health or a nuisance.

A stall from which food was sold and which was in such a condition that it might cause disease might fall within these provisions although more likely to be dealt with under other provisions. [65]

The "best practicable means" defence (considered below) is available to nuisances arising on trade or business premises.

(b)   smoke emitted from premises so as to be prejudicial to health or a nuisance.

Section 79(7) defines "smoke" so as to include soot, ash, grit and gritty particles emitted in smoke.

The "best practicable means" defence extends only to smoke emitted from a chimney.

(c)   fumes or gas emitted from premises so as to be prejudicial to health or a nuisance.

This provision would not seem to be applicable in relation to street trading since it only applies to emissions from private dwellings. [65a]

(d)   any dust, steam, smell or other effluvia arising on industrial, trade or business premises and being prejudicial to health or a nuisance.

If any kinds of street trading do give off a smell, the tort is committed if the smell is either prejudicial to health or a nuisance. Establishing that this is so may not be straightforward. As Silvester argues [66] the common effects of smells are psychological or emotional. Because, as we have seen , the legislation requires risk of infection or similar, it is unlikely that most smells will be

---

[65] If it were "premises". Other controls on hygiene may be found in the Food Safety Act 1990 or the Food Hygiene (Markets, Stalls and Delivery Vehicles) Regulations 1966 SI 1966/791.

[65a] Section 79 (4).

[66] [1986] JPL 571.

"injurious to health" and so, in practice, the smell will have to be a common law nuisance.

As in paragraph (a) the best practicable means defence is available in respect of nuisances arising under this paragraph.

(e)   any accumulation or deposit which is prejudicial to health or a nuisance.

Accumulations and deposits within the Act include such matters as stable dung; [67] rotting seaweed; [68] and a pile of smouldering cinders and ash [69] The offence is only committed where the accumulation or deposit is either a nuisance or prejudicial to health. No nuisance is committed unless the enjoyment of neighbouring property is interfered with and so, as we have seen, a pile of inert material such as broken glass, tin cans tarmacadam and builder's rubble falls outside the section. Such a pile will only become indictable if there is a risk to health posed by the threat of disease, vermin or the like. The possibility that persons coming on to the land may be injured by the deposit is insufficient by itself. [70]

The "best practicable means" defence is available provided that the nuisance arises on industrial, trade or business premises.

(f)   any animal kept in such a place or manner as to be prejudicial to health or a nuisance.

There is some confusion whether a prosecution may be brought simply because an animal is noisy. In *Galer v. Morrissey*, [71] it was suggested that liability may only arise if the animals were, for example, smelly as well as noisy. A wider view was, however, expressed in *Coventry City Council v. Cartwright* where Lord Widgery C.J stated that a noisy animal could be just as much prejudicial to health as a malodorous one. [72] This reasoning seems

---

[67] *Smith v. Waghorn* (1863) 27 JP 744.

[68] *Proprietors of Margate Pier v. Margate Town Council* (1869) 33 JP 437.

[69] *Bishop Aukland Local Board v. Bishop Aukland Iron & Steel Co.* (1882) 10 QBD 138.

[70] *Coventry City Council v. Cartwright.* [1975] 1 WLR 845.

[71] *Galer v. Morrissey* [1955] 1 All ER 380.

[72] *Supra* n. (70) at p.853.

more attractive. [73] Even if *Galer* does properly state the current law, it should not be forgotten that noise could constitute a nuisance at common law and thereby fall within this paragraph.

The problem of animals and noise may also be dealt with under local by-laws with which these provisions may overlap. [74] The procedure for enforcing by-laws, however, suffers from the lack of power to serve an abatement notice. (below)

(g)   noise emitted from premises so as to be prejudicial to health or a nuisance.

Noise is one of the most serious and commonly encountered forms of pollution. That it can cause injury to health has been judicially recognised; [75] and the courts seem to be willing to adopt a liberal interpretation of the legislation in order to control the effects of noise pollution.

The "best practicable means" defence is available to nuisances under this paragraph caused by an act or omission on industrial, trade or business premises.

It may also be noted that noise caused by loudspeakers used to promote street sales may also be controlled under s.62 of the Control of Pollution Act 1974 (as amended). The use of loudspeakers is generally prohibited altogether between 9pm and 8am: at other times, loudspeakers cannot be used to advertise any entertainment, trade or business (subject to various exceptions). Ice cream and other vendors of perishable food may, however, advertise that the food is on sale on the vehicle (other than by means of words) between noon and 7pm.

"Street" is defined under the 1974 Act to mean a highway and any other road, footway, square or court which is for the time being

---

[73] There are also indications that noise pollution has been recognised as a significant problem since *Galer*, and that judicial attitudes have hardened: *R v. Fenny Stratford Justices ex p Watney Mann* (Midlands) Ltd. [1972] 2 All ER 888; *Southwark LBC v. Ince* (1989) 153 JP 597. These decisions raise some doubt as to whether *Galer v. Morrissey* would now be followed.

[74] By-laws may be made under s.235 Local Government Act 1972. The model by-law provides that "No person shall keep within any ...premises any noisy animal which shall be or cause a serious nuisance to residents of the neighbourhood."

[75] *Coventry City Council v. Cartwright* [1975] 2 All ER 99; *Southwark LBC v. Ince* (1989) 153 JP 597.

open to the public. In *Tower Hamlets LB v. Creitzman* [76] the offence was committed where the trader occupied space in a covered market and played loud music through loudspeakers. The stall was held to be in a "square" where it was situated in a space beneath a building which was open on three sides. This illustrates the broad interpretation which the courts are willing to give to legislation to control nuisances in order to protect the public.

Section 62 has been amended by the provisions of the Noise and Statutory Nuisance Act 1993 which allows a local authority, by resolution, to adopt the scheme enacted in Schedule 2 of the 1993 Act. This gives the authority a discretionary power to consent to the use of loudspeakers where they are not used for the purpose of advertising any entertainment, trade or business. If the loudspeakers are not so employed, consent for their use may be sought from the local authority.

In the Metropolitan Police District it is also an offence to blow any horn or other noisy instrument for the purposes of calling persons together, selling or obtaining money. [77] This appears to target two separate evils. It prohibits not only noisy instruments used for advertising but also those used for acquiring money, perhaps through busking.

(ga) noise that is prejudicial to health or a nuisance and is emitted from or caused by a vehicle, machinery or equipment in a street.

Since noise which does not emanate from premises cannot be controlled under para. (g), an important gap in the scope of the legislation as originally drafted was partly closed by the insertion of paragraph (ga) by the Noise and Statutory Nuisance Act 1993, s.2. In particular the paragraph overcomes some of the difficulties exposed such decisions as in *Tower Hamlets Borough Council v. Manzoni and Walder* [77a]. However, paragraph (ga) only partially closes this gap in the legislative code by enabling an abatement notice to be served in respect of noise nuisance caused by any vehicle

---

[76] (1984) 148 JP 630.

[77] Metropolitan Police Act 1839 s. 54 (14). The Metropolitan Police District includes Greater London, the City of London, Inner and Middle Temple and small parts of Herts, Surrey and Essex which border it.

[77a] Supra n (51).

(not being mere traffic noise), or by any machinery or equipment (including a musical instrument) in the street. Noise caused by the cries of pedlars, for example, would still appear to be immune from these controls since it would not emanate from "equipent". Nevertheless, this provision is capable of significantly curtailing noisy street trading activities where these constitute a nuisance or are otherwise prejudicial to health.

Any vehicle, machinery or equipment falling foul of this provision may be removed by an authorised officer of the local authority or immobilised if unattended.

Persons aggreived by a noise nuisance within this paragraph may complain to the magistrate.

(h)   Any other matter declared by any enactment to be a statutory nuisance.

A variety of forms of nuisances are caught by this paragraph. It is sufficient to note here the provisions of s. 268 (2) of the Public Health Act 1936 which enacts that a nuisance arises where a tent, shed or similar structure used for human habitation is so overcrowded or lacking in sanitary condition as to be prejudicial to health.

The defence of "best practicable means" is unavailable in a prosecution instituted under this paragraph.

The "Best Practicable Means" Defence
As we have seen it is sometimes a defence that the "best practicable means" have been used to prevent or counteract the effects of the nuisance. The burden of proof is on the person seeking to justify the *prima facie* nuisance.

What is practicable depends upon the current state of technical knowledge, local conditions, and to financial implications. [78] The latter were relevant in *Wivenhoe Port Ltd. v. Colchester Borough Council,* [79] where the defendant argued that it would lose profitability if it was forced to take additional steps to avoid the nuisance. Whilst exorbitant expenditure would not fall within what was "practicable", a *prima facie* nuisance   would not

---

[78] Section 79 (9).
[79] [1985] JPL 175.

necessarily be excused where mere loss of profitability was involved. The profit margin might be just as much affected by the inefficient running of the company. To allow it to avoid dealing with a *prima facie* nuisance simply to preserve its remaining profit margin would be to force the community to subsidise that company's activities. As the commentator notes,[80] what is practicable for the firm might be different from what is practicable to society in general.

Competence to Bring Proceedings
By s. 82, "any person aggrieved" by a statutory nuisance is entitled to complain direct to the local magistrates about the nuisance. Who is a "person aggrieved" is a matter discussed generally below. [81] It would include someone who suffered injury to health , loss or whose enjoyment of property was prejudiced by the nuisance.[82] This means that those who suffer directly as a result of street trading which results in a statutory nuisance are empowered to take action on their own initiative in the courts to abate the nuisance.

Procedure
The statutory procedure allows for the service, by the local authority, of an abatement notice. This enables action to be taken without resort to court proceedings; and in many cases this will be sufficient to end the matter. The person on whom the notice is served has twenty-one days in which to appeal to magistrates against the notice. Contravention of an abatement notice (unless on industrial trade or business premises) is an offence [83] punishable by fine up to level 5 on the standard scale. Further disobedience will attract a further fine of up to one fifth of the the level 5 amount for each day on which the offence continues after conviction. For offences on trade, industrial or business premises, [84] (and this may arguably extend to street traders trading from barrows and stalls and vehicles) the fine may be of an amount not exceeding £20,000.

---

[80] Ibid.
[81] Below p. 367.
[82] *Sandwell Metropolitan BC v. Bujok* [1990] 3 All ER 385.
[83] Section 80 (4).
[84] Section 80 (6).

There is no further provision for fines calculated on a daily basis following conviction.

CHAPTER 3

BY-LAWS

Street trading is frequently regulated under local by-laws. These are laws made in conformity with an enabling statute which operate and have the force of law within the area of a local authority. To be valid a by-law must be confirmed by the Home Secretary or other Minister designated as the confirming authority.

Many statutes empower local authorities to make by-laws. Some of these may, in effect, create a zoning regime under which street trading, or certain kinds of street trading are prevented from taking place in designated areas; others may control the manner in which trading is conducted, or they may impose obligations in the interests of public health and safety.

It is proposed briefly to note some of the enabling powers which may result in by-laws relevant to street trading and thereafter to consider general requirements for the validity of by-laws and how an invalid by-law may be challenged by the aggrieved trader.[1]

By-Laws and Street Trading

(i) Street Trading by Children and Young Persons

By-laws may be made to control street trading by young people under the Children and Young Persons Act 1933, as amended by Employment Act 1989, s10 and sched. 3.

The amendments brought in by the 1989 Act mean that no child may engage or be employed in street trading unless a local

---

[1] See, e.g., *Kruse v. Johnson* [1898] 2 QB 91, 96, per Lord Russell of Killowen C.J.

authority has enacted by-laws authorising it. [2] These by-laws may enable children who have attained the age of fourteen years to be employed by their parents. Those of a younger age may not be employed or be engaged in street trading.

A range of further controls may also be promulgated in by-laws. The local authority is empowered to require the child to obtain a street trading licence; [3] and the conditions under which this is granted may also become regulated. The times, days and places in which trading is permitted may also fall to be controlled; and the authority may "regulate in any other respect the conduct of the child whilst engaged or employed in street trading."

Children may not take part in street trading on Sundays.

(ii) The Sale of Food

Whilst it was in force, s. 15 of the Food Act 1984, enabled local authorities to make by-laws ensuring the safety of food by establishing regulations governing the handling wrapping and delivery of food. This power was repealed in the Food Safety Act 1990 [4] but by-laws made under the 1984 Act which were already in existence at the date of repeal remain in force.

(iii) Walkways

Rights of way which are sheltered from the elements are sometimes used by street traders. Some of these places are subject to by-laws made under the Highways Act 1980 s.35. This power enables a highway authority or district council to reach an agreement with the owner of a building that "walkways" for the use of the public may be created over, through, or under parts of a building. Where such a walkway has been created, the Act enables a local highway authority- or district council- to make by-laws regulating the use of the walkway, and the times at which the

---

[2] Children & Young Persons Act 1933, s. 20 as amended. A child in relation to England and Wales means a person who is of compulsory school age for the purposes of the Education Act 1944.
[3] But under the street trading licensing schemes, no licence may be granted to a person aged under 17 years and so the effect of this provision is unclear.
[4] Sched 4 para 7.

way may be used. Of particular significance for the street trader is the provision in s.35 (6) (c) of the 1980 Act which enacts that the by-laws may control the placing of any thing or any structure in, on or over any walkway.

(iv) Pleasure Fairs

The regulation of pleasure fairs by by-laws may occur under Public Health Act 1961, s.75 which has been extended by the Local Government (Miscellaneous Provisions) Act 1976, s.22

By-laws can be used to ensure the safety of the means of access to and from both pleasure fairs and roller skating rinks. The hours of operation of these places may also be regulated. More generally the controls may deal with the suppression of nuisances, and the preservation of sanitary conditions, cleanliness, order and public safety at these places. Measures to reduce the risk of fire may also be introduced.

(v) Pleasure Grounds

The use of public walks and pleasure grounds can also be controlled by by-laws. The power to do this is conferred by the Public Health Act 1875, s.164. The power is a wide one enabling the authorities to "regulate" local pleasure grounds and to provide for the removal of offenders from the ground. The power extends to the control of trading activities an example of which can be seen in the case of *Staden v. Tarjanyi* [5] discussed below. Local authorities cannot, however, impose conditions on the use of pleasure grounds which go beyond the by-laws so as to prohibit trading which supports "political activities". [5a]

---

[5] (1980) 78 LGR 614.
[5a] *R v. Barnet LBC ex p Johnson* [1990] The Times, September 1990.

(vi) Commons

By-laws for the prevention of nuisances and the preservation of order on common land may be promulgated by the local authority as part of a "scheme" for the regulation and management of the common. [6] Trading on village and town greens has been discussed earlier. [7]

(vii) Esplanades

In order to prevent "danger, obstruction, or annoyance to anyone using the esplanades or promenades", by-laws may regulate "the selling and hawking of any article commodity or thing thereon " as well as prescribing the nature of traffic which may use them. By-laws may also make provision for the preservation of order and good conduct among persons using the esplanades. [8] By-laws made under this power are likely to be encountered quite frequently because clearly the sea-side esplanade crowded with holiday makers can provide a lucrative market for street traders.

(viii) Nuisances

The Public Health Act 1936, s.81 provides for the promulgation of by-laws to prevent the occurrence of nuisance from, *inter alia* filth, dust, ashes and rubbish. Traders directly responsible for such nuisances could fall foul of such by-laws. In practice litter caused by take-away food stalls is often a more serious problem, but one created by the anti social conduct of the trader's customers. This problem may be more satisfactorily addressed under the anti-litter measures of the Environmental Protection Act 1990. [9]

(ix) Travellers

A local authority may make by-laws designed to promote cleanliness in, and the habitable condition of, tents, vans, sheds

---

[6] Commons Act 1899, ss.1 & 10.

[7] Above p. 4.

[8] Public Health Acts Amendment Act 1907, s.83.

[9] *Infra.* Ch. 2.

and similar structures used for human habitation This power may be used in particular to prevent the spread of infectious diseases by the occupants and, more generally, to prevent nuisances arising in connection with the use of such forms of habitation. [10]

(x) Markets

A local authority which maintains a market has powers to enact by-laws regulating the market. [11] These powers arise either under a special Act incorporating the Markets and Fairs Clauses Act 1847, s.42 or under the Food Act 1984, s.60. Under the former, by-laws may also regulate various matters including the prevention of nuisances and the regulation of trading hours. Provision may also be made to protect buyers from false weights and measures and unfit food. The undertakers have a discretion to fix the penalty for a breach of a by-law, but the penalty must not exceed £5. [12]

The power conferred by the Food Act 1984, s.60 extends to all local authorities regardless of whether they acquired or established the market under the 1984 Act or its predecessors. By-laws may be made regulating the use of the market place, and the buildings, stalls etc. within it and for the prevention of fires, [13] nuisances and obstructions in the market place or in its approaches. Porters and carriers coming to the market, may find their charges regulated by by-laws. By-laws made under this provision are subject to confirmation by the Secretary of State for the Environment. Because this power is rarely used the Government has invited views as to whether it should be abolished.

By-laws may also be enacted specifying articles commonly sold in the market which cannot be sold outside the market in market hours.[14]

---

[10] Public Health Act 1936, s.268; Public Health (Control of Disease) Act 1984, s.56.

[11] The Food Act 1984 extends only to markets; the 1842 Act to markets and fairs.

[12] Section s.43.

[13] Inserted by Food Safety Act 1990 s .52, and sch. 2 para 10.

[14] 56 of the 1984 Act, considered, *infra*. The prohibition extends throughout the distance spcified in the by-law.

(xi) Street Collections

Street collections for charitable purposes may be controlled by by-laws under the Police, Factories &c (Miscellaneous Provisions) Act 1916, s.5. By this means the places where and the conditions under which a person may be permitted in any street or public place to collect money or to sell articles may be regulated.

The Act does not, however, affect anything done in the ordinary course of trade.

(xii) "Good Rule and Government"

One of the most important and wide ranging powers to make by-laws is conferred the Local Government Act 1972, s.235 by which district councils and councils in London boroughs may make by-laws "for the good rule and government of the whole or any part of the district or borough....and for the prevention and suppression of nuisances therein" provided that no similar provision has already been made under any other enactment. The Secretary of State, who is the confirming authority for by-laws made under this section, has drawn up a code of model by-laws designed to promote consistency between local areas. Of these, some are relevant to street trading. For example, the regulation of noisy hawking; music near houses, churches and hospitals; wireless loudspeakers; shooting galleries; advertising vehicles; defacing pavements; broken glass; flags; wilful jostling; advertising bills; and noisy animals is possible under the code. By-laws made under the code may be difficult to challenge since it reflects judicial decisions.

The Validity of By-Laws

Intra Vires

Conformation of the by-law by the relevant authority cannot endow a by-law with the status of law unless the by-law is within the scope of the enabling power. [15] For example, a statute which

---

[15] *Ipswich Taylor's* Case (1614) 11 CO Rep 53; *Kruse v. Johnson, supra* n.1 at p.108.

allowed the making of by-laws for the removal of "filth" did not legitimate a purported by-law instructing the occupiers of premises to remove snow from the footpath in front of their premises since snow in its natural state was not "filth"[16] . The by-law must also be reasonable, free from ambiguity and not repugnant to the general law.

Reasonable

Since there may be different perceptions of what is reasonable [17] The courts should be slow to condemn by-laws as unreasonable since they represent the acts of a democratically accountable body. In *Kruse v. Johnson*, Lord Russell C.J. thought that by-laws should be "'benevolently' interpreted. Nevertheless if a by-law were:

"found to be partial and unequal in (its) operation as between classes; if (it was) manifestly unjust; if (it) disclosed bad faith; if (it) involved such oppressive or gratuitous interference with the rights of those subject to (it) as could find no justification in the minds of reasonable men, the court might well say, 'Parliament never intended to give authority to make such rules; they are unreasonable and *ultra-vires*." [18]

An example of an unreasonable by-law can be found in *Staden v. Tarjanyi* [19] in which a by-law purporting to forbid the flying of hang gliders "in the pleasure ground" was unreasonable because its effect was to assert control over the entire airspace above the pleasure ground. There must have been an altitude above which hang gliders could fly without interfering with any activity taking place on the ground. The District Council could only reasonably assert control of the airspace below that altitude.

Staden suggests that where a by-law goes beyond the minimum interference necessary to achieve its legitimate objective the courts may regard it as unlawful. By-laws have also been struck down

---

[16] *R. v. Wood* (1855) 5 EI +BI 49.
[17] See, eg *Scott v. Pillinger* [1904] 2 KB 855.
[18]*Supra* n. (1) especially at p. 99.
[19] *Supra* n. (5).

where they impose too onerous a burden, [20] or where their effects are so wide that a reasonable and socially useful activity is ostensibly prohibited by it. [21]

An important, although old, case in the street trading context is *Elwood v. Bullock* [22] which concerned the validity of a by-law purporting to restrain any person from erecting a booth in any public place. It had been the immemorial custom for local victuallers to place stalls upon the highway during a fair, leaving room for public passage. The by-law was struck down as unreasonable since the custom was of ancient origin and itself reasonable.

Free From Ambiguity

The by-law should adequately inform those who are bound by it of their obligations and will fail if of indeterminate scope. This was the case in *Scott v. Pilliner* [22] in which a by-law, aimed at controlling street betting, prohibited, amongst other matters, the selling of newspapers which were devoted wholly or mainly to giving information as to the probable result of races *or other competition* (emphasis supplied).

This was unreasonable and too broad since the purported prohibition would prevent distribution of information on such innocuous matters as the probable result of an athletics competition.

Repugnant to the General Law

A by-law is invalid if it is repugnant either to the fundamental principles of the common law or to a provision of a statute. For example, in *London Passenger Transport Board v. Sumner* [23] a by-law penalising non-payment of a fare was void since it lacked a a *mens rea* requirement. In *Powell v. May* Lord Goddard C.J. considered that repugnancy would arise where a by-law purported

---

20 *Arlidge v. Mayor of Islington* [1909] 2 KB 127.
21 Johnson v. Mayor of Croyden (1886) 16 QBD 708.

22 (1844) 6 QB 383.
23 [1904] 2 KB 855.

to permit that which a statute expressly forbad, or where it sought to forbid that which a statute expressly permitted. [24]

Nevertheless, a by-law may go beyond the provisions of the general law and still be valid. This means that it could prohibit, for example, acts which a statute had not made unlawful. In *Gentel v. Rapps,* [25] the by-law provided that "no person shall swear or use offensive or obscene language...in...any carriage" on a tram. The by-law, which was held to be valid, covered *all* such words whether or not they caused "a nuisance or annoyance to others"; it thus extended the effect of the Town Police Clauses Act 1847 but was not repugnant to the general law.

Challenging an Invalid By-Law

Two questions confront the street trader prosecuted under an invalid by-law. First, will the court necessarily strike down the by-law? Second, if it will, how should the challenge be made?

Striking Down and Severance

If the by-law is *ultra vires* in its entirety the court will quash it. More difficult questions arise where part of the by-law falls within the enabling legislation and part does not. The question in such a case will be whether the court will sever the offending part leaving the remainder intact.

This issue was extensively considered by the House of Lords in *DPP v. Hutchinson* [26] which deserves consideration in some detail. The case concerned the prosecution of two "Peace Campaigners" under a by-law which purported to prohibit entry to a military airfield. Under the enabling Act, the by-law could not prejudice commoner's rights, but the by-law under which the women had been convicted made no such saving. Neither of the women, however, sought to assert commoners rights.

In the House of Lords, Lord Bridge with whom the majority agreed, re-stated the fundamental principle that a court has no

---

[24] (1935) 154 L.T. 108.
[25] [1946] KB 330, 365 Lord Goddard C.J.
[26] [1902] 1 KB 160.

jurisdiction to modify or adapt the law to confine it within the scope of the enabling Act.

He stated the orthodox doctrine that a court may sever the invalid part of a by-law where the valid clauses operate independently of the invalid one. Thus where a by-law contains a number of separate clauses only one of which was *ultra vires*, the court could strike out the invalid clause leaving the valid clauses unaffected. This, he held, involves two tests, the first of which is "textual", and the second "substantial". A by-law is textually severable if "a sentence, a phrase, or a single word may be disregarded as exceeding the lawmaker's power, and what remains of the text is still grammatical and coherent. A (by-law) is substantially severable if the substance of what remains after severance is essentially unchanged in its legislative purpose, operation and effect." [27] He added that there would be cases in which the textual test could not be satisfied, but the by-law would be severable notwithstanding this if it passed the "substantial test". [28]

Lord Bridge further explained that when textual severance is possible, the test of substantial severability is satisfied when the valid text is unaffected by, and independent of, the invalid. But when the court must modify the text in order to to achieve severance, this can only be done when the court is satisfied that it is effecting no change in the substantial purpose and effect of the impugned provision.

Only four of the twelve clauses of the Greenham Common by-law were valid. Textual severance was not possible because the valid provisions were ancillary to, and thereby dependent on, the invalid ones. Moreover the by-law was not substantially severable. Its purpose had been to place an absolute prohibition on unauthorised access to the base to meet the demands of security. A by-law which respected the rights of commoners to free access to all parts of the base "would be (a by-law) of a totally different character". [29] They would not be capable of serving the purpose of absolute security which the Greenham Common by-laws were

---

[27] [1990] 2 All ER 836. The decision is discussed by Professor A W Bradley [1990] PL 293 "Judicial Enforcement of *Ultra Vires* Byelaws: The Proper Scope of Severance".
[28] *Ibid* at pp.839-40.
[29] *Ibid* at p. 845.

intended to serve. The by-law thus fell in its entirety, and the appellant's convictions were quashed.

Procedure

A trader prosecuted under an allegedly invalid by-law is not always at liberty to challenge it in the criminal court by way of defence to that prosecution. In some cases, he must initiate separate judicial review proceedings in order to have the by-law declared invalid. The crucial question is when this is so.

Collateral proceedings

A collateral challenge arises where the invalidity of the by-law is raised by way of defence to a prosecution for its alleged breach. The by-law may be invalid in either of two cases. On the one hand, it may be "substantively" invalid because, on its face, the enacting authority had no power to make it, or because it is "patently" unreasonable. On the other, it may also be tainted by a procedural defect such as a failure to consult. The means by which the by-law may be attacked depend on which of the above grounds the attack is based.

(i) Substantive Invalidity
A criminal court hearing a prosecution for a breach of a by-law has a jurisdiction to decide whether the by-law is substantively invalid. Doubts had earlier arisen in this matter after the decision in *O'Reilly v. Mackman*.[30] However, the Divisional Court in judicial review proceedings in *R v. Reading Crown Court ex p Hutchinson* [31] held that a criminal court was bound to consider the question of invalidity when raised as a defence. Such a tactic could not be an abuse of the process of Court since the prosecution and not the accused had been responsible for instituting the proceedings. Moreover, it was felt that injustice would arise if the rule were otherwise because an accused would then be forced institute separate and expensive High Court proceedings in order to appeal a conviction resulting in perhaps a small fine.

---

[30] *Ibid* at p.846.
[31] [1983] 2 AC 237.

(ii) Procedural Invalidity

The principle in *Hutchinson* has no application where the by-law is impugned on the grounds that the enacting authority has failed to comply with a procedural requirement governing its enactment. A trader wishing to mount such a challenge must initiate proceedings for judicial review and bear the expense of so doing. This is because the authority responsible for enacting the by-law is not a party to a criminal prosecution and in such a process would be denied the opportunity of defending the procedure leading to the enactment of the by-law. The court would therefore be unable to decide the issue for lack of sufficient evidence. No such problem arises in the case of substantive *ultra vires* because the question can be resolved by an examination of the by-law and the enabling enactment. [32]

It seems that this does not apply where there are allegations of "*mala fides*" affecting the enactment of the by-law. This could still be considered by the criminal court. It is not, however, clear what constitutes *mala fides* for these purposes. A deliberate failure to consult may be described as bad faith, but would this found the jurisdiction of the criminal court. It is likely that this was not intended. [33]

The distinction between substantive and procedural invalidity is an unfortunate one for the trader. In so far as procedural invalidity is concerned, the distinction erodes the principle that a citizen confronted by *ultra vires* administrative action is entitled to ignore it and remain passive until proceedings are taken against him. [34] Such a rule places the trader at a disadvantage because he must take the initiative of instituting judicial review proceedings and bear their expense.

---

[32] [1988] 1 QB 384; cf *Quitlynn Ltd v. Plymouth CC* [1988] QB 114, distinguished in DPP v. Hutchinson.

[33] *Bugg v. DPP* [1992] The Times, September 11th.

[34] *Ibid per* Woolf L.J. with whom Pill J agreed.

PART II

MARKETS AND FAIRS

CHAPTER 4

INTRODUCTION

Markets enjoy a timeless popularity, perhaps because they provide a more diverse and exciting shopping experience than the anonymous modern shopping mall. People enjoy the variety of goods that stalls and pitches offer as well as the characters who operate them. Goods priced more attractively than in shops lure the bargain hunter who may enjoy the search as much as the purchase.

The profit that a market can generate for its owner has attracted significant entrepreneurial interest in modern times. Yet it is no straightforward matter to organise markets without encountering problems with the law. Attempts at organising new markets have been numerous; not all have been successful.[1]

The Evolution and Purpose of Markets

Markets as a means of trade have origins at least as early as the Roman occupation. Anglo-Saxon Laws often insisted that buying and selling took place before witnesses. [2] The witnesses were necessary to protect the buyer from claims that the goods he had bought had been dishonestly acquired. Unwitnessed sales were perhaps too easily disputed, and furnished a potential flashpoint for violence and bloodshed. Laws [3] were designed to ensure the Peace by encouraging buying and selling to take place in market towns, (although, if witnessed by the portreeve or other trustworthy man, sales could still take place outside the town).

---

[1] *Infra* Ch. 6.
[2] See Pollock and Maitland "The History of English Law" 2nd edition 1968, p 59; Edgar iv, 6; Canute II 24; 1 Edw 1; 2 Athelastan 12.
[3] Such as 1 Edw 1; 2 Athelstan 12.

Transactions within the market were more easily subjected to public scrutiny: title to goods would be observed to pass from seller to buyer, a consequence of importance not only to the parties to the transaction but also the public at large. [4]

Markets also provided a means of establishing a fair or market price of goods [5] thereby removing a further flash point for violence. Thus markets and fairs contributed to a stable and peaceful society.

Because markets were so important to the maintenance of the Peace, their creation was normally an exercise of the royal prerogative. In one sense the franchise of market can be regarded as a mechanism for delegating to private individuals a law and order function which would otherwise have been the responsibility of the State. They were an intelligent use of State power because it would have been impossible for the State to achieve its goals without co-operation at a local level, and such co-operation could best be ensured by the self-interest of the operator of the market in seeking private gain. Therefore the burden of the public responsibility of the market was made more attractive by the profit that the market would generate for the owner. The franchise brought monopolistic rights to ensure commercial supremacy through the exclusion of competitors. Often there was a right to take toll [6] on goods sold in the market. Moreover, the market owner could prevent the holding of rival markets within the common law distance [7] which meant that goods coming to market would be sold in his market and so provide him with toll. The purpose of this lifting of the rules of free competition was only justified where this public interest was served.

The franchisee, however, was not merely a private entrepreneur but in a real sense a public delegate for, after creating a market, the Crown did not renounce its supervisory responsibilities. Market owners were burdened with continuing obligations [8] as well as rights. Failure to fulfil these obligations

---

[4] See *Duke of Bedford v. St. Paul Covent Garden Overseers* (1881) 51 LJMC 41, 55, per Bowen J.

[5] *Per* Lord Mansfield C J in *Hill v. Smith* (1812) 4 Taunt 520.

[6] *Infra*, Ch. 7.

[7] *Infra*, Ch. 6.

[8] For example, there might be a duty to relocate the market if the space available were insufficient. *Infra*, Ch. 8.

might result in the loss of the franchise after which the right to conduct the market reverted to the Crown.

Thus it can be seen that proof of a grant from the Crown, or at a later date, proof of a statutory right of market, became the methods by which lawful markets were established.

The Nature and Attributes of Markets

(i) Lawful Markets

It is important to understand that at common law "market" has a special meaning different from its popular meaning. As already indicated, it refers to a franchise or statutory right of market. There can be no lawful market without a franchise or grant of market either from the Crown, acting under its prerogative powers,[9] or from Parliament. An authoritative judicial definition is to be found in the judgment of Chatterton VC in *Downshire v. O 'Brien*:[10]

"A market is properly speaking the franchise right of having a concourse (a gathering) of buyers and sellers to dispose of commodities in respect of which the franchise was given."

A "Concourse" of Buyers and Sellers

A "concourse" means a coming together of buyers and sellers, a concourse of both, not separate concourses of each. A shop cannot be a concourse of buyers and sellers since here buyers come "independently and at their own convenience to particular premises with the object of buying from or selling to, the occupier of these premises"[11]

---

[9] Bl Comm 1, 274.
[10] (1887) 19 LR Ir 380, 390.
[11] Per Lord Keith in *Scottish Co-operative Wholesale Society Ltd v. Ulster Farmers' Mart Co. Ltd.* [1960] AC 63, 85-86.

Privileges

If the market has been created by grant or franchise (or prescription) the owner of the market has certain privileges including the right (in some cases) to restrain rival markets within the common law distance of six and two third's miles. This means that the right of market is akin to a monopoly right. Its consequence is that the organisers of new informal markets may be at risk of possible action by existing right-holders.

A Lawful Market is Open to All

All persons are entitled to attend a lawful, public market or fair for the purpose of buying or selling within it since the purpose of a grant of market is the benefit of the public. [12] Market organisers should always leave room for casual traders.

(ii) "Informal" or "Unofficial" Markets

Where a market is held without the authority of a right of franchise or by statute it is an "unofficial" or "informal" market. As such it lacks the privileges of a franchise or other grant and may be restrained by others who hold market rights within the common law distance.

Any concourse or gathering of buyers and sellers may amount to an informal market regardless of whether the activity is described as a "market". A market may occur in law at certain types of auction, [13], or at a car boot sale. [14] A market was also held to occur where the organisers purported to organise a "club". This is because the courts focus on the true nature of the gathering. A "sham" label will be disregarded. [15] If a concourse of buyers and seller occurs, the activity is a market in law.

---

[12] *A-G v. Horner No. 2* [1913] 2 Ch 140; *Sevenoaks DC v. Pattullo & Vinson* [1984] 1 All ER 544,551. This does not apply to informal markets held on private premises.

[13] Eg, *Fearon v. Mitchell* (1872) LR 7 QB 690.

[14] A car boot sale was "clearly" a market in *Newcastle-upon-Tyne City Council v. Noble* (1991) 89 LGR 618; see also, *Fitzpatrick v. Secretary of State for the Environment* (1988) JPL 564).

[15] *Stafford Borough Council v. Elkenford* (1976) 75 LGR 337; *Solihull v. Maxfern Ltd.* [1977] 1 WLR 127.

The vulnerability of informal markets and fairs to forced closure at the hands of the holder of market rights in the locality is a problem shared by ancient and modern informal markets alike. Even if it was created before a franchise or statutory market, an informal market held within the common law distance may be closed down. This is important when it is realised that many established, indeed ancient, fairs started as "hiring fairs", "statute" fairs or "mop" fairs. These grew up when masters and servants gathered to discover what the wages, (fixed by local justices under the Statute of Labourers 1351), for the coming year would be. These customary markets and fairs were not created by grant and so were never lawful. They have none of the attributes of a lawful market, and those who trade within them are more vulnerable to legal controls. Traders operating within them, for example, cannot claim a lawful authority for obstructing the highway: without a grant, there is no right of market. In *Simpson v. Wells* [16] the appellant was convicted of an offence after he had placed a stall on the highway at a "statute sessions" which was found to be of great antiquity. He argued unsuccessfully that the right to trade should be inferred from custom and in particular that the fair had been held for more than 20 years. [17] Because the fair had a known origin, however, no prescriptive rights could arise.

Private sector entrepreneurs will normally only be able to create informal markets today because grants under the royal prerogative seem no-longer to be made, and procuring the passage of a private Act of Parliament is enormously expensive. Acquiring an existing franchise or right of market is a different matter. The creation of an informal market is considered further below.

The distinction between "informal" and "lawful" markets is an unsatisfactory one. If a trader, not knowing the history or origin of a market or fair regularly trades there, places a stall on the highway, but leaves room for public passage, he is liable to be indicted for obstruction if the fair was originally a statute fair. On exactly the same facts no conviction would be possible if it were established that the fair originated in a franchise fair. This is because an obstruction occurring in pursuit of a right of market is not

---

[16] (1872) LR 7 QB 214.
[17] *Infra*, p. 71 *et seq.*

an unreasonable user of the highway. [18] It seems objectionable in modern times that the legal status of certain trading should be made to depend upon matters which are of largely antiquarian interest. This is a matter which deserves reform.

The Nature and Atributes of Fairs

The distinction between a market and a fair is of more than academic interest. Some statutes, [19] provide controls which are relevant only to "fairs", so the fair will have to be distinguished from a market.

A fair possesses many of the legal characteristics of a market. It is essentially a large market or festival held once or twice a year perhaps on the day of the patron saint of the village. A fair denotes an event of a larger scale than a mere market. In contrast, a market is held weekly or perhaps even more frequently.

There has been some controversy whether a a purely "pleasure fair", that is, one in which no commodities are sold, can be a fair in law [20] has produced divergent views. This is unlikely to cause difficulty in most cases because even the incidental sale of commodities, such as normally occurs in most modern fairs, seems to be sufficient. [21]

---

[18] *A G v. Horner* (1886) 11 App Cas 66. Although it is uncertain whether market rights could be created over an existing highway: *infra*.

[19] Eg, Metropolitan Police Act 1839, s.39; Metropolitan Fairs Act 1868; the Fairs Acts 1871 and 1873.

[20] *Collins v. Cooper* (1893) 9 TLR 251; *Walker v. Murphy* [1914] 2 Ch 293.

[21] *Collins v. Cooper, per* Bruce J.

CHAPTER 5

THE CREATION OF A MARKET OR FAIR

The means by which market rights may be created are of central importance for all who are concerned in market trading. This applies not only to to entrepreneurs seeking to establish new markets, but also to street traders. Their rights are also at issue because the street trading licensing schemes only exempt markets created by grant, presumed grant or those created under statute. If any market does not have such a legal pedigree, it is at best an "informal" one and the traders who operate within it may be required to obtain street trading licences.

It is now appropriate to consider in more detail the creation of markets. We shall first consider the creation of "lawful" markets and then "informal" ones.

Lawful Markets and Fairs

Lawful markets and fairs are established by grant, presumed grant, or under statute. Establishing the lawful origin of the market will be essential in founding a claim to the rights of market. Of these, the principal is the right to undisturbed enjoyment of the right of market which, amongst other matters, embraces the right to restrain the "levying" or holding of certain rival markets.

A right to take toll, although a separate franchise right, may also be claimed in the case of some, though not all, markets.

1. Creation of a Market or Fair by Grant

The right to create a franchise forms part of the prerogative powers of the Crown. The franchise was created by charter or letters patent. The power to create new franchises remains but has not been used in recent times.

The Crown has no power to grant new market rights which would prejudice rights conferred in an earlier grant unless the consent of the existing market owner is obtained. [1] The rights of the earlier beneficiary have priority. Any purported grant which removes this priority is *prima facie* void [2] and traditionally may be repealed by a *scire facias*. [3]

A franchise right of market which is repealed by a *scire facias* means that the market right reverts to the Crown; the right is not destroyed, and the market may still be held.

It seems that a new grant may be possible if an existing market owner does not exercise his right. If this is correct, it is because a market is created for the benefit of the public. [4] It was held in *Re Islington Market Bill* that a new grant would also be possible where the existing market was limited by metes and bounds and was unable to furnish sufficient accommodation to meet demand. This was, however, subject to the important *caveat* that the new grant should be designed so as not to interfere with the existing market.

Whilst the power of the Crown to grant franchises by letters patent has not been surrendered, procuring such a grant in practice is

---

[1] *Re Islington Market Bill* (1835) 3 Cl & F 513.

[2] *Ibid.*

[3] The writ of *scire facias* is available from the Crown Office to repeal a grant which was improperly made, or where the conditions of a grant have not been fulfilled: *per* Lord Langdale MR in *R v. Prosser* (1848) 11 Beav. 306, 317. The continued existence and availability of the writ has recently been confirmed: *Crown Estate Commissioners v. Mayor and Commonalty and Citizens of the City of London*, Times 11th May 1992; *City of Gloucester v. Williams*, Times 15th May 1990; see also *Tamworth Borough Council v. Fazeley Town Council* 77 LGR 238.

The Attorney General must exercise his discretion to grant his consent or fiat before the writ can issue: an applicant has no right to a writ of *scire facias*. When giving his consent, the Attorney may seek an indemnity as to his costs. The Attorney General's decision does not seem to be subject to judicial review: *R v. Prosser supra*; *Gouriet v. UPW* [1978] AC 435; but this may be subject to the decision of the House of Lords in Council for the *Civil Service Unions v. Minister of the Civil Service* [1985] AC 374 and an exercise of prerogative power was reviewed in *R v. Home Secretary ex p Bentley* [1993] The Times, 8th July.

There appears to be no modern reported instance of the Attorney General intervening *ex officio* to seek a *scire facias* although it remains open to an individual to invoke the procedure with the Attorney General's consent.

[4] *A-G v. Horner No. 2* [1913] 2 Ch. 140.

unlikely to be a straightforward and inexpensive matter. The advantages of seeking a such a grant are, however, that the market would be endowed with the right of monopoly within the common law distance of six and two thirds' miles.

An alternative method of acquiring this right of monopoly is to acquire an existing franchise which is no-longer exercised. This might be purchased from the existing right-holder. Even this is not, however, a guarantee that the right can actually be exercised. As we shall see, the revival of a former market may bring the new owner into conflict with the planning authority. This is considered below. [5]

2. By Prescription and Custom

Failure to adduce any evidence of franchise will not necessarily defeat a claim to a lawful market or fair at common law. A claim may be established by custom or prescription.

The law may give effect to local custom or usage as a means of clothing long established user with legal right. A prescriptive right arises where the court presumes a lost grant creating the right asserted. In effect, it brings forth new rights. To do this the law has indulged in certain fictions.

Presumed Grant

At common law, a grant of a franchise of market may be presumed where user as of right has continued since time immemorial. The year 1189 has been fixed as the limit of legal memory, and any use which can be established as having continued since before that date cannot now be challenged. It is deemed to have all the privileges of a franchise because the origins of the use are presumed to be in a grant the evidence of which has been lost. [6]

User in Excess of Twenty Years

The burden of proving that a user has continued since time immemorial is almost impossible to discharge. The courts have therefore allowed a presumption of immemorial user to arise if

---

[5] P. 77 *et seq.* Note *Spook Erection Ltd v. Secretary of State for the Environment* (1988) 86 LGR 736.

[6] *Bryant v. Foot* [1867] LR 2 QB 161, 180-181.9.

there has been "uninterrupted modern usage", [7] and twenty or more years usage will suffice to raise this presumption if the use is not otherwise explained or contradicted. [8] Less than twenty year's usage may also suffice if there is other evidence to support the right claimed. [9] It seems that the longer the period of use the more difficult it becomes to displace the presumption.

A presumption of immemorial usage may also be made if it can be established as far back as living memory. For example, in *R P C Holdings Ltd v. Rogers* [10] Harman J. relied on the presumption where living memory extended back over half a century but the periods of user which witnesses recalled could not, if tabulated, cover a continuous period of twenty years

Evidence of twenty years user raises a presumption which is, however, capable of being rebutted if it can be shown that the right claimed did not exist at some period after 1189. Thus if it can be shown that there was a time after 1189 when the right of market did not exist, this is sufficient to rebut the presumption. This rule proved fatal in *Hulbert v. Dale* [11] where it was shown that the alleged right of way commenced within the previous century. On this evidence clearly no presumption of immemorial user could be made!

Further, no presumption arises where there is evidence of a custom which is inconsistent with the right of market claimed. This derives from *Perry v. Eames* [12] where an attempt to restrain the erection of a building on the grounds that it would interfere with a right to light founded on prescription failed because the custom of the City of London that no right to light could be acquired in this manner. Thus if it were sought to establish a market as of right at a given time and a given place, proof that the market was, as a matter of custom, held at a different time or a different location would prevent the presumption of immemorial user being raised and a claim based on prescription would fail.

---

[7] Per Parke B *Jenkins v. Harvey* (1835) 1 C M & R 877, 894.
[8] *R v. Joliffe* (1823) 2 B & C 54; *Darling v. Clue* (1864) 4 F & F 329. Market rights are not within the Prescription Act 1832.
[9] *Bealey v. Shaw* (1805) 6 East 208.
[10] [1953] 1 All ER 1029.
[11] [1909] 2 Ch. 570.
[12] [1891] 1 Ch. 658.

Lost Modern Grant

The doctrine of lost modern grant can be invoked where a presumption raised by long user of a market or fair will fail because there is evidence that at some time since 1189 the market or fair in question could not or did not exist. There is authority that the doctrine can only be raised where something prevents the acquisition of the right by custom or long user. [13]

The doctrine presumes that a grant was made at some time after 1189 but that it has subsequently been either lost or destroyed. The doctrine is essentially a legal fiction since the presumption will be made even though the court is aware that in all likelihood no grant was ever made. Although described as a "revolting" doctrine by Lush J in *Angus & Co. v. Dalton* [14] its existence demonstrates the judicial policy of supporting, in so far as it is possible, user which has been enjoyed for a substantial period.

Normally twenty years user is sufficient to raise the presumption of lost modern grant [15] provided the user is not otherwise explained. [16] An alternative explanation caused difficulty in *A-G v. Horner* [17] where the court was not able to presume a lost grant entitling a market to be held on additional days each week because there had been a charter under which that right could have been claimed but this had been made void by statute. [18]

No Grant Made

Whereas a claim based on a presumption of immemorial user will fail if it can be shown that at some time after 1189 the right claimed could not or did not exist, it seems that proof that there never was a grant or charter in fact will not destroy the presumption of lost modern grant. This proposition has, however,

---

[13] *Bryant v. Lefever* (1879) 4 CP D 172, 177.

[14] (1877) 3 QBD 85, 94.

[15] *Penwarden v. Ching* (1829) M & M 400; *Dalton v. Angus & Co.* (1881) 6 App Cas 740, 779.

[16] *A-G v. Simpson* [1901] 2 Ch. 671, 698, per Farwell J.

[17] (1884) 14 QB 245.

[18] Lindley LJ *Ibid.*at 267 stated that the market could still have been conducted on the additional days; it would simply have lacked its right of monopoly. Problems would arise, in a similar case, however, if it was sought to trade on the highway because a right of market constitutes lawful excuse for a *prima facie* obstruction.

been subject to considerable disagreement [19] but this now seems to represent the law. [20] The reason why the presumption cannot be rebutted by evidence that no charter was ever granted was explained by Lindley L.J in *Dalton*:

"The theory of an implied grant was...... as a means to an end. It afforded a technical common law reason for not disturbing a long continued open enjoyment. But it appears to me contrary to the reason for the theory itself that to allow such an enjoyment to be disturbed simply because it can be proved that no grant was ever in fact made." [21]

For this reason, a person seeking to displace the presumption has an onerous burden. [22]

3. The Creation of Markets and Fairs by or Under Statute

A market or fair can be created by local or personal Act of Parliament, or established under a statutory power given to local authorities under a general Act of Parliament.

A Local or Personal Act of Parliament

Parliament can confer a right to a market by local or special Act. This is one of the means by which new market rights can be created for the benefit of the entrepreneurial market organiser. [23] An Act of Parliament is more powerful than a grant by charter since it can disregard existing market rights. Any market or fair so created cannot therefore be challenged on the grounds that it disturbs a pre-existing market. Nevertheless, Parliament will not normally enact legislation which interferes with existing rights without the

---

[19] *Angus v. Dalton* (1877) 3 QBD 85; (1878) 4 QBD 162; (1881) 6 App Case 740.

[20] *Tehidy Minerals Ltd v. Norman* [1971] 2 QB 528, 552 where Buckley J. treated the House of Lords in *Dalton* as having confirmed the decision of the Court of Appeal on this point.

[21] (1881) 6 App Cas at 765.

[22] *Dalton supra.* n. (19) at pp 172, and 186.

[23] Such an individual may be able to operate an informal market with the consent of the local authority where the latter owns the market right, but this market will not have the monopolistic "right" of market.

consent of the owner. [24] Promoters must give public notice of their intention to seek statutory powers, and it is possible for existing market owners to oppose the Bill.

Markets which are created by private enactment will normally have all the incidents of a common law market except in so far as these are inconsistent with the provisions of the Act itself. [25] The Act in question will usually incorporate either the whole or part of the Markets and Fairs Clauses Act 1847 which was designed as a model code for the management and regulation of markets.

Promoting a measure of this kind is, however, notoriously expensive and this would serve as a deterrent to all but the most resourceful organiser of markets. The House fees are currently £10,000 to which must be added the advertising costs, printing costs and the costs of employing Parliamentary Agents, to draft and promote the Bill. If the Bill is opposed, Counsel's fees will probably be added to these other costs.

Other Statutory Powers
Local authorities are the beneficiaries of powers to create "statutory" markets. [26] One of the most important of these powers is conferred by the Food Act 1984, s.50 which enables an authority to establish a market (but not a fair) within its area, or to either purchase or lease an existing market (whether it be a franchise or statutory market) by agreement. [27] A local authority cannot acquire a market right by compulsory purchase. [28] In establishing a new market, a local authority cannot interfere with any rights or privileges enjoyed by any person within the local authority's area without that person's consent. [29]

---

[24] Where this rule is not followed, see *Pickin v. BRB* [1974] 1 All ER 609.

[25] *Manchester City C v. Walsh* (1986) 84 LGR 1.

[26] If a franchise market is acquired, and only the rights of the franchise are exercised, the market remains a franchise market. The market becomes a statutory one, however, where the local authority exercises any of its statutory powers in respect of the market, for example to alter the days on which it is held: *Manchester City Council v. Walsh* 1986 84 LGR 1.

[27] London boroughs have similar powers: London Government Act 1963 s 54 (1) (a) as substituted by the Food Act 1984, s 134 and Sched 10.

[28] The power of compulsory purchase of land under s.110 expressly excepts the acquisition of markets under s.50 (1).

[29] Section 50 (2).

The meaning of this provision is not clear. The better view is probably that the right of enjoyment of a market could extend over the area in which the owner can restrain the levying of a rival market, that is six and two thirds' miles. This is supported by Pease and Chitty, [30] and, with respect, it seems to be the better view, although other interpretations are possible. [31] If this does represent the law, a local authority seeking to establish a market within the common law distance of an existing market would require the consent of the market owner. The right could be purchased under s 50 (1) (b).

However, if a local authority has already created a market under the 1984 Act, or legislation which preceded it, it has no power to restrain the creation by a neighbouring local authority of a new market within its area. The new market is not deemed to disturb any right of the authority. [32]

It is different where the local authority has merely taken over a franchise market. Here the right to prevent the levying of a rival market within the common law distance survives even as against another local authority.[33]

Wharves
Local authorities also have a power to provide wharves, stations, lairs, sheds, and other places for the landing, keeping, sale, slaughter or disposal of imported or other animals under s.54 of the Animal Health Act 1981. Such are markets under the Markets and Fairs Clauses Act 1847 and a substantial part of that Act is incorporated into the Animal Health Act 1981. [34]

4. The Creation of Informal Markets

As we have seen, new informal markets may arise where a "concourse" or gathering of buyers and sellers is organised without

---

[30] *Pease and Chitty's Law of Markets and Fairs* at p. 268.
[31] *Ibid.*
[32] Section 50 (3) of the 1984 Act.
[33]Section 50 (3). This may be reformed: see *infra*.
[34] Excluded from the 1981 Act are sections 6 to 9 and 52-59 which cover matters for which special provision is made under the 1981 Act. See the 1981 Act s 54 (2).

the authority of a grant, presumed grant or statute. It does not matter under what guise the market is created: whether a "bazaar" or "car boot sale", or even a "club", it may still constitute a market in law.

Many difficulties confront those wishing to establish new informal markets. New informal street markets lack lawful authority and are likely to be an obstruction of the highway leaving the traders liable to prosecution. Further, such street markets do not benefit from the exemption from the street trading licensing schemes. This exemption only applies to "lawful" markets and not to informal ones. This means that the continued existence of the market may depend upon the discretion of the local authority. Traders operating within it will also be required to obtain a licence from the local authority. This again is a discretionary matter and a fee is normally payable.

An informal market may also be an unlawful disturbance of the market rights of another-perhaps the local authority for the area, and may be forced to close by the owners of a neighbouring established market. The nature and extent of the monopolistic rights of lawful markets is considered below. [35] In essence, the owner of such a right of market may suppress all informal markets within the common law distance of six and two thirds' miles. The would-be organiser must therefore discover whether any such right exists. If it does, his operation is at risk unless he obtains the consent of the right holder. In many cases the right-holder will be the local authority which may be prepared to grant its consent subject to the payment of a fee. [36]

Even if consent is obtained, a new market will almost *ex hypothesi* represent a change of use of the land on which it is to be sited. This means that it is likely to constitute "development" and will require planning permission. It is now proposed to consider the impact of development controls on new markets.

Markets and Development Control

Planning authorities have far-reaching powers to take enforcement action against markets lacking planning permission, and there is

---

[35] See especially Ch. 6.
[36] This seems to be the practice in Birmingham, for example.

much evidence that they are prepared to use them. Enforcement action is not confined to markets in the popular sense: car boot sales, bazaars and other forms of "market" may all infringe development controls.

For most would-be organisers, development control probably represents the most significant obstacle to the creation of a new market business. Both the creation of new markets as well as the revival and re-location of old ones may fall within the discretionary powers of the local planning authority. This is because, in many instances, there will be a material change of use of the site or planning unit either when a new market is created, (or a car boot sale run) or an existing market re-located. [37] The local authority, in effect, enjoys the power to licence market creation, even if it does not in a private law sense own the market rights in that area. If it owns those market rights it may not need to resort to planning powers to close down a new market.

The power to grant planning permission is a discretionary one. Should permission be withheld the market activity is unlawful and can be restrained by enforcement action taken under the planning legislation or, in extreme cases, by the grant of an injunction. [38]

Development
The concept of "development" is a central one in the scheme of development control for it defines those activities for which planning permission must be sought. If an activity is not "development" it evades the controls of the planning system. In certain limited cases that which is "development" may attract a deemed grant of planning permission if it falls within the scope of the General Development Order 1988 (GDO).

There are two elements to the "development" concept.

(i) "Operational Development"
Operational development means the carrying out of building, engineering, mining or other operations in, on, over or under land. [39]

---

[37] Eg *Stafford Borough Council v. Elkenford* (1976) 75 LGR 337.

[38] Eg *Runnymede BC v. Ball* [1986] 1 All ER 629.

[39] Town and Country Planning Act 1990, s.55 (1).

It clearly embraces the erection of a building. A "building" means "any structure or erection or any part of a building" but purely temporary structures are not buildings.[40] Stalls which are not fixed into the ground and which are removed after a market has closed are not likely to be buildings. Bringing them onto the land would not in itself require planning permission under this limb of "development". [41]

(ii) A Material Change of Use
Development also occurs where there is a material change of use of any building or other land. It is this limb of "development" which may cause problems for those seeking to establish new markets for, *ex hypothesi*, the existing use of the site in question will not be concerned with markets or fairs. Establishing such a new market use will normally be a material change of use and so attract the need to seek planning permission. [42]

"Intensification" and Market Expansion
Even existing uses which expand may be subject to control by virtue of the uncertain and controversial doctrine of "intensification". Where an existing use is "intensified" it may require planning permission, but only if it constitutes a material change of use. [43]

It seems, however, that the increased use of a market would not normally be sufficient to constitute a material change of use. There may be circumstances where this would be otherwise; arguably, if the operation had merely comprised a few stalls (falling short of a market) , and was intensified so as to become a market by the introduction of many more stalls, a material change of use may have occurred. If this is so planning permission for the market would be required.

Permission could also be necessary if a market expanded beyond the boundaries of its existing site.

---

[40] Section 336.
[41] *James v. Brecon CC* [1963] 15 P & CR 20 (fairground swing boats not fixed to the ground were not buildings.)
[42] *Stafford BC v. Elkenford* (1976) 75 LGR 337.
[43] Eg *Brooks & Burton v. Secretary of of State* [1977] 1 WLR 1294. Note also the remarks of Lord Donoldson in *Royal Borough of Kensington and Chelsea & Secretary of State v. Mia Carla Ltd.* [1981] JPL 50.

Permitted Development: Temporary Markets

The requirement to seek planning permission is lifted in the case of temporary open air markets. Planning permission is unnecessary because the Town and Country Planning General Development Order 1988 Schedule 2 Art. 4 Class B permits the use of any land as a market for not more than 14 days in total in any calendar year. This exception is designed to benefit *ad hoc* markets or fairs. [44]

The deemed permission also allows "moveable structures", such as stalls to be used in connection with the temporary market.

What Constitutes a Market?

It should first be noted that the GDO seems to apply only to markets and not to fairs properly so called. In deciding what is a temporary market the courts follow the orthodox approach and may disregard any label applied by the organiser. For example, in *Fitzpatrick v. Secretary of State for the Environment,* [45] a car boot sale was held to be a temporary market. It could thus only operate for 14 days in any year in the absence of an express grant of planning permission. [46]

The saving for temporary markets does not apply if the land in question is a building or within the curtilage of a building. Indoor markets are thus subject to the need to seek planning permission in the normal way even if they are merely a "temporary" occurrence.

"Temporary?"

If it is always intended that the market be permanent it does not acquire the deemed permission under the GDO; in other words, it cannot lawfully be operated even for 14 days: planning permission must be sought for it *ab initio.* [47]

Where Permission Can Still Be Required

Even if a market is temporary, the authorities may give "directions" effectively curtailing the benefits of the GDO

---

[44] *Jarman v. Wetherill* (1977) 75 LGR 537 which concerned a coin or stamp fair held on a single day which would have been the kind of market falling within the General Development Order 1988 had it not been held inside a building.

[45] [1988] JPL 564.

[46] See also [1993] JPL 407 concerning a car boot sale in the Green Belt.

[47] *South Bucks District Council v. Secretary of State for the Environment* [1988] EGCS 157.

exception altogether. This may occur under Article 4, if the Secretary of State or the local planning authority are satisfied that "it is expedient that development should not be carried out unless permission is granted". If this is so, either may give "directions" that the benefits of the GDO be disapplied in a particular case. If trading continues thereafter it may ultimately be restrained by injunction. [48]

An Article 4 direction may be given before the annual quota of 14 days has been exhausted even though the market has commenced. This is because in the interval between the "temporary" markets the land returns to its "normal" use for that period. New development takes place when the land is again used as a market and this requires permission. Art 4 is available to restrain any resumption of a temporary use once it stops and the land reverts to its normal use. [49] Once the direction has been given there is no permission in place to legitimate the recommencement of the market operation.

Compensation
An Article 4 direction disapplies the deemed planning permission under the GDO. In effect it makes it necessary to seek an express grant of permission. Compensation may be payable where this planning permission is refused so long as in doing so the local planning authority is refusing permission for development formerly permitted. This means that the developer, or market organiser, must not in his request for planning permission seek more than was formerly granted under then GDO. [50] Thus three conditions must be satisfied before compensation may be obtained: (i) an Article 4 direction must have withdrawn the deemed permission under the General Development Order thus making an express grant of planning permission necessary if the market organiser wishes to continue operating the market; (ii) an application for that permission must be made but framed only to cover that which had formerly been permitted before the Article 4 direction (operation of the market for 14 days per year); (iii) a refusal by the planning

---

[48] *Thanet District Council v. Ninedrive Ltd.* (1978) 76 LGR 320.

[49] *South Bucks District Council v. Secretary of State* [1989] JPL 351.

[50] Section 108 of the Town and Country Planning Act 1990.

authority to grant that permission, or a decision to grant it subject to conditions.

In *Strandmill Ltd v. Epping Forest DC,* [51] the market organiser failed to secure compensation because, after the Article 4 direction, planning permission was sought to operate the market each Sunday. Since this was a wider form of permission than had been formerly permitted under the General Development Order a duty to compensate did not arise.

Other Powers in Relation to Temporary Markets
If it so resolves, the council of a district or a London borough has an additional power under s.37 of the Local Government (Miscellaneous Provisions) Act 1982 to require those intending to organise temporary open-air markets to give not less than one month's notice of their intention to do so. A "market" for the purposes of this section means a concourse of buyers and sellers held otherwise than in a building or on a highway which comprises not less than five stalls, stands, vehicles or pitches. [52] A person holds such a market if he charges a rent or fee for any such pitch, stall etc. from persons wishing to trade in the market. The duty to notify also binds any occupier of land to be used as the proposed site for the market. The purpose of this power is to allow the council to investigate whether the market will indeed be a temporary arrangement. It is not clear from s.37 what constitutes a "temporary" market for these purposes.

Breach of the duty to notify is an offence punishable by fine not exceeding level 4 on the standard scale.

Markets conducted with the benefit of a grant of planning permission, or markets and fairs held under a grant, presumed grant or statute are outside the operation of the section and do not need to be notified.

Development and Market Revival
If land was used for the purposes of a market or fair on the "appointed day", 1st July 1948, when the Town and Country Planning Act 1947 came into force, it is deemed to have planning permission. This means that markets and fairs held on that date

---

[51] [1992] EGCS 41.
[52] Section 37 (6).

can continue to be held as of right for the purposes of development control. If after that date the market falls into desuetude and the owner later seeks to revive it on the same site, it appears that no grant of planning permission is required.

Problems arise where the franchise entitles the market owner to operate a market within the district rather than within the "metes and bounds" of a particular site within the district. If he attempts to revive the market and at the same time to relocate it to a different site (permitted by the franchise) it seems that planning permission is required. This is so even where the market is to be returned to its original site if that site was not used for market purposes on "the appointed day".

This appears from *Spook Erection Ltd v. Secretary of State* [53] where a franchise market not limited by metes and bounds had been held in a certain street until 1923. It was then moved to another part of the town and fell into desuetude after 1956. In 1976 it was sought to revive the market on its original site whereupon the local planning authority served an enforcement notice. The owner asserted *inter alia* that the franchise entitled him to hold the market in any place within the district.

The Court of Appeal held that because, on July 1st 1948, no market had been held on the original site, it was no-longer possible to do so without a grant of planning permission.

Appeals and the Enforcement Process
If an enforcement notice is served against the operator of a market, he has the right to appeal to the Secretary of State who may (*inter alia*) grant planning permission. [54] Whilst the appeal is in process the owner may continue to hold the market notwithstanding the enforcement notice. In such a case the local authority may wish to restrain the operation of the market by issuing a stop notice. [55] It

---

[53] [1988] 2 All ER 667.

[54] Sections 172, 174 and 177 of the Town and Country Planning Act 1990.

[55] Section 183 of the 1990 Act. A stop notice prevents the carrying on of any activity included in breach of development control during the compliance period. Under s. 172 (5) an enforcement notice only takes effect on a specified date which must not be less than 28 days from when it is served (s. 172 (6)). This period before the enforcement notice takes effect is the compliance period. Stop notices therefore prevent the activity in breach during this period and beyond if the enforcement notice is subject to an appeal.

cannot normally do so, however, where the market began at a date more than twelve months earlier. This is so even if the market has operated unlawfully in that period. [56]

No such restriction applies where the local authority seeks an injunction to restrain the continued unlawful operation of the market, and this kind of proceedings may provide an important means of law enforcement if the service of a stop notice is not possible. [57]

---

[56] *Scott Markets v. Waltham Forest London Borough Council* (1979) 77 LGR 565.
[57] The local authority's power to seek an injunction is considered at p. 358.

CHAPTER 6

DISTURBANCE

Introduction

A market owner has the common law right to restrain a "disturbance" of the right of market. [1] This involves a number of consequential rights including the right to restrain the operation, or "levying", of a rival market within the common law distance. A rival market operator can sometimes be restrained from competing with the established market.

(i) Suppression of Rival Markets

This right generates considerable controversy. It endows the market right with a monopolistic character which many now regard as obsolete. At the time of writing, as part of its programme of de-regulation, the Government has invited views on possible reforms designed to stimulate local enterprise. [2] At present what is contemplated is the removal of the monopolistic rights of local authority owned markets, as well as local authorities' statutory powers to restrain certain sales outside the market. The legislation necessary to do this could be introduced into Parliament early in 1994. It is not proposed to alter the market rights of private market owners. Fairs are also thought to be excluded from the scope of the possible reform. At the time of writing,[3] no decision has been reached on any of the matters.

---

[1] This is so whether the right originates in a grant, by prescription, or by statute *Newcastle v. Noble* (1991) 89 LGR 618; *Manchester City Council v. Walsh* (1986) 84 LGR 1.

[2] See the consultation letter circulated by the Department of the Environment, 16th August 1993, and Clauses 21 and 22 of the Deregulation and Contracting Out Bill 1994.

[3] 3rd December 1993.

Arguments in favour of the abolition of the right of monopoly essentially stress that monopolistic markets were specifically designed to inhibit free competition. The reasons for this, as we have seen, are purely historical. But the issues are not entirely one sided. Local authorities often employ their monopoly of franchise as a means of preventing the uncontrolled growth of informal markets in inappropriate areas by those over whom it exercises no control. The consumer is thus protected against fly-by night traders setting up markets in unsuitable locations.

One counter-argument is that existing planning laws are sufficient to meet this need. The exercise of such limited powers by an elected body and subject to the scrutiny of the courts by way of judicial review may be more satisfactory than allowing new markets to be suppressed in the exercise of monopolistic powers derived from private law. If this is accepted, some reform of the General Development Order might be necessary to impose greater controls on temporary markets. [4] It is true that an Article 4 direction is available to disapply the deemed planning permission otherwise acquired by the General Development Order, but this may not allow local authorities to intervene at a sufficiently early date; [5] and the market organiser may acquire rights to significant compensation. [6]

But this does not conclude the issue. As the Government recognises, the monopoly also serves an economic purpose. By licensing "rival" market operators in return for a fee, local authorities often generate significant income for the purposes of their general revenue. This may itself be controversial (depending upon one's political standpoint) because the licensing fees can be seen either as a further burden on business enterprise or a means by which businesses contribute to the communities in which they derive their profits. Whatever view is adopted, it is nevertheless clear that the abolition of the monopoly will force local government to rely upon local taxation to make up the shortfall in revenue thereby transferring what is now a burden on business to the local taxpaying community.

---

[4] *Supra* p. 80.

[5] Especially if notice under s.37 of the Local Government (Miscellaneous Provisions) Act 1982 were not given.

[6] *Supra* pp. 81-82.

The Government's present proposals raise further problems. It is unclear why, as a matter of principle, the continuation of monopoly rights in private market owners serves the public interest. [7] As we have seen, such arguments as there are for continuing the monopoly seem only to apply to local authority markets where it can be exercised to further the interests of good government of the local area. Arguments for reform bear most heavily upon privately owned rather than local authority markets which stifle competition to further the private interest of the owner rather than the inhabitants of the local area.

The partial nature of the proposed reforms means that the existing law on disturbance cannot be ignored. It must be stressed, however, that the possible effects of European Community Law could also have a significant impact on the enforceability of those market rights which survive any future reforms. This is considered below.

(ii) Selling Goods Outside the Market

Whilst the power to restrain a disturbance by levying a rival market is the most valuable benefit of market rights, it should not be forgotten that a disturbance may also arise in certain circumstances where goods are sold outside the market, or where goods are sold by sample in the market with an intention to evade tolls. Each of these may create a right of action in the market owner. This is another area which may be subject to reform.[7a]

Disturbance by Levying a Rival Market

It is tortious to interfere with the right of the owner to hold the market or fair and to take the profits from it. This is so whether the market was created by franchise or statute. [8] Common law

---

[7] There may be a duty to compensate private market owners if their rights were abolished.

[7a] See now clause 22 of the Deregulation and Contracting Out Bill 1994.

[8] Subject to the terms of special Act creating the market. This is so notwithstanding earlier judicial doubts: see Pickford L.J in *Hailsham Cattle Market v. Tolman* [1915] 2 Ch 1 at 7. The law is now stated in *Manchester City Council v. Walsh* (1986) 84 LGR 1; *Wakefield City Council v. Box* [1982] 3 All ER 506; *Northampton Borough Council v.*

rights are in addition to the protection afforded to the market under the statute. [9]

The right entitles the market owner, in certain circumstances, to restrain the levying of a rival market or fair situated within the common law distance of six and two thirds' miles of his or her own market. If it is beyond that distance, the rival market is too "remote" and is presumed to do no injury to the franchise market. This is so even if a "remote" market or fair causes great loss in fact.

It will be recalled, however, that a franchise creating a new market or fair is itself void if it disturbs the franchise rights of an existing market or fair. [10] If the new market is created by statute, however, it cannot be set aside on these grounds.

What Constitutes a Rival Market?

The Importance of Substance and not Form

As we have seen, whether an activity constitutes a rival market is a question of fact and depends upon all the circumstances of the case. [11] The crucial distinguishing feature of a market is that it is "a concourse of buyers and sellers to dispose of commodities." [12] This means that wherever such a gathering occurs within the common law distance of an established market, a rival market may arise.

Substance and not form is of the essence so that a market organiser cannot disguise what is in fact a rival market by a misleading description. In *Stafford Borough Council v. Elkenford* [13] the organisers sought to disguise the operation of a Sunday market by purporting to operate a "club". The court had no difficulty in disregarding the label attached to this operation.

Midland Development Group of Companies (1978) 76 LGR 750; *Leicester Corporation v. Maby* (1971) 70 LGR 209; *Manchester Corporation v. Lyons* (1883) 22 Ch. D 287.

[9] See, for example, *Wakefield City Council v. Box* [1982] 3 All ER 506.

[10] *Re Islington Market Bill* (1835) 3 Cl & Fin. 513.

[11] *Morpeth Corporation v. Northumberland Farmers' Auction Mart Co. Ltd* [1921] 2 Ch. 154 at p 161.

[12] *Downshire v. O' Brien* (1887) 19 LR Ir 380, 390 *per* Chatterton V-C.

[13] (1976) 75 LGR 337.

As we have seen, markets take many forms: car boot sales, which are increasingly popular, [14] auction sales, "bazaars" , "antiques fairs" and other similar operations may all constitute a market where a concourse of buyers and sellers is assembled. Such activities can be restrained by the owner of market rights if they occur within the common law distance of his or her market or fair.

Because the definition of a market is unsatisfactory, the courts encounter problems in distinguishing a market from other forms of commercial activity in border-line cases. Difficult cases are founded upon value judgments as much as principle.

Auction Sales as Rival Markets
An auction, is not *inherently* a market because it merely provides a means of fixing the price of goods offered for sale. Nevertheless, if a sufficient concourse of buyers and sellers is assembled, a market is created.

Difficulties in distinguishing the two are compounded by the similarities they share: each provides facilities for others to sell their goods, in contrast to the shopkeeper who normally sells his own goods from such premises. Markets and auction sales alike are often preceded by an invitation to the public to buy and sell and this invitation may give rise to a concourse of buyers and sellers. [15] The fact that an auction sale takes place before one person does not prevent a market from arising because sales before one individual were a feature of early markets [16]

Ultimately, whether a market is created is a question of fact. In *Corporation of London v. Lyons, Sons and Co. (Fruit Brokers) Ltd.*[17] fruit was sold by auction close to Spitalfields market but only on behalf of two sellers. This was lawful because it created a concourse of buyers, but not of sellers. It would have been otherwise if a concourse of sellers was established. This is far from satisfactory because it threatens many established and reputable

---

[14] *Newcastle v. Noble* (1991) 89 LGR 618. *Fitzpatrick v. Secretary of State for the Environment* [1988] JPL 564.

[15] The importance of this may be seen in *Kingston upon Hull City Council v. Greenwood* (1984) 82 LGR 586, 597; *Manchester City Council v. Walsh* (1986) 84 LGR 1, 12.

[16] *Elwes v. Payne* 12 Ch. D. 468, 473, Sir George Jessel MR.

[17] [1936] 1 Ch. 78.

auction businesses which are not, in substance, rival markets. [18] These cases illustrate that the test for identifying a market is a necessary but not a sufficient formula: something more should be required.

"Shops" as Rival Markets

Trading in a shop, properly so called, [19] does not normally create a concourse of buyers and sellers and so is not a rival market. Nor does trading in a shop amount to disturbance by selling outside the market. [20]

Problems have arisen where traders have been offered individual "shops" or "units" with storage facilities within larger buildings. Organising such a venture has been held in *Kingston-Upon-Hull v. Greenwood*[21] and *Manchester City Council v. Walsh*[22] to constitute the organising of a rival market even though the development of a shopping mall does not. The courts' approach in these cases is not altogether satisfactory.

In each of these cases the court approached the problem by distinguishing the activities of the individual traders from those of the organiser. Even if the individual traders were operating from shops so that a prosecution for disturbance would not lie against them individually, this did not prevent the organisers from levying a rival market. The organisers held no stock and were not selling anything [23] and so were not shopkeepers. In each case they had facilitated a concourse of buyers and sellers because of the invitation to the public at large to buy and to sell in the premises.[24]

---

[18] *Ibid* at p141.

[19] *Infra.*

[20] *Mayor of Manchester v. Lyons* (1882) 22 Ch.D. 287. But a custom may prevent such trading: *Mayor of Manchester v. Lyons, ibid* at p 306; *Mayor of Macclesfield v. Pedley* (1833) 4 B & Ad 397; *Mosley v. Walker* (1827) 7 B & C 40 esp 56 discussed *infra.*

[21] (1984) 82 LGR 586.

[22] (1986) 84 LGR 1. A similar example of the *modus operandi* seems to have occurred in *Aberdare Markets and Town Hall Co. v. Bolwell & Hayward Ltd.* (1992) 90 LGR 613.

[23] (1984) 82 LGR 586, 617.

[24] See also *Aberdare Markets and Town Hall Co. v. Bolwell & Hayward Ltd.* (1992) 90 LGR 613.

This was held to be a factor strongly indicative that a market had been created. [25]

Also of relevance was the nature and size of the individual units and the proximity of the individual sellers one to another. The degree of control retained and exercised by the owners was important. Even if the traders had some security of tenure this was not inimical to the idea of a market.[25a]

Important questions were not satisfactorily resolved by these decisions. These issues again expose the deficiencies of the unrefined definition of what constitutes a rival market. For example, if a developer of a shopping complex promotes a vigorous advertising campaign seeking both traders to occupy small individual shops and buyers to come to those shops does he thereby operate a rival market? *Walsh* and *Greenwood* suggest that he might although this would be a somewhat bizarre result.

These decisions also seemed to cast doubt upon franchised operations within large department stores. The Court, however, stated:

"We regard this as an unrealistic approach to the problem and have no doubt that with the application of common sense there will be no difficulty in differentiating (operations such as "Affleck's Palace and Harrods)". [26]

This is unsatisfactory because the principles do seem to invite such unrealistic results.

The reality is that the courts place reliance upon the origins of the traders in question. Enterprises which provide facilities for those who normally operate as market or street traders (such as "Affleck's Palace") constitute rival markets. Similar enterprises which franchise non-street trading businesses may not be rival

---

[25] An interesting comparison with *Walsh* and *Greenwood* is *Haynes v. Ford* [1911] 2 Ch 237 where a former market trader moved to a substantial building and carried on a wholesale business in practically the same way as he had done whilst trading in the market. Here the Court of Appeal held that he conducted his business in his own shop.

[25a] Where units are leased to individual traders a market is not necessarily created, however: *East Staffordshire B.C. v. Windridge Pearce (Burton-on-Trent) Ltd.* [1993] EGCS 186.

[26] (1986) 84 LGR 1, 12.

markets even though the franchisees similarly operate in units within a larger operation.

Street traders who vacate the streets and operate from High Street premises may still find their enterprises frustrated by the law on disturbance and so be forced back into the street trading proper. This seems confused in terms of social policy because, unless trading in a lawful market, their businesses might then be stifled by the regulatory powers of the local authority.

The Common Law Distance

The right of monopoly allows the owner of a lawful market (in some circumstances) to force the closure of a rival if the latter is situated within the common law distance of his own. This right is intended to prevent competition from rivals drawing away buyers and sellers within the catchment area of the franchise market.

Notwithstanding earlier doubts, it is now tolerably well settled that the common law distance is six and two thirds' miles.[27] Maddocks J in *Newcastle upon-Tyne City Council v. Noble*[28] thought that the basis of the rule was to be found in Bracton [29] and is derived from Bracton's division of market day into three periods. Two- thirds of the day would be devoted to the journey to and from the market and the remaining third to conducting business there. A reasonable days walking, for an average person, would be about twenty miles. Thus the notional maximum outward journey would be six and two-thirds' miles. [30]

The difficulty with the rule is that Bracton calculated the distance from the "base" or dwelling of the person attending the market. The distance is actually measured from the franchise

---

[27] *Birmingham City Council v. Anvil Fairs.* [1989] 1 WLR 312. This appears to have the support of the Court of Appeal in *Sevenoaks DC v. Pattullo & Vinson* [1984] 1 All ER 544. In contrast, a charter granted by King Edward III to the City of London stated that thereafter no right of market would be created within 7 miles of the City of London: see *GER v. Goldsmid* (1884) 25 ChD 511. This was thought to support the view that the distance should be 7 miles.

[28] (1991) 89 LGR 618.

[29] *De Legibus et Consuetedinibus Angliae* MDXL vo. III p. 198 (Trans. Thorne).

[30] Pease has, however pointed out that different standards of measurement complicate the search for an early authoritative statement of the rule: see 32 LQR 199.

market. This lead Maddocks J to describe the rule as "arbitrary"[31] because a market could be established beyond the common law distance and still draw people away from the franchise market. For example, in a case where a rival market is seven miles from the franchise one, (and so immune from control) a person living four miles from the franchise market may still be nearer to the rival one which is three miles from his home. The rival would be detrimental to the franchise market and yet be immune from control by the right-holder.

Other objections to the rule also emphasise the different modes of transport which would enable some of those attending the market to travel greater distances anyway.[32] The rule is, however, so well entrenched that legislation would be necessary to abolish it.

Measuring the Common Law Distance
There was little authority on whether the distance should be measured radially - "as the crow flies"- or by the shortest road. Maddocks J. in *Newcastle-upon Tyne City Council v. Noble*,[33] having considered the "arbitrary" nature of the rule thought that since it was to be regarded merely "as a broad and simple" rule, the former was the correct method.

From what point should the measurement be taken? This is not a difficulty where the market area is defined in the grant by "metes and bounds", in other words where its site is narrowly defined. The difficulty arises in the case of a grant which enables the market holder to conduct it in any place within the district, borough or "vill". In *Birmingham City Council v. Anvil Fairs*,[34] Browne-Wilkinson V-C held that the measurement should be taken from the place in which the market was actually conducted and not the boundary of the authorised area. This means that if a franchisee exercises his implied right to move his or her market to another site within the district[35] an informal market which had

---

[31] (1991) 89 LGR 618, at p. 625.
[32] Eg *per* Lord Parker of Waddington in *Hammerton v. Earl of Dysart* [1916] 1 AC 57, 88.
[33] (1991) 89 LGR 618.
[34] (1989) 1 WLR 312.
[35] *Infra.* Ch. 8.

been held just outside the common law distance could subsequently find itself in jeopardy.

Similar problems would arise for an informal market if a local authority created a new market under s.50 (1) of the Food Act 1984. This would be so even if the rival market were outside the local authority's district. [36]

What Constitutes Disturbance

A market conducted outside the common law distance inflicts no cognisable injury on the franchise market regardless of when it is held. Rival markets or fairs conducted *within* this distance may constitute a nuisance actionable by the market owner. The rules governing such actions differ according to whether the rival market or fair is held on the same day as the franchise market or fair or on different days.

Hale C.J'S commentary on Fitzherbert's *Natura Brevium* [37] contains an oft-cited statement which is regarded as an authoritative statement of the law. He wrote:

"If the market be on the same day it shall be intended a nuisance, but if it be on another day it shall not be so intended and therefore it shall be put is in issue whether it be a nuisance or not."

"Same Day" Market
There is an irrebuttable presumption that a rival market held on the same day as the franchise market and within the common law distance is a disturbance to the franchise holder. [38] There was some authority that a same day market was only a *prima facie* disturbance, but this seems no longer to be good law. [39] Such a market is actionable *per se* and without proof that any loss was actually inflicted on the franchise market. This is because the

---

[36] *Halton BC v. Cawley* [1985] 1 WLR 15. But note the possible reforms contained in Clause 21 of the Deregulation nd Contracting Out Bill 1994 which would remove the right of the local authority to suppress the operation of the rival market.

[37] 7th edition (1730).

[38] *Tamworth BC v. Fazeley Town Council* (1978) 77 LGR 238, approved in *Sevenoaks v. Pattullo & Vinson* [1984] 1 All ER 544; also *Morpeth Corporation v. Norhumberland Farmers' Auction Mart Co.* [1921] 2 Ch 154; *Yard v. Ford* (1669) 2 Saun 172.

[39] *Re Islington Market Bill* (1835) 3 Cl & Fin 513, 515.

franchisee is to be regarded as having a legal right by virtue of the franchise. Just as trespass to land is actionable without proof of damage, so interference with a market right is deemed to cause loss because "every injury imports a damage." [40]

The evidential advantage of not proving loss may be important where the franchisee has no right to take toll in the market, for without the right to toll it may be more difficult to establish that loss has been inflicted. [41]

Where the Market is Held on Different Days
Where the rival market is held on different days within the common law distance, proof that it causes actual loss to the franchise market is essential. The plaintiff in *Yard v. Ford*[42], who held a franchise market in Newton Abbott on Wednesdays succeeded in proving loss where the defendant levied a rival market on Tuesday in Ashburton within the common law distance. Loss was established because, after attending the defendant's Tuesday market, the jury found that buyers and sellers would have no need of the plaintiff's one held the following day.

Loss can be demonstrated where, for example, the rival deprives the lawful market of tolls or stallages, rents or licence fees. [43] But it is not necessary to show that such economic loss has been inflicted on the market owner. The rule is satisfied if damage can be shown to his stall-holders as, for example, where the rival market threatened the already marginal viability of stalls by depriving them of customers. [44]

---

[40] Per Holt CJ in *Ashby v. White* 2 Ld Raym 938. This is subject to the qualification that damages recovered may be nominal: *Stoke-on-Trent City Council v. W & J Wass* [1989] 87 LGR 129.

[41] See the *Morpeth Corporation case, supra* n. (36). But even without this right the owner may normally still claim stallage, and if fewer traders attend the market profits will diminish.

[42] (1669) 2 Saun 172.

[43] *Birmingham Corporation v. Perry Barr Stadium Ltd.* [1972] 1 All ER 725. Here the Corporation licensed market organisers to operate markets within an authorised area in return for a fee. An unlicensed market would endanger their revenues.

[44] *Northampton BC v. Midland Development Group of Companies Ltd.* (1978) 76 LGR 750, esp 754.

No cause of action arises where a rival market which is held on a different day causes no loss to the franchise market. [45]

Defences to a Civil Action for Disturbance

(i) Consent of the Market Owner

The owner of the right of market is entitled to licence rival markets and a fee may be charged for this permission. One recent example of this can be seen in *Birmingham City Council v. In Shops Centres plc*[46] illustrating how Birmingham City Council licenses private market operators in return for a fee or a percentage of the gross income derived from the market. [47]

A failure to enforce the right against a rival may give rise to an inference of implied consent, but as already noted, the plaintiff market owner would have to act unconscionably before injunctive relief would be denied.

(ii) Statute

That the rival market is operated under the authority of an Act of Parliament is a good defence. When promoting a Bill seeking market powers, the promoters will be required to advertise their intention and the holder of existing market rights will have the opportunity of contesting the Bill.

(iii) A Lack of Room in the Market Place

The owner of the market has a duty to provide sufficient space for all those who are ready to buy and sell within the market place. If sufficiently popular the market place will become so full that no further sellers can be admitted into it. It is now settled that insufficient space in the market is no defence where another

---

[45] But a local authority may use planning powers to restrain rival markets where planning considerations permit this.

[46] Court of Appeal, 1st June 1992. Unreported LEXIS.

[47] See also *Birmingham Corporation v. Perry Barr Stadium Ltd.* [1972] 1 All ER 725.

purports to operate a rival market. [48] This means that a rival
entrepreneur is not at liberty to furnish space for other traders
alleging that the established market lacked sufficient room for
them.

However, if insufficient space has been provided, or space
within the market place has been devoted to other purposes, the
owner of the market has no action against a person selling outside
the market provided that the seller does so because of the lack of
space in the market place and no rival market is organised. [49] This
seems also to apply to sellers who are refused access to the market
for reasons other than lack of space. [50] If space is available in the
market, it is fraud on the market to sell outside it. [51]

(iv) Market No-Longer Held

A failure to conduct a franchise market can amount to a breach of
the grantee's public duty and may be a ground for a repeal of the
franchise either by an Act of Parliament or by a writ of *scire
facias*.[52] If the right is forfeited by *scire facias*, the franchise
could be vested in another who is prepared to conduct the market.
Until repeal, however, the market rights remain intact. [53]

It follows that the owner of market rights could maintain an
action for disturbance by a rival market or by sales outside the
market even when his own is no-longer held. This is, however,
subject to the *caveat* that such a breach of duty would affect the
quantum of damages[54] and it is not certain that a court would be
prepared to grant the discretionary remedy of an injunction in these
circumstances.

Similar principles apply in the case of a statutory market.
Failure to conduct the market would not destroy the *right* to conduct

[48] *Mosley v. Walker* (1827) 7 B & C 40; *Re Islington Market Bill* (1835) 3 Cl & Fin 513;
Great Eastern Rly v. Goldsmid (1884) 9 App Cas 927; *Tamworth Borough Council v. Fazeley
Town Council* (1979) 77 LGR 238.
[49] *Prince v. Lewis* (1826) 5 B & C 363.
[50] *Corporation of London v. Lyons, Sons & Co (Fruit Brokers) Ltd* [1936] 1 Ch. 78.
[51] *Bridgland v. Shapter* (1839) 5 M & W 375.
[52] *Re Islington Market Bill* (1835) 3 Cl & Fin. 513.
[53] *Wyld v. Silver* [1963] Ch 243, upholding Lloyd-Jacob J. [1961] Ch 561.
[54] *Stoke-on-Trent City Council v. W & J Wass Ltd.* (1989) 87 LGR 129.

it. The right would remain in the statutory owner until removed by Act of Parliament.

Remedies

Where there has been a disturbance of the market, the owner is entitled to damages for the loss sustained as a result of the disturbance and, in appropriate circumstances, an injunction to restrain further interference with the right of market.

As we have seen, the levying of an unlawful same day market is actionable without proof of loss. If no loss has in fact been sustained, an injunction and perhaps nominal damages are the most appropriate remedies since damages alone will normally be inadequate. [55] Interlocutory relief is also available, and where such relief has been granted no further question of damages will normally arise.

Similar principles apply in the case of a different day rival market except that, where an interlocutory injunction is sought, proof of actual loss is normally essential to support a claim either for an injunction or for damages. [56]

Where interlocutory relief is sought the balance of justice and convenience allows the court to grant relief where there is a mere likelihood of loss. [57] In *Leicester Corporation v. Maby* [58] Goff J. held that the holding of a rival market on the day following the franchise market was sufficient since it was "calculated to damage the right of the corporation" as owners of the market and gave rise to reasonable grounds for "apprehending" damage.

In the case of both a same day rival market and one held on a different day, in respect of any period when no injunction has been in force it is possible to recover substantial damages if actual loss can be proved. If the evidence will not support such a claim, only nominal damages may be recovered. [59]

---

[55] *Ibid.* See also *Sevenoaks DC v. Pattullo & Vinson* [1984] 1 All ER 544.

[56] *Leicester CC v. Maby* (1971) 70 LGR 209.

[57] *Birmingham Corporation v. Perry Bar Stadium Ltd.* [1972] 1 All ER 725.

[58] (1972) 70 LGR 209, especially pp 214-5.

[59] *Stoke-on Trent City Council v. W & J Wass Ltd.* (1989) 87 LGR 129.

Injunctions: Delay and Acquiescence
If the right holder acquiesces in the infringement of his rights, or is guilty of delay-or laches- in enforcing his right, the court may deny him equitable relief in the form of an injunction. Mere inactivity is not by itself enough because "quiescence is no acquiescence". [60] The test is whether it would be "dishonest or unconscionable" for the plaintiff to insist upon enforcing his right [61] The degree of laches or acquiescence sufficient to deny relief will vary according to the circumstances. Laches or acquiescence which would not suffice to deny the plaintiff a permanent injunction may be sufficient in the case of an interlocutory injunction [62] In a case in which a local authority allowed an unlawful rival market to continue without effective protest for a period of eight months, it was held to be inappropriate to restrain it by an interlocutory injunction pending the trial. [63] In other cases, however, it seems that delay may only bar permanent relief where the limitation period has been exhausted. [64]

Disturbance by Selling Outside the Market

Common Law

It is a disturbance of the market right for a trader to sell his goods outside the market with intention to evade tolls payable on goods sold inside the market. [65] The rule also prohibits a sale by sample in the market of goods which are left outside it in order to evade tolls.

---

[60] *Lamare v. Dixon* (1873) IR 6 HL 414, 422.
[61] *Shaw v. Applegate* [1977] 1 WLR 970, 978, Buckley L. J; see also *per* Goff LJ at 980.
[62] Snell, Equity, 29th ed., 1990, p. 666.
[63] *Warwick Corporation v. Maby* (No.2) (1971) 116 Sol. Jo. 137.
[64] *Morpeth Corporation v. Northumberland Farmers' Auction Mart Co. Ltd.* [1921] 2 Ch. 154, 163 Sargant J.
[65] Tolls are usually levied on buyers and not sellers: 2 Co Inst 221; *Leight v. Pym* (1687) 2 Lutw 1336, *infra*; but note that statute may impose different rules, as, for example in *Bridgland v. Shapter*, *infra*.

A leading case is *Bridgland v. Shapter* [66] where the defendant acted unlawfully by leaving the sheep he intended to sell at a public house a short distance from the market place and then entering the market in search of buyers. This enabled him to evade tolls otherwise payable on the sale of the sheep. [67]

If there is no intention to evade toll, the rights of the market owner are not infringed, and no tort is committed. Accordingly, where an action was brought against the buyer of wheat sold to him by sample (the bulk being left outside the market and so not liable to toll) the action failed because it could not be shown that the buyer had intended to evade toll. He could not compel the seller to bring the bulk into the market. [68] This means that whilst it is normally a disturbance to sell by sample in the market with the intention of evading tolls, it will not be unlawful to purchase by sample unless the buyer conspires with the seller to evade tolls. [69]

Similarly, as we have seen, no disturbance occurs where the market place is too full to admit the trader wishing to sell there provided he does not seek to organise a rival market. [70] Trading outside the market is only permissible in so far as it caters for the excess of demand for the lawful market. The owner of market in effect loses some of the rights of monopoly *vis a vis* those who are excluded from the market.

Statutory Protection Against Disturbance of the Market

Section 56 of the Food Act 1984 allows local authorities to enact by-laws prohibiting certain sales outside their markets during market hours. This power is liable to be abolished if the Government proceeds with reforms.

Under this provision it is currently an offence for a person (other than a pedlar holding a certificate under the Pedlar's Act

---

[66] (1839) 5 M & W 375.

[67] This was a civil suit which established that the defendant's conduct was a fraud upon the market.

[68] *The Bailiffs of Tewkesbury v. Diston* (1805) 6 East 438.

[69] *Ibid.*

[70] *Re Islington Market Bill* (1835) 3 Cl & Fin 513; *Prince v. Lewis* (1826) 5 B & C 363. NB, however, the Food Act 1984, s.56, and the Markets and Fairs Clauses Act 1847, s.13,. The former may be repealed by the enactment of the Deregulation and Contracting Out Bill 1994.

1871) who on a market day and during market hours, sells or exposes for sale any articles (a) which are specified in a by-law made by the market authority, and (b) which are commonly sold in the market. The offence is committed if the sale or exposure for sale takes place within the authority's area and is within such distance of the market as the authority declares in the by-laws.

An offence is punishable by a fine not exceeding level 2 on the standard scale.

It is essential that the articles sold or exposed for sale are specified in a by-law. If no by-law has been promulgated, no offence is committed. The body responsible for enacting by-laws is the market authority. Such an authority is defined in s.61 as a local authority maintaining a market which was established or acquired under s.50 of the 1984 Act or corresponding provisions of earlier legislation.

Unlike the offence under s 13 of the Markets and Fairs Clauses Act 1847 which is considered below, the offence is only committed where the articles are sold during market hours.

There are savings for a sale or exposure for sale in a person's own dwelling place or shop, and also for door to door sales, provided the sale takes place to someone resident in the premises.

As in the case of s.13 of the Markets and Fairs Clauses Act 1847 it is only where "articles" are sold or exposed for sale that the offence is committed. In this and other statutory context the meaning of the word has caused some difficulty.

Articles
Lord Goddard C.J once held that "articles" should include only inanimate objects. [71] In contrast, a horse was held to be an "article" in the *Llandaff and Canton District Market Company v. Lyndon* [72] in the context of a local Act designed (*inter alia*) to prevent the levying of a rival market. Although Lord Goddard's interpretation is an attractive one, there is a danger in construing words employed in one statutory context in the light of that applicable in a

---

[71] *Daly v. Canon* [1954] 1 WLR 261, 263. Lord Goddard CJ was considering the meaning of "article" in the context of the Public Health Act 1936, and followed Moore CJ in *R (Urban D C of Portadown) v. Armagh Chairman and Justices* [1931] NI 209). A goldfish was not an "article" for the purposes of that Act; cf fresh fish in *Loftos v. Kiggins* (1890) 55 JP 151.
[72] (1860) 8 CB (NS) 515.

different context. It may be that in this context the word is intended to have a wider meaning covering all marketable goods specified in the-law. The point should perhaps be regarded as open.

Exposed for Sale

No actual sale is necessary if the goods are exposed for sale. This occurs where the article is exposed to view [73] even when wrapped.[74] Exposure may also occur where a trader using a delivery vehicle has completed his or her round and his returning to the depot. [75]

A delivery to a customer in a course of dealings does not normally constitute "exposing" the goods for sale even if the customer may refuse the goods [76] and they could be sold to anyone who asked for them *en route*.[77] It would have been different if the goods were "cried" about the town. [78]

Sales in Dwelling-places and Shops

No offence under s.56 is committed where articles are sold or exposed for sale by any person within his own dwelling place or shop. The meaning of this provision is lamentably obscure partly because the Act lacks a definition of these terms.

Dwelling place

"Dwelling place" probably has a wider meaning than "dwelling house". In *Llandaff and Canton District Market v. Lyndon* [79] Erle C.J considered that all within the curtilage of a dwelling house could be deemed to be part of it and this should apply *a fortiori* to a dwelling place.

A "Shop"

No offence occurs where trading occurs in a shop. Ultimately whether trading takes place in a "shop" is a question of fact [80] and

---

[73] *Crane v. Lawrence* (1890) 25 QBD 152.

[74] *Wheat v. Brown* [1892] 1 QB 418.

[75] *Keating v. Horwood* (1926) 135 LT 29.

[76] *Newton* in *Makerfield UDC v. Lyon* (1900) 81 LT 756.

[77] *Philpott v. Allbright* (1906) 94 LT 540.

[78] *Ibid.*

[79] (1860) 8 CB (NS) 515, 520.

[80] *Wallace v. Dixon* [1917] 2 IR 236.

depends upon the statutory context. [81] Broad guidance as to the meaning of this term may be found in s.74 of the Shops Act 1950 which states that a "shop includes any premises where any retail trade or business is carried on." The *caveat* must immediately be entered, however, that a "shop" may have a wider meaning in the market context because a wholesaler has been held to trade from a shop. [82]

The court in *Pope v. Whalley* [83] purported to offer certain guidelines to identify a "shop". Of primary significance would be the suitability of the structure for storing goods and whether it had a stable and substantial character. It should also be possible for potential buyers to go inside it. For these reasons stalls and barrows are not normally, shops.

Whilst, however, the capacity for storage, especially overnight storage, is normally a necessary condition, as Mellor J recognised in *Pope v. Whalley*, [84] such a criterion cannot be decisive of the question in all cases. Businesses offering services, such as, for example, a shoe repair business, would not trade from a "shop" if storage were the exclusive criterion. [85] As a corollary, warehouses *would* become shops by virtue of their storage facilities, and this would plainly be an odd result. [86] It is plain that the presence of storage facilities can only be a broad indicator of whether a "shop" exists.

A Stall Distinguished

Since goods cannot normally be stored on a stall overnight once trading has ceased, they are not normally "shops". [87] Furthermore

---

[81] *Ibid.*

[82] *Haynes v. Ford* [1911] 2 Ch. 237; *cf M & F Frawley Ltd v. The Ve-ri Best Co. Ltd.* [1953] 1 QB 318.

[83] *Pope v. Whalley* (1865) 6 B & S 303.

[84] *Ibid.* at p313.

[85] Eg *Wallace v. Dixon* [1917] 2 IR 236 where premises were held to constitute a "shop" in a case where buyers merely ordered coal to be delivered from a depot in a different location. No coal was ever stored on the premises.

[86] *Edlorado Ice Cream Co. Ltd v. Clark* [1938] 1 KB 715.

[87] *Pope v. Whalley* (1865) 6 B & S 303; *Pike v. Jones* (1922) 128 LT 373; *Greenwood v. Whelan* [1967] 1 QB 396.

trading once or twice a week from a market stall lacks sufficient continuity.[88]

A stall does not become a shop even if fixed in the ground and subsequently enclosed to so as to resemble a "traditional building" (sic). [89] but it might be different if, as a matter of fact and degree, it had a stable and substantial character.

It seems that the courts have not been consistent in their approach. In *Dennis v. Hutchinson,* [90] Lord Trevethin C.J held that an amusement stall was capable of being a shop if the evidence had shown the existence of retail sales. In contrast to the *Cowlars* case,[91] no objection was raised that the stall lacked sufficient permanence. Although this decision rested on its facts, it does appear to place a greater weight on the nature of the activity taking place at the stall as opposed to the permanency of the operation. That this is so again highlights inconsistencies in the approach taken by the courts.

Commodities and Services
It may be argued that traders offering services as well as those offering commodities may trade from "shops", but this is not normally the approach taken by the courts.[92] This is, however, unlikely to cause difficulty for the offence under s.56 prohibits only the exposure for sale of "articles" . Businesses dealing in services would not therefore fall foul of the 1984 Act.

Mobile "Premises"
Mobility has sometimes been fatal to the existence of a "shop". Two decisions are illustrative of the inconsistency of the judicial approach. In *Cowlars Co-operative Society v. Glasgow Corporation*[93] the court held that a mobile shop was not a "shop" even though it was not of an itinerant variety. It traded on a piece of vacant ground on which the appellants had taken out a 99 year

---

[88] *Summers v. Roberts* [1944] KB 106.
[89] *Pope v. Whalley supra* n. (83).
[90] [1922] 1 KB 693.
[91] *Cowlars Co-operative Society v. Glasgow Corporation* [1957] SLT 288.
[92] Eg, *M & F Frawley v. The Ve-Ri Best Co. Ltd.* [1953] 1 QB 318; *Erewash BC v. Ilkeston Co-operative Society* (1988) 153 JP 141.
[93] *Supra* n. (91).

lease. The van was towed to this site each week-day morning and away again each evening. Despite the regularity of such trading activities and the finding that the vehicle had all the attributes of a shop except that it was not fixed to the soil, the court held that its lack of "fixity" (by which it was meant the possibility that it might be moved) was sufficient to disqualify the vehicle. From this reasoning it follows *a fortiori* that a mobile shop which does not trade from door to door is not a "shop" and it may disturb a market. [94]

In contrast in *Wiltshire v. Baker,* [95] it was held that a barge moored on a canal was capable of being a shop depending on the use of the vessel. The fact that it might sail away, was not thought to be relevant if it was used as a shop.

If the *Cowlars* decision is followed, mobile traders are at risk of committing an offence under s.56 of the 1984 Act or s.13 of the Markets and Fairs Clauses Act 1847 if they trade in prohibited articles. This appears to be so notwithstanding the social utility of preserving these forms of trading. [96]

"Units" Within Larger Buildings
As we have seen, the creation of "units" within larger premises has been unsuccessfully attempted to avoid disturbance by the organiser of rival markets. It is possible that such units could be shops", [97] so that individual traders might not commit an offence under s.56 of the 1984 Act and s.13 of the 1847 Act. The issue is not clearly decided, however, and there are difficulties considered below.

A shopkeeper's own goods?
Early decisions emphasise that the shop-keeper will normally only escape a penalty if he trades in his own goods. [98] It has subsequently been held that a trader does not cease to be a shop-

---

[94] *Stone v. Boreham* [1959] 1 QB 1.

[95] (1861) 11 CB (NS) 237.

[96] See *Caswell v. Cook* (1862) 11 CB(NS) 637, 652.

[97] Depending on the facts: *Northampton B C v. Midland Development Group of Companies Ltd.* (1978) 76 LGR 750 ; *Manchester City Council v. Walsh* (1985) 84 LGR 1; *Kingston-upon-Hull City Council v. Greenwood* (1984) 82 LGR 586, but see below on the effects of the traders having only a contractual licence of the unit.

[98] *Mayor of Manchester v. Lyons* (1882) 22 Ch.D 287.

keeper if he sells goods belonging to others, for example on commission, [99] but the matter is not beyond doubt.[100]

"His own shop"
Both s. 56 of the 1984 Act and s.13 of the 1847 Act state that a person can only benefit from the exception if the articles are exposed for sale in the persons "own dwelling place or shop". The question arises as to kind of tenure will suffice.

There is some authority that the premises must be under the control of someone who holds a legal estate in the land and who sells his own goods in the shop. [101] There is little doubt that a person holding the freehold of the premises or a lessee would therefore fall within the saving in s.56 of the 1984 Act.[102]

It is uncertain whether licensees have a sufficient interest in land to benefit from the saving. Walton J. in the *Northampton* case[103] expressly contrasted the legal status of a licensee with those who had a legal estate in land. Only the latter, it seems, could trade from their "own" shop. And further doubt on the matter was expressed by Nourse J in the *Greenwood* case [104] where it was suggested that the absence of security of tenure in the trader was a factor denoting a market.

An early decision on the point is *Perkins v. Arber* where a trader in pigs dealt from an inn yard. It was held that he was not trading from his own premises since the pig pens in the inn yard were not in his own exclusive occupation. In delivering a judgment in which the other judges concurred, Blackburn J stated: "In order to come within the (exception) the place must be the (trader's) own premises, that is to say, his own house or shop, which this pen was not." [105]

---

[99] *Haynes v. Ford , supra* n. (82).

[100] *Northampton Borough Council v. Midland Development Group of Companies* (1978) 76 LGR 750.

[101] *Ibid.*

[102] For tenants see, for example, *Ashworth v. Heyworth* (1869) LR 4 QB 316; *Haynes v. Ford* [1911] 2 Ch 237).

[103] (1978) 76 LGR 750, 752.

[104] *Supra*, n. (97).

[105] (1873) 37 J.P. 406, 407.

The point, however, is not beyond doubt because in the *Walsh* case it was accepted that at least some of the licensees of the units could have been shop-keepers and that they might have had a defence to a charge of disturbing a market. The law on this point requires clarification.

Pedlars
No offence is committed by certificated pedlars who sell marketable goods within the area. What constitutes trading as a pedlar is considered in more detail below. [106] It is sufficient at this stage to note that the saving for pedlars creates an important immunity from prosecutions for disturbance.

Further Statutory Protection of Markets
Local Acts of Parliament have often been promoted to create market rights or to confirm ancient manorial or franchise rights already in existence.[107] Local enactments (each known as the "special" Act) often incorporated either in whole or in part the Markets and Fairs Clauses Act 1847. This was designed to provide some uniformity in market regulation. Although the 1847 Act was intended to create an adoptive code, its provisions may be modified by the provisions of the special Act, perhaps to extend the protection of the market against disturbance. [108]

Section 13 of the 1847 Act creates a statutory offence of disturbance by selling outside the market. The Government has invited views as to whether this offence should be abolished. It is currently punishable by fine currently at level one of the standard scale.

S.13 enacts:

"After the market place is open for public use every person other than a licensed hawker who shall sell or expose for sale in any place within the prescribed limits except in his own dwelling place

---

[106] Below p. 180 *et seq.*
[107] See, for example, *City of Birmingham v. Foster* (1894) 70 LT 371; *Manchester City Council v. Walsh* (1985) 84 LGR 1 at 5.
[108] Eg, *Hailsham Cattle Market Co. v. Tolman* [1915] 1 Ch 360.

or shop, any articles in respect of which tolls are by the special Act authorised to be taken in the market shall (be liable to a penalty)".

The section has far-reaching effects. It seeks to restrain all street trading in tollable articles unless either the seller is a hawker (which includes a certificated pedlar) or the trading takes place in a shop or dwelling-place. Its prohibition is not confined to sales in market hours.

To the extent that the prohibition concerns "articles" sold outside the market and contains savings for sales in dwelling places and shops, the provision overlaps with s.56 of the Food Act 1984. The meaning of these words is unlikely to differ significantly from the meaning given to those words under s.56. Reference should therefore be made to the preceding discussion of s.56 of the 1984 Act. It is proposed to focus here upon the unique features of s.13.

What Constitutes A Sale Within the Prescribed Area?
If the sale agreement is concluded inside the prescribed area but the tollable articles are delivered in a place outside it, the offence would seem to be committed. [109]

For the purposes of the section, a sale takes place where the agreement is made and not where the goods are delivered. [110] In *Lambert v. Rowe* [111] both sale and delivery took place in the prescribed area but the agreement was reached in the farmer's dwelling place and thus did not disturb the plaintiff's right of market.

The Prescribed Area
The prescribed area within which the offence may be committed is the area specified or contemplated in the special Act creating the market. Where such an instrument, enacted in 1822, prohibited certain sales in the "town of Rochdale" this was held to refer to the current boundaries of the Town. [112]

---

[109] *Bridgland v. Shapter* (1839) 5 M & W 375).
[110] *Stretch v. White* (1861) 25 JP 485.
[111] [1914] 1 KB 38.
[112] *Kilmister v. Fitton* (1885) 53 LT 959.

Tollable Articles

No offence is committed unless the special Act permits tolls to be taken and that the article sold or exposed for sale is tollable.

It is important to distinguish a right to toll from a right to charge stallage. A right to levy toll is a right to demand a sum of money in respect of goods sold in the market. It is often contrasted with stallage which is the right of the owner of the soil to charge the market trader for the use of his or her land. A right to stallage is not a right to toll.

The courts will examine the substance of the right conferred. This means that even if the special Act refers to a right to "toll" it is not conclusive if what is intended is a charge for exclusive occupation of a part of the market. [113]

The Enforceability of Market Rights

As we have seen, the owner of a right of market may restrain rivals from operating "rival markets" within the common law distance of the established market without his consent. [114] Market traders selling outside of the established market may similarly disturb the market right. Thus market rights are endowed by law with an almost monopolistic status, not only distorting competition but actually eliminating it altogether. Competition may also be distorted if a number of market owners adopt the same practices controlling those who they licence to operate "rival" markets.

The question arises as to whether such rights and practices are compatible with the modern competition rules and, in particular, those of the European Community. [115] If applicable, these rules could have profound consequences for market owners who might be

---

[113] *Caswell v. Cook* (1862) 11 CB (NS) 637.

[114] This is so unless the rival was created by Act of Parliament or the rival market operates on different days and causes the franchise market no damage.

[115] It is unlikely that the provisions of the Fair Trading Act 1973, s.7, which deals with monopoly situations in the provision of services, would be infringed. Market owners, in licensing other operators, are unlikely to offer a service within the meaning of the Act: *Gloucester City Council v. Williams* (1990) 88 LGR 853. The courts have also held that under UK law monopolistic market rights may be fully exploited: *Simonite v. Sheffield City Council* [1992] 1 EGLR 105.

unable to suppress the activities rival market organisers and traders.

Market Rights and the Treaty of Rome

Article 86
Essentially, the competition policy of the European Community is designed to enhance both economic activity and efficiency by allowing the free movement of goods and services throughout the European Community. This demands that there should be no barriers to entry into a given market. As we have seen, market rights allow for rigid barriers to be erected. A monopoly, in so far as it imposes such barriers, is the anti-thesis of a model based on free competition.

One of the legal bulwarks of the EC competition policy is Article 86 of the EC Treaty which provides (in part) :

"Any abuse by one or more undertakings of a dominant position within the common market or in a substantial part of it shall be prohibited as incompatible with the common market in so far as it may affect trade between Member States."

The remainder of Art. 86 lists examples of the manner in which abuses may occur. This list is not exhaustive.

The relevance of Art. 86 to the English law of markets has yet to be explored. Its significance should not, however, be under-estimated. If it is found that a market right is exercised in violation of Art. 86, it will be unenforceable. This means that it will neither be possible to restrain rival markets nor, possibly, to restrain the activities of street traders selling outside the market. This is because Art. 86 is directly effective and as such is a part of the corpus of English law.

The possibility that the exercise of market rights *could* violate Art 86 has been considered in one unreported English case, *Birmingham City Council v. In Shops Centres Plc.* [116] This concerned a motion by Birmingham City Council for an interlocutory

---

[116] 20th May 1992 Hoffman J. and on appeal, 1st June 1992 LEXIS.

injunction to curtail an alleged infringement of its market rights by the defendant. The latter operated two markets under licence from the Council. The operation of one of these markets was uneconomic and so, without obtaining the consent of the Council, the defendants proposed to open a new market on a different, unlicensed, site. It was this market which the City Council sought to restrain by interlocutory injunction.

One of the grounds on which the motion was resisted by the defendants was that the exercise of monopoly rights by the City Council was an abuse of a dominant position contrary to Art. 86. No evidence was adduced at this interlocutory stage to support this argument. Nevertheless, Hoffman J. treated the point as an arguable one because it was possible that such evidence could be found by the time the matter came for trial. The balance of convenience, however, meant that he was prepared to grant an interlocutory injunction to the Council on the grounds (*inter alia*) that the Art. 86 point was unlikely to be resolved without a lengthy reference to the European Court of Justice. In these circumstances, to leave the plaintiffs with only a remedy in damages would not be just.

The case was unsuccessfully appealed by the defendants. The Court of Appeal, like Hoffman J. at first instance, treated the Art. 86 point as an arguable issue to go to trial although at this interlocutory stage there was no evidence to support it. This means that although there is no decision on whether Art. 86 may be applied so as to render market monopolies unenforceable, the Courts seem prepared to treat the point as an arguable one. The question now is whether, given sufficient evidence, such an argument could actually succeed. Before examining this issue it must be noted, however, that adducing evidence required to demonstrate that market rights do affect trade between Member States- a requirement of Art. 86- is likely to make Art. 86 proceedings expensive and possibly unpredictable.

Article 86 does not prohibit the possession of a dominant position, but the abuse of that position. Dominance must be established in the common market as a whole or a substantial part of it. Moreover, whilst proof of abuse and dominance are necessary they are not sufficient conditions to establishing liability: it must also be shown that these affect trade between Member States. Can these requirements be fulfilled in the case of market rights?

A market owner would seem to enjoy sufficient dominance *prima facie* to fall within Art 86. Dominance was defined in *United Brands Co. v. Commission* (Case 27/76) as

"a position of economic strength enjoyed by an undertaking which enables it to prevent effective competition from being maintained in the relevant market by giving it the power to behave to an appreciable extent independently of its competitors...." [117]

Since market rights ostensibly legitimate the suppression of competition in the relevant market area, the exercise of market rights seems to be a perfect example of dominant market behaviour.

Dominance must be exercised in what is called the "relevant product market". Although this may give rise to difficulties in other contexts, it would seem to be easily satisfied in the case of market rights. The market owner is dominant in so far as he possesses the right to conduct all markets within the common law distance. Market organisers can only operate in this area with the consent of the right-holder. The "product" is therefore the provision of markets by the "licensing" arrangements the right-holder may be willing to make (but is not obliged to make) within the common law distance.

Dominance must also be exercised within the relevant geographical area. As Green, Hartley and Usher explain [118] this requires a dominance in a substantial part of the common market. As they argue, a producer supplying the needs of 90% of the UK market thereby obtains a dominant position in the UK. But such local dominance would only account for 15% of the demand within the common market. This is not a position of dominance. However, it must not be forgotten that Art. 86 prohibits abuse of a dominant position within the common market *or a substantial part of it.* Moreover it has been held that the abuse of a dominant position within the territory of a single Member State is sufficient to fall within Art. 86. [119]

---

[117] [1976] 2 CMLR 147. See also *Michelin v. Commission Case* 322/81 [1983] ECR 3461.

[118] *The Legal Foundations of the Single European Market* (Oxford 1991) p260.

[119] *Bandengroothandel Freischebrug BV v. Nederlansche Branden Industrie Michelin NV* (Before Commission) [1982] 1 CMLR 643, paras 31-38, especially 34.

Moreover dominance with the relevant geographical area is an issue which cannot easily be severed from the idea of the relevant product market. For example, if a particular product were only available and consumed within a relatively small region of the European Community, abuse of a dominant position in relation to the availability of that product might fall within the prohibition in Art. 86 even though the geographical area in question might be comparatively small:

"For the purpose of determining whether a specific territory is large enough to amount to 'a substantial part of the Common Market' within the meaning of Art. 86....the pattern and volume of the production and consumption of the said product as well as the habits and economic opportunities of vendors and purchasers must be considered." [120]

It would also be necessary to establish, of course, that the local dominance affected trade between Member States.

If it is possible to define both the relevant product market and the relevant geographical area as the area of an individual market owner's monopoly, it is not inconceivable that a market owner could enjoy the necessary dominance. Such a conclusion may be possible because as right-holder, he or she can exclude any would-be entrepreneur seeking to organise markets in his area. [121] No substitute "supply" would be available to the entrepreneur since the control by the market owner of market activities in his area may be absolute. [122] There are, however, substantial difficulties in reaching such a conclusion. These are considered below.

Whether local monopoly rights could in practice constitute a dominance within the relevant geographical area and affect trade between Member States fell to be considered in *Bodson v. Pompes funebres des regions liberees*. [123] Under French law, certain funeral services could be supplied directly by the communes or through undertakings given a concession by the communes. The largest

---

[120] [1975] ECR 1663, 1977.
[121] At least for trading on the same day.
[122] See the *Michelin* case above as an example of how the inability to gain substitute supplies defines the relevant product market and geographical market.
[123] (Case 30/87) [1988] ECR 2479.

undertaking was Pompes funebres generales SA. Of the 5000 communes which granted concessions to private contractors, this undertaking held the concession in 2800 cases. 45% of all burials in France were conducted by Pompes funebres generales SA or its subsidiaries. Since 1972 the sole concession in Charleville-Mezieres had been granted to a subsidiary of Pompes funebres generales SA. The subsidiary applied for and obtained an interim injunction to restrain a Mme Bodson from providing funeral services in competition with them. Mme Bodson appealed alleging (*inter alia*) that the subsidiary was thereby abusing a dominant position. The action thus raised directly the relevance of Art. 86 in cases of local monopolies.

The question concerning the applicability of Art. 86 was referred to European Court for a preliminary ruling under Art 177. It is noteworthy that the European Court of Justice decided first that Art. 86 is applicable where the absence of competition is facilitated by legal rules. This means that although market rights are legal monopolies they do not by that fact alone become immune to Art 86 proceedings. Whether the prohibition in Art. 86 is in fact violated will depend upon the actual impact of the monopoly upon a market and in particular whether it constrains traders from other Member States from entering the market.

The court stressed that in order to ascertain whether a dominant position exists, the population covered by the monopoly right is more important than the geographical area over which it extends. This is clearly of great significance in the context of market rights which are characteristically local. Rights which extend through large population centres are more likely to be found to be dominant.

In considering whether trade between Member States was affected the Court offered significant guidance. It noted that the Commission had taken the view that the activities of the Pompes funebres generales group could only have had a "imperceptible effect" upon transactions with other States. The Court rejected this and ruled that an abuse of a dominant position may occur where there is damage to the effective competitive structure of the common market. This may occur where the common market is partitioned restricting the freedom to provide goods and services which is essential to the operation of the single market. This is of course of particular relevance in the present context where the "market" is highly partitioned: a market organiser from another Member State wishing to organise markets in the UK might find substantial geographical areas of the UK barred to him by virtue of the market rights enjoyed by others.

After emphasising the importance of the "structure" of the market, the court then stated:

"Accordingly, it is for the national court to consider whether....the activities of the group of undertakings holding concessions, and the monopoly they enjoy over a large part of the territory of a Member State, affect the importation of goods from other Member States or the possibility for competing undertakings established in other Member States to provide services in the first mentioned Member State." [124]

Whether a dominant position existed in the *Pompes funebres* case would be a question of fact for the national court but the following were identified as relevant factors to be applied in this case:

(i)   the size of the market share held by the group which is shielded from competition as a result of the monopolistic concession.

(ii)   the influence of that monopoly on the supply of goods and services outside the monopoly;

(iii)   the position of the group in communes where no concessions had been granted and the market share held by the group in other Member States.

(iv)   the financial resources of the group and whether, for example, the group belonged to a powerful conglomerate of undertakings or groups of undertakings.

The Court thus concluded that Art. 86 does apply where a number of communal or local monopolies are granted to a single group of undertakings if their market strategy is determined by a

---

[124] Para 25.

parent company "in which those monopolies cover a certain part of the national territory."

Applying this ruling in the case of market rights, it seems that Art. 86 could be deployed in certain cases to frustrate a market monopoly and open a market area to free competition. This would be more likely if an undertaking or group of undertakings acquired a significant number of market rights and thus established a network over a much larger area, rather as the Pompes funebres generales and its subsidiaries acquired a large number of concessions affecting a substantial slice of the French population. If market rights were concentrated in this manner, evidence of damage to the effective competitive structure of the common market might be possible.

An argument might also be constructed under which the Art 86 prohibition could extend to the exercise of individual market monopolies. It would have to be shown that the market owner was dominant in a substantial area of the common market and that this dominance affected trade between Member States. It might be possible to satisfy the latter of these requirements in so far as a would-be market organiser from another Member State could find it impossible to establish a market in an area controlled by a UK market owner unwilling to licence others. It is less clear, however, whether an individual market owner exercising his monopoly achieves a dominance over a substantial part of the common market. Such a local market monopoly, confined as it is to a minute area of the common market, may not achieve such dominance. "Substitutes" might be available to the would-be market organiser, in so far as he might obtain a licence to operate a market, albeit in other areas, possibly even neighbouring areas.

But this need not necessarily conclude the position. It might be possible to advance an alternative argument to bring individual market monopolies more clearly within the prohibition in Art. 86. Such an argument would stress that the combined effect of all separate market monopolies taken together is to partition the market and so to prevent competition. This is because the collective effect of all separate market monopolies restricts the opportunities both for competitors to create rival markets and for street traders to sell outside the established markets. These markets rights, if taken together, extend over a substantial part of the national territory. In many areas of the country it is not possible to create new markets without *prima facie* disturbing the market rights of the existing monopolists. The task of identifying areas in which market rights do not exist is also virtually an insurmountable one since it involves considerable and expensive antiquarian investigations. Thus it seems that whilst dominance may not be achieved by one market right holder, the combined effect of all market rights taken together could be a dominant position. This is so regardless of the fact they normally operate separately.

Art. 86 seems to contemplate that such an anti-competitive structure may fall within its scope. It states : "Any abuse by one or more undertakings of a dominant position...." This suggests that dominance achieved by the combined effect of many monopolies may be unlawful. The novelty of this argument is that Art. 86 has generally been employed where there is an concentration of market power in a few hands. As we have seen, it is possible to argue that Art. 86 has a wider application than this.

If individual market rights can fall within Art. 86 those rights could be rendered unenforceable if abused. Some abuses are exemplified in Art. 86:

(a)   directly or indirectly imposing unfair purchase or selling or other unfair trading conditions;

(b)   limiting production, markets or technical development to the prejudice of consumers;

(c)   applying dissimilar conditions to equivalent transactions with other trading parties, thereby placing them at a competitive disadvantage;

(d)   making the conclusion of contracts subject to acceptance by other parties of supplementary obligations which, by their nature or according to commercial usage, have no connection with the subject of such contracts.

Although the existing case-law does not provide a close analogy with the issue under discussion it may be argued that an abuse may occur where market rights are used to enforce a monopoly and so exclude competitors either seeking to create rival markets or to sell outside the market. [125] If the dominance was achieved by an undertaking or group of undertakings holding many market rights, and suppressing all would-be competitors there would be some similarities to the issues in *Pompes funebres generales*. Second, if rivals were permitted to operate under a licensing scheme but the scheme was operated so as to unfairly disadvantage some market organisers as against others, this might also constitute abuse. Finally, the imposition of unfair charges or other unfair terms on the licence holders might also violate Art. 86. This is particularly important because there have been suggestions that some fees charged by local authorities for market operation have been excessive. [126]

Article 85
The exercise of market rights may also be inhibited by the effects of Art. 85 which states:

1.   "The following shall be prohibited as incompatible with the common market: all agreements between undertakings, decisions by associations of undertakings and concerted practices which may affect trade between Member States and which have as their object or effect the prevention, restriction or distortion of competition within the common market...."
    Any agreements or decisions prohibited under this Article are automatically void.
    The prohibition bites upon "agreements", "decisions by associations of undertakings" or "concerted practices".
    All agreements are potentially included whether they are binding contracts or agreements which are merely binding in honour only. [127]
    The prohibition on "decisions by associations of undertakings" is designed to cover the activities of trade associations and other

---

[125] The consequences for the rival trader would be similar to those of a refusal by a dominant undertaking to sell to or deal with a competitor which can constitute abusive behaviour: Cases 6 and 7/73, *Commercial Solvents v. Commission* [1974] ECR 223; but *cf* the exercise of intellectual property rights which are not abusive practices: Case 85/76 *Hoffman-La Roche v. Commission* [1979] ECR 461.

[126] See the consultation letter of 16th August 1993 circulated by the Department of the Environment.

[127] *ACF Chemiefarma v. Commission* (Case 41/69) [1970] ECR 661.

collectivities where these are designed to be anti-competitive, for example by co-ordinating the activities of members. Those associations with public responsibilities are also included here. [128] This might be relevant if local authorities operating markets receive recommendations on the circumstances in which other markets should be permitted to operate and the terms on which they should do so.

More important is the idea of "concerted practices". This is wider than "agreement" and was defined in *ICI Ltd v. Commission (Dyestuffs)*[129] as a form of co-operation between undertakings where no agreement has been reached, yet where practical co-operation is substituted for the risks of competition. Parallel behaviour provides evidence of a concerted practice so that where terms of business are effectively harmonised between different undertakings a concerted practice may exist. An example of this may occur where similar price increases covering the same goods are announced at almost the same time. [130] Hence, where market owners only licence rivals on the same or substantially terms, there may be evidence of concerted behaviour. Similarly, Art. 85 may be relevant where market operators "shadow" each other's policies governing the circumstances in which other markets will be allowed to operate.

Article 85 does not, however, seem to apply to agreements or concerted practices between local authorities granting market licences to rival operators where they "act in their capacity as public authorities". [131] This suggests that where local authorities merely licence rival operators as a means of regulation of market activity in their areas there may be no breach of Art. 85 even if there is parallelism between authorities in the arrangements made.

It is different where the local authority licences markets as a commercial operation and seeks to derive profit by doing so. Here it

---

[128] Eg, *Pabst & Richardz/ BNIA* OJ 1976 L 231/24.
[129] (Case 48/69) [1972] ECR 619.
[130] *Ibid.*
[131] Case 30/87 [1988] ECR 2479).

seems that Art. 85 is applicable because the authority is not acting in its capacity as a public authority, but as a commercial entity. [132]

The difficulty in applying these rules is that a local authority which licences markets in its area is likely to do so both for the purposes of profit and to further the public interest in ensuring effective regulation. It is not yet clear how the courts will approach mixed motives of this kind. A broad approach by the Court might bring a significant number of local authorities within the scope of Art. 85 since licensing arrangements are often intended to generate revenue for the general purposes of the authority.

Article 85 is also only applicable where the agreement etc. affects trade between Member States and has as its object or effect the prevention or restriction or distortion of competition. If these requirements are not satisfied the matter falls only within the scope of domestic competition rules.

A detailed treatment of these requirements is beyond the scope of this work, but it should be noted that an agreement or practice which *potentially* affects trade between Member States is caught by Art. 85. [133] Another indication of the broad interpretation which is given to Art 85 can be found in the rule that an effect on trade between Member States may occur where an agreement concerns only trade within one State. [134] This may mean that, for example, an agreement by several market owners not to licence rival market operations in their market areas of the UK may fall within Art. 85. since it would structure UK market operation along national lines; market operators from other EC countries could not set up in competition in those areas.

If a market owner licences one rival market operator with an undertaking that no other operator will be similarly licensed in that area it seems Art. 85 may be applicable. This appears from *Etablissements Consten SA v. Commission* [135] where Grundig offered Consten an exclusive dealership in its products in France. Consten was not to export Grundig's products to any other country.

---

[132] *Gloucester City Council v. Williams* (1990) 88 LGR 853 contains suggestions that a local authority might not be acting commercially even when deriving profits from a market, but the point is not unambiguous.

[133] *La Technique Miniere v. Maschinebrau Ulm GmbH* (Case 56/65 [1966] ECR 235.

[134] *Re Italian Flat Glass* [1982] 3 CMLR 366.

[135] Cases 55 & 58/ 64 [1966] ECR 299.

Grundig's dealers in other countries would not export to France. The agreement had partitioned the market and prevented competition in the wholesale distribution of Grundig's products. This case confirms that any agreement to exclude competitors from an area could undermine the creation of the single market and may fall within Art. 85.

The applicability of Articles 85 an 86 has yet to be fully explored by the Courts, but if it were held that the monopolistic rights of market owners, or their practices in licensing other market operators, violated EC law there would be far-reaching consequences for the enforcement of market rights under English Law. [136]

---

[136] For a more detailed discussion readers should consult Richard Whish "*Competition Law*" 3rd edit. (1993); Bellamy & Child, "*Common Market Law of Competition*" (1987); Green, Hartley and Usher "*The Legal Foundations of the Single European Market*", Oxford (1991); Goyder "*EC Competition Law*" 2nd edit. (1993).

CHAPTER 7

MARKET REGULATION - 1

The purpose of this and the following chapter is to examine the powers of the market owner to regulate the market place and the terms upon which market traders operate within it. First, however, it is important to explore the nature of the legal relationship between the market owner and traders, and to consider how, in the case of local authority markets, the courts are increasingly willing to intervene to control this relationship.

A. The Legal Relationship Between Traders and the Market Owner - General Principles

The public has a common law right to come into a lawful market to buy and to sell. [1] Those who come into the market to sell do not normally enter into a contractual relationship with the market owner. The common law right does not entitle them to exclusive occupation of the market place; if a trader does so, the owner of the soil of the market place is entitled to charge a fee for the privilege of occupying a part of the land. He can recover this under a contract, whether this be express or implied from the circumstances.[2]

The terms of the contract are a matter for agreement between the stallholder and the market owner. In practice these terms are, in effect, imposed on the trader who wishes to conduct business in the market. Market trading in many markets, and in particular those operated by local authorities, is subject to the "regulations" of the market. These regulations can provide the terms of the

---

[1] Eg *Scott v. Glasgow Corporation* [1988] AC 470; *R v. Barnsley MBC ex p Hook* [1976] 1 WLR 1052. No such right arises in informal markets conducted on private land.
[2] *Mayor of Yarmouth v. Groom* (1862) 1 H & C 102.

contract between the stallholders and the owner. If, however, a trader is unaware of the regulations, perhaps because he has not been given a copy of them, they do not become part of the contract. [3]

The relationship between stallholders and the owner of the market [4] is therefore *prima facie* regulated by the private law. The role of the law under this *laissez-faire* model is merely to interpret and to uphold bargains freely struck. Notions of freedom and sanctity of contract dictate that the courts should not interfere to control the legal relationship for the benefit of either party. Moreover, principles of public law, such as the procedural rights consequent upon the duty to act fairly, or the substantive controls preventing "unreasonable" decision-making, have no application. Unfair treatment is lawful if clothed in contractual authority.

This model is fundamentally flawed. It ignores the inherent inequality of bargaining power between the parties. Traders are not normally in a position freely to negotiate the terms on which they will take a stall in a market. If they do not agree to the terms on offer they are not free to set up in competition. Market rights are monopolies; the market owner can invoke legal redress to prevent competition from rival markets traders seeking to sell outside the lawful market. If traders wish to sell to the population within the area controlled by the owner they must accept the terms offered by the operator of the market.

Possible Limits on Laissez Faire to Vindicate Public Policy

This *laissez faire* model has been revised in other contexts in which the courts have been willing to impose controls on a dominant party in a contractual relationship. The courts seem especially willing to do this where there is an inequality of bargaining power between the parties, and there is an argument that this should be so in the case of markets. In other contexts, the rules of natural justice have been imposed as a matter of public policy on organisations exercising contractual powers, [5] or as a term implied into a

---

[3] *Rickard v. Forest Heath District Council* 1 May 1991 (unreported).

[4] Or of the soil of market place.

[5] See, in the case of social clubs, *Fisher v. Keane* (1878) 11 ChD 353; professional associations, *Law v. National Greyhound Racing Club Ltd.* [1983] 1 WLR 1302; trade unions, *Stevenson v. United Road Transport Union* [1977] ICR 893.

contract.[6] If the source of a duty to observe natural justice is an implied term, it seems that it could be ousted by an express term. [7] This is not so if natural justice or other principles of public law are imposed as a matter of public policy. [8] If so, a term of the contract which conflicts with a requirement of public law may be void. [9]

Public law principles may also regulate a relationship where no contract exists between the parties and is thus an emanation of public policy deployed to regulate the exercise of private power. [10]

Where the courts have considered the relationship of stallholder and market owner these arguments do not, however, appear to have been explored. It seems that the courts will not, as a matter of general principle, restrict the exercise of contractual power by the market owner. The owner is free to impose such terms on the stall-holder as he or she sees fit because the relationship is one of contract. Accordingly, in *Gloucester City Council v. Williams*[11] the court held that even a local authority franchisee was at liberty to restrict the classes of goods sold at individual stalls. A stallholder who disregarded those restrictions could be evicted from the market.

Fox L.J. observed:

"In the present case there are no customary, statutory or chartered rights which would displace the (principles of the private law). The result, in my opinion, is that, at common law, the owner of the soil is entitled to stipulate for such terms as he thinks fit when granting a licence to occupy a stall."

---

[6] Eg *Per* Asquith LJ in *Russell v. Duke of Norfolk* [1949] 1 All Er 109; *Lawlor v. UPW* [1965] Ch 712.

[7] *Roebuck v. NUM* [1977] ICR 573.

[8] *Radford v. NatSOPA* [1972] ICR 484.

[9] *Ibid.*

[10] *McInnes v. Onslow-Fane* [1978] 3 All ER 211.

[11] (1990) 88 LGR 853. Note that arguments based on *Wheeler v. Leicester City Council* [1985] AC 1054 do not appear to have been advanced.

Judicial Review Where a Local Authority Exercises Contractual Powers

Whilst neither entirely consistent nor satisfactory, there is an emerging line of authority which suggests that local authorities may be subject to judicial review in the exercise of their contractual powers in relation to markets. Where this applies, it means that a local authority could not, for example, disregard the duty to act fairly, take into account irrelevant considerations in fixing rents, nor otherwise act unreasonably in the *Wednesbury* sense [12].

This line of authority seems to recognise that - at least in some circumstances- a local authority is not in an analogous position to that of a private individual. It only has the powers which have been conferred upon it by statute, and whether it exercises statutory power, or powers enjoyed under a contract which a statute entitles it to make, all powers are possessed solely in order that they may be used for the public good. [13] Adherents to this view assert that the exercise of contractual power by a local authority market owner is subject to public law principles designed to subject these powers to the rule of law in much the same way as the local authority's statutory powers.

The decisions are not consistent and repay a close examination.

The first was *R v. Barnsley MBC ex p Hook* [14] where a market trader was banned for life from trading in a statutory market operated by the local authority after a minor incident of misconduct. The council's defence *inter alia* asserted that it had exercised a power rooted in private law, and could not be subject to judicial review. In essence, the Council argued that the court could not inquire into the legality of the ban since as market owners they had the power to determine the applicant's licence. Even if they had violated his private law rights they argued that it would not alter the validity of his removal from the market, although it might give rise to an action for damages.

The Court rejected this contention and held that this exercise of power was amenable to judicial review. According to both Lord

---

[12] *Associated Picture Houses Ltd. v. Wednesbury Corporation* [1948] 1 KB 223.

[13] See *Wade Administrative Law* Law 6th edit (1988) p.400; Slade LJ, *Jones v. Swansea City Council* [1990] 1 WLR 55.

[14] [1976] 1 WLR 1052.

Denning MR [15] and Scarman LJ [16] , the applicant's rights were not simply a matter of contract or licence. Because the public has a right under the common law to buy and sell in a market, and these rights are imposed as a matter of general law, the trader had rights protected under public law. Each of their lordships seemed to suggest, however, that had the relationship been purely one of contract, judicial review would not have been possible. Where, however, the facts reveal a sufficient "public law element", judicial review is available. [17]

The existence of the "public law element" was also seen to be crucial in *R v. Wear Valley District Council ex p. Binks* [18] where again the court was willing to overturn the council's contention that their decision was rooted exclusively in private law. Here, without either consultation or warning, the council gave a street trader operating in a market place owned by the council notice to quit. It asserted that public law had no application in this case because the common law right of resort to market only applied in a statutory or franchise market and not an informal one such as this (if indeed it was a market at all).

Taylor J, rejected this submission. Because the trading took place on land to which the public had access at all times, his lordship found that the necessary public interest existed. Further, the public had an interest in the decision of the council with regard to whom they licence and whom they do not licence in the market place. [19]

An even wider approach seemed to be signalled in *R v. Basildon District Council ex p Brown* [20] where intervention did not appear to depend upon proof of a "public law element". Here a local authority terminated the licence of a stall holder in its market by giving three months notice in accordance with the terms of the

---

[15] *Ibid.* at p. 1057.

[16] *Ibid.* at p. 1060.

[17] Where the decision making body is not a public body and its powers derive only from contract, judicial review is not possible. *R v. Jockey Club ex p Agha Khan* (1993) 143 NLJ 163. It is possible to distinguish the position of a local authority from that of the Jockey Club because the latter only possesess the powers which are conferred on them by statute.

[18] [1985] 2 All ER 699.

[19] *Ibid* at p. 703.

[20] (1981) 79 LGR 655.

licence. Here again the council had deployed the familiar argument that the termination had been an exercise of contractual powers under private law and could not be scrutinised on judicial review. The attempt to oust public law principles was buttressed by argument that the market was not a statutory market but an "unofficial" one lacking those common law market rights which would have placed it on a footing with *Ex p. Hook*.

In contrast with his approach in *Ex p. Hook* , Lord Denning MR (dissenting as to the result) held the matter to be reviewable because the local authority was a body established by statute and possessed only such powers as statute gave it. This view demonstrates that, at least for Lord Denning MR, local authorities ought to be subject to review in the exercise of their contractual powers regardless of whether a distinct "public law element" is present. He added, however, that if necessary he would hold that the market was a public market and this would provide sufficient justification for review.

For Templeman L.J. the status of the market was unimportant. Whether a statutory or "unofficial" market, the exercise of powers by a local authority would be regulated by the same public law principles. On the facts, however, the council had not acted unreasonably.

Dunn L.J dismissed the applicant's appeal on the grounds that the stallholder's rights were contractual and not public. This was so because the market was not a statutory market. *Ex p. Hook*, he observed was "clearly right" suggesting that if a sufficient public law element was present, judicial review would be possible.

Despite *Ex p Brown* , the existence of a sufficient public law element was treated as jurisdictional in *R v. Durham City Council ex p. Robinson*. [21] Nevertheless, the parties could not establish that jurisdiction by agreeing that a public law element was present; it was a matter to be established in evidence.

Thus the balance of authority suggests that the courts are increasingly willing to scrutinise the exercise of contractual powers by local authorities where some element of public law can be established. How far review will be constrained by the need to establish a "public law element" will clearly depend on how the

---

[21] [1992] The Times 31st January.

courts interpret this requirement. If Taylor J's view in *Ex p. Binks* that a public law element can be found where a market is held on land on which the public have access at all times, the practical difficulties posed by the requirement are significantly lessened.

As Professor Arrowsmith has argued, [22] however, reliance on the special public law element as the rationale of exercising judicial review may be regretted. Why should the trader's legal relationship with the council depend on whether he happens to trade in a place to which the public has access or, alternatively, in a market in which there has been at some period a common law right of resort to market? In cases in which these kinds of factor are not present the trader's rights may be severely restricted and yet he might equally be the victim of what would otherwise be regarded as an excess or abuse of power. As Professor Arrowsmith argues, the law imposes obligations on contracting parties in many other contexts. Why should this not be done, as a matter of general principle, in the case of a local authority? The unsatisfactory answer to this is perhaps that the courts in the market context have been uncertain whether their proper role is rooted in active intervention or the ideals of *laissez-faire.*

As Professor Arrowsmith suggests, judicial review should apply as a matter of general principle in all cases in which a public authority exercises contractual powers.

B. Market Levies

The reveneue generated for the market owner by the market may be derived from rents (more traditionally known as stallage) paid by stall holders in return for their use of the land, and tolls which, if payable at all, were normally exacted from the buyer as a levy on goods sold in the market. In more modern times, because of the practical difficulties in collection, tolls are often payable by sellers. It is now proposed to examine the powers of the market owner to recover such revenue and the extent to which such powers are limited by law.

---

[22] (1990) LQR 277.

Historical Introduction

The extent to which the law should control the level of charges is a controversial issue linked to the purpose for which markets exist. It will be recalled that in earlier times market owners were almost delegates of the State's function in maintaining law and order; they were not simply private entrepreneurs subject to the principles of free competition. The rationale of the monopoly of market was that it would ensure the viability and thus existence of the market *for the benefit of the public.* This was recognised by the courts. [23] Thus market owners performed a public function over which the Crown never renounced a supervisory role. [24] This public function constrained the owner's power to raise revenue from the market: but how far did this limitation extend?

Regulation at Common Law
A little known but undoubted line of authority demonstrates that the common law courts asserted a power to control prices charged by those who had sufficient market power to withstand the ordinary forces of competition. This amounted to an *ad hoc* method of price regulation and protected the public from the adverse economic effects of certain monopolists. In the interests of public policy, the courts imposed an obligation on those with market power to charge only reasonable prices. One strand of the cases illustrates that this was so where the defendant enjoyed a private right of property affected with a public interest. This is of particular interest in market cases where a franchise is an incorporeal hereditament and where the public have a common law right of resort to the market.[25] It is thus an example *par excellence* of private property rights restricted by public duties. The courts held that where private property was overlaid with a public interest, the owner could not dispose of that private property freely.

---

[23] See, eg, *A G v. Horner No. 2* [1913] 2 Ch 140, 198 *per* Hamilton L.J. and although a franchisee of a market has a duty to operate the market, it seems that he may not be compelled to do so if the market cannot be run profitably: *A G v. Colchester Corporation* [1955] 2 QB 207; *cf* Scott J in *Gravesham BC v. British Railways Board* [1978] Ch 379, 402.
[24] There may be circumstances in which a failure to conduct a market justifies a repeal of the grant: *Re Islington Market Bill* (1835) 3 Cl & Fin 513. See generally Ch. 9.
[25] *R v. Barnsley MBC ex p Hook* [1976] 1 WLR 1052.

Allnut v. Inglis provides a pertinent illustration of the principle. Here the London Dock Company, enjoying a monopoly under a licence from Parliament to receive certain wines, was held to be unable to exclude a wine importer who would not pay their scheduled but unreasonable prices. Lord Ellenborough began his judgment by stating the general principle that private property rights *prima facie* entail a right freely to dispose of those rights,[26] but added that if a property owner enjoys a monopoly he must "perform the duty attached to it on reasonable terms." [27] This was so because the monopoly was imposed for the benefit of the public as well as for the Company. Thus the principle was established that where private property right was dedicated to the use of the public, the owner could only charge what was reasonable. [28]

This principle would seem to apply equally to the regulation of market levies generally; indeed the courts did only permit the recovery of reasonable tolls. This was because toll could not be avoided if a purchase was made in the market.

The principle was never applied, however, to stallage or rents, (as opposed to tolls) because the market trader has no right to a stall (but he does have a right to sell in the market). In deciding to take a stall in the market (as opposed to hawking in the market) he was seen as exercising a choice and so had to pay what the owner demanded. This reasoning has traditionally allowed *laissez faire* principles to apply to stallage but not to tolls. It is now proposed to consider the rules applying to each kind of levy.

Toll

The Nature of Toll
Coke defined toll as "a reasonable sum of money due to the owner of the fair or market upon sale of things tollable within (it)." [29]

---

[26] (1810) 12 East 527, 537.
[27] *Ibid* at p.540. He also stated that if others were licensed to receive wines so that the public had a choice the restriction might not apply.
[28] The Court relied upon the writings of Lord Hale: see Hargrave, Law Tracts (1787) discussed by McAllister (1929-30) 43 Harv. Law Rev 759.
[29] 2 Co Inst 220.

Toll, properly so called, is a levy payable on goods sold in market. [30] Originally it was seen as a charge made of buyers for the prospect of undisputed ownership which a purchase in a public market offered. [31] Toll was thus levied on goods and was normally payable by the buyer and not the seller.

Because toll was collected from buyers it posed enormous problems of collection. Gradually market owners seem either to have abandoned the system of tolls, preferring instead to replace the lost revenue by increasing stallage,[32] or to have switched the burden of tolls to sellers. In *A-G v. Horner No.2* [33] this practice was held not sufficient to give the owner a power to demand toll from sellers as of right.

The Right to Toll

(i) By Grant
The right to take toll is *not* an incident of a market or fair; in other words it is not a right which is inherent in a grant of market, but a separate franchise appurtenant to a grant of market or fair. Without evidence of a grant or franchise of toll, no right can be asserted. [34] Many markets were toll free.

There is no right to toll except on market days specified in the grant. If the market day is changed unlawfully, no toll can be recovered. [35]

(ii) Prescription
The doctrine of prescription or presumed lost grant may enable the courts to enforce a long usage of taking tolls even if no evidence of a grant can be found. A lawful origin may be presumed for the usage. The court may, for example, presume that the highway on which

---

[30] or sometimes unsold, *infra.*
[31] *Duke of Bedford v. St. Paul Covent Garden, Overseers* (1881) 51 LJMC 41,55, Bowen J.
[32] One reported example of this is *Swindon Central Market Co. Ltd v. Panting* (1872) 27 LT 578.
[33] [1913] 2 Ch 140.
[34] *Heddy v. Weelhouse* (1598) Cro Eliz 558; *Kearton v. Robinson* (1965) 63 LGR 341, 342-3, although a right may arise by prescription.
[35] *Duke of Newcastle v. Worksop Urban Council* [1902] 2 Ch. 145.

the trading takes place was dedicated subject to the right to exact tolls for trading thereon. [36]

Evidence that the amount of toll has varied over the years is not fatal to a claim based on a presumed grant. Such variations may be consistent merely with the change in the value of money. [37]

Tollable Goods

Normally toll is payable on goods actually sold in the market-place although prescription and custom may establish a right to levy toll on goods brought into the market regardless of whether actually sold. [38] At common law, goods not brought into the market are not subject to toll. [39] The consequence of these rules is that no toll is normally payable on the bulk of goods if sold in the market by sample. [40]

Amount of Toll

(i) Toll in Markets Created by Grant

Historically, market owners were too willing to set unduly burdensome tolls and this eventually resulted in legislative intervention. The Statute of Westminster 1275 [41] enacted that the taking of "outrageous tolls" could lead to the forfeiture of the franchise of market. This regime was buttressed by the common law which accepted that the regulation of tolls could not be left to market forces alone. The resulting controls are based on the standard of reasonableness. A grant, (unless made by Act of Parliament) permitting the taking of toll cannot create a right to demand an unreasonable toll, nor can an owner levy an unreasonable toll in pursuance of his grant. This means that if the grant specifies the toll and it is found to be unreasonable the right of toll is void.[42] No toll is payable.

---

[36] *Lawrence v. Hitch* (1868) LR 3 QB 521.

[37] *Wright v. Bruister* (1832) 4 B & Ad. 116.

[38] *Duke of Bedford v. Emmett* (1820) 3 B & Ald. 366.

[39] *Kerby v. Whichelow* (1700) 2 Lut. 1498, at p 1502, *per* Powell J.

[40] *Hill v. Smith* (1809) 10 East 476; but see *infra* p. 100 on disturbance.

[41] 3 Edw 1 c.31.

[42] *Heddy v. Weelhouse* (1597) Cro. Eliz 558.

Where no toll is specified in the grant, the courts have allowed a reasonable toll to be recovered since, to do otherwise, would deny the franchise (in so far as it relates to toll) of all operation and effect. [43] In such a case, and subject to what is reasonable, it is then for the owner of the market to fix the toll. Within this limit the courts seem prepared to allow market forces to operate.

(ii) Right to Toll Acquired By Prescription

If the right to toll is claimed by prescription, the court may presume a lost grant either of a specified toll, or of a reasonable toll. The latter would be the outcome most sought by market owners since it would allow them to increase tolls according to the change in the value of money, although such an increase must always be reasonable. [44] It is not fatal to a claim based on prescription that the amount of toll has varied over the years provided the evidence supports the right claimed. Slight variations are therefore normally immaterial.[45]

Increasing Tolls

Unless the amount is fixed, either by the grant or by prescription, the toll can be increased [46] but cannot exceed what is reasonable. If the amount is not fixed in the grant, evidence that a uniform level of toll has been claimed for a substantial period will not necessarily prevent a reasonable increase.[47]

Reasonableness

What is reasonable is the touchstone of the power to demand toll. Reasonableness is a question of law, and the onus of proof lies on the person seeking to challenge the toll to show that it is unreasonable.[48]

It now seems clear that commercial considerations can influence the setting of tolls and stallages. As Hamilton L.J. observed in

---

[43] *Stamford Corporation v. Pawlett* (1830) 1 Cr. & J 57.

[44] *Wright v. Bruister* (1832) 4 B & Ad. 116.

[45] *Duke of Beaufort v. Smith* (1849) 4 Ex 450.

[46] *Lawrence v. Hitch* (1868) LR 3 QB 521..

[47] *Mills v. Mayor of Colchester* (1868) LR 3 CP 575.

[48] *Wright v. Bruister supra*, n.(44).

Horner No.2 [49] the market owner is entitled to have regard to the costs of levying the market, his rent, rates, and taxes. He is entitled to recover his outlay and, it is submitted, make a profit. If this were not possible, the market would cease to operate and this would be detrimental to the public interest.

In the case of a franchise of toll, evidence of long usage and the buyers' acquiescence in it is "cogent evidence" that the toll is reasonable. [50] This seems to import the private law principles of waiver or acquiescence into this field. This also hints at judicial ambivalence concerning the doctrinal basis of intervention. If intervention is necessary to control unreasonable tolls as a matter of public policy, it seems inconsistent to suggest that inactivity by toll payers could bar relief. Their failure to act may be explicable on grounds other than acquiescence, such as the cost of taking court proceedings.

As in the case of any private franchisee, a local authority exercising a franchise right of market will not be at liberty to demand an unreasonable toll. There are, however, other statutory powers to impose charges. A local authority operating a market under any local enactment may make such charges as it may from time to time determine. [51] Where a market is established or acquired under the Food Act 1984, the authority has a similar power to demand such charges as it may from time to time determine. [52] Although it is more likely that these powers would be employed to impose stallage rather than toll, a power to toll is not excluded. The exercise of such statutory powers is subject to the general duty to act reasonably [53] and this would prevent the levying of an unreasonable toll in the purported exercise of these statutory powers.

---

[49] [1913] 2 Ch 140, 198.
[50] *Gard v. Calland* (1817) 6 M & S 69.
[51] Local Government (Miscellaneous Provisions) Act 1976. s. 36 (2).
[52] Section 53.
[53] *Infra* Ch. 17.

Stallage or Rent

The Nature of Stallage

Whilst buyers and sellers have a right to come to market to trade, the seller becomes a trespasser if he attempts to gain an exclusive occupation of part of the soil of the market. [54] Permission is therefore required from the owner of the soil to use or to place any stall or barrow in the market. The fee normally charged for this consent is the rent or stallage.

If a stall is erected without permission an action will lie for stallage upon an implied contract. [55] Stallage is thus a matter of agreement, either express or presumed. It does not depend upon royal grant, but arises *ratione terrae.* [56] Whereas toll is payable to the owner of the market, stallage is payable to the owner of the soil or the person who is entitled to possession of the market place.

There is no rule that the market place must be vested in the owner of the market right; he is entitled to hold the market on land on which he has a tenancy or even a mere licence to hold it. [57] However, there is some authority that if the market owner does not have exclusive possession of the soil of the market place he is not entitled to charge stallage.[58]

Stallage cannot be imposed on a seller who does not seek to trade from a particular site in the market place. The "hawker" may sell his goods free of charge. Such a rule could cause difficulties in practice because a "hawker" is entitled to place his goods upon the ground when weary. [59] Similarly, when making a sale he could find himself in one site for a substantial period, especially if his goods are so popular that he is, in effect, selling continuously. [60] It must be a question of fact as to when he or she becomes liable to stallage.

---

[54] *Northampton Corpn v. Ward* (1745) 2 Stra. 1238.

[55] *Mayor of Newport v. Saunders* 3 B & Ad. 411.

[56] *A G v. Colchester Corporation* [1952] 1 Ch. 586, 594-5.

[57] *A G v. Horner* (1884) 14 QBD 245.

[58] *Lockwood v. Wood* (1841) 6 QB 31. Note, however, *A G v. Horner* (1886) 11 App Cas 66.

[59] *Mayor of Yarmouth v. Groom* (1862) 1 H&C 102, especially *per* Martin B at 111.

[60] This same difficulty faces someone acting as a pedlar, *infra* p. 180 *et seq.*

Stalls in the Market Place
There is no duty in the market owner to provide stalls, [61] but there is an incentive to do so in order to encourage traders to take them and thus pay stallage. In one extreme case it seems that the entire market place was covered in stalls to deny any space to the "hawkers". This was condemned as unlawful. [62] Owners should permit casual traders to operate.

The Amount of Stallage
We are here concerned with the regulation of the amount which the owner of the soil can demand as stallage. The applicable rules will depend upon whether the owner is merely subject to the private law, in which case the issue will turn on the extent to which the courts will control the exercise of contractual powers, or whether, in the case of local authorities, powers derived from contract are constrained by principles of public law.

(i) Rights to Stallage under Private Law
At issue here are markets which are not owned by local authorities and where the right is enjoyed by virtue of grant or presumed grant.[63]

If the amount of stallage is fixed by charter or by prescription, these amounts cannot be exceeded. The amount recoverable can also be determined by local custom which may permit recovery of a reasonable sum or, the custom may itself prescribe the amount recoverable. [64]

If the amount is not otherwise prescribed, the amount payable is determined by an agreement, either express or implied, between the stallholder and the owner of the soil. The orthodox view is that the owner is free to increase the stallage payable and the increase cannot normally be impugned on the ground that it is unreasonable. It is simply a matter of free bargain.

---

[61] *Brackenborough v. Spalding UDC* [1942] AC 310.

[62] *R v. Burdett* 1 Ld Raym 149.

[63] Markets owned by private individuals or companies which are created by private Act of Parliament are subject to the Markets and Fairs Clauses Act 1847. There is no power to exceed the limits therein prescribed. See *infra*.

[64] *A G v. Colchester Corpn.* [1952] Ch 586, 595; *Percy v. Ashford Union* (1876) 34 LT 579; *Bennington v. Taylor* 2 Lut. 642.

Influenced by principles of *laissez-faire*, the courts have been reluctant to strike down bargains freely concluded. This reasoning has been influential even in modern times and exposes the stallholders to very significant increases in stallage without redress. That the courts have favoured abstentionism in such cases contrasts starkly with their intervention to control unreasonable tolls.

A significant illustration of the extent of private law powers is *A-G v. Colchester Corporation*. [65]. It is noteworthy here that the court applied private law principles notwithstanding that the market owner was a public authority.

In this case the Corporation owned both the right of market and the soil of the market place. It increased stallage charges forcing those not resident in the borough to pay significantly more than traders residing locally. These charges were also considerably higher than in markets elsewhere. Danckwerts J., apparently persuaded by *laissez-faire* principles, dismissed the action on the grounds that stallage was a voluntary payment. The trader, who had the option of trading without a stall, became a stallholder for his own convenience.

His lordship seemed, however to impose some limits on the charging power. The public, for example, appears to have an interest in preserving the range of goods available for purchase in the market. If the charges were so high that traders dealing in certain classes of goods were driven from the market, the court might have intervened to declare the charges unreasonable. [66] Such an issue did not arise in the *Colchester* case because the local traders were able to meet the normal demands of the buying public.

(ii) Markets Operated by Local Authorities: Judicial Review
Local authorities may exercise statutory powers or powers rooted in private law when setting stallage. This means that the source of their power in relation to a market may lie either in public or in private law.

---

[65] *Ibid.*
[66] *Ibid.* at pp. 602-3.

(a) Stallage Fixed Under Statutory Powers

The amount of rent or stallage may be ascertained under statutory powers rather than private law powers. [67] We have already seen how, under s.53 of the Food Act 1984, an authority which has acquired or established a market under s.50 may impose such charges as they from time to time determine. "Charges" are defined to include both stallages and tolls. [68] But excluded are rents charged by a market authority for the letting of accommodation for a period of more than one week. These are a matter of agreement between the parties. This must, however, be subject to what follows on the expansion of judicial review.

A further statutory power to charge arises where a local authority maintains a market under a local, or "special" Act. This may incorporate the provisions of the Markets and Fairs Clauses Act 1847. S.36 of this Act provides that the authority may alter the relevant tolls or stallages provided any amount in the special Act is not exceeded. But this is of little consequence because the local authority now has power to disregard any limits laid down in the special Act. It may make such charges as it determines from time to time notwithstanding any provision of the local Act. [69] This gives it a discretionary power to increase charges or to charge differential rates subject only to the limitation of reasonableness imposed by the general law. Although setting rents is a commercial operation, it is now clear that it is subject to judicial review. [70] There would therefore be no difficulty in challenging an *ultra vires* decision.

General principles of Administrative Law [71] ensure that the powers in these Acts cannot be exceeded. In determining rent levels, the authority is amenable to judicial review on the grounds of irrationality, illegality or procedural impropriety. [72] This may generate both substantive and procedural rights. An increase may

---

[67] Statutory powers to charge have already been noted, *supra* n (51).
[68] Food Act 1984, s.61.
[69] Local Government (Miscellaneous Provisions) Act 1976 s36 (2).
[70] *R v. Birmingham City Council ex p Dredger* [1993] The Times, January 28th.
[71] *Infra.*
[72] *Council of Civil Service Unions v. Minister of the Civil Service* [1985] AC 374, *per* Lord Diplock at p. 410.

be challenged because it is unreasonable, or it may be vulnerable by virtue of the process by which the decision to increase stallage was reached. [73]

A well-known example illustrating how the courts are prepared to scrutinise the charging power occurred in *Ricketts v. Havering LBC.* [74] Here the local market authority had increased charges in order to achieve parity with charges elsewhere. Moreover, Central Government policy aimed at reducing expenditure forced the authority to consider other means of raising revenue for the Borough. The increases were attacked as *ultra vires*, but the challenge failed since the court accepted that the market could make a profit and that this profit could lawfully supplement other forms of local government revenue. It was accepted, however, that any excessive or unreasonable increase would be challengeable.

This recognises that in an appropriate case the *amount* of stallage may be challenged on the grounds of unreasonableness. It is not entirely clear what this means in practice. Reasonableness is not self-defining. What is reasonable is dependent upon what factors the courts is able to consider.

Unreasonable Stallage or Rent?
The *Colchester* case suggests that an increase in rent which is so severe that traders dealing in certain classes of goods (presumably where profit margins are tighter) could not continue to trade thereby denying the public access to their goods, such an increase would be unlawful. It is not clear whether any increase which had less dramatic consequences than these would necessarily be reasonable.

---

[73] Eg if irrelevant considerations were taken into account. Note an action commenced by writ may apparently be available as an alternative in some circumstances notwithstanding the principle in *O' Reilly v. Mackman* [1983] 1 AC 237, and this seems to be so even though the traders seek to impugn the local authority's decision on the grounds of a breach of natural justice: *R v. Durham City Council ex p Robinson* [1992] The Times 31st January.

[74] (1981) 79 LGR 146.

(b) Stallage Fixed Under Private Law Powers

There are circumstances in which a local authority can use its private law powers to fix rents and stallages. This may arise where a franchise of market is vested in the local authority. [75] In settling the terms upon which it is prepared to allow traders to use its markets, it is exercising private law powers in much the same way as an individual franchisee.

As we have seen, there is a line of authority which holds that a public authority may be subject to public law principles even in the exercise of private law powers provided that some "public law element" is involved in the case. None of the case-law so far has dealt with the application of this principle to the question of stallage. It nevertheless, seems open to the courts to apply public law principles to restrict the freedom of local authorities to increase stallage. If this were so, it would mean that a decision to increase stallage for a "improper" purpose, or in breach of a duty to act fairly or otherwise unreasonably may be challenged by way of judicial review.

The *caveat* must be entered, however, that where the court has considered increases in stallage it has applied orthodox private law principles even where the market owner is a local authority. It will be recalled that this was so in the *Colchester* case although, even here, *laissez faire* was not accepted unequivocally. More recently in *Simonite v. Sheffield City Council* [76] a local authority was held to be fully entitled to exploit its monopolistic property rights in its market subject only to market forces.

Thus doubt continues to surround the powers of the local authority franchisee. This is a matter is of vital importance to many market traders and urgently requires clarification from the courts. In particular. it is important to know whether decisions such as that in the *Colchester* case and *Simonite* should be read subject to *Ex p Hook*, *Ex p Binks* and *Ex p Brown*.[77]

---

[75] The Food Act 1984, ss 50 & 53 allow such markets to be acquired. In such circumstances the market is still a franchise market: *Manchester City Council v. Walsh* (1986) 84 LGR 1.

[76] 1992] 24 EG 134.

[77] *Supra* p. 126 *et seq.* The inconsistency in the judicial approach may be noted when these decisions are also read alongside *Gloucester City Council v. Williams* (1990) 88 LGR 853.

There are, however, important reasons of policy why judicial review should be available. In particular the rights of the trader should not be made to depend on whether he or she happens to trade in a market which the local authority regulates under statutory powers. The juridical nature of the power involved in market regulation should make no difference to the limitations on the powers of local authorities.

Differential Charges

Because some market stalls occupy a more favoured position in the market place than others it is possible to charge different rates to reflect this. [78] This is so provided that any limits on stallage charges, whether imposed by custom, charter or statute, are not exceeded. [79] It is different, however, if the levy is "toll" properly so called. Differential tolls would not be enforced. [80]

Where judicial review is available to control an increase in stallage or rent, it could similarly restrain *ultra vires* differential charges in local authority markets. The courts could examine the legality of the reasons why differentials were operated. By analogy with *R v. Lewisham ex p Shell UK Ltd*, [81] a decision to increase the rents of those who had political links of which the local authority disapproved might be *ultra vires.*

(c) Leases and Licences

Although as we have seen, the relationship between the owner and individual stallholder is normally a matter of contract or licence, the power of the local authority market owner may be restricted by public law principles where a "sufficient public law element" is involved. For example, in *Ex p Hook* [82] the termination of the stallholders licence was ineffective when the rules of natural

---

[78] *Duke of Bedford v. Emmett* (1820) 3 B & Ald. 366, especially *per* Bayley J. at p. 371.

[79] *Hungerford Market Co. v. City Steamboat Co.* (1860) 3 E & E 365.

[80] *Supra.*

[81] [1988] 1 All ER 938. See also *R v. Barnet LBC ex p Johnson* [1990] The Times, Sept. 6th; *R v. Ealing LBC ex p Times Newspapers Ltd.* (1987) 85 LGR 310; *Wheeler v. Leicester City Council* [1985] AC 1054.

[82] *Ex p Hook* [1976] 1 WLR 1052.

justice were breached. Thus the private law principles of contract and licence may be buttressed by public law principles in appropriate cases so as to prevent a stall-holder from being unlawfully ejected from the market. These rules provide important protection for stall-holders in local authority markets. But these are not the only rules which apply. Whether the stallholder operates in a privately owned market or a local authority one, there may be other, statutory, rules which buttress the legal relationship with the market owner.

Business Tenancies: Security of Tenure

Where the stallholder has a tenancy of his stall rather than a mere licence he may enjoy more extensive rights to have the tenancy renewed.

Security of tenure is an important right because the continued ability of the trader to pursue his business depends on being able to trade in the market. The right to renew the tenancy ensures that the business can continue after the tenancy has expired. Part II of the Landlord and Tenant Act 1954 also reformed the common law rule that, on granting a new lease, a landlord is entitled to stipulate whatever terms he thought fit. Under the 1954 Act the lease must be renewed at a commercial rent. The legislation does not, however, regulate the lease during the period of its term. What follows is an outline of the essential provisions of the legislation.[83] It should be noted, however, that the Law Commission has recently recommended reforms to this part of the 1954 Act. [84]

In practice, the protection afforded by the relevant parts of the Act, [85] can be disapplied. Where the tenant enjoys a term of years certain, on a joint application from landlord and tenant, the court may authorise an agreement excluding the tenant's rights under those provisions.[86] It has been held that a fixed term of less than a year is a term of years certain for these purposes. [87]

---

[83] Readers are referred to Hill and Redman's Law of Landlord and Tenant Vol 1.
[84] Law Comm no. 208, November 1992.
[85] Sections 24 to 28.
[86] Section 38.
[87] *Re Land and Premises at Liss, Hants.* [1971] Ch 986.

The Scope of the 1954 Act
The rights under the Act apply to most tenancies including periodic and weekly tenancies. This provision benefits many market traders and stallholders having weekly tenancies. A tenant holding premises under a tenancy at will, whether express or implied, is, however, excluded. [88] A tenancy for a term certain of six months or less may also be excluded. This is not an invariable rule and is considered below.

A fundamentally important exception excludes licensees from the scope of the Act. The stallholder must hold a tenancy and not a mere licence. [89] A detailed analysis of the distinction between a lease and a licence falls outside the scope of the present work. It is sufficient to note that the grant of exclusive possession of the premises for a fixed or periodic term will normally result in the grant of a tenancy. Exclusive possession of the premises is the essence of a lease. [90] If the grantee acquires use of the stall without exclusive possession of it, this will operate as a licence. The grant of exclusive possession will, however create only a licence if the grantor has no power to grant a lease. Exclusive possession is the right to exclude all others from the stall, including the landlord.

Whether a lease or a licence is created is always a question of substance and not form so that, even if the agreement is described as a licence, it may operate as a tenancy where exclusive possession is conferred. [91]

Also excluded from the operation of the Part II is a tenancy for a term certain not exceeding six months unless there is a provision for renewing or extending the term, or the tenant has been in occupation for a period which, together with any period during which any predecessor in the carrying on of the business carried on by the tenant was in occupation, exceeds twelve months. [92]

---

[88] *Wheeler v. Mercer* [1957] AC 44; *Hagee London Ltd v. A.B. Erikson and Larson* [1976] QB 209.
[89] *Shell-Mex and B.P. Ltd v. Manchester Garages Ltd.* [1971] 1 WLR 612.
[90] *Street v. Mountford* [1985] AC 809.
[91] See more generally, Megarry and Thompson, *Megarry's Manual of Real Property* 7th edit., 1993.
[92] Section 43 (3) as amended.

The Mechanism of the 1954 Act
First the Act provides that a tenancy falling within the Act will
continue, even though the date for its expiry has passed, unless the
provisions enacted for its termination have been followed. [93] One
consequence of this is that where negotiations for renewal have
continued beyond the expiry date of the lease, the tenancy is
continued. It can only be ended in accordance with the Act. If the
statutory procedures are not followed the tenancy continues on the
terms on which it was granted.
    The usual means of termination is by the landlord giving notice
in the prescribed form under s.25. [94] The notice must state that the
landlord objects to the granting of a new lease [95] and it must set out
the grounds of his objection. These must fall within s.30. [96] The
notice must also require the tenant to notify the landlord within
two months after service of the notice, whether he is willing to
give up possession. If the tenant does indicate such a willingness he
loses all right to renewal. [97] His rights are also lost if he fails to
serve the statement within the two month period. [98]
    Time limits for the serving of the s.25 notice are of central
importance. The notice must be served not less than six months and
not more than twelve months from the date of termination, but this
is subject to s.25 (3). This provides that the termination date must
not be earlier than the date on which the tenancy could have been
ended at common law by notice to quit or by effluxion of time. In the
case of a term of years certain, this is the term date. In the case of a
periodic tenancy, the date of termination must not be earlier than
the date the landlord could have terminated the tenancy by a
notice to quit served on the same day as the s.25 notice.
    The renewal procedure may also be initiated by the tenant
acting under s.26. The tenant's request for a new tenancy may be
served not more than twelve months nor less than six months before

[93] Section 24(1).
[94] The form is prescribed by the Landlord and Tenant Act 1954 Part II (Notices)
Regulations 1983 (SI 1983/133) as amended. A form "substantially to the like effect" is
acceptable: *Tegerdine v. Brooks* (1977) 36 P & CR 261.
[95] If the landlord does not object the Law Commission has recommended that the
landlord set out his proposals for the terms of the new tenancy (para 2.34).
[96] Section 25(5).
[97] *De Havilland (Antiques) Ltd v. Centrovincial Estates (Mayfair) Ltd.* [1971] 2 All ER 1.
[98] The Law Commission recommend that this counter-notice be abolished: para 2.39.

the date the new tenancy is to commence and this cannot be earlier than the date of expiry of the current term. This provision is only available to tenants with a term certain exceeding one year. Those having a periodic tenancy cannot initiate a renewal. [99] The tenant must set out his proposals for a new tenancy including the rent he is willing to pay. [100]

The provision is a useful one for, once a tenant has served a request, the landlord cannot serve a notice to end the lease. [101] If the landlord wishes to end the tenancy at the end of the term and delays in serving a s.25 notice until the last moment , the tenant can make a request under s.26 giving twelve months' notice and so ensure that the lease is continued under the existing rent for six months.

The landlord may oppose a s.26 request by serving a notice on the tenant within two months of the tenant's request stating the grounds- which must fall within s.30 of the Act- upon which his objection is based. Failure to serve the notice within the two month period entitles the tenant to a new tenancy. [102]

If the parties are unable to agree on the terms of renewal, the tenant must apply to the court. This is possible either where the landlord has served a notice to terminate the existing tenancy under s.25 or where the tenant has requested a new tenancy under s.26. The application must be made according to time limits established under the Act. If the tenant requests a new tenancy he must apply between two and four months after making his request. If the landlord has served a notice under s.25 the tenant must apply between two and four months after the serving of the notice. If made outside these limits, the court will not entertain the application.

The grounds on which the landlord can resist an application for a new lease are laid down in s.30. If the landlord fails to establish any of these grounds the court must grant a new tenancy. Amongst the grounds included in s.30 are:

(a)   The tenant's failure failed to comply with the repair and maintenance obligations under the current tenancy;

---

[99] The Law Commission recommended that there should be no change to this rule: para 3.20.
[100] Section 26 (3).
[101] Section 26 (4).
[102] Section 26 (6).

(b)   The persistent delay of the tenant in paying due rent.

(c)   The tenant has committed other substantial breaches of obligations under the tenancy.

(d)   the landlord will provide suitable alternative accommodation on reasonable terms;

(e)   the tenancy is a sub tenancy of part of the premises within a superior tenancy and the landlord wishes to dispose of the premises as a whole because he would gain substantially greater rent;

(f)   the landlord wishes to regain possession for construction or demolition work.

A landlord also is entitled to possession if he intends to occupy the leased premises for the purposes of his own business. The landlord must have owned his interest for at least five years before he can invoke this ground. [103]

Where a new tenancy is granted by the court it may be for a new term not exceeding fourteen years and may be on such terms as the court considers reasonable in all the circumstances.

Rent
The court can also establish the rent. This must be an open market rent which means the rent which might be obtained from a willing lessor in the open market and having regard to the terms of the tenancy. Rent obtainable in comparable stalls is of relevance and the court may rely upon expert evidence. The Act directs that certain factors are to be ignored. These include first the fact that the tenant or his predecessors in title have been in occupation. This prevents the court from considering the possibility that the sitting tenant might be prepared to offer more than what would otherwise be the open market rent in order to remain in occupation of the stall. Second, the court disregards goodwill attaching to the stall by reason of the tenant's business and also certain improvements made by the tenant.

---

[103] Section 30 (2). For a further discussion see Hill & Redman *loc cit* B514 *et seq.*

Relevant factors in the case of a market stall, are the length of the tenancy, the position of a particular stall and the trade which may be carried on there because these will govern its profitability and its attractiveness to prospective tenants. The tenancy may also be more valuable if it carries a right of assignment.

The courts also seems prepared to recognise that a market organiser-even if a local authority- is fully entitled fully to exploit its right of market in fixing rents. Arguments emphasising that the courts should control the use of monopoly power for the benefit of traders and customers alike have not found favour in this context as can be seen in *Simonite v. Sheffield City Council*.[104] Here the court held that the local authority market owner owed no duty to stall holders to restrict the rent charged. This decision gives full rein to *laissez faire* principles and again betrays judicial ambivalence about its role in relation to monopoly power.

The Rights of the Market Organiser Under the Landlord and Tenant Act 1954

The rights of the stall-holder in the market may be dependent on those of the market organiser where the organiser is a tenant. If the organiser's tenancy cannot continue under the Act, the market may cease to operate. Much may therefore turn on whether the tenant-organiser qualifies for protection under the 1954 Act.

The difficulty for market organisers lies in s.23 which applies the protection of the Act "to any tenancy where the property comprised in the tenancy is or includes premises which are occupied by the tenant and are so occupied for the purposes of a business carried on by him.." If each *stallholder* enjoys exclusive possession it has been held that the market organiser is not in occupation of the market premises and cannot acquire security of tenure.[105] This means that the landlord was entitled to oppose the granting of a new tenancy to the market organiser.

In principle the result might differ where the stall holders are merely licensees without exclusive possession of their stalls. The market organiser could then be said to retain "occupation" of the premises and so seek renewal of his tenancy.

---

[104] [1992] 24 EG 134.
[105] *Graysim Holdings Ltd v. P.& O. Property Holdings Ltd.* [1992] EGCS 108.

(d). Other Regulatory Powers in Statutory Markets

By-Laws

In addition to general licensing and contractual powers, local authorities have powers to regulate their markets by means of by-laws. District councils and councils of a London borough have a general power to enact by-laws for the good rule and government of their area and to suppress nuisances. [106] In principle these by-laws may apply to markets not owned by the local authority. Other powers arise under the Food Act 1984, and any special Act which incorporates s.42 of the Markets and Fairs Clauses Act 1847. These have been considered in Chapter 3.

Regulation of Street Markets Under Street Trading Licensing Schemes

Whilst various statutes empower local authorities to regulate street trading,[107] each statutory regime has a saving for trading conducted in lawful markets established under statute, grant or presumed grant. [108]

Trading in informal or "unofficial" markets may thus fall within the licensing schemes- and traders must obtain a licence- whilst trading in lawful markets and fairs is exempt. As we have seen, the distinction between a lawful market and an informal one depends upon the manner of its creation and can give rise to complex investigations. It is desirable that this distinction be reformed because licensing authorities will have powers under the licensing schemes in respect of some markets but not others.

---

[106] Section 235 of the Local Government Act 1972.

[107] District Councils may adopt the "street trading code" in Schedule 4 of the Local Government (Miscellaneous Provisions) Act 1982. In London boroughs (but not in the City) Street trading is regulated under the London Local Authorities Act 1990, and in the City, under the City of London (Various Powers) Act 1965 and 1987. Considered

[108] See 1987 Act, s21; s..41 of the 1990 Act; and para 1 (2) (b) of Schedule 4 of the 1982 Act.

CHAPTER 8

MARKET REGULATION - 2

The previous chapter examined aspects of the legal relationship between buyers and sellers in the market and the market owner. This chapter will consider other aspects of market regulation and in particular the rights and duties of the owner in relation to the market place and the hours of trading.

1. The Market Place

(i) The Location of the Market or Fair

As we have seen, market rights may lawfully be created by Crown grant, by prescription or by statute. "Unofficial" markets, by which it is meant those conducted without lawful authority, are in a separate category. The location of the market depends upon its legal pedigree and, in either case, may be subject to the development control powers of the local authority.

Lawful Markets
Markets created by grant or statute may be created either with or without "metes and bounds". The former is one in which the site of the market place is established and prescribed by the instrument creating the market. More usually, a grant of market entitled the market owner to conduct a market within a particular "vill", manor, city, borough parish or other district. [1] Such a market would be one without metes and bounds.

---

[1] *Gingell, Son & Foskett Ltd v. Stepney Borough Council* [1906] 2 KB 468; aff'd [1909] AC 245. For example, the relevant grant in *Curwen v. Salkeld* (1803) 3 East. 538 permitted the market to be held *"infra villum de Workington"*.

Market created without "metes and bounds"
Where the site of the market place is not specified in the grant, the market place can be located at any suitable site within the district or manor or "vill". The owner of the market is entitled to exercise a judgment as to the most appropriate site within the district in which the market should be operated. [2] This need not be land in his ownership; it may be land over which he has a lease, or even a licence, to conduct the market.[3] At common law, the only limitation on his choice of site is that it should be a suitable, or "convenient" market capable of providing reasonably sufficient accommodation.[4]

Two consequences flow from this: (i) since the grant specifies no single site, there is a power of removal of the market from one site to another within the district and, as we shall see, there may be a duty to remove it as circumstances change; (ii) the owner must, so far as is reasonable, select the eventual site to meet the current and anticipated demands of the public who attend there for buying and selling, and may be required to move it if demand increases. This is considered further below.

Where the right to hold a market is acquired by prescription, the market place may normally be sited anywhere within the manor. [5] As we have seen, there may also be a presumption that if such a market is held on the highway, the highway was dedicated subject to the exercise of the right of market. [6]

Enlargement of District Boundaries
Although strictly, it is a matter of construction of the grant and the enactment enlarging the boundaries, the courts seem to be willing to construe such instruments as permitting a re-location which was not within the contemporary boundaries of the district or manor so as to preserve a market which serves the current needs of the local

---

[2] *Dixon v. Robinson* (1687) 3 Mod. 107.
[3] *A G v. Horner* (1884) 14 QBD 245, 254.
[4] *Re Islington Market Bill.* (1835) 3 Cl & Fin 513; also *per* Lord Watson in *Edinburgh Magistrates v. Blackie* (1886) 11 App Cas 665, 679.
[5] *De Rutzen v. Lloyd* (1836) 5 Ad & El 456; *Gingell, Son & Foskett Ltd. Stepney Borough Council, supra;* see also Holroyd J in *R v. Cotterill* (1817) 1 B & Ald. 67, 81.
[6] *Gingell, supra* n. (1).

population in the most appropriate modern site. [7] Such a policy was expressed most eloquently by Holroyd J in *R v. Cotterill:* [8]

"It is a general rule in the construction of Charters, that such a presumption shall be made *ut res magis valeat quam pereat,* that is, the object of the grant shall be attained rather than defeated...."

Market limited by "metes and bounds"
A market limited by metes and bounds is one in which the particular site of the market place is prescribed by the instrument creating the market. The old Covent Garden Market provides the most famous illustration of this. [9]

If the market is limited by metes and bounds the market owner's duty is to endeavour to provide sufficient room within the limits available. If the market has diminished and no-longer occupies the entire market place, the part unused may be set aside for other purposes, [10] but must be restored if demand so requires. No action will lie for disturbance by selling out of the market unless this is done. [11]

There is no implied power to re-locate a market limited by metes and bounds to an alternative site. This creates problems if the market place is too confined for the demands placed upon it. A new grant or Act of Parliament could, however, make provision for a new site. A local authority owning a market confined by metes and bounds might alternatively use its discretionary power under s.50 of the Food Act 1984 to establish a new market.

Informal Markets
Informal or unofficial markets are neither created under statute nor the royal prerogative. They may be conducted on private land with the consent of the landowner, subject to the development control

---

[7] *Curwen v. Salkeld, supra* n. (1); *Mayor of Dorchester v. Ensor* (1869) LR 4 Ex 335.
[8] (1817) 1 B & Ald 67, 81.
[9] See, eg *Prince v. Lewis* (1826) 5 B & C 363, 365.
[10] *Ibid.* at pp. 371, 373; *Jones v. Lewis* [1989] The Times, June 12th.
[11] *Prince v. Lewis, ibid.*

powers of the local authority. If not a temporary market, planning permission will normally be required to create a new market. [12]

As we shall see, there is no right to conduct an informal market on the highway because it is not clothed in market rights.

The Highway as the Market Place [13]

Markets Conducted as of Right: Lawful Markets

It is doubtful whether a grant under the prerogative could validly create market rights over an existing highway. [14] Of course, as a matter of theory, such a right could be established by Act of Parliament. If a highway was laid out after the franchise market was established a conditional dedication of the highway may be presumed. [15]

No offence is committed by market traders setting up stalls on the highway in furtherance of the established right of market because the *de facto* obstruction, is conducted with lawful authority or excuse. [16] The courts also appear generally to construe statutes regulating highways as not rendering unlawful anything which is lawfully done in pursuit of market rights. [17]

The relationship between market rights and the statutory regulation of highways can be seen in *R v. Starkey* [18] where a trader was indicted for obstruction of the highway after he had continued to trade in the place in which a market had been held prior to its purported removal to another site. The removal being found to be invalid in law, it was held that market rights continued to extend to the former market place. No offence was committed by his continuing to trade there.

---

[12] Discussed at p. 78 *er seq.*

[13] The general principles concerning trading on the highway are considered in Ch. 1.

[14] See *A G v. Horner* (1884) 14 QB 245, 258; cf, Ld Esher MR, 258, Lindley L.J 264-5.

[15] *A-G v. Horner* (1886) 11 App Cas 66.

[16] See *GER v. Goldsmid* (1884) 9 App Cas 927 especially *per* Lord Selborne LC at p 942; *A G v. Horner*, (1886) 11 App Cas 66. There may be difficulties in establishing the existence of market rights in the case of expansion: see *infra*.

[17] *A-G v. Horner ibid.; cf Gloucestershire CC v. Farrow* [1985] 1 WLR 741.

[18] (1837) 7 A & E 95.

Informal Markets
Street markets which have no legal pedigree cannot normally benefit from these rules; trading therein is an unlawful obstruction of the highway. This appears, for example, in *Simpson v. Wells* [19] in which the trader's claim to be able to trade on the highway as a customary right was rejected since "statute" fairs, which are one kind of informal market, are not held from time immemorial and generate no claim of right. [20]

Exception if there is a Qualified Dedication of the Highway
Sometimes both the market and the highway are of immemorial age. Here it is possible that the public has only acquired a conditional dedication of the highway subject to the customary market. [21] In such a case, the public's right is a limited one and takes effect subject to the rights of the traders. This principle is a controversial one for only rarely is there ever evidence that the highway was actually subject to a conditional dedication. More usually, the court is prepared to presume a conditional dedication in order to save certain long-established customary trading. The distinction between trading which benefits from these rules and that which does not can appear to be arbitrary as can be seen from what follows.

A qualified dedication was found to have occurred in *Le Neve v. The Vestry of Mile End Old Town*. [22] Here the occupiers of various properties had for many years made use of a strip of land used as a public highway between the actual highway and the footway for the purposes of their trades. The Vestry, claiming to exercise statutory powers, removed the obstructions placed on the land. The court was prepared to presume that the traders had occupied this land with the permission of the lord of the manor and that the public had only ever acquired a right of free passage conditional upon the rights of the traders. These rights were not removed by the statute regulating the highway. It is interesting that it only had to be established that the custom may have had a lawful origin; no actual lawful origin needed to be proved.

---

[19] (1872) LR 7 QB 214.
[20] *Elwood v. Bullock* (1844) 6 QB 383 was distinguished. See further p. 10.
[21] See also Chapter 1.
[22] (1858) 8 E & B 1054.

A conditional dedication cannot be presumed, however, where the highway is an immemorial one and the trading only arose within living memory. [23] The presumption can only be made where the highway can be presumed to be of later date than the right asserted.

These rules have arbitrary consequences. A custom which grows up within the time of memory can be lawful provided its lack of legal pedigree cannot be established. It may then be presumed to have a lawful origin. [24] An equally ancient custom which suffers from having a known origin cannot become clothed in market rights; trading therein may be an obstruction of the highway. *Le Neve* can thus be contrasted with *Simpson v. Wells* [25] in which customary trading in a fair which originated as a "statute" fair was not a legitimate user of the highway because its origins were known. In modern times it is difficult to support this distinction because it seems of little importance now whether a market can be presumed to have originated in a grant pre-dating the reign of King Richard I or a practice originating in the fourteenth century enactment of the Statute of Labourers.

The operation of these presumptions has a fictional quality to it. That the livelihood of individual traders should depend upon it is a matter of regret. The focus should instead be placed upon whether the use made of the highway is a reasonable one taking into account, as Lord Denman CJ stated in *Elwood v. Bullock,* [26] the benefit the public may derive from the market, its duration and the degree of obstruction it causes. This approach would treat all customary and lawful markets alike. [27] Any other approach is an attempt to forge a distinction without a difference.

---

[23] *Spice v. Peacock* (1875) 39 JP 581.
[24] As in *Le Neve, supra* n. (22) and *Elwood v. Bullock, supra* n. (20).
[25] (1872) LR 7 QB 214.
[26] *Supra. n.* (20) at p. 411.
[27] Modern unofficial markets would still be subject to the local authority's development control powers.

(ii) Changing the Location of the Market

Franchise Markets
In the case of a market established by grant, or presumed grant, provided the market is not limited by "metes and bounds", the owner has a power to alter the location of the market place within the limits of the instrument (or presumed instrument) creating the market right. As we have seen, the only restriction on this power at common law is the duty to provide a suitable site to meet the demand for the market. This common law power is, of course, circumscribed by the development control powers of local authorities. Removing the market to a new site may well constitute a "material change of use" of the chosen site in which case the removal can only proceed lawfully if planning permission is obtained. [28]

There may, however, be circumstances in which the owner of a market is under a duty to expand the existing market place, or even to find a new site for the market in order to meet the demand which exists for it.

(a) Expansion of the Existing Site
Subject to the possible need for planning permission, the expansion of the existing site presents few difficulties where the market place lies within a larger area which is vested in the market owner. He may also be able to acquire an interest in the land over which expansion is contemplated.

Any expansion onto the highway is likely to cause difficulties. First, even if the market is a lawful one, the market may well constitute an obstruction or public nuisance; second, if the owner of the soil is not the owner of the market right problems may arise if consent to use the land is withheld. [29] The former problem can only be overcome if the highway is one over which market rights extend. This was so in *A G v. Horner* [30] but in this case the difficulty concerning the consent of the owner of the soil of the highway was not satisfactorily resolved. In the Court of Appeal,

---

[28] P. 82 *et seq.*

[29] In the case of highways maintained at the public expense, the soil of the highway vests in the highway authority: Highways Act 1980, s. 263.

[30] (1886) 11 App Cas 66.

Cotton L.J thought that a public authority owning the soil would not be granted an injunction to restrain the expansion of a market which was of benefit to the public. [31] In the House of Lords, Lord Selborne thought that the ownership of the particular streets in question was not known, there was no evidence that the owner withheld consent and so the issue of consent did not arise. [32]

After this decision it seems at least open to argue that the consent of the highway authority may be necessary where expansion onto the highway is otherwise possible. Whether relief could be obtained where consent was withheld is a difficult question especially where the market is of public benefit.

(b) Removal of a Franchise Market to a Different Site
Removal may be necessary as the franchise market becomes more popular or as the commercial life of a district follows the growth and development of a town. In either case, the old market place may no-longer be convenient.

Where the market is not limited by metes and bounds there is an implied power to re-locate the market. It is a right incident to the grant; [33] and the power may be exercised even if the market has been conducted on one site for a considerable period. [34] If the market is limited by metes and bound the owner is merely under a duty to devote the entire market place to market uses. There is no implied power of removal.[35]

It must be a question of fact when the problem of lack of space becomes sufficiently acute to trigger the duty to re-locate. It seems that this may occur once persons seeking a standing place or stall are unable to do so. [36] This also seems to follow from the opinion of Littledale J. in the *Islington Market* case [37] where he observed that the grantee of a franchise must provide convenient accommodation "for *all* who are ready to buy and sell in the public market" (Emphasis supplied). It would, however, be unduly harsh and

---

[31] (1884) 14 QBD 245, 263.
[32] 11 App Cas 66, 78.
[33] *Curwen v. Salkeld* (1803) 3 East 538.
[34] *Ibid.*
[35] *Re Islington Market Bill* (1835) 3 Cl & Fin 513.
[36] *Goldsmid v. GER Co.* (1883) 25 ChD 511, 543, per Cotton L.J.
[37] *Supra* n (35) at p. 518.

unrealistic to require an owner to consider removal immediately a would-be stallholder is turned away. A more satisfactory approach might be to require removal where the owner could reasonably foresee that the problem of overcrowding is likely to be an enduring rather than a merely temporary difficulty.

The owner of the market is not excused from his duty to remove merely because he does not own land onto which the market may be removed and expanded. The franchise of market can be operated on land which is not vested in the market owner. [38] The market owner is under a duty to endeavour to acquire an interest in land which would entitle him to conduct the market in a more convenient site if such land is available within the area of the grant. [39] The grant of franchise may be cancelled on a *scire facias* if no removal takes place. This is not the case in a market created by statute which is not liable to forfeiture.

Once a valid removal has occurred the public and market traders lose the common law right of resort to the former site; if they attempt to continue to trade on the old site without the consent of the owner they are liable to be treated as trespassers. It is possible for the owner of the former site to consent to the continuance of market trading, but he cannot purport to do so as a franchise market. [40] It would be an "unofficial" market since the right of market has been transferred to the new site.

Unlawful Removal

It follows from the principles already discussed that a market cannot be removed to an inconvenient site. If it is, the removal is unlawful, and it is a ground for a repeal of the grant by a *scire facias*. There are also other ways in which a purported removal may be bad. These are considered below.

(i) New Site Outside the Scope of the Grant
The purported re-location to a place outside the scope of the grant, for example, outside the boundaries of the district, is also unlawful. This may provide grounds for a repeal of the grant. Further, it is

---

[38] *A G v. Horner* (1884) 14 QBD 245.
[39] *Mosley v. Walker* (1827) 7 B & C 40,55, per Bayley J.
[40] *Sevenoaks DC v. Pattullo & Vinson Ltd.* [1984] 1 All ER 544.

ineffective to transfer the rights of the public from the "old" site. If traders continue to use that site they do not commit a trespass; nor, it seems will an indictment will lie in nuisance for the continued placing of a stall on the former site if this is a public highway. [41] The market rights of the public still attach to this site. Moreover it seems that the owner is still entitled to suppress rival markets. [42]

(ii) A Re-Location Which Prejudices the Rights of the Market Traders
Removal seems also to be unlawful unless the market on the new site is operated on no less favourable terms than previously. If it purports to deprive traders of rights enjoyed in the old market, the removal may be bad. An example of this is *R v. Starkey* [43] where the lease of transfer of the market imposed a new charge on traders merely for exposing goods for sale which, by itself, made the purported removal unlawful.

Where individual traders have legal rights to trade in a particular site, the court may give effect to this right even if this amounts to a veto over the power of removal. In *Ellis v. Bridgnorth Corporation* [44] the plaintiff was entitled to maintain an action for the unlawful disturbance by the Corporation of the right to sell free of toll and stallage. From time immemorial he and previous occupiers of his house, which was situated where the market was held, had erected stalls opposite their houses and exposed goods for sale. This activity had been free of toll and stallage. The Corporation purported to move the market a short distance away thereby causing the plaintiff to suffer loss.

It was held that the removal was bad and that the plaintiff could enforce his prescriptive right to trade outside his house. The original site thus continued to be the lawful site of the market.

Naturally the court is confronted with a conflict of interest in a case of this nature. The public authority may have reasons rooted in the interests of a wider public, in relocating the market, whilst the individual right-holders, the owners of property adjacent to the highway, have an interest in maintaining the *status quo*. By

---

[41] *R v. Starkey* (1837) 7 A & E 95.
[42] *Middleton v. Power* (1886) 19 LR Ir. 1.
[43] *Supra* n. (41).
[44] (1863) 15 CB(NS) 52.

holding the balance in favour of the individuals it is possible that the interests of the wider public are not given effect. This may be criticised because markets exist to serve the public interest.

Relocation of Statutory Markets
Any power of removal of a statutory market would be subject to the terms of the special Act. Where a local authority has acquired a franchise market without metes and bounds, it may continue to enjoy the inherent common law power of removal. If the acquired franchise market is one with metes and bounds there is no common law power enabling removal, nor is there a power to do so under the 1984 Act. It seems that in such a case, the local authority would have to rely on its power under s.50 to establish a new market rather than remove the old one. Planning controls may be relevant in any of these cases since it would be likely that the removal or creation of a market would involve a material change of use of the contemplated site. [45]

Removal and Local Authority Development Control Powers
Although the franchisee may enjoy a power inherent in the grant to remove the market to another part of the district, this is subject to the development control powers of the local planning authority and may require planning permission. In practice this may have the effect of severely curtailing the franchisee's freedom. Possible difficulties can be seen in *Spook Erection Ltd. v. Secretary of State,*[46] which has already been considered.[47]

2. The Rights of the Public in the Market Place

Whether a market has been created by grant, prescription or statute, all members of the public acquire a right under the common law to come into the market to buy and to sell. [48] The market owner has no general power to exclude any group or class of individuals

---

[45] *Supra*, p. 78 *et seq.*
[46] [1988] 2 All ER 667.
[47] *Supra*, p. 83.
[48] *R v. Barnsley MBC ex p Hook* [1976] 1 WLR 1052; *Northampton Corporation v. Ward* (1745) 2 Stra. 1238.

from using the market. If there are limits on the kinds of goods which are normally sold in the market, sellers must only or expose for sale goods of the type normally sold there. [49]

As has already been discussed, the common law right of resort to market does not carry with it a right to a stand or stall, nor indeed to exclusive occupation of part of the market place by any trader. This means that there is no automatic right to place any structure on the soil, nor even to place any baskets in which goods are carried to market on the soil if the intention in so doing is to trade from a particular site within the market. [50] A trader wishing to occupy a stall or stand must obtain the consent of the market owner and may become liable to rent or stallage.

Should a market lack a legal pedigree, it is an "unofficial" market and the public do not acquire the right to come onto it. Any individual or class of individuals they may be excluded from it if the consent of the owner is withdrawn. [51]

Sales in the Market

Whilst part of the market place may be set aside for certain kinds of sale, [52] the market owner has no common law power to fix the terms upon which sales are to be agreed nor upon the manner used in fixing the price. Traders are free to choose the manner of doing business which may be the most effective and convenient. [53] Auction sales within the market are thus permissible although they may be confined to an area within a particular area of the market place [54].

---

[49] *Scott v. Glasgow Corporation* [1899] AC 470, especially at p. 475.

[50] *Mayor of Yarmouth v. Groom* (1862) 1 H & C 102.

[51] Eg, *R v. Basildon District Council ex p Brown* (1981) 79 LGR 655 CA *per* Templeman L.J. at 666.

[52] *Scott v. Glasgow Corpn.* [1899] AC 470.

[53] *Corporation of London v. Lyons, Sons & Co (Fruit Brokers) Ltd.* [1936] 1 Ch 78, see especially *per* Romer L.J at 128.

[54] *Ibid.*

3. **Where the Market Place is Too Large for the Market**

If the market place is too large for the current demand for the
market, the space unused may be employed for other purposes. It
must be restored if necessary for the market, however. [55] In a
market operated by a local authority, the market rights will
remain in the unused space unless effectively removed by resolution.
This means that the space unused for market purposes may remain
in law available for market trading. A prosecution for unlicensed
street trading ostensibly because trading took place outside the *de
facto* market place would not be sustainable in such circumstances. [56]

4. **Market Days and Hours**

(i) Franchise Markets and Fairs

The grant will normally prescribe the days on which the market
may be conducted. The owner has no general power to alter these
days; nor may he hold the market, on the additional days as a
franchise market. In *A-G v. Horner,* [57] Lindley L.J. considered that,
despite this rule, a market owner is at liberty to allow trading on
days other than those in his grant; if he does so the market merely
lacks the right of monopoly on those days. This may be so, but
difficulties would arise if trading did take place. First the trading
would not be clothed in market right. If it took place on the
highway, it could constitute an unlawful obstruction. Moreover, it
seems that enforcement proceedings may be brought by the
Attorney-General against the owner to restrain the purported
change. It seems, however, that the Attorney-General is unlikely
to intervene except by way of the relator action although his power
to bring *ex officio* proceedings is not lost. [58]

A change in the market day, or the holding of the market on
additional market days may acquire legal validity if a lost grant

---

[55] *Prince v. Lewis* (1826) 5 B & C 363; *Jones v. Lewis* [1989] The Times June 12th.
[56] *Jones v. Lewis* [1989] The Times, June 12th.
[57] 14 QBD 245, 266
[58] Statistics reveal that intervention by way of *ex officio* proceedings is rare: [1992] PL
130, 135.

authorising such changes can be presumed. [59] No such presumption was made in *A-G v. Horner* where the market originated in letters patent of Charles II because, as Lindley L.J. observed:

"The cases which have been referred to in support of presumption from long usage will be found to have been cases where the origin of the right has been lost in obscurity, and there has been nothing but evidence of immemorial user. Here that is not so." [60]

"Uninterrupted modern usage" could be enough to raise a presumption of a lost grant of a change of day, [61] but this presumption is rebutted if it can be shown that at any time after 1189 the right did not exist. [62] Accordingly, a change of day occurring in the last five or six years is insufficient to raise a presumption of lost grant. [63]

Fairs

The Secretary of State has a statutory power to alter the days on which a fair is held. The number of days over which a fair is held may also be changed. The Secretary of State may act after receiving representations by district councils or London borough councils that the alteration would be "for the convenience and advantage of the public".[64] Such representations may also be made by the owner of the fair.

Where the representation is made by the local authority, the owner has a right to be notified of it.

In the Metropolitan Police District [65] fairs shall not be conducted for business or amusement between the hours of eleven pm

---

[59] *Mayor of Penryn v. Best* 3 ExD 292.

[60] (1884) 14 QBD 245, 266. The other judges decided that the additional days claimed were consistent with the market owner acting under a void charter of James II.

[61] *Jenkins v. Harvey* (1835) 1 C M & R 877.

[62] *Hulbert v. Dale* [1909] 2 Ch 570.

[63] *Newcastle (Duke) v. Worksop UDC* [1902] 2 Ch. 145, 158.

[64] Local Govt Act 1894, s 21 (3), s.27 (1) (e); Local Government Act 1972 ss 1 (10), s179 (3) ; and the London Government Order 1965 SI 1965/ 654 art. 3 Sch 1.

[65] Greater London not including the City, Inner and Middle Temple, along with some parts of Essex, Hertfordshire and Surrey: London Government Act 1963, s 76 (1) (a)-(d).

and six am. [66] If this prohibition is breached the each trader is liable to a fine not exceeding level 1 on the standard scale.
This provision does not apply to markets properly so called.

Statutory Markets

Where the market is created by statute the times and days on which the market is held are those prescribed therein and may be altered in so far as the statute permits this.
If a local authority acquires a franchise market by exercising its powers under s.50 of the Food Act 1984, it may alter the days and times on which the market is held in accordance with s.52 of the 1984 Act. [67]
Once the franchise market has been acquired, any exercise of the statutory power to change the days converts the market to a statutory one which means that any rights acquired under the franchise may only be exercised in so far as they are consistent with and have not been removed by the Food Act 1984 or any other relevant statute. [68]

---

[66] Metropolitan Police Act 1839, s.38.

[67] Section 52 states: "A market authority may appoint the days on which, and the hours during which, markets are to be held." This power is limited by general restrictions on trading hours, such as those contained in the Shops Act 1950.

[68] *Ellis v. Bridgnorth Corpn.* (1861) 4 LT 11; *Manchester v. Lyons* (1882) 22 ChD 287; *Leicester Corpn. v. Maby* (1972) 70 LGR 209; *Manchester City Council v. Walsh* (1986) 84 LGR 1.

CHAPTER 9

EXTINCTION AND LOSS OF MARKET RIGHTS

The abuse of the market franchise, or its neglect, may give rise to forfeiture of the market right. The rules are different in the case of a statutory market. Here the abuse of the market rights conferred will not render the market right liable to forfeiture by a writ of *scire facias.* [1] Statutory markets are thus considered separately.

Grounds for Forfeiture of Market Rights

1. Franchise Markets

Forfeiture of franchise rights may arise in a number of different circumstances:

(i) Non-User of the franchise
Because the Crown, in granting a franchise of fair or of market, exercises a prerogative power for the benefit of the public at large, it follows that the continued failure to hold a market defeats the purpose of the grant and is injurious to the public interest. Non- user of the franchise may therefore give rise to its forfeiture. [2] It may be repealed by a *scire facias.*

(ii) Unlawful Change of Market or Fair Day
Although the alteration of the market or fair day or days does not, by itself, forfeit the franchise, [3] it provides grounds upon which

[1] *New Windsor Corporation v. Taylor* [1899] AC 41.
[2] *Case of Leicester Forest* (1607) Cro Jac. 155 per Coke C.J.
[3] *Peter v. Kendal* (1827) 6 B & C 703, 710, per Bayley J.

the grant may be repealed by a scire facias. [4] If the grantee purports to hold the market or fair on *additional days,* there is some authority that the Attorney-General may take proceedings to restrain this, [5] but the franchise would not seem to be placed at jeopardy. Lindley L.J once stated that the market owner *could* continue to hold the market on the additional days, but he would not enjoy the right of monopoly. If correct, on such occasions the market would not have a legal authority and, as has already been noted, if trading took place on the highway, it could constitute an unlawful obstruction of it. [6]

(iii) Insufficient Accommodation
It has already been noted [7] that the continued failure to provide space for the public may lead to forfeiture of the grant. [8] It has been suggested that such a failure is an offence. [9] However, the rule is that the want of space does not *ipso facto* forfeit the grant. Until proceedings are taken all the rights of the franchise remain; the franchisee may, for example, restrain the levying of a rival market within the common law distance [10]

(iv) Abuse of Franchise of Toll
In contrast to the right of market which exists for the benefit of the public, a right to take toll exists for the private benefit of the franchisee. Accordingly, a failure to take toll is neither a ground of forfeiture of the right of market nor of the franchise of toll.

The franchise of market may be repealed where the owner exacts excessive, "outrageous" or unreasonable tolls. As we have seen, this does not apply to unreasonable stallage since these charges may in principle be avoided where the trader declines the opportunity of having a standing place or stall. In statutory

---

[4] *Newcastle (Duke) v. Worksop Urban Council* [1902] 2 Ch. 145.
[5] *A G v. Horner* (1884) 14 QBD 245.
[6] *Ibid.* at p. 267.
[7] *Supra* at p. 158.
[8] *Re Islington Market Bill* 3 Cl & Fin 513, 519.
[9] *Ibid.*
[10] *GER v. Goldsmid* 9 App Cas 927.

markets operated by local authorities, however, it has been argued that stallage charges may be liable to judicial review. [11]

(v) Illegal Removal

A purported removal of a market to a place unauthorised by the grant may lead to forfeiture of the market right. Similar consequences may flow where the removal is to an inconvenient site.

2. Statutory Markets

A right of market or fair created by statute can only be destroyed by Act of Parliament. An example of how this might occur can be seen in *Gloucester County Council v. Farrow* [12] where a right to hold a market on a public highway not exercised for a period in excess of twenty years was held to have been extinguished by the Highways Act 1980.

In the absence of a statutory repeal, any excess or abuse of the statutory powers conferred may be restrained by proceedings brought at the instance of the Attorney-General. [13] In principle such proceedings may be brought *ex officio* or by way of the relator action at the instance of individual traders. There is some authority that they may also have *locus standi* in their own right as individual "persons aggrieved" in such a matter. [14] Furthermore, one or several traders may also bring proceedings representing all other traders in the market. They are competent to do so only if they have the same interest in the matter as those represented, [15] but such a common interest may be found in so far as the plaintiffs and traders represented are all traders in the same market. Accordingly, if market owner has committed various kinds of abuse not all of which affect the representatives in their individual

---

[11] *R v. Birmingam City Council ex p Dredger* [1993] The Times, January 8th; cf *Gloucester City Council v. Williams* (1990) 88 LGR 853 where *AG v. Colchester Corpn.* [1952[] 1 Ch 586 was followed, but no argument was addressed to the court on whether the exercise of private law contractual powers were amenable to judicial review.

[12] *Infra.*

[13] *A-G v. Tynemouth Corporation* (1900) 17 TLR 77.

[14] *Infra.* p. 367 *et seq.*

[15] RSC Ord 15 r.12.

capacity, it seems that they may nevertheless be competent representatives of all market traders in the market. [16]

Abandonment of Market Rights

Market No-longer Held
Subject to the possible need to seek planning permission, [17] a market which has fallen into desuetude can normally be revived. As a matter of general principle, it seems that the right of market cannot be abandoned by mere disuse. This is so because the right benefits the public. [18]. Disuse does provide a ground for repeal of the grant, however. The right may also be removed by Act of Parliament.

Abandonment of the Right to Conduct a Street Market
It seems that the franchise right to conduct a market on a public highway may be lost if the right is not exercised for a period of twenty years or more. The franchise right of market can then only survive if the market could be held elsewhere within the district. This rule may also apply in the case of statutory markets which have not been held for a period of twenty years or more.

This appears from *Gloucestershire County Council v. Farrow* [19] where the plaintiff council successfully restrained the defendant from reviving a weekly market on the highway. The market had its origins in a charter of Henry I but it had not actually been conducted on the site since about 1900. The right to hold the market was held to have been lost by virtue of s.31 of the Highways Act 1980 which, properly construed, meant that private rights over the highway could only limit the public right of passage if the private right had been asserted during the previous twenty years.

As Holgate comments, [20] this decision appears to qualify the judgment of Lord Denning MR in *Wyld v. Silver* [21] that a right of market cannot be lost by mere disuse. Holgate's point has some

---

[16] *Bedford (Duke of) v. Ellis* [1901] AC 1.
[17] Where the market has not been held on the site since before 1st July 1948.
[18] *Wyld v. Silver* [1963] Ch 243 per Lord Denning MR at 254, *per* Harman L.J 263.
[19] [1985] 1 WLR 741.
[20] [1963] Ch. 243.
[21] *Supra* n. 19.

force, but it must not be forgotten that the right is extinguished only if the right of franchise is limited to the highway in question. The market may be conducted on another site elsewhere in the district provided the new site is not a public highway. [22]. Any such removal would be subject to possible need to obtain planning permission. [23]

Abolition of Fairs

General
Under powers conferred by the Fairs Act 1871, s.3 [24] the Secretary of State, acting on a representation of a district council or London borough may order that a right to hold a fair be abolished "for the convenience and advantage of the public". Such representations may also be made by the owner of the fair.

The power of abolition can only be exercised, however, with the written consent of the owner of the fair or of the owner right of toll.

Fairs in the Metropolitan Police District [25]
If a fair is held on any ground in the Metropolitan Police District other than that on which it has been held in the seven immediately preceding years, the owner or occupier the site of the fair may be summoned before a magistrate and made to establish their right to hold the fair. If this cannot be established the magistrate can declare that the fair is an unlawful one. Thereafter the police, [26] may remove stalls etc. and take into custody any person who attempts to trade, as well as those "resorting to such ground with any show or instrument of gambling or amusement."

---

[22] A point emphasised by Fox L.J., *ibid* at p. 746.

[23] *Spook Erection v. Secretary of State for the Environment* (1988) 86 LGR 736.

[24] As amended by the Local Government Act 1894,s 21 (3), 27 (1) (e), the Local Government Act 1972, s 1 (10), 179 (3), and the London Government Order 1965 SI 1965/ 654 art. 3 (24), Sch 1.

[25] The district embraces Greater London not including the City, Inner and Middle Temple, along with some parts of Essex, Hertfordshire and Surrey - London Government Act 1963, s. 1 (a) - (d).

[26] After the display of notices for a minimum period of six hours.

Conviction of any of these offences carries a fine not exceeding level 1 on the standard scale. [27]

Similar powers exist under the Metropolitan Police Act, 1839, s.39. The police may ascertain whether any fair held in the Metropolitan Police District is lawful and not conducted for longer than the permitted period. Where a fair is suspected of being unlawful, the owner or occupier of the ground where the fair is sited may be summoned to establish his right to hold it. If it is found to be unlawful, or held for an unlawfully protracted period, it may be prohibited by notice (or confined to its lawful duration). Any breach of the notices entitles the police to break up the fair. Anyone purporting to trade unlawfully may be convicted of an offence and punished by a fine not exceeding level 1 on the standard scale.

These provisions would clearly have the effect not only of abolishing existing informal fairs but also of preventing the creation of "informal" or unofficial fairs. Markets are exempt these provisions. For these purposes it is therefore important to be able to distinguish a market from a fair.

---

[27] Metropolitan Fairs Act, 1868 s.2 as amended.

PART III

STREET TRADING: THE LICENSING SYSTEMS

INTRODUCTION TO THE LICENSING SYSTEMS

Lawful street trading is normally dependent upon the possession of a licence from the appropriate authority. By this means, trading is regulated by the State which exercises control over whether the individual can trade at all and, if so, under what conditions. Licenses therefore have an enormous economic consequences; any revocation, for example, would cut very deeply into the economic life of the trader. How the courts treat licensing is thus a matter of great significance.

This exposes a familiar difficulty about the proper limits of State control over individual liberty. One model emphasises the role of the market in determining who should be allowed to trade. Such a view places emphasis upon the autonomy of the individual and individual freedom. It demands only limited regulation and emphasises the need to achieve fair standards, both in matters of substance and procedure in licensing matters. A licence is regarded as akin to private property. The granting of a licence would be a matter of strong presumption. Regulation would be strictly limited and subject to procedural controls. Revocation, even if for the sake of an overriding the public interest, would be compensated.

Arguments that access to the ranks of street traders is a privilege and not a right, a matter of the benificence of the State, down-play procedural and other protections for the would-be trader. Under this model the State only has a duty to act fairly which requires little more than impartiality and rationality in its decision-making. The agency administering the licensing scheme should have as free a hand as possible to act in the public interest, and this demands that individual enterprise be regulated in a manner consistent with an overriding general public interest.

A third model, *upon which the following licensing regimes are essentially based*, achieves a compromise between these two extremes. It recognises that street trading falls short of a cognisable right and may be denied where the public interest so demands. Individual justice is achieved by emphasising that there are enforceable limits on the exercise of statutory discretion in licensing matters, but that these limits can be drawn to give due weight to the public interest. An annual licence need not be renewed, but if renewal is not to take place, the administrators will have to show cause why this is so and adhere to fair procedures before reaching their decision. Similarly, revocation is possible where the public interest, as statutorily defined, so dictates, and no right to compensation arises.

CHAPTER 10

STREET TRADING: THE STREET TRADING CODE

1. Introduction

The regulation of street trading outside the City of London and the London boroughs has traditionally been regarded as a local issue most appropriately regulated by the authorities administering justice in a local area: the magistrates, the police or the local authority. Regulatory structures evolved in a piecemeal and unco-ordinated manner as local authorities sought to promote private legislation to meet the problems of their areas. Regulatory provisions were found in a labyrinthine system of local enactments and by-laws as well as the over-arching provisions of the general law. The complexity of the system made it inaccessible and difficult to operate.

Following local government re-organisation, local authorities outside London re-examined their existing powers to seek the re-enactment of as many of them as remained useful. By placing these provisions in a general measure, the Local Government (Miscellaneous Provisions) Act 1982,[1] Parliament saved district councils the expense of individually promoting private legislation. The new street trading code would be widely operated and would substantially harmonise the street trading regulation outside London.[2]

The code is not a compulsory part of the Act; district councils are permitted to adopt the code and apply the measures contained

---

[1] Section 3 and Schedule 4, known as the "street trading code". The Government proposes to review the operation of the code as part of its de-regulation programme.
[2] These matters are fully discussed in the debate to the second reading of the Local Government (Miscellaneous Provisions) Bill HC Debs. 6th series Vol 13 cols 903-972.

within it. Adoption is by achieved by resolution [3] and apply the measures contained within it. Nothing compels them to do so, and a few have not adopted it, preferring instead to rely on local legislation.   However, because the code has been so widely adopted, it provides the focus of the present chapter.

Where the code applies, it is an offence to engage in unlicensed street trading. Street trading is defined [4] to mean "the selling or exposing or offering for sale of any article (including a living thing) in a street." Only those actually offering goods for sale which are present in the street fall within the regulatory scheme. [5] Services do not fall within its regime. Neither does it apply to a contract made on the street unless it is made by persons actually dealing in goods which are physically present. This means that, for example, the activities of street photographers are not subject to the licensing provisions if the photograph is not immediately delivered to the purchaser.[6]

The definition of street trading is subject to the provisions of sub-paragraph (2) which immunises certain trading from control under the code. This will be considered below.

Trading which does not take place on a "street" within the meaning of the Act is clearly exempt the provisions of the code even if the code is adopted in the local area. Paragraph 1 offers a partial definition of "street" which is stated to *include* any road, footway, beach or other area to which the public have access without payment. It also includes a motorway service area.

Because "street" embraces land to which the public have access without payment, the definition is wide enough to bring traders not actually operating in streets within the licensing system. By including private land to which the public has free access, the code can extend to such events as indoor markets and fairs conducted on private premises. This may have important consequences for unofficial markets, car boot sales and similar activities; but the provision may be evaded if the organiser adopts the simple expedient of demanding a nominal fee for entry onto the land.

---

[3] Section 3.

[4] Subject to various exceptions in Para 1 sub para 2 of Schedule 4. *Infra.*

[5] *Newman v. Lipman* (1950) 49 LGR 457.

[6] *Ibid.*

2. Exempt Trading

The code falls short of providing a comprehensive regulatory system. Certain forms of trading, some of which appear to have been continued from earlier enactments, are exempted from its controls. This means that a trader whose activities are exempt from the provisions of the code may lawfully carry on his activities without first having to obtain a street trading licence or consent. The "zoning" restrictions are also inapplicable: the exempted trader is free to trade anywhere within the district and even in a street in which street trading would otherwise be prohibited. It does not follow, however, that the trader is exempt all licensing requirements; for example, the pedlar must normally obtain a pedlar's certificate before acquiring exemption from the street trading code. Whether these exemptions still serve the public interest is a controversial issue. [7]

The burden of proof in establishing that the relevant trading falls into an exempted category will be on the trader claiming the benefit of that exemption. [8]

(i) Markets and Fairs

Anything done in a market or fair is *prima facie* exempt from control under the code. [9] However, the market or fair must be a lawful one created by statute, grant or presumed grant. This places outside the exception any market or fair lacking this legal pedigree, such as an informal or unofficial market. Trading in such a market is still "street trading" and a licence must be sought. [10] Even markets and fairs of some antiquity may not be able to benefit from the exception; for example, those which originated in "hiring" or "mop" fairs would not qualify because they were neither created by grant nor statute; [11] and the courts do not seem to

---

[7] See *infra*.

[8] Section 101 of the Magistrates' Court Act 1980. *Jones v. Lewis* [1989] The Times, June 12th provides an interesting example of how the burden may nevertheless shift.

[9] Para. 1 (2) (b).

[10] Note that even if the unoffical market is held on private property and not on the highway, the traders may still need to seek licenses because "street" is defined to include any place to which the public have access without payment: para. 1(1).

[11] *Supra*, p. 67.

be prepared to presume a lawful origin. This is a rather unfortunate consequence of the definition in the Schedule. Some detailed investigations may have to be conducted in order to discover the origins of the market or fair. Moreover, in modern times it seems unsatisfactory, indeed almost arbitrary, that the rights of the trader *vis a vis* the local authority should depend on whether a long established market happened to have been created by grant or grew up as a matter of custom.

Where market rights exist, the exemption applies. It is possible for a market *de facto* to be conducted within a smaller area than that over which the market right extends. This means that a trader selling outside the *de facto* but within the *de jure* area of the market is still, in law, able to benefit from the exemption. If unlicensed, he cannot be prosecuted for an offence under the code [12]

In a local authority market, the council may only restrict the *de jure* area of the market (and so confine the right of market) by resolution. [13]

(ii) Pedlars

The Benefits of Trading as a Pedlar
Trading as a pedlar offers the trader a significant and useful means of circumventing the controls of the code. In the modern age it is surprising that this should be so. The reasons why such a privilege should be continued in a statute of such a modern date are not immediately obvious.

The Schedule exempts from control "trading by a person acting as a pedlar under the authority of a pedlar's certificate granted under the Pedlar's Act 1871."

As we shall see, a pedlar is defined as an itinerant trader. He travels and trades on foot. Liberated as he is from the constraints of the code he is free to trade without regard to its restrictions. This not only means that he does not require a street trading licence, but that he is also free from the "zoning" rules. He is free, for example, to trade even in a prohibited street. The saving for pedlars thus somewhat weakens the controls for, having decided that a street within its area is unsuitable for street trading, and thus having

---

[12] *Jones v. Lewis* [1989] The Times, June 12th.
[13] *Ibid.*

designated it as a prohibited street, a district council is liable to find that a *bona fide* pedlar is, notwithstanding the designation, free to continue street trading in that very street. In theory, this exemption is tolerable because the pedlar should move on after making a sale. As we shall see, the reality may be somewhat different; and nothing prevents the pedlar from repeating visits to the prohibited street.

Perhaps the most significant advantage for the pedlar is that it provides a means of evading the significant charges made for street trading licences and consents. Although now subject to judicial scrutiny, these remain significantly higher than the cost of a pedlar's certificate. [14] Thus the status of pedlar offers enormous advantages to the would-be street trader. But who may be a pedlar?

S.3 of the Pedlar's Act 1871 defines a pedlar as follows: "any hawker, pedlar, petty chapman, tinker, caster of metals, mender of chairs, or other person who, without any horse, or other beast of bearing or drawing burden, travels and trades on foot and goes from town to town or to other men's houses, carrying or selling or exposing for sale any goods, wares, merchandise immediately to be delivered, or selling or offering his skill in handicraft."

It has been held [15] that a trader may act as a pedlar even if he is not travelling from town to town on foot. Accordingly, where salesmen went by car to a town and then proceeded to sell from door to door, it was held they were acting as pedlars because in passing along each street they were "travelling". A trader who barters goods for other goods, such as a rag and bone man, may also act as a pedlar. [16] It is not necessary that the trader derive his entire living or even a substantial part of it from peddling provided he actually trades as a pedlar. [17]

To qualify as a pedlar, however, it is insufficient merely to possess a pedlar's certificate: the saving only exempts a trader who acts as a pedlar at the material time. [18]

---

[14] The fee for a certificate - the maximum duration of which is one year- is currently £12.25 (Pedlar's Certificates (Variation of Fee) Order 1985, SI 1985/2027).

[15] *Sample v. Hume* [1956] 1 WLR 1319.

[16] *Druce v. Gabb* (1858) 6 WR 497.

[17] *Murphy v. Duke* ([1985] 2 All ER 274.

[18] *Sidonio v. Turk* (1964) 62 LGR 467.

Acting as a Pedlar: Trading from a Fixed Position?
Traders who use a vehicle to travel from town to town and who then sell on foot from a fixed position, or "pitch", in the town have encountered problems in acting as pedlars. Traders such as these are perhaps the most important group who may wish to qualify as pedlars. It has been argued that they may do so. [19] According to one argument, a pedlar may trade from a fixed position because a pedlar may be a "hawker" under the 1871 Act. A "hawker" is defined by s.2 of the Hawkers Act 1888, to mean "any person who...sells or exposes for sale any goods etc. in or at any house, shop, room, booth, stall or other place whatever hired or used by him for that purpose." Thus, for the purposes of the 1888 Act, it was clear that a hawker could trade from a fixed position, and under the Pedlar's Act 1871, a pedlar may be a hawker.

The better view, however, is that there is now no distinction between a hawker and a pedlar. The 1888 Act was repealed by the Local Government Act 1966 and this repeal extends to the above definition of "hawker". Moreover, the Pedlar's Act 1871, s.6 seems to envisage that "hawker" and "pedlar" could have the same meaning; [20] and the limitation requiring both travel and trading on foot applies to each. This limitation causes difficulties for stationary traders as may be seen from what follows.

Whether certificated pedlars can lawfully trade from a fixed position without a street trading licence has received the attention of the court in two cases heard together by the Divisional Court, *Watson v. Malloy* and *Watson v. Oldrey*. [21] These significantly qualify the statutory definition of a pedlar. In *Oldrey* the trader, who held a pedlar's certificate, sold wrapping paper from a portable stand which she stationed in a prohibited street after travelling to the town in a motor vehicle.

In *Malloy* the trader, who, like Oldrey, travelled from town to town, had been operating from a portable stand in a consent street without a street trading consent. On the day in question his application for the renewal of his pedlar's certificate had not been decided. There was therefore no certificate in force on that day.

---

[19] *Police Review*, 1st January 1993.
[20] Halsbury's Statutes vol 27 p. 417.
[21] [1988] 1 WLR 1026.

An information was laid against each of the traders alleging that they were guilty of an offence under Schedule 4 of the 1982 Act in so far as they had engaged in street trading without the authority of the City Council. Justices dismissed the information, holding *inter alia*, that each benefited from the privileged status of a pedlar. Their trade, it was held, was generally of a peripatetic nature so it was unimportant that they operated from a pitch. The prosecutor appealed.

In allowing the appeals, the Divisional Court held that the activities of the defendants were not, at the relevant time, those of pedlars. The 1871 Act required the pedlar to "travel and trade on foot". The effect of the conjunctive "and" was to make the legal definition of "pedlar" synonymous with the popular view which would regard a pedlar as an individual who sells whilst on the move. Hutchison J observed:

"If the distinction is to be encapsulated in an aphorism, one might say that a pedlar is one who trades as he travels as distinct from one who merely travels to trade. I do not mean that he must not stop.....the chairmender stops in order to mend chairs: but the feature which makes him a pedlar is that he goes from place to place, mending a chair here and a chair there: He comes to the owners of distressed chairs, rather than setting up his pitch and allowing them to come to him." [22]

This means that the trader who stands by a portable stall, that is, who trades on foot in that more limited sense, is not a pedlar. He must move. Essentially this requires a pedlar to go to his customers. He is permitted to stop and then to trade, but he is not permitted to set up a stall in a pre-selected location inviting customers to come to him. In *Watson v. Oldrey*, the court reasoned that if this were not so, market traders would be pedlars and this conclusion was clearly not one permitted under the code. The court's decision, in effect, prevents the pedlar from operating from a pitch.

This has been applied in Scotland, so that a trader holding a pedlar's certificate who traded from a stall inviting customers to come to him rather than moving from place to place was not within

[22] *Ibid.* at p. 1032.

the statutory exemption because he was not acting as a pedlar. He was therefore bound to seek a street trader's licence.[23]

These decisions in fact create significant practical and theoretical difficulties. At a practical level, it was accepted that a pedlar may lawfully stop and trade, but for how long? At what point is the exemption lost? If the pedlar's goods are popular, a crowd may gather to buy his goods. He may then occupy one site for a considerable period. It would be bizarre if he then lost the benefit of the exemption. The solution probably depends upon the purpose for which the stop takes place: it would be lawful to stop after a customer has approached; it may be lawful to stop for a rest; but the exemption is lost if the pedlar stops to invite customers to come to him. The problem is that these distinctions are difficult to draw in practice.

At a theoretical level, one important issue remains unresolved. It concerns the provision for market traders in the 1871 Act. Market traders are given exemption from the need to obtain a pedlars certificate under s.23 of the Pedlars Act 1871. The existence of this provision suggests that Parliament did regard their activities as similar to those of pedlars and was thus forced to make special provision for them lest they fell within the statutory definition of a pedlar. In other words Parliament's view seems to have been that trading from a fixed position did not prevent a market trader from falling within the *prima facie* definition of a "pedlar" and so special provision had to be made to prevent this. If this reasoning is correct, this somewhat weakens the conclusion in *Watson* that a pedlar is *only* someone who sells whilst on the move. It might also embrace traders who do stop from time to time in one pre-selected location as market traders do. Otherwise the provisions in s.23 of the 1871 Act would have been unnecessary.

Policy issues clearly influenced the decision in *Watson v. Malloy* suggesting that the courts may not be sympathetic to arguments placing many would-be pedlar's outside of the licensing system. Hutchison J emphasised this policy issue most clearly:

---

[23] *Normand v. Alexander* [1993] Scotsman, February 11th, a decision reached under the Civic Government (Scotland) Act 1982.

"If the defendant (Mr Malloy) is a pedlar then the restrictions imposed on street trading are virtually ineffective." [24]

There is, no doubt, some force in this argument. But arguably the problem lies in the design of the legislation and the remedy should lie with Parliament and not the courts.

In practice, it is possible that many traders may succeed in structuring their activities in order to fulfil the definition of "pedlar". This has been judicially acknowledged. In *R v. Taylor* [25] His Honour Judge Proctor held that a trader operating in a shopping precinct- a "prohibited street"- was lawfully acting as a pedlar. The trader generally walked through towns selling as he went. On this occasion he was going through the precinct, but it seems that had stopped in one place to sell for up to ten or fifteen minutes whilst members of the public bought goods from him. It was held that although he was in a stationary position he continued to act as a pedlar. Ultimately it was a question of fact and "undue lingering" would take him outside the scope of the pedlar's exception.

It may be that, with little inconvenience many traders will still benefit from the exemption. Provided that they walk up and down a street in search of customers, perhaps pausing from time to time to rest or to sell, they would seem be acting as pedlars. This means that the pedlar's exemption may still furnish effective means of avoiding the consequences of the code.

The Need for a Certificate
The would-be pedlar, will need to comply with the licensing legislation governing pedlars. Section 4 of the 1871 Act states that no person shall act as a pedlar without the necessary certificate. [26] Breach of this requirement renders the offender liable to a penalty not exceeding level 1 on the standard scale.

---

[24] [1988] 1 WLR 1026, 1031.

[25] Manchester Crown Court 7th July 1989, (unreported). I am indebted to Mr Barry Hudson for a note on this decision.

[26] Pedlar's Act 1871, s.4. This provision may be replaced as part of the Government's de-regulation programme.

It is not difficult to obtain a pedlar's certificate. The chief officer of police, by s.5 of the 1871 Act, [27] has a *duty* to grant the certificate provided that the applicant has resided in the district for at least a month and that the officer is satisfied that he or she is over 17 years of age, of good character and "in good faith intends to carry on the trade of a pedlar." This duty may be contrasted with the discretionary power of a local authority to grant a street trading consent. It seems that it is also in this respect that the pedlar enjoys a more favoured status: subject to fulfilling the limited statutory conditions he can acquire a certificate as a matter of right.

The certificate may not be lent or transferred to another trader.[28] Anyone seeking to borrow a certificate issued to another is guilty of an offence. [29]

An applicant may appeal to the magistrates for the district against a refusal to grant or renew a certificate. [30] In order to invoke the appellate process the applicant must within one week of the refusal give to the chief officer of police notice in writing of the appeal.

The court may make any order which it considers to be just including an order for costs. If it decides, in effect, to quash the refusal and to grant a certificate this has the same effect as if granted by the chief officer of police.

The holder of a certificate may peddle his wares within any part of the United Kingdom [31] although this does not entitle the pedlar to breach any by-law. [32]

Those Pedlars Who do not Require a Pedlar's Certificate
Traders such as commercial travellers, those who trade in lawful markets or fairs, and those dealing in vegetables, fish, fruit or

---

[27] By s.22 of the Pedlar's Act 1871, anything authorised to be done by the chief officer of police may be done by any police officer under his command authorised by him.
[28] Pedlar's Act 1871, s.10.
[29] *Ibid.* s.11.
[30] *Ibid.* s.15.
[31] Pedlar's Act 1881.
[32] A pedlar is not entitled to trade in certain goods including , gunpowder: Explosives Act 1875 ss 3, 39; and stamps: Stamp Duties Management Act 1891, (but excluding postage stamps: Finance Act 1966, s.48; Post Office Act 1969, s.141, Sch 11, pt II; Interpretation Act 1978, s.16 (1) sch.2.)

victuals [33]are not required to obtain a pedlar's certificate. [34] This creates problems for those of them who would be eligible for the exemption under the code. [35] The reason is that the code only creates the exemption for:

"a person acting as a pedlar *under the authority of a pedlar's certificate granted under the Pedlar's Act 1871.*" (Emphasis supplied).
Without such a certificate, the exemption is unavailable.

This may not, however, conclude the matter. s.23 of the 1871 Act merely states that it shall not be "*necessary*" for the traders mentioned in that section to obtain a pedlar's certificate. It does not preclude them from seeking one. If this is correct, traders exempt under the 1871 Act should apply for a pedlar's certificate so as to obtain the benefit of the code's exemption.

Revocation of a Pedlar's Certificate
A pedlar may be liable to be deprived of his certificate if he is convicted of any offence. [36] If interpreted literally this seems to be extremely wide since the commission of any offence would be a ground for revocation. The matter would, however, be within the magistrates' discretion. There is no discretion if a pedlar is convicted of begging: the certificate must be revoked.

Conclusion
Pedlars are exempted from the regulatory scheme of the street trading code and would appear to enjoy significantly greater privileges than other street traders. Not least of these is that he or she is free to trade even in prohibited streets and that the fee for the certificate is a mere £12.25. The police have a duty to grant a certificate to traders fulfilling the statutory conditions; and in most cases this is likely to present few difficulties. Once a certificate is obtained, a trader can acquire the benefits of trading as a pedlar

---

[33] Victuals includes any ingredient in food, such as, for example, yeast: *R v. Hodgkinson* (1829) 10 B & C 74.
[34] Pedlar's Act 1871, s.23.
[35] I.e., not market traders because they are not peripatetic.
[36] Pedlar's Act 1871, s.16.

provided he goes in search of his customers, although this does not mean that he can never stop either to trade or rest. The rules essentially prohibit the pedlar from taking up one stationary position.

Other Exempt Trading

The following are exempted from the need to obtain a street trading licence or consent:

(i) Trading in a trunk road picnic area provided by the Secretary of State under s.112 of the Highways Act 1980.

By virtue of this provision, the Secretary of State may provide picnic sites on land adjoining or in the vicinity of certain trunk roads. [37] Although the Minister has a power to manage such a site, provisions, for example, for meals and refreshments must be provided by others (not including a council) who enter arrangements with the Minister to do so. As these sites are regulated in this manner it was unnecessary to extend the provisions of the code to them.

(ii) Trading as a newsvendor

This is also exempt from the provisions of the Code by paragraph 1 sub-para (2) (d).

Difficulties will arise where the newsvendor trades in other items in addition to newspapers and magazines. In such a case [38] the exemption is lost and the trader must seek a street trading licence in the ordinary way. This so regardless of what other goods are sold or exposed for sale. The trader must act solely as a newsvendor if he is to preserve the exemption.

---

[37] An exception is made for "special roads" reserved to special, classes of traffic, such as a motorway: s.16 of the 1980 Act. Motorway service areas are regarded as falling within the scheme of the code: see the definition of "street" in paragraph 1 (1) of Schedule 4.

[38] Sub para. (3) (a).

The trader is also required to trade from a stall or receptacle which conforms to certain size restrictions. If a larger stand is employed a licence must be sought. [39]

(iii) Trading Carried on at a Petrol Filling Station

This saving enables proprietors of filling stations to continue to offer on their forecourts a range of goods to motorists and others without seeking a street trading licence. Were this saving omitted such trading would have fallen within the scope of the Schedule because the forecourt would as a place to which the public have access to without payment, would be deemed to be a "street" for the purposes of the Schedule.

(iv) Trading in and Around Shops

Since the public has access to a shop [40] without payment they might have fallen within the scheme of the code but for this saving. The exemption extends also to trading which takes place in a street adjoining premises used as a shop where trading is part of the business of the shop. This appears designed to remove from the code stands and stalls placed on the street outside corner shops and the like. This does not mean that such a use of the highway is lawful. A trader who positions a stall or display outside his shop and on the highway may be obstructing it. [41]

(v) Roundsmen

Roundsmen such as milkmen, coalmen and the like who offer or expose goods for sale may trade lawfully without a street trading licence or consent. It may be that this exemption is only available

---

[39] The limits are that the stall or receptacle must neither exceed one metre in length and width nor two metres in height, nor occupy a ground area of more than 0.25 square metres, nor stand on the carriageway of a street.
[40] For a discussion of the meaning off "shop", see p. 102 *et seq.*
[41] *Wolverton UDC v. Willis* [1962] 1 WLR 205; Town Police Clauses Act 1847, s.28.

to the trader who has recognised customers in a street with whom he is already carrying on business as a trader. [42]

(vi) Services to the Public Provided under Part VIIA of the Highways Act 1980

The significance of s.115 of the Highways Act 1980 in this context is that it allows a council, or anyone else it authorises, to place "structures" such as booths or kiosks on the highway so as to provide a service to the public. Permission to do so can be conditional and include an obligation to meet the council's reasonable charges. Since these powers in effect licence trading operations, there was no need to include them within the regulatory structure of the street trading code.

(vii) Charity Collections

For the purposes of the code, street trading does not occur where money is raised for charitable or "other purposes". [43]

3. Controls on the Place in which Trading may Occur

"Zoning"

The Code is structured so as to permit district councils to "zone" their areas for street trading purposes. This zoning scheme operates to prohibit street trading altogether, or to confine it to certain designated areas.

By paragraph 2 of Schedule 4 of the 1982 Act, a district council may designate any street in their district according to the following categories.

---

[42] *London Borough of Islington v. Panico* (1973) 72 LGR 51, decided under a similar provision of the London County Council (General Powers) Act 1947. This seems a narrow interpretation because a roundsmen seeking new business might be outside the exemption.

[43] The Police, Factories etc, (Miscellaneous Provisions) Act 1916, s.5.

(i) Prohibited Streets

If a street is designated as a prohibited street, all street trading therein is prohibited. [44] A trader who breaches this control commits an offence under paragraph 10 and is liable on conviction to a fine not exceeding level 3 on the standard scale. [45]

Streets are sometimes designated as "prohibited streets" to exclude traders from areas of special historical importance or conservation areas within the district.

(ii) Consent Streets

The council may alternatively designate a "consent street" which prohibits street trading in such a street without the consent of the district council. [46] The regime for granting consents gives the council more extensive discretionary powers than is the case for street trading licences.

The system of consents is designed principally to regulate itinerant traders including those who either operate from vehicles, or barrows. [47] In practice the "consent" system will most often apply to those selling from vehicles. It is a more stringent system than the quasi-judicial one applicable to street trading licences. In particular it targets trading from mobile snack bars which can cause significant road safety problems if sited in unsuitable locations. [48]

(iii) Licence streets

The district council may alternatively designate a street as a "licence street". This has the effect of prohibiting street trading in that street unless the trader obtains a licence granted by the district council. The licensing system (as opposed to the system for consents) is intended to apply to those who trade from a fixed

---

[44] Para. 1 (1).

[45] Para 10 as amended by the Criminal Justice Act 1982, s.46.

[46] Para. 1 (1). It is an offence punishable by a fine not exceeding level 3 on the standard scale to trade in such a street without a consent: para 10.

[47] This may even include those who carry their wares, per Timothy Raison HC Debs. 6th series, vol. 13. 25th November 1981, col 905. See also para 10 (1) (d) (i) & (ii); also *R v. Bristol City Council ex p. Pearce* (1985) 83 LGR 711.

[48] Samuels, *Controls on Street Trading: Mobile Snack Bars* (1986) 150 LGR 211. Permission to trade from a *stationary* van, cart, barrow or other vehicle, or from a portable stall may be included in a consent in accordance with para 7 (8) so the division in the Act between itinerant and non-itinerant trading is somewhat blurred.

position, that is, from a stationary barrow, a cart, a or stall. [49] A trader who disregards the designations, for example , by trading from a stationary barrow in a consent street without permission, commits an offence punishable by fine not exceeding level 3 on the standard scale. [50]

Procedure for Designating Streets

The designation of a street must be made by resolution. Prior to passing such a resolution various statutory consultation and notification requirements apply.

Under paragraph 2 (3) the council must publish a notice in the statutory form of their proposals in a local newspaper. This means that the notice should include a draft of the resolution and state that representations concerning it maybe made in writing to the council within a period of not less than 28 days from the publication of the notice.[51]

The notification of the chief officer of police and the highway authority responsible for that street is also necessary [52] unless the street is to be a licence street and is maintained by the highway authority, in which case the *consent* of the highway authority is also required. [53] If the street is owned by any "relevant corporation" their consent will also be necessary. [54] The "relevant corporations" are (a) the British Railways Board; (b) the Commission for the New Towns; (c) a development corporation for a new town; (d) an urban development corporation established under the Local Government Planning and Land Act 1980; and (e) the Development Board for Rural Wales. [55]

If, after having taken into account any representations it has received, the council passes its resolution, it must publish a notice to that effect in a local newspaper in two consecutive weeks. [56] The

---

[49] This appears to follow from para 10 (1) (d).
[50] Para. 10 (1) (d).
[51] Para. 2 (6).
[52] Para. 2 (3).
[53] Paras. 2 (3)(c), 2 (4) (b) (ii).
[54] Para. 2 (3) (c).
[55] Para. 2 (5).
[56] Para. 2 (9).

first publication must be at least 28 days before the day specified in the resolution for the coming into force of the regulatory scheme. [57]

Under para 2 (11) the council has further powers in relation to streets designated or to be designated as a licence street. Here the council may stipulate the number of days on which traders will be expected to trade. It may decide that licences will not be granted to those who intend to trade on fewer days. These requirements may be imposed either in the initial resolution or in any subsequent resolution. If this step is taken in a subsequent resolution rather than the one in which the street is designated *ab initio* the council must follow some but not all of the procedures required for the *ab initio* designation. [58] These are that it must publish a notice in the statutory form in a local newspaper inviting representations. If the resolution is passed, a notice to this effect must be published in a local newspaper in two consecutive weeks and subject to the same rules as to time as applied on the initial designation.

4. The Licensing Power

4.1. Street Trading Licences

It is to be noted that we are concerned here with street trading licences, not street trading consents.

Applications for a Street Trading Licence
The applicant for a street trading licence, or the licensee who seeks to renew his licence, must make his application in writing to the district council stating, *inter alia* the description of the goods in which he wishes to trade, the place in which he intends to do so, and the proposed days and times of day in which he will operate. In addition to these and other matters specified in para 3, the trader may be required to furnish such other information as the council may require.

The power to demand information about the goods to be offered for sale is important because the application may be denied, [59] if

---

[57] Para. 2 (10).

[58] Para. 2 (12).

[59] Para. 3 (6) (b).

there are "enough" traders trading in the street either in shops or otherwise in the goods in which the applicant desires to trade. The idea of sufficiency in this provision is not further defined in the Act. The open-textured nature of the drafting does, however, appear to allow local authorities to shield "established" rate paying shop keepers from competition on the grounds that they provide sufficient access to the goods in question. It is not clear, however, whether the availability from the trader of the same goods at lower cost is a relevant factor. [60]

A district council is under a *duty* to grant an application for a street trading licence, or to renew an existing licence, unless they are satisified that grounds exist for a refusal. [61] In some instances even if these grounds do exist, the council may still award the licence upon special terms. [62] The controlled nature of this discretionary power limits the powers of local authorities to refuse licences.

If there is competition for a limited number of licences (or consents) the council should not award the licence (or consent) merely on a "first-come-first-served" basis. Some consideration must be given to the merits of each application. [63]

Grounds for the Refusal of a Licence
The grounds for refusal fall into distinct categories. In the first are "mandatory" grounds by which the district council has no power to grant (and must refuse) a licence; [64] in the second are "general " grounds unrelated to the merit of the individual applicant; [65] and in the third "suitability" reasons which have some bearing on the suitability of the applicant as a potential licensee. [66]
The grounds are as follows:

---

[60] On the unhappy relationship generally between street traders and some local authorities see remarks of S. Hughes, MP HC Debs. 6th series vol. 165, cols 1112, 1113-1114, 25th January 1990.

[61] Paras. 3 (5); 6 (1).

[62] Para. 3 (7).

[63] *Perilly v. Tower Hamlets LBC* (1972) 70 LGR 474, overruling *Stepney v. Schneider* (1960) 58 LGR 202.

[64] Para. 3 (4).

[65] Para. 3(6) (a) and (b).

[66] Para.3 (6) (c)-(g).

(i) "Mandatory grounds"

The district council has no power to grant a licence to any person under the age of 17 years, nor for trading in a street relation to which a control order has been made. [67] The council has no discretion in these cases: the application must be refused. [68]

"Control Orders"

A local authority has no power to grant a street trading licence (or consent) where a "control order" under s.7 of the Local Government (Miscellaneous Provisions) Act 1976 is in force. Such an order, subject to important exceptions, prohibits road-side sales on the highway specified or sale from a stall or vehicle within 15 metres of any part of the highway. Exemptions from these provisions benefit *(inter alia)*, itinerant traders such as delivery roundsmen, the provision from a lay-by of refreshments for travellers or the sale of agricultural produce from the land on which it was produced.

(ii) General Grounds

Under this and the next category the district council has a duty to grant the application unless "they consider that the application *ought to be refused* on one or more" of the following grounds. [69] The words highlighted seem to suggest that the existence of one or more of these grounds is not by itself sufficient *per se*. The council has to be satisfied that the application "ought to be refused" by virtue of that reason. This may allow the applicant to explain or mitigate conduct which might otherwise have resulted in a refusal of his application. For example, it is not difficult to envisage cases where, notwithstanding the existence of a reason under, for example, sub- para (e), - that the applicant has persistently failed to pay fees or charges due to the licensing authority- the council may feel that this is insufficient to warrant a refusal of a licence. The applicant may have sufficiently explained his neglect and satisfied the council that arrears and future payments will be made when due. In such a case it may be that prior neglect may not be a case in which the application *ought* to be refused.

---

[67] *Infra.*

[68] Para. 3 (4).

[69] Para. 3 (5) emphasis supplied.

The "general" grounds in paragraph 3 (6) are:

Para 3 (6) (a) *that there is not enough space in the street for the applicant to engage in the trading in which he desires to engage without causing undue interference or inconvenience to persons using the street.*

This provision recognises that street trading is not to be prevented merely because it results in *some* inconvenience to persons using the street. Licences may only be withheld if the interference is "undue". This begs value judgments about the competing interests of those who trade and benefit from the trading on the one hand and other highway users on the other. How much interference is permissible depends on how important the street trading is perceived to be. This is a matter for the district council. [70]

Para 3 (6) (b) *that there are already enough traders trading in the street from shops or otherwise in the goods in which the applicant desires to trade.*

This provision has already been noted. This provision enables the authority to protect the interests of existing traders and shop-keepers. Whether this is unquestionably advantageous is open to dispute. There is an argument that this provision excludes new traders gaining access to the market even if they were prepared to compete in terms of price or quality. *Ex hypothesi* , there is enough space for them to trade, so it is open to question whether the public interest is served by this provision.

(iii) Grounds Relating to the Suitability of the Applicant/Licensee

Para 3 (6) (c) *that the applicant desires to trade on fewer days than the minimum number specified in the resolution which designated the street as a licence street, or any other subsequent resolution.* This is a measure designed to ensure that where street trading is acceptable the public should gain the greatest benefit from it. It requires a commitment from traders in return for the privilege of holding a licence.

---

[70] Subject to acting reasonably in the *Wednesbury* sense; see *Associated Provincial Picture Houses Ltd v. Wednesbury Corpn.* [1948] 1 KB 223.

Para 3 (6) (d) *that the applicant is unsuitable to hold the licence by reason of having been convicted of an offence or for any other reason.*

To justify the withholding of a licence, the offence, or "other reason" contemplated by the sub-paragraph should be one that brought into question the applicant or licensee's suitability as a licence-holder. The repeated and deliberate commission of even minor offences, such as parking offences committed in the course of earlier trading, could be relevant in this context. [71]

Para 3 (6) (e) *that the applicant has at any time been granted a street trading licence by the council and has persistently refused or neglected to pay fees due to them for it or charges due to them under para 9 (6) for services rendered by them to him in his capacity as licence-holder.*

Para 3 (6) (f) makes a similar provision for street trading consents.

Para 3 (6) (g) *that the applicant has without reasonable excuse failed to avail himself to a reasonable extent of a previous trading licence.*

The code specifies certain cases in which, instead of refusing an application, the council may grant it but on terms different from those sought. [72] This is so where the refusal might have occurred by reason of a lack of space, or where there are enough traders in the goods the applicant proposed to sell, or where the applicant had unreasonably failed to use the benefit of a former licence. The special terms may allow the trader to operate for fewer hours or in a restricted class or classes of goods.

Procedural Safeguards

Where the council proposes to refuse to grant or renew a licence the code confers certain mandatory procedural rights on the trader concerned. These process rights depend to a significant extent upon the notice procedure.

---

[71] *Manchester Corporation v. Penson* (1969) 68 LGR 225. Convictions for obstruction of the highway or similar offences could also be relevant.

[72] Para. 3 (7).

This procedure requires the district council to serve a notice on the applicant or licence-holder specifying the grounds on which its decision would be based and offering the applicant/licence-holder the opportunity to make representations. [73] To qualify for this right the trader must require the district council to allow him to make representations and he must inform the council of this within 7 days of receiving the notice. [74] The notice should state that he has this right.

There is no statutory right under para 6 (2) to an oral hearing. Normally written representations should suffice to comply with the general law. But there may be circumstances in which an oral hearing should be granted. [75]

The notice procedure significantly buttresses the rights of applicants and traders because once a notice has been served, the district council has no power to reach a decision in the matter unless it can establish that the requirements of paragraphs 6 (3) and (4) are satisfied. These are essentially rules intended to prevent traders from abusing the procedural guarantees simply to cause unnecessary delay. Nevertheless, the council can only reach a lawful decision if one the following provisions is fulfilled. First, a decision can be taken if the trader has actually made representations concerning the proposed decision. If the trader has not asserted his right to make representations the council can only decide the matter if the 7 day period in which he might do so has expired.

If a trader has asserted his right to make representations, the council is empowered by 6 (4) to decide the matter if it has allowed the trader a reasonable period in which to make his representations and he has failed to do so within that period. [76]

---

[73] Para. 6 (1) and (2).

[74] The day the notice is received is not included in the calculation: *Carapanayoti & Co Ltd v. Comptair Commercial Andre & Cie SA.* [1972] 1 Lloyds Rep 139.

[75] The rules of natural justice and acting fairly are considered in Ch. 16.

[76] What is reasonable is a question of fact. The complexity of the case which the trader may wish to advance would be one relevant factor.

Appeals Against the Refusal of a Licence

If the district council refuses either to grant or to renew a street trading licence, any "person aggrieved" may appeal against the decision so long as the reason or reasons for the council's decision falls within one of the categories designated under paragraph 3 (6) (d)-(g).

The appeal lies to the magistrates' court within the area in which the street for which the licence was sought is situated. The justices may make such order as they think fit.[77] A right of further appeal lies to the Crown Court which, in respect of the appeal, has similar powers to the magistrates' court.[78]

Restrictions on Appeal

An appeal will only lie where the reasons for the council's decision fall within designated categories. Because the council is under a duty to serve a notice specifying the grounds on which the decision might be based, the applicant or licence-holder should be aware of what the reasons for the refusal are and will have had the opportunity to make representations on this matter to persuade the council to grant the licence. If this right has been exercised unsuccessfully, reliance must be placed upon the appeal mechanism. An appeal is only possible where the reason or, if there is more than one, all reasons, fall within the permissible reasons in the code.

These reasons are contained in paragraph 3 (6) (d) to (g). These have already been noted.[79] It follows that no appeal is possible where the refusal is based on grounds in 3 (6) (a)- (c) which relate to lack of space in the street, or that there are sufficient traders in the goods proposed to be sold, or the applicant proposes to trade on fewer than the minimum required days. Proceedings by way of judicial review are the only means by which a refusal on these grounds may be challenged.

---

[77] Para. 6 (7).
[78] Paras. 6 (6) and (7).
[79] *Supra.* p. 197.

The Scope and Effect of a Street Trading Licence

Once granted or renewed, a licence is normally valid for 12 months from the date of the grant or for such shorter period as the council may determine in the licence.[80] The licence grants a conditional permission to trade. Most importantly, the trader may be obliged to trade for the minimum number of days specified in the designating resolution.

Although the trader is empowered to employ assistants, [81] there seems nevertheless to be an obligation to trade personally since a licence may be revoked if the licence-holder has without reasonable excuse failed to avail *himself* of the licence to a reasonable extent [82] (emphasis supplied). Much will turn on the interpretation of the word "himself". One interpretation suggests that the burden is a personal one. An argument that this provision merely requires the licence-holder to make use of the licence, but not personally to do so, is, however, also possible. It should be noted, however, that the similarly worded provision in s 21 (3) (f) of the London County Council (General Powers) Act 1947 entailed an obligation personally to trade. The requirement was not merely for personal responsibility for the stall; personal supervision of it was essential. [83]

Other conditions of trading are established by the "principal" or "subsidiary" terms of the licence. [84] The licence is required to specify the street in which trading is permitted and the times at which this is so. It must also specify the class or classes of goods which the trader is entitled to offer for sale. [85] If trading is only to be permitted in a particular place in the street the licence must also stipulate this.[86] Terms relating to these matters are known as "principal terms". [87]

---

[80] Para. 4 (6).
[81] Para. 8.
[82] Para. 5 (1) (d).
[83] *R v. Southwark Crown Court ex p Watts* [1992] C.O.D. 140.
[84] Para. 4
[85] Para. 4 (1).
[86] Para. 4 (2).
[87] Para. 4 (3).

Councils also have power to impose "subsidiary" terms on the licence-holder in so far as it appears to them to be reasonable to do so. Para 4 (5) enacts that these subsidiary terms may include, amongst other matters, conditions relating to the size and type of stall; and they may impose a requirement that the trader identifies himself on the stall. Subsidiary terms may also address refuse and litter problems: the licence may either prohibit the leaving of refuse altogether or specify how much may be left and at what place.

The licence does not confer an inalienable right to trade. If the district council resolves that the street in which the trader is licensed to trade should become a prohibited street, the street trading licence ceases to be valid once the designation of the street takes effect. [88]

Variation of the Terms of Street Trading Licences

The rules governing variation depend upon when the variation occurs and the kind of term it is proposed to vary. Problems of interpetation also arise from the drafting of the relevant paragraphs.

Terms may be varied when the trader applies to renew his licence. If the change affects one or more of the "principal" terms of the licence the variation can only take place if the council follows the notice procedure to which reference has already been made. [89] These procedures do not apply where the variation extends to a "subsidiary term". Nor does it seem that there is any restriction on the occasions on which a subsidiary term can be varied.

As in the case of a refusal to grant or renew a licence, the council cannot reach a final decision on the variation of a principal term until the trader has actually made representations or has not exercised his right to arrange for representations to be made within the permitted time limit. [90] If the trader has replied "requiring" to be heard on the matter, the council cannot proceed until representations have actually been made or, if they have not, a

---

[88] See further pp. 394-395.
[89] P. 198. Paras 6 (1) and (2).
[90] Para. 6 (3).

reasonable period has expired without the trader exercising his right. [91]

The code also provides for variation of a principal term as an alternative to revocation. For this reason the circumstances in which variation is possible are linked to those in which the licence might otherwise have been revoked. Para 5 (1) sets out the grounds for revocation (see further below) and these are:

(a)   "that there is insufficient space in the street for the licence-holder to continue to trade without causing undue interference to traffic or other users of the street

(b)   that the licence-holder is unsuitable to hold the licence by reason of having been convicted of an offence or for any other reason;

(c)   that, since the grant or renewal of the licence, the licence-holder has persistently refused or neglected to pay fees due to the council for it or charges due to them (for services rendered to the licence-holder); or

(d)   that, since the grant or renewal of the licence, the licence-holder has without reasonable excuse failed to avail himself of the licence to a reasonable extent."

The council may decide to vary the principal terms of a licence either by reducing the times at which trading may take place or by limiting the classes of goods which may be offered for sale where the licence may otherwise have been revoked for a reason in para 5 1 (1) (a) or (d). [92] Thus these two reasons appear to be the only ones in which variation is possible as an alternative to revocation.

This is not, however, beyond dispute. Difficulties of interpretation arise because of para 6 (5) (c) which confers the right of appeal against a decision to vary the principal terms of a licence whilst it is still in force. The problem is that para 6 (5) (c) appears to suggest that an appeal is only possible where variation is for a reason contained in para 5 (1) (b) to (d). This naturally implies that a variation is possible in such cases otherwise there would be no

---

[91] Para. 6 (4).
[92] Para 5 (2).

need to confer a right of appeal. There is no right of appeal if the variation were for a reason under para 5 (1) (a).

An appeal is also only possible where, if more than one reason is stated, all fall within 5 (1) (b)-(d). This may be open to abuse since, literally read, para 6 (5) (c) removes the right of appeal where any other ground for variation is included.

Where the licence is renewed, the rights of the trader are different. A right of appeal only exists where the grant is subject to principal terms different from those in the previous licence where the only reason for the change was that the trader failed without reasonable excuse to use to a reasonable extent the previous licence.[93]

Time Limit for Appeal
A right of appeal must be exercised within 21 days of the date when the decision to vary was notified to the applicant or licence-holder. [94]

Revocation of Street Trading Licences

Grounds on which Revocation may Occur

Subject to following the notice procedures discussed above, [95] a council may at any time revoke a street trading licence if one or more of the grounds in para 5 (1) are available. These have been outlined above.

As already noted, variation instead of revocation may occur where the a ground for revocation exists under para 5 (1) (a) or (d) above. The council may either reduce the number of days on which trading is permitted, or restrict the kinds of goods in which trading can take place.

---

[93] Para. 6 (5) (b).
[94] Para. 6 (5) (c).
[95] *Supra*, p. 198.

Appeals Against Revocation
A right of appeal to the magistrates' court lies against the decision of the local authority to revoke a street trading licence provided the grounds for revocation are only those enumerated in para 5 (1) (b) to (d). [96] Judicial review provides the only means of challenging a revocation on the ground of insufficient space.

An appeal must be commenced within 21 days of the date on which the trader was notified of the council's decision.

4.2 Street Trading Consents

The Power to Grant Consents
The system of consents is a more stringent system conferring fewer rights on the trader than that which applies in the case of street trading licences. Consents are more likely to authorise mobile street trading such as that which takes place from hot dog and other mobile snack bars.

The grant of a street trading consent is a matter which falls within the discretion of the district council: it may grant the application "if they think fit" [97] provided that the applicant is not under 17 years of age, or the application does not relate to any trading on a highway in relation to which a control order has been made. [98]   The consent may permit the holder to trade from a stationary van, cart, barrow, or other vehicle, or from a portable stall. [99]

The effect of this paragraph is that, subject to the above-mentioned limits, the district council may grant or refuse an application on any grounds it sees fit. In particular, and in contrast to the provisions regulating the grant of licences, there is no limitation on the grounds on which the application may be refused. The district council is entitled to have regard to any matters which

---

[96] By the inclusion of an additional ground not within those cognisable grounds, the right of appeal would seem to be lost. This is, however, an interpetation which is extremely unattractive.

[97] Para. 7 (2).

[98] Para. 7 (3).

[99] Para. 7 (8).

it considers to be relevant subject only to the requirement that it must act reasonably. [100]

Applications for a Street Trading Consent
The information which may be required by the district council in support of an application for a street trading consent is not prescribed in the Schedule. Nor does it seem that the application need, as a matter of law, to be made in writing. The effect of this is to allow the council a discretion to prescribe for themselves (subject to the general law) the matters which information must be supplied and which will be taken into account.

Procedure Governing the Granting of Street Trading Consents
Those seeking a consent are denied the extensive procedural protection enshrined in the rules governing street trading licences. There is no statutory procedure requiring the district council to notify the applicant of any objections. Nor is there any right of appeal against the decision of the council in the matter. The rights of applicants are only those embodied in the general law.[101] The extent of these rights depends normally upon whether the council is dealing with an application for a licence, whether it is a case of renewal of an existing licence, or whether the council is seeking to deprive a trader of the benefit of an existing licence. [102] In this context we are concerned with the rights of an applicant for a street trading licence.

In such a case the district council will be under a duty to act fairly. This merely affords minimum standards of procedural fairness, compelling the council to act without bias and not to reach a decision which is tainted by any arbitrary or perverse policy.[103] The applicant for a consent must also be notified of the substance of any objections to the granting of a consent and an opportunity to respond to those objections. These representations must be fully

---

[100] *Associated Provincial Picture Houses v. Wednesbury Corporation* [1948] 1 KB 223.
[101] *Infra* Chapter 16.
[102] *McInnes v. Onslow-Fane* [1978] 1 WLR 1520.
[103] *Ibid.* at p. 1528.

considered by the council. This need not be by way of an oral hearing. [104]

These general principles were followed and applied in *R v. Bristol City Council ex p Pearce* [105] where the denial of an oral hearing provided one of the grounds for a challenge to a council's decision to refuse consents although written representations had been before the relevant committee when it met in public session. The court refused to hold that the council had acted *ultra vires* because, under the general law, the council would have a discretion as to how they would hear representations from the applicant. It followed that there was no obligation to allow representations to be made orally, nor was the council required to give reasons for their refusal of a consent. The court further held that if written representations were submitted it would be presumed that they had been considered unless the contrary were established in evidence.

Ex p Pearce also decided that even existing traders- such as the applicants in this case- are treated in law as first time applicants when the code is first promulgated in an area. In other words, prior trading under the previous regime does not generate a legitimate expectation that a consent will be granted under the code.

The Scope and Effect of a Street Trading Consent
The district council may attach such conditions to the street trading consent as they consider reasonably necessary [106] and, in particular, conditions designed to prevent obstruction of the street, danger to those using it or "nuisance or annoyance". In so far as these conditions may address matters likely to cause "annoyance", conditions may address any effects of the street trading on the neighbourhood which might fall short of a nuisance in law.

The power to attach conditions to the consent may be exercised when the consent is granted ab initio or when it is renewed. This means that a consent-holder cannot be certain that a consent will be renewed on the same terms as those previously enjoyed. Further, para 7 (6) provides that the council may vary the conditions of a street trading consent at any time. There are no procedural

---

[104] *R v. Bristol City Council ex p Pearce* (1985) 83 LGR 711, 723. The decision is noted by Samuels, "Control of street trading: mobile snack bars." (1986) 150 LGR 211.
[105] *Ibid.*
[106] Para. 7 (4).

safeguards for the consent holder. It seems that the council is only bound by the general duty to act fairly when exercising this power.

Unless the consent stipulates to the contrary, its holder cannot trade from a van or other vehicle or from a stall, barrow or cart. The council may expressly permit such trading, however. [107] If it decides to do so, the consent may be conditional upon the holder obeying restrictions as to the places in which he can trade and the times at which trading may take place. [108]

Revocation of Street Trading Consents
A consent may be revoked at any time in the council's discretion. [109] The trader does not benefit from any statutory procedural safeguards before a consent is revoked. Nevertheless, in the absence of statutory procedures, the rules of natural justice must be observed before a revocation can occur since the council would be interfering with an existing privilege.[110]

Appeals
No right of appeal lies in respect of the refusal, revocation or variation of a street trading consent. The council has a discretion in these matters which is subject only to the principles exercised by the courts in judicial review proceedings.

5. Fees and Charges

The level of fees and charges imposed on street traders by the regulatory authorities in the past represented one of the key areas of potential conflict. Licence fees could once have represented significant overheads over which the traders had no control. In extreme cases, increases in fees and charges prejudiced the viability of traders' businesses; their livelihoods were often at issue.

---

[107] Para. 7 (8).
[108] *Ibid.*
[109] Para. 7 (10).
[110] *McInnes v. Onslow-Fane, supra* n (102); *R v. Bristol City Council ex p Pearce, supra* n (104) esp, at pp 715-6. Glidewell J observed that the refusal or grant (sic) of a consent could be attacked on the grounds of a breach of the rules of natural justice where appropriate. If so, a right to natural justice ought to follow *a fortiori* in the case of a revocation.

The Power to Recover Fees

The council is empowered to charge "such fees as they consider reasonable" for the grant or renewal of a street trading licence or consent. [111] On a literal interpretation the power is drafted subjectively and purports to make the council the judge of what is reasonable. In fact, the power of the council is not so extensive. As we shall, the power is limited by general principles of Administrative Law.

It should be noted that the Act distinguishes "fees" from "charges". The cost of a licence or consent is the "fee" paid for it. The council also has a power to impose "charges" under para 9 (6). These refer to the charges made for services provided to the trader by the council. These "charges" are considered separately.

The fee, whether it be for a licence or consent, must be a reasonable one: the discretion is the same in each case, although, of course, this does not mean that the same charge will necessarily be made for licences and consents respectively. The matter does not, however, end there. The Act goes further in informing the council of some factors which should influence the level of fees. Paragraph 9 states that the "council may determine different fees for different types of licence or consent" [112] and having regard to such matters as the duration of the licence or consent, the street in which trading is authorised, and the kinds of article in which trading is proposed.[113] This allows the council to take into account the profitability of the particular trader's business and set an appropriate fee. This encourages a diversity of trading. Other limitations are imposed by the general law.

Policy Issues
What constitutes a reasonable fee begs the question of what purpose the fee serves. We can only know what is reasonable if we understand why a fee is to be imposed. The Act is silent on this and so, in the absence of statutory guidance, local authorities appear to have adopted different policies in this matter. Some have taken the view that the fee allows the council to create a "level playing

---

[111] Para. 9 (1).
[112] Para. 9 (2).
[113] Para. 9 (2) (a) - (c).

field" between highly rated shop keepers and street traders. On this view substantial licence fees are appropriate in order to increase the overheads of traders so as to create "fair" competition. This view sees rival shop keepers as the indirect beneficiaries of the charging power.

Others view the power as an extension of the powers of control and regulation. Substantial fees may be set under this view to deter trading and thus promote free passage along the highway. Reduced levels of trading also minimises possible nuisance effects.

A different argument stresses that the purpose of the fee is merely to recover the costs of operating the system. [114] Under this view, the purpose of the power to charge is merely to make the system self-financing. In so far as this policy sought only to impose the minimum of burdens on street traders, it sees no need for further barriers to street trading activity beyond those already expressly enacted.

Finally, there have been those who would treat the licence or consent as a commodity to be sold in the market place for the highest price the market could bear. This policy sought to protect the interests of local taxpayers by raising the maximum revenue possible. Such an approach treated the licence almost as a private franchise right vested in the local authority to be exploited for its "private" advantage. It sublimated wider issues of public interest in having access to a diversity of street trading and not just the most profitable.

These policy options were diverse and were capable of exerting profoundly different influences on the eventual level of fees. In order to discover the proper purpose of the power to charge fees, some brief reference must be made to the principles of the general law. It is important to understand that although the power to charge is ostensibly unfettered, like all discretionary power it is limited by considerations of reasonableness. This has a special meaning in law. In fixing the fee, the district council must have regard to relevant considerations and must not be influenced by irrelevant ones. The fee determined must itself be reasonable and must not be one that no reasonable authority could impose. [115]

---

[114] See, e.g., the City of London (Various Powers) Act 1987, s.10.

[115] *Associated Provincial Picture Houses Ltd. v. Wednesbury Corpn.* [1948] 1 KB 223. See further Ch. 17.

Fees Must Relate to the Cost of the Scheme
The limits on the power to impose fees and charges were fully canvassed in *R v. Manchester City Council ex p. King*,[116] a decision which settles for the first time the scope and purpose of these powers. In this case, the City Council resolved to increase charges for street trading licences by over 1000%. This charge was set having regard to various matters, including the fees charged for stalls in council owned markets, the tenders received from traders seeking to trade in council owned stalls, and the proximity of the street traders to the city centre which is the major regional shopping centre. The traders affected were not given an opportunity to present objections before these charges were fixed. The suspicion arose that, at the very least, the increase in fees was designed substantially to reduce the number of street traders in central Manchester, although the council denied that this was so.[117]

In considering the purpose of the charging power the council had adopted the latter of the alternative policy options canvassed above. It claimed that the fiduciary duty owed to local tax payers[118] required it to maximise its income from licensing and thus to charge what the market could bear. Evidence was adduced that the fees were reasonable: the number of street traders had increased since the fees were raised. Moreover they were within the range of fees charged by councils in other comparable districts.

On behalf of the traders it was argued that the charges were unreasonable within the meaning of the *Wednesbury* principles [119] because the decision was one no reasonable authority could have reached. The fees were too high and would have a grave impact on existing and potential traders. It was further argued that the purpose of the charging power was to promote the policy and objects of the Act [120] by encouraging a diversity of street trading including those traders who ran less profitable lines.

It was also asserted that the fees fixed by the council were tainted by a breach of the rules of natural justice in so far as the

---

[116] (1991) 89 LGR 696.
[117] *Ibid.* at pp 702, 704.
[118] Eg *Bromley BC v. GLC* [1983] 1 AC 768; *Roberts v. Hopwood* [1925] AC 578.
[119] *Supra.* n (115).
[120] See, e.g., *Padfield v. Minister of Agriculture* [1968] AC 997.

traders had not been given the opportunity to make representations before the decision was reached.

Thus the parties divided *inter alia* on the purpose power to impose fees. Each realised however, that the legitimacy of the licence fees would depend upon its purpose. This was the major issue which confronted the court and which is of significant interest to all concerned in the street trading system.

The court held that the council had no power to set fees at a level which would raise general revenue. Roch J, with whom Nolan LJ agreed, stated: [121]

"The fees charged, in my judgment, must be related to the street trading scheme operated by the district council and the costs of operating that scheme. The district council may charge such fees as they reasonably consider will cover the total cost of operating the street trading scheme or such lesser part of operating the street trading scheme as they consider reasonable. One consequence of the wording used is that, if the fees levied in the event exceed the cost of operating the scheme, the original decision will remain valid provided that it can be said that the district council reasonably considered such fees would be required to meet the total cost of operating the scheme."

Nolan L.J added that the Act was not a fiscal measure. Its policy and object was to control street trading. Para 9 (1) (the power to demand payment of a fee) merely enables "the council to charge a reasonable fee for the service which they render in granting or renewing licences and consents. Paragraph 9(2) enables the council to charge different fees to different traders, depending on the type of goods which they sell and the place where they sell them, with a view to ensuring so far as possible that the public are supplied with the right goods in the right place. But the level of fees overall must be related to the cost to the council of operating the street trading scheme." [122]

He pertinently observed that if Parliament had intended the licence to be an income producing asset the consequences would be far-reaching. The authority had a monopoly over the granting of

---

[121] (1991) 89 LGR 696, 709-10, 711, 712.
[122] *Ibid* at p 712.

licences throughout Greater Manchester and could force traders to meet the council's perceptions of what the market could bear. The implication of this would be that traders would be forced to conduct their business only in the most profitable lines.

The court decisively concluded therefore that the fee must be designed *ab initio* only to recoup the costs of the operating the code. This includes the cost of administering the licence scheme as well as the costs of prosecuting offenders. [123] The district council must assess what those costs will be and fix the fee only with the purpose of meeting those costs. An operating profit may be *intra vires*, but only if it is an unintended result; in other words it would have to be shown that it arose from an over-estimate of those costs at the time the fee was set.

This was sufficient to dispose of the case, but it may be noted that the court further held that the rules of natural justice were not normally applicable to the setting of licence fees unless a legitimate expectation of consultation could be established on the particular facts of an individual case. [124]

The decision is an important one because the limits imposed on the charging power under the general law ensure that traders henceforward should only bear the minimum burden of the cost of operating the licensing scheme. In effect the licence fee is only a means by which the council is re-imbursed for its expenses. The decision is also important because the judgments emphasised the public importance of street trading in bringing affordable commodities within reach of the less well-of. It further recognised the stimulus of competition injected by a variety of street trading.

Procedural Rules Governing the Fixing of Fees
The Schedule does not require consultation in the matter of fixing fees properly so called. Nor, as we have seen are procedural rules normally imposed under the general law. In *Ex p King* it was held that the code did not require representations from traders before the licence fees were fixed. Moreover, the applicants in that case

---

[123] But at p. 706 in *Pearce* Roch J stated that an element for prosecution costs could constitute a "charge" for services rendered to the licence-holder thereby triggering the consultation and notification procedures in para. 9 (8) even though the council is ostensibly determining a fee and not a charge.
[124] This issue is considered in Chapter 16.

lacked a legitimate expectation of being heard since there was no prior promise that a hearing would be given, nor any administrative practice of consultation prior to reaching a decision in these matters. Of course, the position might have been different had these matters been established.

As we shall see, para. 9 does require the council to abide by certain procedures before determining or varying the amount of charges properly so called. These are the charges imposed for the provision of services to traders. Of course, a single "fee" may be charged to embrace both "fees" and "charges"! This clearly complicates the question of which procedures, if any, are applicable. This is considered below.

Charges

The Scope of the Power to Charge

In this section we are principally concerned with "charges" properly so called (and not fees). The specific power to make a charge is narrowly drawn. It contemplates the recovery of reasonable charges in respect of such services as the collection of refuse, the cleansing of streets and other services rendered to the trader in his capacity as *licence-holder.* [125] Under this paragraph the council can only recover the costs of providing services rendered to the *licensed trader.* General street cleansing, which is not a service rendered specifically to any individual trader, seems to be outside the scope of this provision. [126] These general costs can be recovered through the licence *fee* . The difference between these two charging powers is that one attracts procedural rules and the other does not.

The council may only impose a *charge* properly so called on *licence-holders* and not those who trade under a consent.[127] The cost of any services rendered to consent holders can, however, be

---

[125] Para. 9 (6).

[126] *R v. Manchester City Council ex p King* (1991) 89 LGR 696, at p. 706, per Roch J.

[127] Para 9 (6), but see below.

recovered through the consent *fee* imposed under para 9 (1). [128] However, consent holders, who are normally mobile traders, are not usually the beneficiaries of such services and so no such charges would be appropriate. Nevertheless, it must not be forgotten that a consent may be so framed as to allow a consent holder to operate from a stationary position [129] in which case the trader's operation is in substance little different from that of a licence-holder. There seems to be no reason why the council should not then re-imburse itself by fixing the consent fee at the appropriate level.

Excluding consent holders from paragraph 9 (6) simply excludes them from statutory procedural protection (considered below) which imposing a charge attracts. This is consistent with the general scheme of the consent system. Thus the statutory procedural rules applicable in the fixing or variation of charges benefit only licence-holders.

However, this does not necessarily conclude the matter. If a component to reflect service costs is built into the consent fee, the rules of natural justice or fairness applicable under the general law, may require the council to allow the traders affected to make representations about an increase in charges if there were a legitimate expectation of consultation in the circumstances of the particular case. [130]

Where a charge is made for services, the code provides that the charge may be included in the licence or consent fee. Charging a single fee comprising both elements (fee properly so called and service "charge") may be less burdensome on a local authority's administration, but, as we shall see, such an approach is not without its difficulties. There is, however, no duty combine the two types of charge . [131]

---

[128] This follows from *ex p King, supra* n. (126). The costs of administering the scheme can determine what is a reasonable fee.

[129] Para. 7 (8).

[130] E.g. if a practice of consultation has arisen: *Council of Civil Service Unions v. Minister for the Civil Service* [1985] AC 374; *R v. Liverpool Corpn. ex p Liverpool Taxi Fleet Operators' Association* [1972] 2 QB 299.

[131] Para. 9 (8).

Procedural Rules

As we have seen, procedural guarantees do not normally apply to the fixing of fees. Some guarantees are, however, available where charges are imposed on licence-holders under para 9 (6).

Before charges for licence-holders can be "determined" (i.e. fixed) or varied, the council must follow the procedures laid down in paragraph 9(9)-(11). It must give licence-holders notice of its proposals and publish a notice of the proposed charges in a local newspaper circulating in their area. This notice must specify a "reasonable" period in which representations can be made. [132] Representations made within this period must be considered by the council.

The drafting of sub para (10) suggests that it is open to anyone to object: the right is not limited to actual or would-be traders. By this means, traders and others have the opportunity of influencing the council's eventual decision; they have a statutory right to be "heard", so that the council can be informed of the effect its proposals may have.

Rules Where the Licence/ Consent Fee and Charges are Combined

It is interesting that the power to charge for services rendered to licence-holders is limited by procedural safeguards for traders, whereas the power to fix the licence or consent *fee* is not normally so limited. [133] The reason why this should be so is not immediately obvious. It does, however give rise to a difficulty. What procedure, if any, applies where the service charges and licence fee are charged as one single fee stated to be the licence or consent fee? Do the procedural rules apply? One possibility is that they do not because, on its face, this is a licence/ consent fee. (i.e. charged under para 9 (1). On the other hand, it can be argued that, because this fee includes an element for service charges which do attract procedural rules, these rules should also apply to the global fee.

In deciding which rules apply, the position of those holding street trading consents is most easily stated. Consent-holders are excluded from para. 9 (6) and so do not qualify for the procedural

---

[132] Para. 9 (10).
[133] See (123) above.

safeguards offered by para. 9 (9). Where seeking to recover the cost
of any services [134] provided to consent holders, the local authority
does not have to notify them, nor publish a notice of its proposals;
nor is it obliged under the statute to consider any representations
they make. Thus, subject to the general law, there is no statutory
duty to consult traders when combining the charges in the case of
consent holders.

The position of licence-holders is more complicated. They do
qualify for the procedural safeguards where charges are fixed or
determined in para. 9 (9). In *Ex p. King*, Roch J considered that
fixing a single fee which embraces an element for service charges
may mean that the council are obliged to follow the consultation
and notification procedures in paragraph 9 (9), (10) and to consider
representations made (9(11)). He stated:

"What considerations do local authorities have to take into
account when determining the level of fees....(for the grant or
renewal of a licence or consent)? The local authority are no longer
confined to the cost of issuing licences. They may take into account
the costs which they will incur in operating the street trading
scheme, including the prosecution of those who trade in the streets
without licences. However, if they take into account those costs,
they may need to comply with the provisions of paragraph 9(8),
(9), (10) and (11) (the consultation and notification requirements) as
the prosecution of those who trade in the streets without street
trading licences or consents may be services rendered by the local
authority to street traders in their capacity as licence-holders
within the meaning of paragraph 9(6)." [135]

This means that where the council builds in an element for such
costs, the licence-holders would have to give notice of the proposed
charges to licence-holders, invite them to make representations
within a reasonable period and ensure that a notice of the proposal
is published in a local newspaper 9 (9)-(11). The council would be
bound to consider any representations made by licence-holders under
this procedure. This procedure is also mandatory where the amount
of any charge is varied.

---

[134] And these may be general or specific. Discussed below.
[135] (1991) 89 LGR 696, 710.

In *Ex p King* the City Council, which imposed a single licence fee, indicated that this fee included amounts to reflect the costs of enforcement, administration and street cleansing. This meant that part of the fee went to "operational services" as a payment towards general street cleansing and litter collection rather than specific refuse collection from individual traders. Roch J considered that this evidence *prima facie* indicated a breach of the procedural rules. [136] When the matter was further investigated, however, it was revealed that it was a condition of each licence that the individual licensee was responsible for the removal of waste and litter generated by his stall and so the general charges were not made for services rendered to the licence-holder in his capacity as a licence-holder under para 9 (6). In other words, there is a distinction between charges for general street cleansing (which do not fall within para 9 (6) and do not attract the procedural rules) and specific refuse collection by the authority from the individual trader (which does fall within para 9 (6) and does attract those rules). Since the Council had only sought to recover "general" service charges they were not obliged to follow the notification and consultation procedures established in sub paragraphs (9)-(11). In other words, these could be recovered as a "pure" fee.

Conclusion

If the licence fee is to include a "charge" element to reflect the uplift in operational costs caused by street trading generally, the authority need not consult traders before fixing or varying the fee. This would be, for example, where traders are individually obliged under the terms of their licences to remove waste and litter. Refuse collection is not then provided to them individually in their capacity as licence-holders any charge may be an element in the "fee" properly so called. If, on the other hand, the council provides a service to licence-holders specifically and in their capacity as licence holder and builds a charge for this into the licence fee, the notification and consultation provisions do seem to apply. They also apply it seems, where an element to recover prosecution and enforcement costs is included in the "fees" charged because this may

---

[136] *Ibid.* at p. 706.

be a service rendered by the local authority to street traders in their capacity as street traders. [137]

6. Offences

Criminal sanctions are available under paragraph 10 to punish street traders in breach of obligations imposed by the code. Accordingly, it is an offence

(i)   to engage in street trading in any prohibited street;

(ii)   to engage in street trading in either a licence street or a consent street unless authorised to do so by the local authority under the provisions of the code.

(iii) to contravene any of the principal terms of a street trading licence.

There is a similar provision where a consent-holder who breaches any conditions included in a consent relating to the times and place in which trading is to be permitted.

It is also an offence to trade as a consent holder in the permitted street but to do so (a) from a stationary van, cart, barrow or other vehicle; or (b) from a portable stall unless permission has been granted to do so.[138] This provision exists because consents are normally granted to itinerant traders and licences to those who normally trade from a fixed position. A consent-holder who, in the absence of express permission, sought to trade from a stationary position would normally commit an offence under the Act.

The trader who knowingly makes a false statement in support of a licence application also commits an offence under paragraph 10.

---

[137] It is, however, possible to take objection to this interpretation. Prosecution and enforcement is surely intended to benefit the public generally and should not be regarded merely as a service for the benefit of street traders.

[138] Under para. 7 (8).

Defence

A trader charged with an offence under the Code has a defence if he can prove that he took "all reasonable precautions and exercised all due diligence to avoid commission of the offence." [139] These words have been held to import a duty to take reasonable care. [140] In this context, it will often be important for the trader to demonstrate that he has taken appropriate steps to comply with the requirements of the code. A trader who has done so, but who has been improperly advised by the relevant authorities should, depending on the facts, be able to rely upon the defence. It must be stated, however, that the defence is narrowly construed. In *Watson v. Malloy* , [141] for example, it was held not to be available to a trader who sought to rely upon the pedlar's exemption whose application to renew his certificate had yet to be determined. Having held a certificate for many years, the trader had no reason to believe that the application would be refused. Nevertheless, Hutchison J regarded the defence in such circumstances as "unsustainable". He added that it was not as if the defendant had sought legal advice on the point. It is open to speculation whether this would have made any difference, however. [142]

Unlike the London Local Authorities Act 1990 [143] which governs street trading in the London boroughs, the code does not confer a power on either the council or the police to seize goods offered for sale as evidence of an offence under the Act.

It should be noted, however, that a highway authority has a common law power to remove obstructions upon the highway, [144] and so may remove stalls or trestles or any other structures used for trading which cause an unlawful obstruction. These and the powers to remove obstructions under the Highways Act 1980 have already been noted. [145]

---

[139] Para. 10 (2).

[140] Under the Hague Rules: *Riverstone Meat Co. Pty v. Lancashire Shipping Co. Ltd.* [1960] 1 QB 536, 581.

[141] [1988] 1 WLR 1024.

[142] *Cambridgeshire and Isle of Ely County Council v. Rust* [1972] 2 QB 426.

[143] Section 38 (4).

[144] *Bagshaw v. Buxton Local Board of Health* [1875] 1 ChD 220; *Reynolds v. Presteigne UDC* [1896] 1 QB 604, as well as under s.130 of the Highways Act 1980.

[145] See Ch.1.

CHAPTER 11

STREET TRADING IN THE LONDON BOROUGHS

1. Introduction

Street trading in the Metropolitan area is separately regulated from that in other parts of England and Wales. Unfortunately, within the Metropolitan area there is no single code of rules governing street trading. Trading in the London boroughs is regulated separately from that in the City of London. With one exception [1] the boroughs now participate in the adoptive scheme under Part III of the London Local Authorities Act 1990; the City under the City of London (Various Powers) Act 1987.

Street trading in the London boroughs is regulated under Part III of the London Local Authorities Act 1990. This is an adoptive measure which furnishes a scheme for the regulation of street trading as defined by the Act in the areas of participating boroughs. The provisions of Part III came into effect on "the appointed day" which was the day fixed by resolution by the borough council for the introduction in its area of the provisions of Part III. [2]

The main purpose of the 1990 Act was to provide a simpler licensing framework than that which existed previously [3] and to bring certain matters within the regulatory framework which had previously been outside it. [4]

---

[1] Camden intends to adopt the scheme in early 1994. Until it does so, its power remain subject to the London County Council (General Powers) Act 1947.

[2] Section 3 (1).

[3] Under the London County Council (General Powers) Act 1947.

[4] HC Debs, 6th series, vol 165, col 1117, 25th January 1990.

The general scheme of the 1990 Act is to impose controls on street trading within the participating borough. "Street trading" is defined as "the selling or exposing or offering for sale of any article (including a living thing) or the supplying or offering to supply any service in a street for gain or reward". [5] Where any article is displayed in the street it is presumed to have been offered or exposed for sale. [6] It is to be noted that the definition of street trading is wider than that which applies under the street trading code and in the City under the City of London (Various Powers) Act 1987 because the 1990 Act extends to services and the latter measures do not. This inclusion of services was no doubt intended to control the activities of such individuals as street photographers. These had been held to be exempt from the 1947 Act which only applied to the sales of "articles or things" in the street. [7] This means that the London boroughs have power to regulate the provision of services on the streets which other licensing authorities lack.

"Street" is only partially defined in s.21. It includes "(a) any road or footway; (b) any other area not being within permanently enclosed premises, within 7 metres of any road or footway to which the public have access without payment; (c) any part of such roadway or footway or area; (d) any part of any housing development provided or maintained by a local authority under Part II of the Housing Act 1985".

Controls available under the 1990 Act operate at two levels. First, the Act enables the borough to create "zones" in which street trading can be permitted. Outside these "zones", non-exempt street trading is a criminal offence. [8]

Controls also operate in the "zones" in which street trading is possible. Within these areas, a licensing scheme operates so that the borough can control what trading takes place there and who may undertake it. In other words, the designation of a street as a licence street confers no right upon an individual trader to indulge

---

[5] Subject to the exceptions in s 21 (2).
[6] Section 38 (2).
[7] *Newman v. Lipman* (1950) 49 LGR 457.
[8] Section 38.

in street trading. His business is normally subject to the discretionary licensing powers of the borough. [9]

Exempt kinds of trading fall outside the scope of the Act and are therefore immune from its controls. Such trading may be conducted lawfully without a licence. One consequence of this is that a decision not to "zone" an area is not absolutely effective to control street trading. Exempted street traders may still operate in areas of the borough which the council regards as inappropriate for other street trading purposes.

2. Trading Immune From the Controls of the 1990 Act

The following kinds of trading activity are not deemed to be "street trading" and so are immune from the controls imposed by the 1990 Act. Exempted trading may be conducted lawfully without a street trading licence and beyond streets designated as "licence streets". The burden of proof rests upon the trader to show that his activities fall within one of these categories. [10]

(i) Pedlars and Costermongers

Certificated pedlars are peripatetic traders. The designers of the Act presumably thought it inappropriate to confine such traders to specific areas or zones, but this is not an uncontroversial matter. "Hawking" activities can have considerable nuisance effects and there are arguments which favour placing pedlars within the controls of the licensing scheme. Who may qualify as a pedlar has already been considered in relation to the street trading code [11] where the point has been subject to judicial decision.

No special saving is made for costermongers within the 1990 Act although some privileges remain. Under the Metropolitan Streets Act 1867, s.6 it is an offence, within a six mile radius of Charing Cross, to place goods or articles on any part of a street to the obstruction or inconvenience of other highway users. This prohibition is lifted from costermongers and itinerant traders by

---

[9] Sections 23 and 38.
[10] Magistrates' Court Act 1980, s.101.
[11] *Supra* p. 180 *et seq.*

the Metropolitan Streets Act Amendment Act 1867 so long as they carry on their business in accordance with regulations made by the Commissioner of Police. This saving benefits only itinerant costermongers and not those who trade from stalls which are stationary during trading hours. [12] An itinerant costermonger holding a pedlar's certificate and acting as a pedlar could, however, fall within the saving for pedlars in the 1990 Act.

(ii) Markets and Fairs

Trading in lawful street markets and fairs is outside the licensing scheme. These markets are those created by grant, presumed grant or acquired or established by statute or order. [13] A trader may claim the benefit of this exception provided the market right subsists in the site in which he trades. A local authority market owner may only validly restrict the extent of market rights by resolution.[14]

Only trading in *lawful* markets and fairs is exempt, and is further restricted to traders who operate with the written authority of the person entitled to conduct the market or who have paid toll in respect of any sales made or stalls occupied in the market. This means that although at common law all members of the public may buy and sell in a market, [15] casual traders who do not have a stall may be required to seek a licence.

Traders in "unofficial" street markets enjoy no such protection. Those trading from a pitch or stand may be required to seek a licence; other peripatetic traders in the market may also be required to seek a pedlar's certificate. [16] That the rights of the trader should depend upon the origins of the market is unsatisfactory.

The limits placed on the saving for markets and fairs means that such events as "collectors fairs", car boot sales, customary Sunday street markets and similar events are all brought within

---

[12] *Baker v. Bradley* (1910) 74 JP 341.

[13] Section 41.

[14] *Jones v. Lewis* [1989] The Times, June 12th.

[15] Eg *A G v. Horner No. 2* [1913] 2 Ch 140; *Sevenoaks BC v. Pattullo & Vinson* [1984] 1 All ER 544,551.

[16] Pedlar's Act 1871, s.23; *Benajmin v. Andrews* (1858) 5 CBNS 299.

the licensing structure if they take place in a street falling within the meaning of the 1990 Act. This is, of course, without prejudice to other forms of control such as those under the Town and Country Planning Act 1990.

(iii) Miscellaneous Exceptions

The other forms of trading outside this licensing structure are diverse but follow closely the exclusions from the street trading code of the Local Government (Miscellaneous Provisions) Act 1982.

(a)   The first exception concerns trading in a trunk road picnic area provided by the Secretary of State under s. 112 of the Highways Act 1980. This also applies under the street trading code and has been considered in that context.

(b)   News-vendors are also exempt perhaps because of the social importance of promoting the free flow of information. However such trading is subject to restrictions. The news vendor must confine his trading only to newspapers or periodicals. If he wishes to offer other commodities he must seek a licence. To benefit from the saving he or she must either trade without a "receptacle" or, if with one, it must not exceed the dimensions established under s 21 (2) (d). [17] The receptacle or stand must not cause undue interference or inconvenience to persons using the street. This suggests that some interference is permissible if it is reasonable in the circumstances.

(c)   Also exempt from the need to obtain a licence are traders concerned (i) in the selling of articles or things to occupiers of premises adjoining any street, or (ii) offering or exposing them for sale from a vehicle which is used only for the regular delivery of milk or other perishable goods to those persons.

This provision is clearly aimed at protecting delivery roundsmen but is poorly drafted. A similar exemption was at issue in *London Borough of Islington v. Panico* [17a] were it was held to

---

[17] Not more than 1 metre in either length or width or 2 metres in height, and the stand should not occupy a ground area exceeding 0.25 of a square metre.
[17a] (1973) 72 LGR 51.

require a trader to show, before he made a sale, that he had customers in the street with whom, he was already carrying on business as a trader. However, if this were established, the trader did not have to show that the purchaser was *de facto* an occupier of premises in the street.

(d)   Under Part VIIA of the Highways Act 1980, s.115 a council has power to place structures such as booths or kiosks on a highway for the purpose *inter alia* of providing a service to the public and may also licence others to do so, often in return for a fee. Where this is done, street trading for the purposes of the 1990 Act is not deemed to take place.

(e)   Part VIIA of the Highways Act also empowers local authorities to provide and operate facilities for recreation or refreshment on a highway. For the reasons outlined in (d) above the operation of these facilities is not deemed to be street trading and falls outside the 1990 Act.

(f)   Charitable street collections, and the sale of articles for charitable purposes are also not deemed to be street trading if what is done is authorised by regulations made under section 5 of the Police, Factories, &c (Miscellaneous Provisions) Act 1916.

(g)   Also outside the scope of the 1990 Act is trading on the highway which is subject to a control order under section 7 of the Local Government (Miscellaneous Provisions Act) 1976 is in force. Trading to which the control order does not apply is, however, within the scheme of the 1990 Act and must be licensed. [18]

(h)   Trading on private land adjoining a street to which the public have access is also exempt if conducted by the owner or occupier of that land or by a *bona fide* employee of such a person. This provision is narrowly construed. It did not benefit a trader, who acting with permission, had set up trestle tables on the forecourt of retail premises and sold T-shirts because, as a licensee, having no power to exclude anyone from the area in which he traded, he was

---

[18]Controls orders have been considered *supra* at p. 22-23.

not the "occupier" of the land. Much will depend on the facts of each case, however, because it was held that, at least in some circumstances, licensees could be in occupation of the land. [19]

3. Designating "Licence Streets"

The Effect of Street Designation

A major cornerstone of the legislation is the power conferred on borough council to create "zones" in which street trading is permissible. Zoning works both positively and negatively. This means that the borough council may *authorise* street trading in certain streets or, in the case of ice cream trading, may designate streets as "prohibited" streets in which trading is not permitted. [20]

The extent to which street trading (apart from the sale of ice cream) becomes lawful therefore depends on the decision of the borough council to designate streets as "licence streets". If a borough council decides to permit street trading in its area, it must pass a "designating resolution" specifying which streets are to be "licence streets". It is in respect of pitches or sites in these streets that traders will be able to obtain street trading licences and thus trade lawfully. In so far as streets remain undesignated, it will not be lawful to trade there [21] unless the trading takes place in a lawful market or otherwise falls outside the scope of the Act.

The power to designate streets is a discretionary one. If the borough council decides to exercise this power, it may also specify the classes of goods or services in which trading in that street will be permitted. Designation may take place by resolution but is subject to certain procedural controls which are considered below.

Where trading had been permitted in certain streets under earlier legislation, these streets are deemed to have been designated as licence streets for the purposes of the 1990 Act.

---

[19] *O 'Gorman v. Brent LBC* [1993] The Times, May 20th.
[20] Section 37.
[21] Section 38.

Procedure

Before a designating resolution is passed the borough council must satisfy various consultation, consent and notification requirements.[22] The Metropolitan Police Commissioner has a right to be consulted about any proposed designation, although the Act does not make clear how much weight should be attached to his advice. If, having obtained such advice, it is decided to proceed to designation, the council must publish a notice containing a draft of the resolution in a local newspaper inviting representations to be made within not less than 28 days. A copy of the notice must also be served on the highway authority. The council is under a duty to consider any representations made to it. [23]

Under the Act, certain streets cannot be designated without the consent of other bodies. For example, if the street is one maintained by a highway authority, its prior consent must be obtained. A similar rule applies where the street is owned or maintained by one of the "relevant corporations" listed in the Act which includes such bodies as London Regional Transport and the British Railways Board. [24]

If a designating resolution is passed, a notice to this effect must be published in a local newspaper in two consecutive weeks, the first notice appearing not less than 28 days before the designation comes into force. [25] Once passed, a resolution takes effect on the day specified within it which cannot be less than one month after the resolution is passed.

The rules discussed above are not confined to the designation of the street; they apply equally where the designating resolution is intended to regulate the classes of goods in which trading is permitted and to the procedure governing the regulation of ice cream trading under s.37.

---

[22] Section 24. The consequence of failing to do so is considered in Ch. 16.
[23] Section 24(8).
[24] Section 24 (6).
[25] Section 24 (10)-(11).

Appeals in Relation to Designations

There is no right of appeal against a decision of the council to designate a street as a licence street. This would not, of course, prevent a challenge by way of judicial review to a designation which was tainted by illegality, irrationality or procedural impropriety. [26]

Appeal rights are, however, granted to any person aggrieved[27] where an existing designation is rescinded or varied, [28] and also in respect of a resolution specifying the types of goods in which trading may take place. An appeal lies to the Secretary of State whose decision is final. The Act does not prescribe a time limit within which the appeal must be brought.

4. Applications for a Street Trading Licence and the Renewal of Licences

Application Cases

Applications for a licence and for the renewal of an existing licence are subject to detailed regulations which entitle the borough council to seek information about the trader, the desired site, and the goods in which he or she wishes to trade. The council has a discretionary power to seek other information in so far as it is reasonable to do so. [29] An applicant who knowingly makes a false statement in support of the application commits an offence punishable by a fine not exceeding level 3 on the standard scale. [30] The application should be accompanied by two photographs of the applicant one of which will be attached to the licence if the application is successful. [31] The licence must be produced on demand

---

[26] *Council of Civil Service Unions v. Minister for Civil Service* [1985] AC 374.

[27] *Supra* p. 367 *et seq.*

[28] Section 30 (11) (a).

[29] Section 25 (2) (e).

[30] Section 34 (2).

[31] Section 25 (3).

to an authorised officer of the borough council. Failure to do so constitutes an offence. [32]

The Power to Grant a Licence
In contrast to previous enactments, the 1990 Act creates a presumption that a street trading licence will be granted. [33] This is important since it signals the recognition of the importance and popularity of street trading in general and in particular in the Capital. [34] The borough's discretion to grant or to refuse a licence is limited. There are cases in which the grant of a licence is prohibited, others in which its *prima facie* mandatory, and yet others in which the local authority may consider the application in its (limited) discretion.

Where the Grant of a Licence is Prohibited
Under s.25 (4) it is prohibited to award a licence (other than a temporary licence) in respect of a street which has not been designated as a licence street, or if the goods or services which it is proposed to offer fall outside the scope of the designating resolution. Nor is it possible to award a licence to a person under 17 years of age. Other prohibitions prevent the grant of a licence for ice cream trading where the trader is already licensed to trade at a corresponding day or time in any other licence street unless the application is made by a company or a partnership. Unincorporated associations are not to be granted licences to trade in ice cream. [35]

Perhaps the most important limitation on the power to license is that concerning available space. The Act prevents a borough council from granting a licence unless they are satisfied that there is enough space in the street for trading to take place without causing undue interference with the flow of pedestrians or other traffic. [36] This suggests that some obstruction is no bar to licensing further street trading. When this provision is read alongside the *prima facie* duty to grant a street trading licence, it seems that the

---

[32] Section 34. An offence is punishable by a fine not exceeding level 3 on the standard scale.
[33] Section 25 (5).
[34] *Supra* n. (4), col 1112 *et seq.*
[35] Section 25 (4).
[36] Section 25 (4) (b).

council must be prepared to tolerate some interference with the right of passage along the highway. In practice, however, much will turn on the question of what is an "undue" interference". This is an uncertain matter, and a refusal on these grounds will almost certainly be difficult to challenge.

Mandatory Cases
When the scheme under the 1990 Act is first adopted, traders who held licences under the previous regime in respect of streets which thereafter become licence streets, have a right to a licence if they apply within two months of the date the street becomes a licence street.[37]

Discretionary Cases
If the application does not fall into a either a "prohibited" or a "mandatory" category, the borough may consider the application in its discretion provided, of course, the council is satisfied that there is enough space in the street without causing undue interference to traffic. But the discretion is limited because the application can only be refused on certain grounds; and under s.25 (9) the borough council is under a duty to give preference to traders who, before the appointed day, had a licence to trade in a street which under the Act is not to be a licence street. Of more enduring significance is the limitation which benefits traders who do not reside in the borough. Section 29 (3) provides that the borough council cannot refuse to grant a licence on the sole ground that the applicant resides outside the borough. A further limitation on the borough's discretion requires it to treat all applicants seeking to carry on ice cream trading on an equal footing, and not, in particular, to discriminate between individuals, partnerships and companies. [38]

In exercising their discretion, councils cannot decide who should receive a licence on a "first come first served" basis. The applications must considered on their merits.[39]

If the application is not within one of the prohibited categories mentioned above, the borough council shall grant the application unless they consider that the application should be refused on one

---

[37] Section 25 (8).
[38] Section 25 (10).
[39] *Perilly v. Tower Hamlets LBC* (1970) 70 LGR 474.

of the grounds listed in 25 (6). This in effect creates a presumption in favour of the grant of a street trading licence. The grounds for refusal in s 25 (6) are essentially as follows:

(a)   *That there are enough traders offering the goods in which the applicant seeks to trade either in the street in which he or she seeks to trade or in any street adjoining this street;*

(b)   *that the applicant, whether by reason of misconduct, or any other sufficient reason is unsuitable to hold the licence.* A trader may be unsuitable if he has repeatedly committed breaches of the criminal law during trading (if an existing licence holder) or during the currency of an earlier licence (if applying for a licence or seeking renewal). It seems that his conduct must show an intention to disregard the law; [40]

(c)   *that the applicant without reasonable excuse failed personally to avail himself fully of a previous street trading licence.* If the borough council finds that the applicant has failed to fulfil this criterion, or that the goods in which the trader seeks to trade are sufficiently available (i.e. a reason under (a)), they may nevertheless grant a licence to trade on fewer days or during shorter hours than those sought by the applicant or to limit the range of goods in which he is permitted to trade. In such a case the trader or any other person aggrieved by the decision may appeal to the local magistrates under s.30 (1) (b) which may make such order as it thinks fit;

(d)   *that a previous licence has been revoked, or could have been revoked, for non-payment of any fees or charges due to be paid to the borough council under the licence;*

(e)   *that the applicant has not specified suitable premises for storage "of any receptacles" or perishable goods in which he proposes to trade when street trading is not taking place;*

---

[40] *Manchester Corporation v. Penson* (1969) 68 LGR 225.

(f)   *that the application is for the grant (but not the renewal of a licence) AND the only space available for trading in that street is in front of a shop which itself trades in the goods specified in the, trader's application.* [41] Similarly, the grant (but not the renewal of a licence) may be refused where the only available space is within the curtilage of a shop not owned by the applicant trader. [42] These provisions are clearly intended to preserve the interests of the shop keepers who are often most forthright in their resistance to street trading from perceived rivals. Nevertheless, such interests do not prevent the renewal of a trading licence in such circumstances.

Temporary Licences

A borough council also has a discretionary power to grant temporary licences under s.31. Such a licence may take effect only for a day or such other period as the borough council determines and this is to be specified in the licence. A temporary licence should be in a similar form and granted on terms similar to those in non-temporary street trading licences, although the council has a power to stipulate such other terms as it considers appropriate in the circumstances.

Temporary licences can be issued when an existing street trading licence holder is not exercising his right to trade. The Act enables his pitch to be granted to another trader on a temporary basis. Such a trading arrangement is a precarious one for the temporary licensee since the temporary licence must include a condition that the right to trade shall cease if the other trader wishes to resume his rights during the currency of his own licence. To do this he must give due notice. This is merely twenty four hours' notice except in cases where the trader has not exercised his rights for a period of at least 14 days. In such a case he must give 7 days notice of his intention to resume trading.

Renewal Cases

Where a trader seeks to renew a licence he or she should normally apply between two and three months before the expiry of the existing licence, although the borough council has a power to entertain late applications for renewal for all licences (except

---

[41] Section 25 (6) (f).
[42] Section 25 (6) (g).

temporary licences) if they consider it reasonable in the circumstances to do so.

The existing licence remains valid for certain periods [43] during the renewal process. The length of this period is determined by the council's decision and whether the trader has appeal rights.

If the council decides to renew the licence on the same terms, the old licence continues until the council actually grants the new licence. If the council refuses to renew the licence, or decides to grant it on different terms from those previously enjoyed, the old licence continues in force until the time limit for appeal has passed or until any appeal has been determined.

These rules apply, however, only where the applicant has a right of appeal and no such right is conferred where the new licence is offered on "standard" conditions different from those in the old licence. [44] The old licence remains in force until the council grants the licence subject to these conditions. [45]

Procedural Safeguards

Representations
If a borough council proposes not to grant or renew a licence on the above s.25 (6) grounds, or if it decides to exercise its power to vary or revoke an existing licence [46] it must give the applicant or licence holder, as the case may be, at least 21 days' notice in writing that it proposes to do so and must state what its objections are. It cannot decide the matter until the period for objections stated in the notice has expired.

The applicant must be given an opportunity to make representations by appearing before the body responsible for the ultimate decision, whether it be the relevant committee, sub-committee, or officer. The council has a duty to consider any representations made by the applicant.

---

[43] Section 30 (8).
[44] *Infra.*
[45] Section 30 and Section 25 (6) (a)-(e).
[46] *Infra.*

Appeals

Rights of appeal under s.30 arise for any "person aggrieved" by a decision not to grant or not to renew a licence on grounds (a)-(e) in s. 25 (6) above. There is no right of appeal where the application (but not a renewal) is refused because the site sought is in front of a shop trading in similar goods, or where the application relates to a site within the curtilage of a shop not owned by the applicant. An appeal lies to the local magistrates and beyond that (at the instance of either the trader or the borough) to the Crown Court under s. 30 (4). Either court may make such order as it thinks fit.[47]

The appeal must be brought within 21 days of the notification of the council's decision.

5. Duration and Scope of Licences

Should a licence be granted, it will be valid for any period up to a maximum of three years.

Conditions

Licences may be granted subject to conditions. Breach of any condition constitutes an offence punishable by a fine not exceeding level 3 on the standard scale. Persistent breaches may also constitute grounds for revocation of the licence under s.28 (1) (h).

The conditions imposed may be varied according to the rules in s. 27 (1). These prescribe that if either the council or the licence holder wish to vary these conditions, this may be done on the 1st January in any year during the currency of the licence, or upon its renewal. Conditions may be varied at any other time at the request of the licence holder [48] but not the borough council.

Under s.27 (3) the borough council is empowered to make regulations prescribing standard conditions upon which licences are granted, and under sub-sect (8) may specify additional conditions in so far as it appears reasonable to them to do so in any individual case.

---

[47] Section 30 (5).
[48] Subject to the borough's discretion.

There is an important difference between standard and non-standard conditions since a right of appeal only entitles an aggrieved applicant to appeal to the magistrates court against the imposition of "additional" conditions and not the standard ones. An appeal against standard conditions lies to the Secretary of State. This is considered further below.

The power to impose both standard and "additional" conditions is, of course, limited by the general principles of Administrative law. Conditions must, for example relate to the control and organisation of the proposed street trading rather than to other unrelated matters. [49] Conditions which go beyond the control and regulation of street trading may be ultra vires and void.

Section 27 (7) stipulates that the standard conditions shall so far as is reasonable include conditions relating to the location in which trading is to take place, the goods which may be offered for sale, as well as the time at which trading may take place. They shall also specify the nature of any "receptacle" and number of receptacles used in by the trader, the arrangements for the keeping of receptacles used for storage or for perishable goods, and regulate the deposit and removal of refuse. An important, but poorly drafted provision in para (h), requires that a standard condition should require a trader to commence trading by a certain time on any day or forfeit his right to trade. The intention seems to be to enable another trader to take his place on that day, but the language of the paragraph is not transparent.

Appeals Against Conditions
Where "non-standard" conditions are attached to the licence, any trader or other person aggrieved may appeal to the local magistrates who may make such order as they think fit. [50] In such a case, the appeal must be brought within 21 days of the notification of the council's decision.

In the case of standard conditions the person aggrieved may appeal to the Secretary of State whose decision is final. No time limit for such an appeal is prescribed in s.30.[51]

---

[49] *Mixnam's Properties Ltd. v. Chertsey UDC* [1965] AC 735.

[50] Section 30 (1) (c).

[51] Section 30 (11).

6. Licensing Fees and Other Charges

A borough council may charge fees, subject to statutory limits, for the grant or renewal of a street trading licence, including a temporary licence. A fee may also be imposed for any change in the conditions on which an existing licence is held where this change is made at the request of the trader concerned. [52]

The level at which charges are set for street trading licences can produce conflict between the local authority, the street traders and the local shop-keepers. What fees and charges are set is normally a matter for the discretion of the local authority and there is often little guidance within the scheme of regulation as to how the discretion is to be exercised. This problem has, however, been addressed by the 1990 Act which limits the discretion of the borough council to decide on the level of fees and charges.

As in the street trading code, the 1990 Act distinguishes the cost of a licence- a licence "fee"- from the cost to the trader of services provided by the council- the "charges".

Charges

In addition to a fee for the licence the borough council may make further charges in order to recover the costs of providing:

(a)   any refuse collection and disposal service provided to the licence holders;

(b)   street cleansing in so far as the need for this is attributable to street trading.

(c)   reasonable administrative costs incurred in the administration of the system of regulation of street trading;

(d)   the costs of enforcing the street trading regulations.

---

[52] Section 32.

Charges for these services may be incorporated into the licence fee. The borough is under no duty to levy two separate charges, but may do so in its discretion.

The Criteria to be Employed in Setting Fees and Charges

Fees

Although the borough council has a discretion in the matter of fees, it must fix the amount according to criteria. By this means, the borough is denied the right to use the licensing system to raise revenue generally.

The criteria which the borough is entitled to consider are established in s.31 (1) and limit it to raising an income from licensing which is sufficient in aggregate to cover in whole or in part the reasonable administrative costs of operating the regulatory scheme. The level of fees can also take into account the costs incurred by the borough in connection with their functions under the 1990 Act but only in so far as these costs have not been recovered by other means.

The licence fee may be recovered in instalments.

Charges

The borough council may impose charges for the services it provides street traders only in so far as these charges are sufficient in the aggregate taking one year with another to recover the reasonable cost of providing the services and only in so far as those costs are not otherwise recovered.

Procedures

It is only in respect of "charges" that certain procedural rights under s.32 arise. Traders have no statutory right to be consulted nor to make representations before licence fees are fixed. Nor is it likely that such a right will normally arise under the general law since the Act has conferred procedural rights in respect of fixing service charges but expressly excluded these in respect of licensing fees. [53] This is not to say that procedural rights in relation to the fixing or varying of licensing fees can never be acquired under the general law. If, as a matter of practice, a borough council normally consulted traders before establishing or varying licensing fees, this may give rise to a legitimate expectation which would entitle the trades to be consulted as a matter of law. A failure to consult could amount to acting unfairly. The subsequent decision to vary the charges would then be *ultra vires* and void. [54]

Before setting the charges for services, traders have a right to be notified of the council's proposals and to make representations about them. Once a decision is reached the council must give notice of the charges in a local newspaper.

Before the council reaches a decision to fix or to vary charges it is under a duty to notify the existing licensed street traders of its proposals. Alternatively, the notice may be given to any body which represents those traders. In addition, notice of the proposals should be placed in a local newspaper. [55]

The notice must specify a period of not less than 28 days from the date of publication of the newspaper within which written representations by or on behalf of street traders concerning the proposed charges can be submitted to the borough council. These must be taken into account before a final decision in the matter is reached.[56]

Once the level of charges is decided, similar notice and publicity requirements operate: traders must be notified of the charges and a notice must be published in a local newspaper. [57]

Appeals

Any person aggrieved by the amount of the licence fee or service charge may appeal to the Secretary of State whose decision is

---

[53] *R v. Manchester City Council ex p King* (1991) 89 LGR 696, although this decision was reached under the terms of the street trading code: Local Government (Miscellaneous Provisions) Act 1982, s.3, sch 4.

[54] See further Ch. 17, especially p. 303 *et seq.*

[55] Section 32 (7).

[56] Section 32 (7)-(9).

[57] Section 32 (10).

stated to be final. [58] No time limit is laid down governing such appeals.

7. Revocation or Variation of Licences

Revocation

A borough council has a discretionary power to revoke a street trading licence. Before doing so it must be satisfied that one of the grounds in s.28 (1) can be established.
These are:

(a)   that circumstances have arisen such that there is insufficient space for the trader to continue to trade without undue interference to the public's right of passage;

(b)   that the trader is trading in an unauthorised class of goods or services.

(c)   the licence holder has without reasonable excuse failed to avail himself of the benefits of the licence. This is considered below.

(d)   the licence holder is on account of misconduct or any other sufficient reason unsuitable to hold the licence; or

(e)   that since the grant or renewal of the licence, the trader has for a period of four weeks or more failed to pay fees or charges due under the licence, or other charges authorised under the Act.

(f)   that since the grant or renewal of the licence the trader has not made adequate storage provision for the receptacles used by him for trading or for any perishable goods in which he trades when trading does not take place; or

---

[58] Section 30 (11).

(g)   that since the grant or renewal of the licence the trader has persistently failed to remove to a place of storage the receptacles used by him for trading; or

(h)   that the licence holder has persistently failed to comply with a condition of his licence.

Trading Personally
A street trading licence may be revoked under s.28 (1) (c) if the licence-holder is an individual who has without reasonable excuse personally failed fully to avail himself of his licence. The inclusion of the word "personally" contrasts with the provision under the street trading code which merely states that revocation is possible if the licence-holder has without reasonable excuse failed to avail himself of the licence...." [59] The inclusion of the word "personally" in s. 28 is arguably *ex abundante cautela* and seems to place beyond doubt that the licence enables the licensee personally to operate as a street trader. This means that the trader who is an individual is under a duty personally to trade. Revocation may only be avoided if the trader is actively concerned with the running of the stall. This means that the licence-holder cannot withdraw from the day to day operation of the business delegating this responsibility to an employee. He cannot rely on employees to operate the stall on his behalf and retain for himself the profits generated. Personal responsibility for the stall is not enough; there must be a personal supervision of it. This responsibility cannot be delegated because it has been judicially stated that the local authority cannot properly control street trading if the licensees are absentees. [60]

Section 36 provides, however, that the licensee may employ any other person to assist him in trading.

The trader-employer is not required to be present throughout all hours of trading and it may not be possible for him to be present if he is obtaining stock from a distant source. If, however, the licence-holder is temporarily absent from the stall, and the

[59] Local Government (Miscellaneous Provisions) Act 1982, Sch 4, para 5 (1) (d).

[60] *R v. Southwark Crown Court ex p Watts* [1992] C.O.D. 140. This decision was reached under the provisions of the London County Council (General Powers) Act 1947 which, although drafted in different terms, is probably to similar effect.

employee fails to comply with any condition contained in the street trading the licence holder is deemed to be responsible for such failure.

Variation

If grounds for revocation exist under any of the first three criteria, ((a)- (c) above) the council may instead vary the terms upon which the licence is held by attaching further conditions to the licence. These conditions may either (a) reduce the number of days or the times of day during which trading may be conducted; or (b) require the trader to relocate either to a different licence street, or to a different pitch or site; or (c) restrict the range of goods and services which the trader may offer for sale.

Variation of licences is also possible in other circumstances which have already been considered. [61]

Procedure

The borough council cannot revoke or vary the terms of a street trading licence unless the trader has received no less than 21 days notice in writing of the council's proposals. The notice must specify the grounds upon which the revocation or variation is proposed. The trader must also be allowed the opportunity of appearing before the body which has the responsibility for decision in the matter. [62] These provisions give statutory form to the common law right to be heard before a licence is revoked or varied. Arguably, however, the right is extended by the provision giving the trader a right to an oral hearing. This is not necessarily enshrined in the rules of natural justice. [63]

Any revocation or variation cannot take effect until the expiry of the period stated in the written notice. [64] The council are under a duty to consider representations made by the licence-holder. If it is decided to vary or revoke the licence, the council must inform the

---

[61] In accordance with Section 27 (1) considered above at p. 235.
[62] Section 29 (1).
[63] *Lloyd v. Mcmahon* [1987] AC 625.
[64] Section 29 (2).

trader of the decision to do so in writing and notify him or her of the right of appeal.

Appeals
A trader or any other person who is "aggrieved" by a decision to revoke a street trading licence on grounds in s.28 (1) (d)-(h) above inclusive has a right of appeal to local magistrates. The appeal must be brought within 21 days of the notification of the council's decision.

There is no right of appeal in respect of a revocation or variation on grounds (a)-(c). [65]

Where an appeal is permitted, it lies in the magistrates' court with a further right of appeal to the Crown Court. [66] Either court has a power to make such order as it thinks fit. [67]

Refunds
If a licence is revoked on the grounds under s28 (1) (a) or (b), the council are under a duty to refund the appropriate part of the licence fee. It will be recalled that these grounds are that there is insufficient space in the street for the licence-holder to trade without undue interference with the public's right of passage along the highway, or that the trader trades in a class of goods which the council wishes to prohibit in street in which he trades. [68]

If a licence is revoked on other grounds, or surrendered, the council has a discretion to refund the whole or part of the fee paid for the licence and charges imposed for council services. [69]

8. Succession

The Problem of Succession

Licences cannot normally be sold or transferred. If prohibited altogether this would erode the tradition of street traders passing

---

[65] Section 30 (1) (a).
[66] Section 30 (4).
[67] Section 30 (5).
[68] Section 32 (11).
[69] Section 32 (12).

on their businesses to family members once they have retired which is a matter of vital importance to many street traders.

The issue of succession exposes a conflict of interests. Nominated succession will tend to make it difficult for newcomers to set up in business in competition. This is particularly so where the street trading opportunities in the borough are few. Against this, street traders, not unnaturally wish to pass on a family business which may have been established with the assistance or support of the potential beneficiary. Reconciliation of these competing interests is not necessarily straightforward: in the third reading debate on the Bill Simon Hughes MP alleged that regulators had indulged in "sharp practice" which precluded family members from continuing the business. [70]

The Act requires the council to grant a licence to the nominated relative (as defined) and so allow that relative to succeed to the street trader's business in the circumstances permitted by the Act. Succession under the Act is not limited to benefiting the younger and rising generation. It is quite possible for the trader to nominate elder members of his family to succeed him. In essence, the Act seeks to regulate the limited circumstances in which succession is possible and to provide safeguards so that the borough council may exclude inappropriate successors in the public interest.

Section 26 defines the circumstances in which succession is possible. This is achieved by restricting the classes of trader who may provide for the succession of the licence; the relatives who are entitled to succeed to the licence; the occasions on which such a transfer is may be sought, and the circumstances when the borough council may veto the process.

(i) Who May Nominate a Successor?

Succession arrangements are only open to individual traders, not to partnerships and companies. Provision is made for the succession at the time the individual trader applies for a licence.[71] This rule may have some influence on the kinds of business structure adopted by a trader. Incorporation may be less attractive where the trader wishes to benefit from the provisions of this part of the Act.

[70] HC Debs, 6th series, vol 165 col 1112, 25th January 1990.
[71] Section 25 (2).

(ii) The Relatives Entitled to Succeed to a Licence

The Act defines the degrees of relationship which may benefit from the succession. The trader's wife, husband, father, mother, grandfather, grandmother, stepfather, stepmother, son, daughter, grandson, granddaughter, stepson, stepdaughter, brother, sister, half-brother or half sister may all succeed to the licence and this is so notwithstanding that the relationship arises through illegitimacy or adoption. [72]

(iii) When Succession is Possible

The succession is only possible in circumstances permitted by s.26. These are where the licensed street trader dies, or retires *having reached the normal age for retirement* or gives up trading due to ill-health. There may be some difficulty in identifying the "normal age for retirement" [73], but it seems that, strictly construed, the borough council might not be obliged to accept the nomination of the successor where the street trader wishes to retire early having achieved a degree of affluence. Early retirement seems to fall outside the scope of s.26 since the nominating trader is unlikely to have reached the "normal age for retirement". Of course, his successor would be able to apply for a licence in the usual way; the council would merely be under no duty to grant it under s.26.
    Succession is also possible in cases where the ill-health of the licence-holder prevents him from continuing to trade provided that he can provide evidence of his ill-health.

(iv) The Council's Power to Prevent Succession

Once the successor has been nominated by the licence-holder, the succession is not of a matter of right. The borough council retains a power to refuse the application, but it can only do so in the limited circumstances set out in s.25 (6) (b) and (e), considered above. These, it will be recalled, relate to a number of possible matters: that by

---

[72] Section 26 (2).
[73] Note employment law on the problems of identifying the normal retirement age for the purposes of unfair dismissal and redundancy: eg *Waite v. GCHQ* [1983] 2 AC 714.

virtue of misconduct or general unsuitability it is undesirable that
the trader should hold a licence; that he or she has without
reasonable excuse failed to exercise sufficiently the right to trade
under a previous licence; that he or she has not paid fees or other
charges due under a previous licence; or that he or she has failed to
provide satisfactory arrangements for storage of receptacles or
perishable goods at times when trading does not take place.

9. Special Provisions for Ice Cream Sales

The zoning of streets or areas of the borough for street trading
purposes provides one of the principle bulwarks of the 1990 Act.
This power allows the borough council to confine most forms of
trading to designated streets or areas within the borough. Whilst
this is appropriate in the case of stationary form of trading, for
example, trading from a pitch or a stall, it is less so in cases where
the trader necessarily goes in search of his business. The Act
therefore makes concessions for peripatetic traders, as in the saving
for pedlars who are placed outside the regulatory framework of the
Act.

Similar considerations apply in the case of ice-cream vendors
whose activities could not in practice be confined to the areas of the
borough designated for street trading purposes. One reason for this
is that the designated areas which are often non-residential would
not be profitable for ice cream salesmen. The 1990 Act therefore
significantly alters the way in which the zoning rules apply to ice
cream sales, although it does not exempt such traders altogether.
The ice cream salesman is not entitled to trade in any street
designated by the borough as a "prohibited street". Further, if the
ice cream salesman wishes to trade in a licence street, he must
apply for a street trading licence. [74]

Before passing a resolution that a street become a a "prohibited
street" the borough should be satisfied that this prohibition is
necessary to prevent obstruction to traffic, or undue interference or
inconvenience to persons using the street. If circumstances change so

---

[74] Section 38.

that the prohibition is no longer necessary, the borough council has power either to rescind or vary the restriction. [75]

The borough is under a duty to consult the Metropolitan Police Commissioner and bodies representing ice cream traders before such a resolution is passed. [76] The council must also follow the procedures applicable when designating licence streets. [77]

Appeals

Any person aggrieved by a resolution to prohibit ice cream trading may appeal to the magistrates' court. [78] The appeal must be brought within 21 days beginning with the second publication of the statutory notice in a local newspaper.

10. Miscellaneous Powers in Relation to Street Trading

The 1990 Act seeks to address some of the anti-social practices of a minority of street traders. Some of these can be prevented by the imposition of conditions in the licence. Where anti-social consequences do occur, the borough council may charge the trader for the cost of remedying the problem. The power to charge for street cleansing which has already been examined is but an example of this.

Section 35 of the Act contains a power to remove the paraphernalia of street trading after trading has ceased. The council may remove the "receptacle" and place it in a place of storage. Before this can occur the trader must be in breach of his obligation to provide storage facilities. [79]

"Receptacle" is defined broadly in s.21. As well as including any "vehicle or stall and any basket, bag, box, vessel, stand, easel, board, (or) tray", it embraces any thing used to display goods or as

---

[75] Section 37 (2).
[76] Section 37 (3).
[77] Section 37 (4). See Section 24 (3)-(11).
[78] Section 30 (1) (e). The meaning of "a person aggrieved" is considered at p. 367 *et seq.*
[79] Section 25 (6) (e). The obligation may be imposed by a condition in the licence.

a container for any commodities or any equipment used in the provision of any service.

Any costs incurred by the borough council in doing so and in placing the "receptacle" in storage can be recovered from the licence holder. Further, if there has been a breach of a condition in the licence, the licence-holder may be prosecuted. [80]

An important practical point concerns the power of the enforcement authorities to remove goods, stalls and barrows used on the street by unlicensed traders. If the unlicensed trader does not benefit from any of the exceptions in the 1990 Act, he is trading unlawfully and commits an offence under the 1990 Act. By s. 38 (4) of the 1990 Act the police or authorised council officer have a power to seize non-perishable goods unlawfully offered for sale and any receptacle used by the trader. The power is not a general power of confiscation since it extends only to the seizure of goods which may be required to be used in evidence in any proceedings. Any items which are not so required, such as the personal property of the trader, cannot be seized.

There may be a power of arrest where the trader has obstructed the highway. [81]

Traders should also be aware of the provisions in s.6 of the Metropolitan Street Act 1867, which prohibits the placing of goods or other articles on the footway or any part of the street so as to cause an obstruction or inconvenience to other users of the highway. Under this Act, however, there is no power to seize goods.[82]

It should not be forgotten that the highway authority has a common law power to remove obstructions without notice. [83] The authority may also exercise statutory powers to remove any obstruction which causes a nuisance and which is also a danger to users of the highway. [84]

---

[80] Section 34 (1).

[81] Highways Act 1980, s.137 as amended by Police and Criminal Evidence Act 1984, s25 (1) (d) (v).

[82] This prohibition was lifted from street hawkers and itinerant traders by Metropolitan Streets Amendment Act 1867, s.1.

[83] *Reynolds v.Presteigne UDC* [1896] 1 QB 604.

[84] Highways Act 1980, ss 143, 149.

CHAPTER 12

STREET TRADING IN THE CITY
OF LONDON

1. Introduction

The principal focus of street trading activities in the City of London is in Petticoat Lane Market, Middlesex Street. Trading is regulated separately from the adoptive scheme which may be applied in the London boroughs. The relevant legislation is the City of London (Various Powers) Act 1965 and the City of London (Various Powers) Act 1987. Eventually, the provisions of the 1987 Act will replace those of the 1965 Act. The latter, however, continues to govern some licences granted under the 1965 Act renewed with the option of one succession to a nominated relative. All new licences are, however, granted under the 1987 Act. This Act allows the Corporation to repeal the surviving relevant parts of the 1965 Act after the death of the last person entitled to the grant of a licence under the 1965 Act. [1] It is accordingly proposed to concentrate here upon the provisions of the 1987 Act.

The scheme of the legislation is the familiar one: street trading in the City is generally prohibited. Street trading is defined as "the selling or exposing or offering for sale of any article or thing in a street. [2] The Act does not therefore extend to exposing or offering for sale of any service. [3] But specific provisions exist to control street photographers who would otherwise have been exempt from the controls imposed under this Act. [4]

---

[1] Or under s.10 of the City of London (Various Powers) Act 1970.

[2] "Street" is not defined in the Act.

[3] Section 6.

[4] *Newman v. Lipman* (1950) 49 LGR 457.

Articles displayed in the street are presumed to have been exposed or offered for sale. [5]

Unlicensed trading is an offence unless it benefits from an exception under the Act. If a licence is granted, a street trader, not being a newsvendor or one of certain itinerant traders, [5a] acquires the right to trade in that part of Middlesex Street between Widegate Street and Sandy Row. Licensed street trading does not take place elsewhere in the City. Newsvendors and itinerant traders are not, however, confined to Middlesex Street.

2. Exempted Trading

Certain forms of street trading are outside of the scope of the licensing scheme: each may be conducted lawfully without the authority of a licence from the Corporation. They remain, however, subject to the controls applicable under the general law. [6] The burden of proof rests upon the trader to show that he falls within the scope of one of these exceptions. [7]

(i) Newsvendors

The licensing scheme is not applied to a "person who exposes or offers for sale newspapers or periodicals in a street" unless he uses a stand or "receptacle". [8] And even if a stand is used, a licence need not be obtained provided that certain conditions are fulfilled. [9] This means that qualifying newsvendors are not confined to the Middlesex Street and need not obtain a street trading licence.

If the trader sells other commodities as well as newspapers he cannot benefit from the exception and must obtain a licence. The first condition is therefore that the trader must trade exclusively

---

[5] Section 18. By s.12 "article of thing" includes any living thing.
[5a] Section 19.
[6] See Ch.1.
[7] Magistrates' Court Act 1980, s.101.
[8] By s.6 "receptacle", for the purposes of Part III of the 1987 Act, includes a vehicle or stall and any basket, bag, box, vessel, stand, easel, board, tray or other structure or thing which is used (whether or not constructed or adapted for such use) as a container for, or for the display of, any article or thing.
[9] Below.

as a newsvendor selling "daily, weekly or Sunday newspapers". The second condition is that any stand or "receptacle" used by the newsvendor must not exceed certain maximum dimensions. [10] Finally the stand must not be placed upon the carriageway of the street.

(ii) Itinerant Traders

Unlike the other licensing schemes, there is no saving for pedlars. An itinerant trader for the purposes of the 1987 Act is a trader "who is for the time being carrying on business with persons residing or employed in premises in, or abutting on, a street". Such a trader need not obtain a licence in "respect of any street trading conducted by him in the course of that business unless he permits any receptacle used by him to occupy a stationary position in the street for an unreasonable time."

The saving is intended to benefit roundsmen and door to door salesmen. It is, however, narrowly construed. [11]

Itinerant costermongers are lawfully entitled to place goods and articles on the street, and these rights are preserved by s.20 of the 1987 Act. The position of costermongers has been considered in the previous chapter. [12]

(iii) Lawful Markets and Fairs

Trading in lawful street markets is normally outside the scope of the Act. A lawful market is defined as one held in pursuance of statute, royal licence, royal charter or letters patent, or as of right from time immemorial. [13] A trader need not seek a licence under the 1987 Act if he trades in the market with the written authority of a person entitled to conduct the market or to receive tolls or stallage. This restricts the common law rule that anyone is at liberty to sell

---

[10] Section 19. It must not exceed 3 ft in height, nor occupy a portion of footway measuring more than 2 feet 6 inches in any direction, nor exceed 3 square feet in area.

[11] See *London Borough of Islington v. Panico* (1973) 72 LGR 51, discussed *infra* pp. 225-226.

[12] At pp. 223-224.

[13] Section 21.

in a market. A licence must be sought unless the required written authority is obtained.

A trader may claim the benefit of the saving for markets and fairs if he trades in an area over which the market right extends. The important issue is the *de jure* area of the market and not the *de facto* one. [14]

3. Licensing Powers

Applications

An application for a licence, or for the renewal of an existing licence, may require the trader to supply detailed information to the Corporation. Amongst other matters, information concerning the type of goods intended to be sold, the nature of the equipment to be used in selling, and the arrangements made for the storage of stock and stall when trading has ceased can be required. This information will inform the Corporation's decision whether or not to grant the application. [15]

Under s.8 the Corporation also has a power to require any other information in so far as it is reasonable to do so; and the current application form asks, for example, whether any other street trading licences are held and whether any similar application has ever been refused.

Any person who, in order to support an application for a licence, makes any statement which he or she knows to be false in a material particular is guilty of an offence punishable by fine not exceeding level 2 on the standard scale [16]. This compares with a fine not exceeding level 3 on the standard scale for a similar offence under the London Local Authorities Act 1990. It seems undesirable that similar conduct should carry a greater penalty in the London boroughs than in the City.

---

[14] *Jones v. Lewis* [1989] The Times, 12th June.
[15] See *infra* for the grounds on which an application might be refused.
[16] Section 16.

Grounds upon which a Licence may be Refused, Revoked or Varied

The Corporation has no power to grant a licence if the applicant is under 17 years of age. [17] In other cases, however, it is under a *prima facie* duty to grant or renew an application for a street trading licence, and it must grant it as soon as reasonably practicable after the application is lodged. [18] This raises a presumption in favour of permitting street trading. If there are competing claims for licences it seems that priority should *not* be given to those who apply first. Each application must be considered on its merits. [19]

The licence cannot be refused merely because the applicant does not reside in the City. [20] If however one or more of the grounds for refusal under s 8 exist the Corporation may decline to grant or renew the licence. These also provide grounds for revocation and, further, enable the Corporation to vary the terms of a licence.

The grounds in s.8 (5) are as follows:

(i)   *the applicant is an unsuitable person to hold a street trading licence by reason of having been convicted of an offence which the Corporation considers to be material to his conduct as a street trader or for any other sufficient reason.* In deciding what offence is "material", the Corporation is under a duty under the general law to act reasonably. A similar limitation applies to the final limb of paragraph (i), that the applicant is unsuitable "for any other sufficient reason". [21] Repeated breaches of the criminal law in the course of trading may furnish grounds for revocation, even if the offences were of a minor nature especially if the trader, by this conduct, has shown an intention flagrantly to disregard the law; [22]

(ii)   *the space available in Middlesex Street market is or has become insufficient to permit the applicant or licensee to continue to*

---

[17] Section 8(4).
[18] Section 8(3).
[19] *Perilly v. Tower Hamlets LBC* (1970) 70 LGR 474.
[20] Section (5) (g) (i).
[21] The scope of this provision would be limited by the general law to reasons which would affect the applicant's suitability as a licence-holder. See Ch. 17.
[22] *Manchester Corporation v. Penson* (1969) 68 LGR 225.

trade without causing undue inconvenience to or interference with traffic in that street;

(iii)   *the Corporation believes that there are enough traders in Middlesex Street dealing in the goods in which the applicant desires to trade whether sold in shops or otherwise.*

(iv)   *the storage arrangements notified by the applicant in his application are inadequate or unsuitable;*

(v)   *the licensee has persistently failed to remove and store the equipment or receptacles used in street trading;*

(vi)   *the applicant or licensee has persistently refused or neglected to pay any charges due to the Corporation.* Establishing a "persistent refusal" is necessary.   It is suggested that what is required is conduct sufficient to show that the trader intends not to be bound by the obligation to pay.

Only a charge which is actually due falls within this paragraph. It is not enough that the Corporation believes it to be due unless it is actually due;

(vii)   *the licensee personally has for a period of not less than four weeks not exercised, or not fully exercised, his rights under the licence.* This paragraph establishes the obligation to trade personally. The important distinction is between personal responsibility for a stall and personal supervision of it. It is the latter upon which the law insists. [23] A trader cannot employ others to run the stall and take no part in its day to day operation. The section does not, however, prohibit the employment of assistants,[24] and where a trader does so he should be permitted to leave the stall for reasonable periods, for example, to obtain stock.

If the Corporation finds that there are already enough traders in Middlesex Street selling the goods in which the applicant trades

---

[23] *R v. Southwark Crown Court ex p Watts* [1992] COD 140.

[24] Under s.9 (e) the Corporation has a duty to prescribe whether the licensee may employ others.

or proposes to trade, it may restrict the licence to one or more types of goods specified in his application. [25]

Procedure

The rights of traders in application cases are less extensive than those of traders who already hold a licence which the Corporation proposes either to vary, to revoke or not to renew. [26] In the latter cases, the Corporation cannot decide to vary, to revoke or not to renew the licence unless at least seven days' notice in writing has been given to any trader who requests such notice that an objection will be taken to the renewal, or that revocation or variation has been proposed.

The trader may then request an opportunity to be heard on the matter, but he must request this within three days of receiving notice of the Corporation's proposals.

The position is different where what is at issue is a right to receive reasons after a decision has been taken. In this case, the applicant for a licence, or the trader whose licence is either varied, not renewed or has been revoked, may require the Corporation to inform him of the reasons for its decision. Reasons must be given with 7 days of the trader's request. [27] The trader should, of course, normally exercise this right since the reasons may furnish grounds for an appeal.

Appeals

A right of appeal to the magistrates' court exists [28] for the benefit of any person aggrieved either by (i) the refusal to grant a licence, (ii) the variation of an existing licence, (iii) the non-renewal of a licence, (iv) the revocation of a licence or (v) by any prescribed condition in the licence. Magistrates may confirm, reverse or vary the decision of the Corporation as well as award costs.

---

[25] Section 8 (6).
[26] Section 8 (5) (g).
[27] Section 8 (7).
[28] Section 11.

Whether appeal rights are exercised has an effect upon the duration of the existing licence. The period for which the licence remains in force depends upon the circumstances.

If it is either a case of the non-renewal of an existing licence, a case of revocation, or a case in which the terms of the licence are varied, the *status quo ante* is maintained until a date specified in the Act. This is determined according to whether an appeal is instituted. If no appeal·is brought against the decision, the current licence continues in force until the 14 day time limit for appeal has elapsed. If an appeal is lodged, the licence is continued in force until the appeal is determined, withdrawn, or fails for want of prosecution. This will be the date at which the court dismisses the appeal for want of prosecution. In the exercise of its discretion, the court may consider whether the trader's conduct has been intentional and contumelious or whether there has been inordinate and inexcusable delay on his part of the trader. [29]

As indicated above, if a trader wishes to exercise a right of appeal he must do so within 14 days from the date on which the Corporation's decision is notified to him.

4. The Scope and Effect of a Licence

Duration

In contrast to licences granted under the London Local Authorities Act 1990, licences under the 1987 Act are annual licences and expire on 31st December in each year. Licences granted during the course of the year are also subject to the same expiry date. [30]

Limits on Trading

(i) "Prescriptions"
In common with other licensing schemes, licences under the 1987 Act include conditions. One difference in this context, however, is that these are known as "prescriptions". The street trading licence must

---

[29] See generally *Birkett v. James* [1978] AC 297; *Department of Transport v. Chris Smaller (Transport) Ltd.* [1989] 2 WLR 578.
[30] Section 8 (9).

"prescribe" the matters set out in s.9. In other words, there has to be provision for these matters, although the detailed nature of this provision remains a matter for the discretion of the Corporation.

By s.9 "prescriptions" may relate to the site of trading, goods which may be sold, the types of "receptacle" from which trading may take place, and whether assistants may be employed by the licensee.

If any trader breaches any prescription of the licence he or she is guilty of an offence punishable by a fine not exceeding level 2 on the standard scale. [31]

(ii) By-laws

The scope of permitted activities is also defined by by-laws which may regulate the matters specified in s.14 of the 1987 Act. By-laws made under the 1965 Act have been continued with additions. For example, by-laws have been enacted governing the manner in which street trading is carried on. [32] The by-laws also control many of the nuisance effects of street trading. Under by-law 15 a licensed street trader must ensure that litter and other waste material is disposed of properly. Other provisions relate to the charges which may be made to street traders; [33] to the manner in which the stall may be lit; the charges made for services, the wearing of street traders' badges, and the production of licences. [34]

By-laws for Photographers

The 1987 Act makes special provisions for street photographers. Section 26 (10) enables the Corporation to make by-laws requiring photographers to produce any consents which legitimise their activities. Little reliance appears to be made on these provisions and the author is unaware of any by-laws made under them.

Licences and Statutes Regulating the Use of the Highway

Authorised trading under the 1987 Act is *prima facie* lawful, but may become unlawful if it infringes the provisions of any of the far-reaching statutory rules governing obstruction of the highway since

---

[31] Section 16.
[32] Eg, by-laws 2-10, regulate the type of stall a trader must use and its position.
[33] *Infra.*
[34] See by-laws 17, 18, 14, 13 respectively.

the relevant part of the 1987 Act takes effect subject to those rules.[35] This would seem to expose traders to the risk of prosecutions for obstruction, but it will be recalled that the possession of a street trading licence normally affords the trader with a "lawful excuse" for his encroachment onto the highway and thus a defence to a charge of obstruction. [36] This protection might be lost if the trader acted outside the scope of his licence, however.

5. Fees and Charges

Fees

Under the 1987 Act the fee for the grant or renewal of a street trading licence is £5. [37] The Corporation has no power under existing legislation to alter this.

If the application for a licence is refused, or the licence is not renewed, this sum must be repaid to the trader concerned. It cannot be retained, as a contribution, for example, towards the costs of administering the licensing scheme since costs these can be recovered by other means. [38]

Charges

The Corporation has a discretion to impose charges and to recover these from traders. [39] Charges may be imposed in respect of costs incurred by the Corporation in (a) the removal of refuse or the provision of other services including street cleansing; and (b) to recover the cost of administering the licensing scheme. In practice a single charge is made to cover both these matters. Bye-law 18, which came into operation on 12th February 1990, provides that the charge shall not exceed £15 per week.

---

[35] Section 20.
[36] Eg, *Hirst & Agu v. Chief Constable of West Yorkshire* (1986) 85 Cr App Rep 143.
[37] Section 10.
[38] Section 10 (2).
[39] Section 12.

6. Photographers

The Scope of the Controls

Those who take photographs of any *person* by way of trade or business have been made the subject of special controls under the 1987 Act. [40] Excluded are those who take photographs of other subject matter. There is, however, a saving for journalists. [41] Further, nothing in the 1987 Act prohibits the taking of any photographs on any land by the owner or occupier of that land, or by any other person with the consent of such an owner or occupier, or the taking of photographs on the highway by the owner or occupier of land fronting that part of the highway. [42] This provision seems to be aimed at photographs taken by professionals in a domestic environment, for example, of a wedding group. Family photography would not be caught by the section anyway since it is not normally undertaken by way of trade or business.

Controls on the regulated activities of photographers adopt the familiar design: areas are "zoned" as those in which photographers may only operate lawfully with the consent of the Corporation. An offence is committed if this consent is not obtained or the trader breaches a condition subject to which consent was given. [43] There is a statutory defence under s.26 (3) (a) if the accused photographer can establish that he took all reasonable precautions and exercised all due diligence to avoid the commission of the offence. [44]

The "zoning" is achieved when the Corporation exercises its discretionary power to designate certain places for the purposes of the regulatory scheme. These places are: [45]

---

[40] Special provision for photographers was necessary to bring them within the scope of the controls: *Newman v. Lipman* (1950) 49 LGR 457.

[41] Section 26 (9) (b).

[42] Section 26 (9) (a).

[43] Section 26 (2).

[44] Although the defence may only be founded upon an allegation that an offence was committed by another if the accused assists in identifying that person, unless the leave of the court is obtained: s. 26 (3) (b).

[45] Section 26 (1).

(a)   a public off-street car park, garden or other park or open space under the management and control of the Corporation;

(b)   a street, parade or way to which the public commonly have access, whether or not as of right; and

(c)   any road or any unenclosed land adjacent to, and within 15 metres of, any road provided that any such place is within Middlesex Street or within 45 metres of any part of this Street which lies within the city.

Procedural rules govern the making of a designation. A notice of the proposed designation must be published in a newspaper circulating in the City, and posted in the place which it is proposed to designate. These notices must invite objections to be made within a stated period not less than 28 days after the giving of the notice.[46] Any objections made must be considered by the Corporation.

Further consultation about the designation must take place with the Commissioner of Police.

If it is decided to proceed with designation, the date for the bringing it into force must be published in a like manner to that described above. The designation cannot, however, come into force until at least 28 days since the publication of these notices. [47]

Once these "consent zones" have been established, a photographer within the meaning of the Act can only pursue his trade with the written consent of the Corporation.

Any such consent may be conditional. Limitations may stipulate the times at which trading is possible and the duration of the consent. [48]

The Corporation may by resolution impose reasonable charges for the grant of consents but the amount of the fee must be limited to the recovery of the expenses incurred in dealing with applications received. [49]

---

[46] Section 26 (7) (a).
[47] Section 26 (8).
[48] Section 26 (4).
[49] *Ibid.*

Appeals

The limitation of the right of appeal is also a familiar one, enabling only a "person aggrieved" within the meaning of the Act to maintain an appeal to the magistrates' court. An appeal lies against the refusal by the Corporation of any consent necessary to lawful trading, the refusal to renew such a consent, the conditions upon which the consent has been given, or the revocation of a consent. The rules which continue a street trading licence in force during the appeal process are also applied to consents. [50]

On appeal, the magistrates may confirm, reverse, or vary the decision of the Corporation and may also award costs.[51]

An appeal must be instituted within 14 days from the day on which the Corporation's decision is notified to the aggrieved trader. [52]

7. Inheritance Provisions

In contrast to the regulatory scheme under the London Local Authorities Act 1990, there is no statutory provision enabling a trader to nominate his or her successor. There was, of course, such a possibility under the 1965 Act. Its omission from the 1987 Act marks an important difference between the rights of traders in the City and those in the London boroughs.

8. Offences

Unauthorised street trading and trading in breach of a condition of the licence are offences under the Act. [53] It is also an offence knowingly in support of an application for a licence to make a statement which is known to be false in a material particular. For these offences, a fine not exceeding level 2 on the standard scale may be imposed.

---

[50] Section 26 (6).
[51] Section 11 as applied by s. 26 (6).
[52] *Ibid.*
[53] Section 16.

There is no power in the authorities to seize the goods offered for sale as evidence of an offence under this section. [54]

It must not be forgotten, however, that unlawful trading may constitute an offence of obstruction under s.137 of the Highways Act 1980. Highway authorities have both common law and statutory powers to remove obstructions from the highway. [55] Further, obstruction of the highway may become an arrestable offence and so in certain circumstances a trader trading unlawfully on the highway may be liable to arrest.[56]

---

[54] See, in contrast, s.38 (4) of the London Local Authorities Act 1990.

[55] Ch 1.

[56] Police and Criminal Evidence Act 1984, s.25 (d) (v).

PART IV

THE REGULATION OF TRADING HOURS

264

CHAPTER 13

TRADING HOURS

The regulation of trading hours and in particular Sunday trading has had far-reaching consequences for street and market traders. Sunday trading has especially been a profitable venture, and much effort has been invested in attempts to defeat the Sunday trading prohibition in the courts. This is now the subject of Parliamentary reform. Other restrictions on trading hours may nevertheless apply.

The Scope of the Controls

(i) A "Shop" and a "Place"

First, statute regulates the hours and times at which trading is permitted in shops. [1] "Shop" for the purposes of the Shops Act 1950, is defined to include "any premises where any retail trade or business is carried on". [2] "Premises" normally connotes a fixed structure [3] and so, because stalls, barrows and similar moveable structures are not normally within the orthodox definition, they are not normally "shops".[4] This interpretation causes difficulties in extending the controls on trading hours to street traders. For this reason itinerant traders are also exempt. [5] It has been lawful for

---

[1] Shops Act 1950 and the Shops (Early Closing Days) Act 1965; Local Government (Miscellaneous Provisions) Act 1982, s.4.

[2] Section 74.

[3] *Cowlars Co-op v. Glasgow Corporation* [1957] SLT 288; *Thanet DC v. Ninedrive Ltd* [1978] 1 All ER 703.

[4] *Greenwood v. Whelan* [1967] 1 QB 396; *Kahn v. Newberry* (1959) 57 LGR 140; cf *Dennis v. Hutchinson* [1922] 1 KB 693 and *Thanet DC v. Ninedrive Ltd* [1978] 1 All ER 703, 710.

[5] *Stone v. Boreham* [1959] 1 QB 1; *Cowlairs Co-operative Society v. Glasgow Corporation Supra* n. 3.

them, for example, to sell non-exempt goods on Sundays and at later hours than would apply in local shops. [6]

However, the courts have not always been consistent in their approach to what constitutes a "shop".[7] The word "premises" has also received different interpretations. It has been held, for example, to include a vessel or "anything of that kind". [8] This suggests that "premises", at least in other legal contexts, may embrace moveable structures.

The regulatory controls are, however, extended to *places* other than "shops". Section 12 of the 1950 Act enacts that " it shall not be lawful in any locality to carry on in any place not being a shop retail trade or business of any class at any time when it would be unlawful in that locality to keep a shop open for the purpose of retail trade or business of that class." This means that if a trader (not operating from a "shop") trades from a "place" within the meaning of s.12, the controls in Part 1 of the Act apply. [9]

Similarly, by section 58 of the 1950 Act, the prohibition on Sunday trading was extended to embrace trading from "places" other than shops.

Whether trading occurs at a "place" depends in part upon its degree of permanency. It is important that trading should be a regular occurence. This is a question of fact and degree. In *Maby v. Warwick Corporation* [10] sufficient permanence was established since the trading took place in a regular weekly market.

---

[6] *Stone v. Boreham* , *ibid; Kahn v. Newberry. Supra* n. (4). The prohibition is only inapplicable, however where such traders do not operate from a "place", *infra*. For similar reasons, late night mobile snack bars are not subject to the same controls as takeaway food shops under the Local Government (Miscellaneous Provisions) Act 1982, s.4 which only apply to "premises".

[7] See above p. 102 *et seq.*

[8] Buckley L.J. *Andrews v. Andrews & Mears* [1908] 2 KB 567,570 571, considering the Workman's Compensation Act 1906.

[9] Section 12 does not apply to newsvendors selling "newspapers". The Act is not clear whether this exemption applies to those who sell newspapers and magasines; in other words is it confined to those who sell only newspapers. It seems that it could not extend to those who sell newspapers and other unrelated goods, for such an interpetation would seriously undermine the policy of the Act.

[10] [1972] 2 QB 242.

Sufficient permanence was also established where a car boot sale was regularly held in a large field adjoining a public house. [11] Lacking sufficient permanence, and thus not a "place" within the meaning of the 1950 Act, were stalls at a one day stamp fair which were erected in the morning and removed in the evening, and so the prohibition on Sunday trading did not apply. [12] Similarly, trading from a costermonger's barrow lacked permanency and so controls on trading hours were inapplicable. [13]

(ii) A Retail Trade or Business [14]

The controls on the trading hours of street traders only apply where they are engaged in a "retail trade or business". It is only where such trading activity takes place that the relevant provisions of the Act are extended to traders not operating in shops but "places". It is therefore important to know how these words have been interpreted.

It has been held that "the expression 'retail trade' ...clearly denotes in its primary sense a business consisting of selling goods to members of the public (as distinct from members of the trade) who resort to the shop or premises where a business is carried on for the purpose of making of purchases." [15] A retail trade primarily suggests a business trading in goods rather than services, but may, nevertheless, include a trade in services provided that the circumstances in which services are retailed are similar to those of

---

[11] *Palmer v. Bugler* (1989) 87 LGR 382. Here the owner of field was charged with aiding and abetting another to contravene s. 47, but the conviction was quashed because the information was bad for alleging that the car boot was a "place" and because of the lack of evidence that sellers did so with sufficient regularity. There was also no evidence that sales took place in the course of a retail trade or business. (See Pill J at p. 391). This means that, in the absence of regular trading by the sellers, the control of car boot sales under the Shops Act 1950 may be difficult.

[12] *Jarmain v. Wetherill* (1977) 75 LGR 537. Note, however, that stalls erected for an indoor exhibtion lasting for 16 days were held to be of a sufficient degree of permanence: *Randall v. D Turner (Garages) Ltd.* [1973] 1 WLR 1052.

[13] *Kahn v. Newberry, supra* n. (4).

[14] Under s.74 of the 1950 Act this is defined to include the business of barber or hairdresser, the sale of refreshments or intoxicating liquours, the business of lending books and periodicals when carried out for the purpose of gain and retail sales by auction. There are then savings for sales of programmes and the like at theatres and cinemas.

[15] *M & F Frawley Ltd v. The Ve-Ri Best Co. Ltd.* [1953] 1 QB 318, 326, Jenkins LJ.

an ordinary retail trade (i.e. concerned with goods). [16] It seems therefore that street traders may be involved in retail businesses even if not concerned exclusively with the sale of goods.

Sales lacking a business or commercial connotation may fall outside of the controls, however. [17] Car boot sales furnish particular problems because members of the public often sell to each other and, unless the there is evidence to enable the prosecution to establish that trading took place in the course of a retail business, the car boot sale may fall outside the scope of the 1950 Act. It would be a question of fact whether Sunday trading at such a sale was unlawful. [18]

Closing Hours

The general provisions as to closing hours apply not only to shops but also to "any place not being a shop (where a) retail trade or business is carried on..." [19] The effect of these provisions is that some static forms of street trading will fall within the ambit of the rules.   These controls are in addition to any others restricting trading hours which may be applied as conditions of street trading licences or consents. Some of those traders who are exempt from the licensing schemes may, nevertheless, be caught by the closing hours provisions of Part 1 of the 1950 Act. Some may be exempted even from these controls. [20] It must be remembered that if these traders do not trade from a "place" the closing hours rules do not apply.

Early Closing Days

Every shop must be closed for the serving of customers not later than 1pm on one week day in every week. [21] The owner of the shop may

---

[16] *Ibid.* at p 326-7; also *Lewis v. Rogers* (1984) 82 LGR 670.

[17] *Palmer v. Bugler , supra* (11) at p 391.

[18] *Ibid.* Note that there were suggestions that only amateur sellers were operating on the site because of evidence that market traders and those seeking to sell new merchandise were excluded from it.

[19] Section 12.

[20] Eg. pedlars who, as itinerant traders, will not trade from a "place".

[21] Section 1 (1).

select which day shall be early closing day. [22] Certain classes of business are exempt from the duty to close early. These are listed in Schedule 1 of the 1950 Act.[23] It is to be noted that the Schedule exempts "fairs". Only "fairs" benefit from this exemption; markets do not. This is another instance in which the distinction remains of modern relevance. It is to be noted that late trading is only possible if the fair is lawfully held. This would seem to confine such trading to those held under grant, or presumed grant.

Further, the general obligation to operate an early closing day can be disapplied where the majority of shops of a particular class wish to be so exempted. If the majority express such a wish the local authority should make the appropriate order lifting from that class of shops the obligation in s.1 of the Act. A local authority in a holiday resort may also suspend the duty to close early for the benefit of all shops or shops of any class for a period not exceeding in aggregate four months in any year.[24]

General Closing Hours

General closing hours are normally established by s.2 of the 1950 Act which provides that every shop shall be closed for the serving of customers not later than 9pm on the "late day" and 8pm on any other day of the week. Earlier hours may, however, be prescribed by a "closing order" made by the local authority. [25]

"The late day" is normally Saturday but the local authority may by order designate another day.[26] Different days may be stipulated for different classes of shops, or different parts of the area or for different parts of the year. [27]

---

[22] Shops (Early Closing Days) Act 1965 s 1 (1).

[23] These include trading in milk, cream, fish, meat, bread, confectionary, fruit, vegetables, flowers, as well as trading in lawful fairs and charitable bazaars from which no private profit is derived.

[24] Section 40.

[25] Below.

[26] Section 3.

[27] Section 33.

Exemptions and Special Provisions

Savings embodied in Schedule 2 permit later trading in certain cases. Of these perhaps the most important for street traders relates to the sale of newly cooked provisions. [28] This has been interpreted to embrace newly baked rolls and bread. [29] Rolls sold one and a half hours after being baked were also included. [30] This exemption benefits those wishing to sell hot food as takeaways at late hours. Of course, the scope of this exemption may be restricted in practice by the terms under which the trader's licence is held. These may require him to cease trading at a time stated in the licence or consent.

Also exempt from the general closing hours is any fair lawfully held or any bazaar or sale of work for charitable or other non-profit making purposes. [31]

Special provision is made for ice cream businesses and (amongst other businesses) those selling sweets, chocolates or other sugar confectionery. By s.6 the closing hour on the late day may be 10pm; on the other days it is 9.30 pm. If a majority of shops affected desire it, however, the local authority may prescribe earlier closing provided that this is not earlier than 8pm. (Traders dealing in smokers' requisites are also a special case but this is unlikely to be of importance for street traders.)

An application may be made in holiday resorts (as well as those in which seasonal sea fishing takes place) for later trading hours to apply. The local authority, if satisfied that this is desired by the majority of shops in its area, may effect this change by order provided that it does not last for more than four months in that year. [32] The order may apply to the whole or any part of the area and to all shops or shops of any class.

The local authority may also prescribe by order later closing (no later than 10pm) in respect of any show or exhibition if the retail business carried on there is only ancillary to the main purpose of the event. [33]

---

[28] Section 2 (3) (b); Sched 2.

[29] *LCC v. Davis* [1938] 2 All ER 764.

[30] *Magistrates of Alloa v. Dalziel* 1955 SLT (Notes) 59.

[31] Section 45.

[32] Section 41.

[33] Section 42.

Further, the general closing hours and closing orders may be suspended by order of the Secretary of State [34] or the local authority provided in the case of the latter that this is for a period of not more than 7 days in the aggregate in the year.

The Government considers the current legislation on closing hours to be anachronistic and intends to reform them when Parliamentary time permits. [35]

Closing Orders

Notwithstanding the provisions of the "general closing hours", a local authority has a power [36] to make a "closing order" which may specify the closing hour throughout the area or any part of it. Such an order may only be made, however, if at least two-thirds in number of the occupiers of shops to be affected by the order approve of it. [37]

The hour of closing specified in the order must not be earlier than 7 pm; but a closing order cannot purport to permit later trading than is permitted under the general trading hours.

Similar exemptions apply in the case of a closing order as in the case of the general closing hours. Accordingly, transactions mentioned in Schedule 2 are exempt as are transactions in lawful fairs.

Mixed Businesses: Early Closing Days and Closing Orders

It will be recalled that businesses of a particular class may be exempted from the obligation to close early on one day each week. Similarly, shop closing hours may be the subject to a closing order affecting a designated class or classes of business. Problems arise where shops operate mixed businesses involving that listed in the relevant order as well as another type of business. A modern

---

[34] Section 43.

[35] Reforming the Law on Sunday Trading- A Guide to the Options for Reform (1993) Cm 2300 para 53.

[36] Section 8.

[37] Section 9. Note that shop keepers have the right to vote on this matter; traders do not unless they operate from "premises" within the meaning of the Act. So although affected by closing hours, they have no statutory right to influence what these hours may be.

example would be that of the supermarket, but it could also apply to some street traders operating mixed businesses.

In relation to the obligation to close early, section 13 (1) provides that if a shop carries on a number of businesses and one of these, if sold exclusively, would enable the shop to benefit from an exemption the shop may remain open on early closing day for the sale of that (exempt) line only subject to any conditions which the local authority may prescribe. [38] Some business, such as supermarkets may not be within the scope of the order since they are not businesses of the class specified within it. [39]

The provisions have been judicially extended to permit trading in cases such as *Margerison v. Wilson.* [40] Here a trader who sold pork sausages, but whose principal business was that of confectioner, was prosecuted for trading during the weekly half-holiday which applied to pork butchers. The justices found that the trader could not be said to be carrying on the trade of selling sausages. The acquittal was upheld on appeal since, even though a considerable amount of sausages were sold, the trader did not fall within the category of pork butcher. This is a lenient decision.

Section 13 (3) permits shops carrying on a number of trades to remain open after the hour specified in the closing order for the trade not specified within it. This enables shops to continue to trade in regard to some ancillary businesses. [41]

A closing order must specify the class of business affected by it by reference to the main business conducted. If a mixed business is not of a kind specified in a closing order, the business may remain open for sales after the hours mentioned in the order because the order has no application to that business. [42] Accordingly, a supermarket was not within the scope of a closing order specifying the trade of a grocer even though groceries were sold.

---

[38] *Redbridge London BC v. Wests (Ilford).* [1968] 2 WLR 145.
[39] *Fine Fare v. Brighton Corpn.* [1959] 1 WLR 223.
[40] (1914) 79 JP 38.
[41] *Fine Fare Ltd v. Aberdare UDC* [1965] 2 QB 39.
[42] *Fine Fare Ltd v. Aberdare UDC, ibid.*

Sunday Trading

Massive resources and not a little ingenuity have been invested in the Sunday trading question in recent years as traders have sought to evade the prohibition on Sunday trading. At the time of writing, the House of Commons has just resolved to reform the law, and it is anticipated that the proposals will find support in the House of Lords. [43] Provided that the Bill becomes law, small shops will be permitted to open on a Sunday without restriction, but it will only be possible for larger shops to open for a maximum period of six hours.

The reforms will permit Sunday trading by most if not all street traders. The scheme of regulation which gained Commons support is that contained in Schedules 2 and 3 of the Sunday Trading Bill. This scheme distinguishes large from small shops. A "shop" is defined to mean "any premises where there is carried on a trade or business consisting wholly or mainly of the retail sale of goods." Traders operating from market stalls and pitches do not operate from "premises"; they would thus be at liberty to trade on a Sunday. Those operating from "units" in larger buildings may be in a different position. It must not be forgotten that in cases like *Walsh* [44] and *Greenwood* [45] street traders have been organised into what are essentially markets with the important difference that the individual traders operate from so-called "units". These may constitute "shops" in law. [46]

In essence the scheme amounts to de-regulation of Sunday opening for shops of less than 280 square metres. Larger shops with an internal floor area of more than 280 square metres will only be able to open for a maximum continuous period of six hours between 10 am and 6 pm provided that they have given the local authority at least 14 days notice that they intend to do so. Special provision

---

[43] It is proposed to outline the law as reformed although, at the time of writing, the Sunday Trading Bill has neither been considered by the House of Lords nor received the Royal Assent.

[44] *Manchester City Council v. Walsh* (1986) 84 LGR 1.

[45] *Kingston-upon-Hull City Council v. Greenwood* (1984) 82 LGR 586.

[46] The point was left open in *Greenwood, ibid.* p. 594, but the possibility that "units" may sometimes be shops was acknowledged in *Walsh* at p. 15.

is made for Jewish traders where the controls would otherwise apply.

Certain businesses which would otherwise be "large shops" are exempted from these restrictions to enable them to open for longer than six hours on a Sunday. [47] Even if operating from units in operations which are essentially indoor markets, traders are unlikely to occupy premises larger than 280 square metres and so are likely to be able to trade lawfully on a Sunday once the Bill receives Royal Assent.

---

[47] These are listed in Sched. 2 para. 3 (1).

PART V

THE SALE OF FOOD: HYGIENE AND REGISTRATION

CHAPTER 14

THE REGISTRATION AND HYGIENE OF FOOD PREMISES

A survey of law of food as if affects street traders is beyond the scope of this book. It is, however, important to note two matters which are of relevance in the present context. The first concerns the requirement to register food premises, including stalls, from which food is sold. The second concerns food hygiene standards affecting mobile shops and stalls.

The Registration of Food Premises [1]

In order to facilitate the enforcement food safety standards, it is essential that enforcement agencies should know which premises are being used for commercial food sales in their area so that proper inspections can be carried out. To achieve this s.19 of the Food Safety Act 1990 enables Ministers to make regulations requiring premises used or proposed to be used for the purposes of a food business to be registered with the enforcement authorities. This enables a record of food premises in a local authority's area to be established; it does not allow the authority to assess in advance the competence of those engaged in food operations; such a scheme would require a general licensing system. The protection afforded to the public falls far short of this.

A food business is defined in s. 1 (3) to mean any business in the course of which commercial operations with respect to food or food sources are carried out. "Premises" includes any place, any vehicle, stall or moveable structure which means that street traders,

---

[1] Discussed Thomas (1992) Law Society's Gazette pt.15, p 19.

whether itinerant or not, will be caught by the requirement to register.

The registration process was introduced by the Food Premises (Registration) Regulations 1991 [2] which came into force for most purposes on 1st February 1992. These require the registration of most premises used for food businesses. The use of premises for the purposes of any food business is prohibited on five or more days (whether or not consecutive) in any period of five weeks unless an application for registration has been made at least 28 days before the commencement of use of the premises. There are detailed exemptions favouring certain premises.

Where moveable premises [3] are used in a market [4] Schedule 1 requires both the market organiser and each trader to register unless, in the case of the latter, the stalls etc. are provided by the controller or organiser of the market. In the case of a local authority market the controller is the local authority; in other cases it is the person by whose authority market premises are used.

By Schedule 3 moveable food premises, [5] such as mobile food stalls, snack bars, or barrows are not required to be registered unless registration is required because they are used in a market. [6]

Permanent premises used for the storage of mobile food premises are also required to be registered. [7] This suggests that it may be necessary to register the place where a stall is normally stored.

Where registration is required, a failure to register means that the premises cannot lawfully be used for the purposes of a food business. Any person using unregistered premises for the purpose of a food business commits an offence punishable by a fine not exceeding level 3 on the standard scale.[8]

---

[2] SI 1991 2825 (amended from 1st January 1993 by the Fresh Meat (Hygiene and Inspection) Regulations SI 1992/ 2037, reg 27.

[3] Defined widely in reg 1 (3) to include all those which are not permanent food premises, for example, stalls, barrows or vehicles. Permanent premises means any land or building.

[4] Defined to include both "official" and "unofficial" markets, that is, those not held under the authority of a grant, presumed grant or statutory authority: reg 1 (3).

[5] Excluding those used in a market.

[6] Ie, under Schedule 1.

[7] Schedule 3.

[8] Other offences are also created; for example in relation to permitting the use of unregistered premises, (punishable by a fine not exceeding level 3); failing to notify a

Food Hygiene and Street Traders

Specific hygiene standards are imposed *inter alia* on mobile shops and stalls. These are laid down in the Food Hygiene (Markets, Stalls and Delivery Vehicles) Regulations 1966. [9] It is proposed briefly to notice some of the key provisions of these regulations which are designed to guarantee the hygiene standards in relation to food sales by street and other traders. [10]

The Scope of the Regulations

The regulations are intended to affect persons who are not directly concerned in the sale and handling of food as well as those who are. Accordingly, those who allow land or premises to be used are bound to observe hygiene standards and may be prosecuted if they do not. This is achieved by regulation 5 (2) which extends the burden of the food hygiene regulations beyond the stall-holder. Any person who provides market premises or who permits land to be used or allows any stall to be erected for the purpose of sale, storage, exposure for sale, or deposit for sale of any food, is bound by obligations in these regulations. Such a person is bound to ensure that the land, or market premises are clean an in proper repair. It is prohibited to allow the premises to be used if there is a risk of contamination of food.

General Hygiene Requirements

Part II of the Regulations lays down general food hygiene requirements. First, no business shall be carried on from any stall which is insanitary. [11] This means that a food business cannot be carried on unless all three of the following obligations are fulfilled. The stall-holder must ensure that the stall is properly

---

change in proprietor, or a change in the food business; failing to register where moveable premises are kept; or failing to notify a change in registered particulars. Furnishing false information etc is punishable by a fine not exceeding level 5 of the standard scale.

[9] SI 1966/791 as amended.

[10] The regulations are now deemed to take effect under s.16 of the Food Safety Act 1990: s.59(3), Sch 4 para 2.

[11] reg 4.

constructed, and that it is not allowed to fall into a such a condition that the food is exposed to the risk of contamination. Further the stall must be sited so as to avoid such a risk.

"Stall" is defined extremely widely and includes any stand, marquee , tent, mobile canteen, vehicle (whether moveable or not) , vending machine, site or pitch, from which food is sold not being food premises. [12] Most street traders are likely to be deemed to trade from a "stall" within the meaning of these regulations.

Regulation 5 (1) buttresses these obligations by imposing a duty to ensure that any stall from which a food business is carried on is kept clean and in such good order as to enable it to be cleaned effectively.

Articles or equipment or containers with which food comes into contact are to be of suitable materials and kept thoroughly clean and must be made of suitable materials and maintained in such good order, repair and condition as to enable them to be thoroughly cleaned. This is to prevent any matter being absorbed into them and thus to avoid any risk of contamination of the food. [13] Regard must be had to the nature and packing of food in judging whether equipment meets the required standards of cleanliness.

Duties in Handling Food
A person who handles food must take all steps as may be reasonably necessary to protect the food from the risk of contamination. This embraces a number of obligations including the duty to keep open food covered while exposed for sale. [14] Open food is food which is not in a closed container of a kind which will exclude the risk of contamination.

Anyone handling food must maintain high standards of personal hygiene, keep cuts and abrasions covered, and refrain from spitting and smoking. If handling open food other than raw vegetables, overclothing must be worn [15] and, if this is liable to

---

[12] reg 2.
[13] It has been held that "risk of contamination" arises where the contamination is injurious to health: *Mac Fisheries (Wholesale and Retail) v. Coventry Corporation* [1957] 1 WLR 1066.
[14] reg 7.
[15] reg. 9.

come into contact with food, it must be kept as clean as is reasonably possible. [16]

Carriage and Wrapping of Food
A person engaged in the carriage of food must not allow food to be carried in a vehicle or container together with any article from which there is a risk of contamination of the food unless he or she takes such precautions as are reasonably practicable to avoid the risk of contamination. No live animal or live poultry should come into contact with the food. [17]

Wrapping paper or other wrapping material must not be used to wrap open food if it is liable to contaminate the food. Printed material other than that specifically designed to come into contact with food should not be used for wrapping open food subject to certain exceptions. [18]

Persons suffering from certain infections and in particular those likely to cause food poisoning must inform the medical officer of the district.

Detailed regulations also exist for the temperatures at which certain foods intended for human consumption are to be kept. [19]

Hygiene Requirements Affecting Stalls and Vehicles
Regulation 13 contains general provisions affecting stalls and vehicles. The first stipulates that the name and address of the person carrying on that business must be displayed legibly and conspicuously upon it and any other address at which it is normally kept or garaged unless it carries a fleet number and is kept or garaged on that person's premises.

No stall is to be stored, in a manner which will make it insanitary. It cannot be stored with any food unless this can be kept free from contamination. Sleeping in vehicles (or stalls) is prohibited unless the vehicle is specifically so designed for the purpose.

---

[16] reg 8.
[17] reg 10 (a).
[18] reg 10 (b).
[19] reg 12.

Supply of Water
Every market or stall from which a food business is carried on must have a supply of "clean and wholesome water" in quantities sufficient to allow compliance with hygiene requirements. [20] There are, however certain exemptions. [21]

Wash-hand basins
Every stall from which a food business is carried on must have wash hand basins with a supply of hot water , soap etc, in numbers sufficient for the use of all those who handle food in connection with the business. [22] This is in addition to a separate sink for the washing of food and equipment used in the business. [23] The position of the basin is subject to detailed regulation. Only cold water need be available if the sink is used exclusively for washing fish, fruit or vegetables. Exemptions are also available from these requirements. [24]

First aid facilities must normally also be available on each food stall. [25]

Facilities for Washing and Sorting Food and Equipment
Apart from the wash-basins, stalls are required to have sinks or other facilities for the washing of food and equipment used in its preparation.[26] These must comply with the detailed provisions of this regulation which concern amongst other matters the provision of hot and cold water, drying facilities etc.

Exemptions
Exemptions from the duty to provide a water supply, wash hand-basin, a sink for washing and cleaning food, and first aid equipment are established under reg 24.

First an exemption is available to a stall used exclusively for the sale of covered food where the stall-holder has notified the

---

[20] reg 15.
[21] *Infra.*
[22] Required by reg. 16.
[23] *Infra.*
[24] *Infra.*
[25] reg 17.
[26] reg 18.

food authority that he is so engaged, or for the sale of roast chestnuts or of hot potatoes.

An exemption from the requirement to provide sinks for the washing of food is available to a stallholder dealing exclusively as a fruiterer, wholesaler of fruit, greengrocer or wholesaler of raw vegetables where the stall-holder has notified the food authority that he is so engaged.

Certificates of Exemption
Under Schedule 2, certificates of exemption may be obtained in two classes of case. The first benefits traders operating from stalls in a market. Such a trader is entitled to be granted a certificate of exemption by the food authority [27] lifting the burden of providing a wash hand basin, a fresh water supply, first aid equipment and a sink for washing food if these facilities are made available by any authority for that market.

The second benefits any stall holder who satisfies the food authority that the facilities otherwise required by these regulations [28] are readily available to his business without payment. Exemptions under this provision cannot however be granted to certain classes of food business, [29] and only limited exemptions from regulation 18 are available for certain others.[30]

Miscellaneous Obligations

Lighting
Every stall from which food is sold is required to be suitably and sufficiently lit.

---

[27] A food authority is defined to mean a district council or London borough council, the common council of the City of London, and as repects the Inner and Middle Temple, the Sub-Treasurer and Under Treasurer respectively.
[28] regs 15, 16, 17 or 18 (a) (b) (c) or (d).
[29] A catering business; the sale of bakery goods and flour and confectionery prepared at the stall; the sale of fried fish and chips; the sale of sugar confectionery prepared at the stall; the sale of ice cream and ice lollies prepared at the stall; the sale of ice cream which is open food.
[30] A butcher or poulterer; a fishmonger; the sale of groceries and provisions which are open food; the sale of bakery goods and flour confectionery which is open food; the sale of cooked meat and butchers' small goods, and the sale of sugar confectionery which is open food. Such businesses are only exempted from the obligation to provide facilities for washing food.

Accumulation of Refuse etc
Refuse cannot be permitted to accumulate at any stall except in so far as this is unavoidable for the proper carrying on of the business.

Covering of Stalls
If open food, apart from raw vegetables, is sold from an open-air stall, this must be covered and screened at the back and sides to prevent the contamination of any open food on the stall.

Receptacles for Waste
Unless the stall-holder is provided with refuse collection services by the licensing authority, he or she must provide a suitable number of covered receptacles for refuse.

PART VI

FUNDAMENTAL PRINCIPLES OF ADMINISTRATIVE LAW

CHAPTER 15

INTRODUCTION

The statutory regulatory regimes are not, by themselves, exhaustive of the legal principles which govern the control of street trading. Fundamental limitations on the powers of local authorities and other public bodies are imposed under the general principles of Administrative Law, which may have a profound effect not only upon the manner in which power is exercised limit but also upon the final outcome of the decision making process.

It is difficult to over-emphasise the importance of these general principles. One recent example may, however, be illustrative. As we have seen, despite the express provisions of the street trading code, which permits a district council to charge "such fees as they consider reasonable" for a licence, [1] the council is only empowered to set licence fees at a level which merely meets the costs of operating the licensing system. [2] This means that one of the most important issues at the heart of the relationship between traders and the authorities, and one which affected the very livelihoods of the former, was resolved by recourse to the general principles of Administrative law. Moreover, the limitation on the power to charge was not evident from the language of the code. The true scope of the council's power could only be understood by an understanding of the general law.

---

[1] Local Government (Miscellaneous Provisions) Act 1982, Sched 4 para 9 (1).
[2] *R v. Manchester City Council ex p King* (1991) 89 LGR 696.

The Scope of Judicial Review: Public and Private Law Controls on Street Trading

The general principles of Administrative law apply to decisions of local authorities and other public bodies in the exercise of their statutory powers. Local authorities also seem to be subject to the scrutiny of the courts by way of judicial review in the exercise of their contractual powers, at least where a "public law element" is involved in their decision. This is a matter which has already been considered. [3]

It must not be forgotten, however, that street trading takes many forms some of which are controlled exclusively under private law where the principles of judicial review have no application. This would be so, for example in the case of a franchise market owned by a private individual or company. A franchise is an incorporeal heriditament and creates a property right protected under private law. Neither the juridical source of the power of regulation, nor the owner, are subject to public law principles. Thus where the franchise is operated by a private individual it seems that the rights of those who trade in the market are subject to the principles of the law of contract. Where, however, the franchisee is a public body such as a local authority the courts have been more willing to hold that public law principles apply where a sufficient "public law element" is present in the factual or legal circumstances.

Constitutional Fundamentals

The keystones of the English constitution are the doctrine of Parliamentary sovereignty and the Rule of Law. Whatever Parliament enacts in a statute the courts must uphold and apply. The courts cannot strike down an Act of Parliament. [4]

---

[3] Above p. 126 et seq.

[4] Eg *Pickin v. BRB* [1974] AC 765; note however that a statute which conflicts with European Community Law is unenforceable: *Simmenthal* [1978]. ECR 629; *R v. Secretary of State for Transport ex p Factortame* C 213/89 [1991] 1 AC 603. See N Gravells [1989] PL 568, [1991] PL 180; Wade (1991) 107 LQR 1.

Although the Rule of Law has a variety of meanings, [5] it requires that all power must be exercised in accordance with the law. As Wade states, there is an constitutional principle of legality.[6]

Whilst Parliament is beyond the control of the courts, Administrative bodies are in a different position. They normally derive their powers from Parliament and are subordinate to it. They must not exceed the powers conferred upon them. If they purport to do so they act without legal authority. The traditional conception of Administrative Law, and in particular judicial review , is that it serves to keep governmental bodies within the true ambit of their powers and to protect the citizen against abuse of power. It ensures that powers conferred upon administrative bodies are exercised lawfully. This is essentially a "containment" theory of Administrative Law and is briefly evaluated below.

Merits and Legality

The mechanism of judicial review is not one for testing the merits of a particular decision. Policy and decision making have, *ex hypothesi*, been entrusted by Parliament to the administration. It is not for the courts to decide upon the merits of the policy adopted. The courts are simply not furnished with a specialist knowledge of the reasons underpinning a decision; nor are they in a position properly to understand its consequences. The limited adversarial process of judicial review is simply not equipped to inform the courts sufficiently for them to arrive at such an understanding. The court's role is merely supervisory: it ensures that, whatever the merits of the decision, it is lawful. If it is, the courts cannot interfere no matter how ill advised the decision is perceived to be. A decision cannot normally be challenged merely because it is wrong. [7]

Thus within the limits of what is lawful, the administrator retains the policy making role, a necessary consequence of which is that he or she enjoys a choice of outcomes within a permitted range.

---

[5] See Wade *Administrative Law*, 6th edition, 1988, Ch.2

[6] *Ibid.*

[7] But only if unreasonable: *Associated Provincial Picture Houses Ltd. v. Wednesbury Corporation* [1948] 1 KB 223.

The extent to which the courts can or should control these outcomes is a matter of high controversy. Those who model judicial review most narrowly hold that any intervention in the merits of the decision is illegitimate if the decision is within the limits of the power conferred. Judicial review, it is maintained, should be confined merely to examining the manner in which a decision was taken. [8] It may ensure that a fair procedure was followed, that the authority had due regard to relevancy and dismissed all irrelevant matter from its consideration, and so on.

The reality of judicial review is that the courts will exercise control at the substantive level as well as at the procedural one. Administrative decisions can be struck down if they are so gravely wrong as to be "irrational" [9] and this necessarily demands intervention upon the merits. What is at issue in these cases is no less than the judicial evaluation of different policy options. Nevertheless the courts have been willing to do this notwithstanding the arguments that to do so usurps the role of the administrator and may give insufficient weight to administrative expertise.

Lord Diplock in the GCHQ case categorised the grounds on which judicial review may proceed as "illegality", "irrationality" and "procedural impropriety". [10] The prohibition on "illegality" requires that the administrator correctly understand and apply the law regulating his decision; "irrationality" embraces "Wednesbury" [11] unreasonableness. This renders ultra vires a "decision which is so outrageous in its defiance of logic or of accepted moral standards that no sensible person who had applied his mind to the question to be decided could have arrived at it." [12] "Procedural impropriety" focuses on the requirements of a fair procedure, whether statutory or common law.

---

[8] There are suggestions of such an approach in Chief Constable of North Wales v. Evans [1982] 1 WLR 1155, 1174.

[9] Supra n (7). See also Council for Civil Service Unions v. Minister for the Civil Service [1985] 1 AC 374, 410-11, per Lord Diplock.

[10] Ibid.

[11] Ibid. Associated Provincial Picture Houses Ltd v. Wednesbury Corpn. Supra n (7).

[12] [1985] AC 374, 410-411, per Lord Diplock.

The Purpose of Judicial Review

The idea of unrestricted discretionary power is inimical to the Rule of Law which demands that all power has legal limits. The administrator cannot be free to exercise his discretion in any manner he sees fit, for example, for private gain. This and many other limits are presumed to have been intended by Parliament to restrict powers which are *ex facie* discretionary. The courts have therefore evolved a system of rules limiting discretionary powers. Power must be exercised, for example, only to further the policy and objectives of the statute in which the power was conferred; it must be exercised according to the rules of procedural fairness, in good faith and only after the decision-maker has considered relevant considerations and ignored irrelevant ones. Moreover the decision must not be so unreasonable that no reasonable body could have arrived at it. [13] Using these techniques the courts uphold the concept of administrative legality and subject all administrative decisions to the Rule of Law. The court's authority for doing so is ostensibly that this reflects the true intentions of Parliament.

Such an approach sees the purpose of judicial review as the "containment" of administrators within the boundaries of the powers granted to them by Parliament. It sees the role of the courts as an objective one under which they are confined to interpreting statutes in order to locate the boundaries of power. In fact this disguises a more creative process since many of the limits are judicially implied. This means in effect that the courts are the architects of administrative legality. It is the judges who decide upon the very boundaries of power.

Critics suggest that these boundaries are essentially judicially imposed preferences masquerading as apolitical and neutral principles. [14] Moreover, remedies available in judicial review proceedings are discretionary permitting the courts considerable flexibility in controlling administrative action. [15] The legality of administrative action is not the sole nor indeed the dominant criterion; considerations of fairness are also at issue and endow judicial decisions with a degree of subjectivity. The indeterminacy

---

[13] See *infra*.
[14] Eg, Hutchinson (1986) 48 MLR 293.
[15] Eg, *Glynn v. Keele University* [1971] 1 WLR 487.

both of principles and outcomes is thus a central dilemma for the administration. Ultimately this is the consequence of a lack of a common perception of the purpose served by judicial review.

Appeal and Review

Although the courts do sometimes become involved in the merits of administrative action, there is a fundamental distinction between appeal and review. As already indicated, the task of the court in exercising judicial review of administrative action is to ensure the legality of the decision. The court is not normally concerned with whether the decision is the right decision, and cannot quash it merely because it believes that it is wrong. The court can only interfere of the administrative body has exceeded its powers. [16]

A further important difference between an appeal and judicial review is that the appellate tribunal may substitute its decision for that of some other body. In judicial review, the court is only concerned with whether the action impugned is lawful or not. If not lawful, it is usually quashed and the matter remitted to the administrator for re-consideration.

Ultra Vires: Void and Voidable

A decision which an administrator has no power to make is one taken without authority. It is a decision which is *ultra vires*. Logically such an unauthorised decision should have no legal effects. It is one which is ostensibly void, meaning that it has never had legal consequences. A declaration that administrative action is invalid thus has retrospective consequences.

Such an analysis is, however too simplistic. Because not everyone is entitled to challenge administrative action, (the challenger must normally have a "sufficient interest") [17] the courts will not intervene when someone lacking such an interest appears before them. This is so even if the administrative decision is *ultra vires*. If no "qualified" challenger comes forward the "void" act

---

[16] For a recent example of this see *R v. Independent Television Commission ex p TSW Broadcasting Ltd.* [1992] The Times, March 30th.
[17] See Ch. 19.

may well have all the legal consequences it would have had if valid.

Less serious defects may make a decision "voidable" rather than void. [18] The decision will be valid until quashed by the courts. Invalidity in this sense has only prospective consequences. [19] but here too, the courts will only declare that a decision is voidable if requested to do so by someone having a sufficient interest in the matter.

[18] *Re F (Infants) Adoption Order: (Validity)* [1977] Fam. 165.
[19] See *Craig Administrative Law*, 2nd edition, 1989, p. 326.

CHAPTER 16

PROCEDURAL RULES GOVERNING THE EXERCISE OF GOVERNMENTAL POWER

Introduction: The Rationale of Fair Procedures

Fair procedures allow those affected by the exercise of power to participate in the decision-making process. Apart from serving perceptions of democracy and individual autonomy, process rights also offer the important practical benefit of informing the decision-maker of all the circumstances bearing upon his decision. This is important because the courts scrutinise the rationality of decisions: all relevant circumstances must be considered before a decision is reached. [1] This means that there must be some process by which the decision maker can ensure that these matters are brought to his attention. Participation by those most affected by the decision provides an important mechanism by which this can be achieved. If both the individual affected and the wider public are aware that the decision-maker is so informed, the accuracy of the decision making - and public confidence in it - are enhanced. More pragmatically, by affording the individual some influence over the outcome, fair procedures make the outcome more acceptable, and reduce the risk of challenge where the decision is adverse to individual interests.

Procedures also assist in informing us about the relationship between the individual and the administration. Participation goes some way to acknowledging the autonomy of the individual by allowing some influence in, if not control over, the outcome of his

---

[1] *Associated Provincial Picture Houses Ltd. v. Wednesbury Corpn.* [1948] 1 KB 223.

case. But the case-law does evidence some tension in deciding the dominant ideological roots of fair process in English law. There has been some confusion in how to resolve the tension between the competing ideologies of individualism and communitarianism. Recognition is given to the former where the individual is entitled to a judicial style hearing before an administrative decision can validly be reached. The street trading code goes some way towards embodying this model in relation to street trading licences. [2] In such cases the individual should have the opportunity to exert an influence over the administration, to argue and defend his interests. Yet the law does not embrace this ideology without compromise: a bias towards subjecting individual interests to those of the community can be seen in the code in relation to street trading consents where few procedural safeguards are enacted. In such cases weight is attached to the communitarian ideal that public bodies (*a fortiori*, elected public bodies) are fully equipped to identify and implement policies beneficial to the wider community with only a minimal recognition of the autonomy of the individual. [3]

The procedures actually required depend to an extent upon the burden they will impose upon the administration and the importance attached to the rights or interests which are at issue. There is, as we shall see, a difference between cancelling an existing licence and denying an initial application for a licence. The burdens of providing full-blown procedural safeguards in all application cases would impose an unmanageable burden on the administration. Accordingly, the courts will assess the administrative burdens of fair procedures and whether they can be effective and beneficial in the circumstance of each case although participation cannot entirely be ignored as a value for its own sake. [4]

[2] Local Government (Miscellaneous Provisions) Act 1982, Sch. 4 para 6.
[3] See generally Hutchinson (1986) 48 MLR 293; Galligan, *Discretionary Powers* Oxford 1986.
[4] *John v. Rees* [1970] Ch 345, 402.

1. Breach of Statutory Procedural Requirements

Authorities responsible for the regulation of street trading are often given discretionary powers which can only be exercised if certain statutory requirements are fulfilled. [5] As Lord Hailsham made clear in *London & Clydesdale Estates Ltd v. Aberdeen DC,* [6] Parliament must have intended those rules to be followed with scrupulous care.[7] If these requirements are breached, however, the question arises as to what consequences follow. The statute itself seldom prescribes these consequences and so the matter must usually be resolved by the courts.

The law on this matter is uncertain and difficult to apply, partly because policy considerations - such as the administrative inconvenience of holding an administrative decision to be invalid - have a significant influence on the outcome. [8] Policy considerations do not always suggest a result favourable to the administration, however. There are often valid arguments that the procedural requirements are safeguards imposed for the benefit of the individual affected by the decision or, possibly, for the public at large. [9] The courts should always be careful to balance the interests of the individual with that of the administration.

Nevertheless, because some procedural failures may be of such a minor character, or may have caused no injustice, the courts may naturally be unwilling to strike down a decision for what might be described as a merely "technical" breach. [10]

Mandatory and Directory Requirements

The consequences flowing from the breach of a particular statutory procedural requirement traditionally depend on whether it is

---

[5] See, eg, the street designation procedure under the street trading code, *supra* n (2) para 2.
[6] [1980] 1 WLR 182, 189-90.
[7] See also *Secretary of State for Trade and Industry v. Langridge* [1991] 3 All ER 591.
[8] Eg. *R v. Paddington Valuation Officer ex p Peachey Property Corpn.* [1966] 1 QB 380.
[9] See eg *R v. St Edmundsbury Borough Council ex p Investors in Industry Commercial Properties Ltd.* [1985] 3 All ER 234.
[10] *Ibid.*

classified by the court as "mandatory" [11] or "directory". There have, however, been recent indications of a reluctance to employ such rigid distinctions. Lord Hailsham in *London & Clydesdale Estates Ltd v. Aberdeen District Council* [12] observed that there are extreme cases in which the authority has flagrantly breached a fundamental requirement, or has merely committed a trivial defect which the courts could ignore. In cases lying between these extremes there is an "inherent discretion" to decide the consequences of the breach. In such cases the individual should challenge the decision in question.

According to the traditional view, however, if a requirement is mandatory, disobedience may make the decision a nullity: but the concept of nullity itself disguises a distinction between decisions which are void and those which are merely voidable. [13] If a decision is "void" it has never had any legal effect; the declaration by the court of the invalidity of the decision therefore has retrospective effect. If the defect makes the decision merely "voidable", it is invalid only from the moment the court declares it to be so. Invalidity has a prospective effect.

If the requirement is not "mandatory" but merely "directory", the error does not result in invalidity. However, the dichotomy between "mandatory" and "directory" requirements is further obscured because remedies in judicial review cases are discretionary. In an *obiter dictum* in *Coney v. Choyce* [14] Templeman J expressed the opinion that even if a requirement were mandatory, the court is not bound to grant a declaration that the decision impugned is invalid. Such views make the outcome in any given case difficult to predict.

Whether a requirement is mandatory or directory is a matter which depends upon the proper construction of the statute in question. [15] The courts examine the subject matter, the importance of the requirement breached, and the relationship that requirement

---

[11]Sometimes "imperitive": *Howard v. Bodington* (1877) 2 PD 203.

[12] [1980] 1 WLR 182.

[13] *Calvin v. Carr* [1980] AC 574, 589-90, per Ld Wilberforce.

[14] [1975] 1 WLR 422, 435-6.

[15] A matter which has been recently re-emphasised by Lord Diplock in *O' Reilly v. Mackman* [1983] 2 AC 237, 275-6.

has to the scheme and purpose of the statute in which it is found. [16] Whether the court should go further and consider the facts of the individual case is unclear. In *Cullimore v. Lyme Regis Corpn ,*[17] Edmund-Davies J thought that question should be resolved without reference to the particular facts of the case, but this was refuted by Lord Hailsham LC in his oft-cited speech in *London & Clydesdale Estates Ltd. v. Aberdeen DC.* [18] In practice, it probably matters little which of these approaches is followed: the court can use its discretion at the remedial stage to take into account the particular circumstances of the case in issue. [19]

Mandatory Requirements
A requirement intended to protect the rights or interests of individuals is more likely to be "mandatory". Requirements which contemplate the consultation of an individual, or which entitle a person to make representations before a decision is made, would normally fall within this category. These process rights are regarded as of such importance that non-compliance would almost certainly lead to the invalidity of any purported decision. [20]

Under the street trading code, the notification and consultation requirements imposed by para 6 (1) in cases of refusal, non-renewal or revocation of licence (amongst other matters) is likely to be held to be of a mandatory character because often the livelihood of the individual and his or her "right" to work is at stake. These are interests to which great importance is attached. [21]

The matter is not, however, entirely beyond dispute because the courts hold that where the overriding rationale of a regulatory scheme is the protection of the public and not the protection of individual rights, a breach of a procedural requirement need not result in invalidity. Under one view, the purpose of the street

---

[16] *Howard v. Bodington* (1877) 2 PD 203, 210-11.

[17] [1962] 1 QB 718.

[18] [1980] 1 WLR 182 at 189-190.

[19] *R v. Secretary of State ex p Association of Metropolitan Authorities* [1986] 1 All E R 164.

[20] Per Lord Diplock in *O' Reilly v. Mackman* [1983] 2 AC 237 at 275-6; *Grunwick Processing Laboratories v. ACAS* [1978] AC 277; see also *Howard v. Bodington, supra* n (16) where the incumbent of the parish had a right to be informed of certain accusations within a statutory time limit. This was held to be "imperitive"; failure to comply with the limit invalidated the subsequent proceedings.

[21] See *Nagle v. Fielden* [1966] 2 QB 633; *R v. Barnsley MBC ex p Hook* [1976] 1 WLR 1052.

trading controls is the protection of the public. The difficulties are well illustrated in the *Langridge* case. [22] Here a statutory requirement that a person applying for a disqualification order against a director of a company notify the latter within 10 days was held, by a majority, to be merely directory. It was relevant that the majority construed the purpose of the provision as one intended merely to notify the director of the application and not to protect his rights.

Nourse L.J, however, delivered a strong dissenting judgment emphasising that a statutory provision whose purpose was to protect an individual "in regard to the commencement and conduct of proceedings which may result in a substantial interference with his freedom to carry on or pursue his chosen trade, profession or calling is mandatory and not directory." [23] The decision exposes the problems in applying principles to particular cases since the relative weight given to the public interest and that of the individual is often subject to value judgments which promote divergent views.

Directory Requirements
There is some authority that where the administrative authority is performing statutory duties, as opposed to exercising statutory powers, the courts will more readily treat the requirement as directory. [24]

Paradoxically, perhaps, even an important provision may be merely directory if a decision to quash a decision taken following its breach would cause serious public inconvenience or injustice. [25] Thus where the striking down of a decision would affect large numbers of individuals and be disruptive to the administration, the requirement is more likely to be directory. [26]

Where a notice must be served, any failure to abide by the statutory form may be excused as directory provided the substance of the required information is communicated. The same result may

---

[22] *Supra* n. (7).
[23] *Ibid.* at p. 604.
[24] *Cullimore v. Lyme Regis Corpn* [1962] 1 QB 718.
[25] *Montreal Street Rly Co. v. Normandin* [1917] AC 170,174.
[26] *Coney v. Choyce* [1975] 1 WLR 437.

follow where the individual intended to benefit from the notice is already likely to be aware of the information it contains. [27]

Non-Compliance with Directory Requirements
Breach of a requirement which is merely directory does not normally result in invalidity provided that there is "substantial compliance" with the provision. In *Coney v. Choice* [28] the breach of a notice requirement was of a trivial character and substantial compliance was held to have occurred.

Lord Diplock in *O' Reilly v. Mackman* [29] was even prepared to suggest that an administrative authority should exceptionally enjoy a *discretion* to depart from a directory requirement. This is doubtful. No administrative body should be at liberty to resolve to depart from rules where Parliament has stipulated that compliance is required. Compliance is not a discretionary matter.

In summary, the decision whether a requirement is mandatory or directory is a complex one. The indeterminacy of the principles and the circumstances in which the courts will refuse relief makes challenge to any breach of the rules one in which the prospects of success are uncertain. Proof of illegality is not by itself sufficient to invite judicial intervention. Arguments based upon administrative exigencies seem to be treated sympathetically and, combined with the residual discretion enjoyed by the courts in granting relief, the rules are sufficiently flexible to allow the courts to reach whatever decision appears suitable on the facts of each individual case.

2. Procedural Rights Implied Under the General Law

So far we have considered the consequences of breaching statutory procedural rules designed to regulate the manner in which administrative power is exercised. The required procedure was laid down in the statute; the task of the courts was to interpret its scope and meaning, and to decide upon the consequences of breach. In this section we are concerned with cases where procedural rules are not specifically enacted and thus whether, and in what circumstances,

---

[27] *R v. St Edmundsbury BC ex p Investors in Commerce and Industry* [1985] 3 All ER 234.
[28] [1975] 1 WLR 422.
[29] [1983] 2 AC 237, 275-6.

they will be implied by the courts. The first issue to be addressed concerns the circumstances in which fair procedures will be implied. If the rules are applicable, it is then appropriate to ask what proceures are actually required in particular cases.

(i) Natural Justice and Fairness

Before considering when the rules apply it is important to refer to the terminology affecting procedural rights. As Megarry V-C stated in *McInnes v. Onslow-Fane* [30] natural justice is a flexible concept embracing a wide range of situations ranging from the "judicial", in which the rights of the applicant are at issue, to the purely "administrative" where no such rights are present. At the "judicial" end of the spectrum, and where significant importance is attached to the rights at issue, the courts tend to refer to "natural justice". Towards the other end of the spectrum, fewer procedural safeguards are required, and the courts refer merely to a "duty to act fairly". There is some inconsistency in this approach since some decisions suggest that , as the applicability of the safeguards has expanded, the term "natural justice" should be abandoned in favour of a comprehensive "duty to act fairly". This is also because "natural justice is but fairness writ large and judicially." [31] However, although this may be useful to an understanding of the case-law, further discussion can be left to specialist books. [32]

When Natural Justice or Fairness Applies

After some doubts, [33] it is now settled that the rules of natural justice are capable of extending to administrative cases [34] including licensing cases. It is no longer relevant to inquire into the nature of the governmental power-whether it is judicial or administrative - but what consequences flow from the decision or administrative action in question.

---

[30] [1978] 1 WLR 1520.

[31] *Furnell v. Whangerai High Schools Board* [1970] AC 660,679.

[32] Eg, Craig *Administrative Law*, 2nd edition, 1989, pp. 207 *et seq.*

[33] Eg, *R v. Metropolitan Police Commissioner ex p Parker* [1953] 1 WLR 1150- revocation of taxi drivers licence lawful even without a hearing.

[34] *Ridge v. Baldwin* [1964] AC 40.

The necessary procedure is always governed by any express requirements of the statute under which the administrator acts. If no rules are expressly enacted the issue turns on the consequences of decision in question. Distinctions are often drawn between the "forfeiture" cases, where the decision takes away an existing licence or trading privilege, the "legitimate expectation" cases, where the applicant seeks the renewal of his licence and, by virtue of having been judged suitable as a licence-holder in the past, enjoys a "legitimate expectation" of renewal, and, finally, the "mere" application cases in which the applicant only has a "hope" that his application will be successful. [35] But, as we shall see, these are not the only cases in which a fair procedure is required.

The distinction must not be applied with undue rigidity because it does not always signify the gravity of the consequences upon the individual. For example, if an application by a family member for a licence to take over a family stall is refused, the consequences are far-reaching. In contrast, the consequences of the withdrawal of a small grant- a classic "forfeiture" case- might not be so serious. Arguably natural justice should apply in the former as much as in the latter case. The courts, as we shall see , have been responsive to these difficulties. Even in "application" cases, the courts have extended the scope of the duty to act fairly. [36]

Where the licensing authority proposes to revoke an existing licence the rules of natural justice apply. [37] Fair procedures are necessary to ensure what Galligan [38] has described as the "accuracy" of the decision, by giving the applicant the opportunity of contesting the evidence against him so that if forfeiture is to occur it occurs in the circumstances intended by Parliament. Similarly, fair procedures are required where the trader has a "legitimate expectation", an example of which occurs where the trader has held a licence and seeks its renewal. The court regards

---

[35] Megarry V-C in *McInnes v. Onslow-Fane* [1978] 1 WLR 1520, 1528 approved by Lord Diplock in *O' Reilly v. Mackman* [1983] 2AC 237.

[36] *R v. Huntingdon DC ex p Cowan* [1984] 1 WLR 501; *R v.Bristol City Council* (1985) 83 LGR 711.

[37] *McInnes v. Onslow-Fane, supra.* n (35)

[38] Op. cit. p332.

this interest as sufficiently important that it should not be denied without consultation.[39]

The renewal cases are but one example of the broader and developing doctrine of "legitimate expectation". Where such an expectation arises it normally creates process rights, but is not always so confined. The doctrine is one that is being developed rapidly by the courts and although its application remains somewhat indeterminate, [40] it can widen the circumstances in which the court will require a decision-maker to abide by fair procedures.

Apart from cases concerning the renewal of a licence, a legitimate expectation may arise from the past practice of the public body. A leading example of this is the GCHQ case [41] where an employer had a well established practice of consulting the recognised trade union concerning alterations in the terms of employment, although the union enjoyed no legal right to consultation. It was held that an expectation becomes enforceable by judicial review where the practice of consultation is so well established that it would be unfair or inconsistent with good administration for the decision-making body to depart from the practice in the case in question.

An agreement that a decision will only be taken after a certain procedure has been followed may also generate a legitimate expectation so that no decision may lawfully be reached without the consultation taking place. This was so in *R v. Secretary of State for Trade ex p Vardy* [42] where an agreement known as the modified colliery review procedure, concluded by British Coal with the coal miners' unions under statute provided for joint consultation machinery on matters relating to the closure of pits. The unions had a legitimate expectation that the procedure would be followed unless and until it was withdrawn by British Coal and a new machinery put in its place. British Coal, acted unlawfully in

---

[39] *McInnes v. Onslow-Fane, supra* n (35).

[40] See, generally, Forsyth, "*The Provenance and Protection of Legitimate Expectations,* (1988) 47 Cambridge Law Journal 238; Craig, "*Legitimate Expectations: A Conceptual Analysis,*" [1992] 108 LQR 7, and also Craig, *Administrative Law,* 2nd edition, 1989, pp 141- 143.

[41] [1985] AC 374.

[42] [1992] *The Times,* Dec 20th.

announcing pit closures without following the agreed consultation process.

Finally, and closely related to the above category, a representation, promise or undertaking by an administrator may also generate a legitimate expectation that the promise/undertaking will be respected. The promise/undertaking may be either that a certain procedure will be followed or that a right or privilege can continue to be enjoyed in the same way as it has been in the past. For example, if a public body has made a particular promise to an individual (or group of individuals) that a certain policy will be followed, the individual may demand that that policy be applied in his case, or that he should be consulted before that policy is altered. Thus the promise generating the legitimate expectation may, according to the circumstances, create procedural rights, or limit the decision making power of the public body. The authority's promise will be enforced so long as this is consistent with its statutory duty. An example of the former type of case is *A-G for Hong Kong v. Ng Yuen Shiu* [43] where the authorities were held to be bound by an undertaking to interview illegal immigrants into Hong Kong and to treat each case upon its merits, even though such immigrants had no legal right to be heard before deportation.

In many cases where a legitimate expectation arises the administrative body is bound to act in accordance with the rules of natural justice, the requirements of which are considered below.

Where what is at issue is an application for a licence unsupported by any legitimate expectation, the rules are somewhat less burdensome. In many "mere" application cases there is often only a duty to act fairly. Such cases normally stand apart because there is not usually a particular allegation or "charge" at issue. General questions of the suitability of the applicant and policy questions such as the number of licences already awarded will be normally govern the prospects of success of the application. These do not cast a slur on the plaintiff's character; some may be wholly unconnected with the applicant. Here the rules of natural justice are inappropriate. The courts are also aware of the administrative burden in imposing the requirements of natural justice in cases of

---

[43] [1983] 2 AC 629.

this kind. Nevertheless the licensing authority will always be bound to act fairly which means that it should reach a rational and unbiased decision and not one reached in pursuit of any arbitrary or capricious policy. [44]

However, these principles have been refined where a particular "charge" or allegation is levelled against the applicant even if the case is merely "an application" case. This means that where an application is to be refused because some particular objection or allegation has been made against the applicant, there should be an opportunity of refuting it. [45] It must not be forgotten, however, that para 6 of the street trading code does fortify the position of the applicant for street trading licences beyond the minimum standards of the general law. [46]

Examples from the Street Trading Code
Where street trading is regulated by statutory rules, it is a matter of construction of the statute whether and to what extent a licensing authority is under a duty to act fairly. The Local Government (Miscellaneous Provisions) Act 1982, may be taken as illustrative of the kinds of issues which arise in deciding the relevance and scope of the general law in the context of street trading.

Where a local authority is fixing the annual fee for licences and consents under Schedule 4 of the Local Government (Miscellaneous Provisions) Act 1982, the rules of natural justice are normally inapplicable. Traders do not have a right to be heard before those fees are established unless the particular circumstances of the case give rise to a legitimate expectation that a hearing would be granted. It makes no difference that the level of fee may affect the viability of a trader's business and place his livelihood in jeopardy. [47]

In so far as the grant and revocation of licences and consents is concerned, procedural requirements are stated to differ according to whether the applicant seeks a licence or a street trading consent. In the case of a street trading licence, the procedures are set out in

---

[44] *McInnes v. Onslow-Fane, supra* n. (35).
[45] Eg *Breen v. AEU* [1971] 2 QB 175.
[46] *Supra* p. 197 *et seq.*
[47] *R v. Manchester City Council ex p King* (1991) 89 LGR 696 .

para 6 of Sched 4 and these have already been noted. [48] These procedures may however be supplemented by the principles of the general law; for example in making representations at an oral hearing , there may be particular cases where the council ought to allow the trader to assisted by a lawyer. In a classic statement of the law, Byles J. stated:

"...although there are no positive words in a statute, requiring that the party shall be heard, yet the justice of the common law shall supply the omission of the legislature." [49]

Thus there may be circumstances where fairness would require additional process rights to be extended to the trader going beyond those in para 6. [50]

In contrast to the detailed provisions affecting street trading licences, Schedule 4 does not specify the procedures to apply in the case of street trading consents. There is no statutory procedure for the applicant to make representations, nor one for receiving objections. Nevertheless, in *R v. Bristol City Council ex p Pearce*, [51] it was held that such requirements may be implied under the general law where the applicant is to be denied a consent because there has been some particular allegation or objection to his or her application.

Here the court had to consider the position of mobile traders who had applied for street trading consents when the council had first adopted the street trading code in its area. Significantly, the court regarded this as a mere "application" case (and not one of a legitimate expectation) which meant that the applicants would only be entitled to the minimum procedural safeguards. Despite this, Glidewell J decided that the licensing authority was obliged to observe the rules of natural justice which meant that it had a duty to act fairly in considering the applications. He followed his own decision in *R v. Huntingdon District Council ex p Cowan* [52] and held that:

---

[48] Above at p. 197.
[49] *Cooper v. Wandsworth Board of Works* (1863) 14 CB(NS) 180.
[50] See further below.
[51] (1985) 83 LGR 711.
[52] [1984] 1 WLR 501.

"The exercise of a licensing function,...by any authority, is one to which the rules of natural justice-including the requirement of giving notice of the substance, at least, of the objections, and giving some opportunity for the applicant to respond to those objections-would normally apply." [53]

This does not, however apply to objections received from their own officers, nor from the police, nor from the county council. In such cases the substance of the objections does not have to be communicated to the applicant. Nor is the authority under a duty to give reasons for its final decision. [54]

After *Cowan* and *Pearce* important process rights will govern even applications for street trading consents in so far as the applicants will have the right to know of the substance of any objections to their application and be able to make representations about them. This does not mean, however, that such process rights will govern all application cases. Apart from the exception governing "in-house" and other "official" objections to an application, it must not be forgotten that where the application is rejected on purely policy grounds the applicant has no general right to make representations about the council's policy. The authority's duty is simply to ensure that it reaches an unbiased decision, and that its policy is a rational one.

Other Circumstances Generating an Entitlement to a Fair Hearing
A fair hearing may be required even where the rights or legitimate expectations of the trader are not at issue. The courts here seem to justify the imposition of procedural safeguards through a more general notion of fair administrative practice. Such emerges from *R v. Great Yarmouth BC ex p. Botton Bros Arcades Ltd.* [55] Here a local planning authority acted unlawfully in not consulting rival traders before approving plans for another amusement arcade where the approval departed from a previous policy of refusing such applications. In considering the matter, the authority had

---

[53] *Ibid.* at p 508.
[54] (1985) 83 LGR 711, 723-4. Note that this may have to be read subject to recent developments on the duty to give reasons discussed at pp. 316-318.
[55] [1988] JPL 18.

allowed the architect for the developers to address the planning committee.

Otton J held that the claim of the rival traders to be heard could not rest upon a legitimate expectation within the principle expounded in *GCHQ* [56] since they had not received a specific promise or undertaking that their views would be taken into account. His lordship held, however, that the special nature of the circumstances, the likelihood that their objections would have been "material" and the fact that the authority had heard the developers meant that, as part of the general duty to act fairly, the traders should have been consulted.

Procedure

If a matter is to be determined according to natural justice or fairness, the issue then is to decide what procedures must actually be followed. The starting point is an examination of the statute which confers the decision-making power. Only those procedural rules which are consistent with its terms will be implied by the courts. Although the courts are ostensibly engaged in isolating and interpreting the intention of the legislature, in essence the judiciary is required to repair the damage by the legislature's failure to incorporate into the statutory regime proper procedures for its just administration.

Administrators will search in vain for a codified statement of the procedural rules. The standard is a flexible and depends upon the circumstances of the particular case. The courts have stated:

"The requirements of natural justice must depend upon the circumstances of the case, the nature of the inquiry, the rules under which the tribunal is acting, the subject-matter that is being dealt with, and so forth..." [57]

"..the rules of natural justice -or of fairness-are not cut and dried. They vary infinitely." [58]

---

[56] *Council of the Civil Service Unions v. Minister for the Civil Service* [1985] AC 374.
[57] Tucker L.J in *Russell v. Duke of Norfolk* [1949] 1 All ER 109, at 118.
[58] *R v. Home Secretary ex p Santillo* [1981 QB 778 at 795 *per* Lord Denning MR.

It must always be remembered, however, that there is no penalty in applying a higher standard than the rules ordinarily require. Judicial intervention strikes at administrative acts vitiated by inadequate procedures.

Fairness lies at the heart of natural justice: "Natural justice is but fairness writ large and judicially". [59] It provides what is essentially the minimum standard of fairness; and the contents of this minimum standard can be identified in a *dictum* of Harman J.:

"First, I think that the person accused should know the nature of the accusation made; secondly, that he should be given an opportunity to state his case; and thirdly,... that the tribunal must act in good faith."[60]

This *dictum* does not exclude other rights from the principle of natural justice: it simply describes what is the minimum standard to be applied. Whether any more is required will depend upon the particular facts of the case. This is considered in more detail below.

The Right to Make Representations

Correct and fair decision making demands that the individual accused should know the case against him, know what evidence has been given, what statements have been made prejudicial to his case and that he should be given an opportunity of correcting them and advancing arguments in support of his own case. [61] He is entitled to know the case he has to meet. He cannot be accused of one offence and found guilty of another. [62] Nor, if particular facts are to be established before a decision is reached, can the authority reach a decision on those facts without giving the trader an opportunity to comment. [63] Whilst all the material facts must be disclosed, it is not necessary that the source of the information be divulged. [64] The

---

[59] *Furnell v. Whangerai High Schools Board* [1973] AC 660, 679.

[60] *Byrne v. Kinematograph Renters Society Ltd.* [1958] 2 All ER 579, 599.

[61] *Khanda v. Government of Malaya* [1962] AC 322.

[62] *Lau Luit Meng v. Disciplinary Committee* [1968] AC 391.

[63] *William Hill (Scotland) v. Kyle and Carrick DLB* (1991) SLT 559.

[64] *R v. Gaming Board for GB ex p Benaim and Khaida* [1970] 2 QB 417.

required information must be disclosed in sufficient time to enable the accused to make his objections. [65]

A Right to an Oral Hearing?

Although English law attaches weight to oral hearings, [66] it would place an impossible burden on the administration if all hearings were of such a character. Since reasoning and writing are not mutually exclusive processes [67] it is often sufficient to satisfy the rules of natural justice if the accused is allowed merely an opportunity to submit written representations in support of his case. Oral submissions are not seen as "the very pith of...natural justice".[68]

The true pith of natural justice is acting fairly. "An oral hearing should be held where, in all the circumstances, the issues cannot fairly be resolved otherwise.." [69] Of particular relevance will be whether the decision making body exercises a judicial function affecting the rights of traders and the question at issue involves substantial issues of disputed fact which cannot be resolved without an oral hearing. [70]

In *Lloyd v. Macmahon* [71] Lord Keith considered that an oral hearing would be "essential in the interests of fairness, for example where an objector states that he has personal knowledge of some fact indicative of wilful misconduct on the part of the (accused)." This is to put the duty at its highest. As Lord Bridge indicated, the nature of the accused's argument may lend itself more readily to written representations particularly where it comprises a large volume of documentary material. [72] And even where there is a *prima facie* duty to offer an oral hearing, it does not follow that in denying it the authority will act unfairly. It will depend on whether the failure to offer an oral hearing denied the accused the

---

[65] *R v. Thames Magistrates' Court ex p. Polemis* [1974] 1 WLR 1371.

[66] *Per* Woolf L.J. in *Lloyd v. McMahon* [1987] AC 625, 670.

[67] *Per* Hamilton L.J in *R v. Local Government Board v. Arlidge* [1914] 1 KB 160-192-3 approved [1915] AC 120.

[68] *Ibid.*

[69] *Per* Taylor L.J. *R v. Dept. of Health ex p Ganghi* [1991] 1 WLR 1053, 1063.

[70] *R v. Army Board of the Defence Council ex p Anderson* [1991] 3 All ER 375.

[71] [1987] AC 625 at p. 696.

[72] *Ibid* at p 706.

opportunity to supplement his written defence in any material respect. [73] Moreover, a failure to offer an oral hearing is more likely to be excused where the accused did not request such a hearing. If, however, such a request is made it may be desirable for the request to be granted. [74]

Procedure at an Oral Hearing

In the context of a statutory tribunal it has been held that it must (a) consider all the evidence which a party wishes to submit; (b) inform every party of all the evidence to be taken into account; (c) allow witnesses to be questioned; (d) allow comment on the evidence and argument on the whole case. [75]

(i) Evidence: The Right to Call Evidence and To Cross Examine
The rules of evidence are not part of natural justice [76] An administrative authority may take hearsay evidence into account provided that the accused trader has an ample opportunity to comment upon it and to refute it. [77]

Natural justice does not confer any *right* to call witnesses, or to cross examine. But the administrative body may have a discretion to permit this, and it must exercise any discretion reasonably, taking into account relevant considerations. It has been stated that mere administrative difficulties are not, by themselves, factors which be taken into account. [78] This probably means that if the proceedings would not be fair unless witnesses were called, the administrative problems such a process may cause cannot be pleaded to deny an opportunity to call those witnesses.

The guiding principle is that the accused trader must have a "fair chance of exculpation". Livingstone has argued persuasively[79] that a failure to exercise this discretion would, in

---

[73] *Ibid* at p. 714.
[74] *Ibid*.
[75] *R v. Deputy Industrial Injuries Commissioner ex p Moore* [1965] 1 QB 456, at p. 488.
[76] *Ibid* at p. 488.
[77] *R v. Hull Prison Board of Visitors ex p St Germain No 2* [1979] 1 WLR 1401, 1418.
[78] *Ibid*.
[79] (1987) 38 NILQ 144, 145.

most cases, be unfair; at least, it may, *prima facie*, be unfair. [80] Where witnesses have relevant evidence there is almost certainly a duty to allow the accused trader to produce them.

Since the administrative body is normally the master of its own procedure, it may limit the number of witnesses which may be called and the extent to which cross examination is permissible.

A trader who does not request the calling of witnesses or cross examination may not be able to challenge the resulting decision; and the proceedings may be deemed to be fair even without such processes being observed. [81]

Calling and cross examining witnesses is generally not required where the matter concerns a preliminary report or an investigation not leading to any penalty. [82] In such cases the duty to follow a fair procedure will be satisfied by offering the opportunity to make written representations. The residual duty to act fairly applies so that the trader must have an opportunity of commenting and correcting what has been alleged against him.

(ii) Representation
Much of the case law is concerned with whether there is a right to legal representation but the question should embrace lay representation as well. The principles applying to each may not necessarily be the same. Turning first to legal representation.

Legal Representation [83]
Lord Denning MR 's view was that legal representation can be crucial to the fairness of the hearing. In some cases the right to appear may be worthless without representation for, as Lord Denning MR stated, whether by reason of a lack of confidence or an inability to deal with complex issues, some individuals are not adequately able to defend themselves. [84]

The issue of a possible right to legal representation is not, however, clear-cut. Arguments against legal representation

---

[80] *R v. Nottingham Prison Board of Visitors ex p Mosley* [1981] The Times, 23rd January.
[81] *University of Ceylon v. Fernando* [1960] 1 All ER 631; *Lloyd v. McMahon supra* (63).
[82] *Re Pergammon Press Ltd.* [1971] Ch 388; *R v. Commission for Racial Equality ex p Cotterell* [1980] 1 WLR 1580.
[83] Livingstone offers a useful discussion: (1987) 38 NILQ 144.
[84] *Pett v. GRA Ltd.* [1969] 1 QB 125, 131.

emphasise that in most straightforward cases it is unnecessary unless a point of law arises, or the individual is not equipped to deal with his own case. Legal representation may also be undesirable because it can give undue weight to arguments based upon individual interests rather than those of public policy. The latter may not be given sufficient weight in a process which favours a narrow adversarial model. Other arguments add that it would also invite an unwelcome legalisation of the administrative process; informality could be sacrificed actually making it difficult for those traders who do wish to represent themselves to do so. Such developments might also be costly in terms of expense and delay.

It is now settled that natural justice does not embody a *right* to legal representation. [85] But this is not the end of the matter. To deny legal representation may still be unlawful where it would be unfair to proceed without it. The reasoning behind such a conclusion lies in a careful distinction between *right* and *discretion*. An administrative body may have a discretion to permit representation. Such a discretion must be exercised reasonably, and representation, whether by a lawyer or friend, must not be unreasonably refused. Factors such as the ability of the accused adequately to present his own case, the seriousness of the matter, whether the livelihood of the trader is at stake, whether any points of law are likely to arise, and the need for reasonable speed determine whether legal representation should be permitted. [86] It should be noted that in the street trading context, the loss of livelihood may well be a consequence of withdrawal of a trading licence. There are numerous dicta in the case-law that this consideration which should weigh heavily upon the discretion to grant representation. [87] It is also unlawful for any body to decide never to allow representation. A decision must be reached according to the circumstances of each case. [88]

---

[85] *Pett v. GRA Ltd No. 2* [1970] 1 QB 46; *Enderby Town FC Ltd. v. Football Association Ltd.* [1971] Ch. 591; *Fraser v. Mudge* [1975] 1 WLR 432; *Ex p. Hone* [1988] 2 WLR 177.

[86] *R v. Secretary of State for the Home Department ex p. Tarrant* [1984] 1 All ER 798, approved by the House of Lords in *R v. Board of Visitors of HM Prison, the Maze, ex p Hone* [1988] 2 WLR 177.

[87] *Pett v. GRA Ltd., supra* n (84); *Maynard v. Osmond* [1977] QB at 252.

[88] *Enderby Town FC v. Football Assoc,.* per Lord Denning MR [1971] Ch 591, 607.

Mere administrative" difficulties are not enough to deny legal representation. [89] The precise effect of such a rule is unclear. It may simply mean that if fairness cannot be achieved without representation, administrative inconvenience cannot be used to deny it.

Lay Representation

If a trader seeks lay representation, many of the arguments designed to exclude lawyers, such as the avoidance of expense and the prevention of the legalisation of administrative procedures, have no relevance. Moreover, even in court proceedings a litigant appearing before the court in person does not require the leave of the court in order to be assisted by a lay adviser. [90]

The principle has recently been re-affirmed in the *Leicester City Justices case* where Staughton L.J stated, "..there are no general grounds for objecting to a litigant in person being accompanied by an assistant, who will sit beside him, take notes and advise *sotto voce* on the conduct of his case. If the court is open to the public, the assistant is entitled to be present in his own right provided that there is room; and if the litigant wishes him as an assistant, he should be accorded priority over the public in general. Any member of the public is entitled to take notes. And I can see no reason why a litigant in person should not, if he wishes, receive quiet and unobtrusive advice from a member of the public." [91]

This means that a lay person may assist in the presentation of the litigation, but he cannot normally conduct it. By analogy it may be appropriate for a trader to be allowed assistance in order better to present his case.

---

[89] *R v. Hull Prison Visitors ex p St Germain (No 2)* [1979] 1 WLR 1401.

[90] *Collier v. Hicks* (1831) 2 B 7 Ad 663 esp 669; *McKenzie* [1970] 3 All ER 1034; *R v. Leicester City Justices* [1991] 3 WLR 368, discussed Thomas [1992] P.L. 208.

[91] *Supra. n.* (90) at p. 380.

A Duty to Give Reasons? [92]

Whilst administrators should have proper reasons for their decisions, English law has traditionally not gone so far as to impose a general rule requiring these reasons to be communicated to the individual affected by the decision. There have, however, been a series of incursions into the general rule which, in one first instance decision, has itself been questioned.

Many arguments have been advanced in support of a general duty to give reasons for administrative decisions. At one level, the proponents of such a duty identify a value in open government and administrative candour. On a more practical level, if reasons are given it is more likely that reasons will then have been properly thought out. This is no doubt a "healthy discipline" for administrators. [93] The resulting exposure of faults in the decision making process tends to support the process of appeal and review. In so far as reasoned decisions avoid a perception by the trader of unfairness and arbitrariness, they also make decisions more acceptable by emphasising their rationality. This enhances public confidence generally.

Opponents of a duty stress that it might inhibit free discussion and place an intolerable burden upon the administration generally. Other arguments warn against the delay and expense that the giving of reasons would cause, and that it would promote a "legalisation" by stimulating appeals and judicial review. Moreover administrators might concentrate on making their reasons judge proof: candour might not inevitably flow from a general duty to give reasons.

Hitherto, a duty to give reasons has not been a general requirement of the rules of natural justice; [94] but exceptions have been created and expanded at a rapid pace, and the point has now been reached where even the general absence of a duty has been

---

[92] Under the street trading code, the trader will often know the reasons for decisions taken against him: above at p. 198.

[93] Report of the Committee on Administrative Tribunals and Enquiries Cmnd 218 (1957) para 98. See also Justice/ All Souls Report on Administrative Justice pp69-71 for a general discussion.

[94] *R v Civil Service Appeal Board ex p Cunningham* [1991] 4 All ER 310; *R v. Gaming Board for Great Britain ex p Benaim and Khaida* [1970] QB 417, 431, also (1970) 33 MLR 154 Akehurst.

refuted. [95] There are now circumstances in which a failure to give reasons may lead to the quashing of the decision in question.

First, it has long been accepted that where a right of appeal exists, it is necessary that reasons be given to facilitate such a right. Often such a duty arises from statutory interpretation, but it has been suggested that similar results flow from natural justice. [96]

Second, the House of Lords in *Padfield v. Minister of Agriculture and Fisheries* [97] indicated that a failure to give reasons may suggest that the decision is irrational if all *prima facie* reasons seem to point in favour a particular decision, but the administrator has adopted a contrary decision without seeking to justify such a course by the giving of reasons. [98] But this only applies where all known factors appear to indicate that the only rational decision would be one different from that reached. The court will not interfere where there were reasons which could have justified the decision even if no reasons were actually given. [99]

A further significant curtailment of the general rule was signalled in *R v. Lancashire County Council ex p Huddleston.* [100] Public authorities must give reasons to the court when a decision is challenged by way of judicial review even if the applicant was not entitled to a statement of reasons. The significant limitation in the *Huddleston* approach is that it only applies where leave has been granted. The applicant who cannot show a *prima facie* case cannot rely on this decision. If the absence of a general duty to give reasons survives, it will bear most heavily on this kind of case.

The Court of Appeal made a further incursion into the general absence of a duty to give reasons in *R v. Civil Service Appeal Board ex p Cunningham.*[101] Here it was acknowledged for the first time that a duty to give reasons could be encompassed by the rules of natural justice. How far the decision will benefit traders in the licensing context is unclear since much emphasis was placed upon the judicial nature of the public function as a pre-requisite of any

---

[95] *R v. Lambeth BC ex p Walters* [1993] The Times Oct 6th.
[96] *Norton Tool Co. Ltd. v. Tewson* [1973] 1 WLR 45.
[97] [1968] AC 997.
[98] *R v. Trade and Industry Secretary ex p Lonrho plc* [1989] 1 WLR 525.
[99] *Cannock Chase D.C. v. Kelly* [1978] 1 WLR 1.
[100] [1986] 2 All ER 941.
[101] [1991] 4 All ER 310.

duty. Javan Herberg has, however, argued [102] for a wider reading of the decision. However, the court in *R v. Lambeth BC ex p Walters* [103] appears to have used this decision as a spring board to impose a general duty to give reasons, at least where the administrative body is bound by a duty to act fairly towards the applicant. This is a welcome development but one which is not easy to reconcile with long established authority.

If *Ex p Walters* does now represent the law, it only imposes a minimum burden. The judge cautioned against setting too high a standard. It was enough for the decision maker to show that he had directed his mind to the relevant issues. Anything more would turn the administrative process into something resembling a judicial one.

It must not be forgotten that a duty to give reasons may also arise on the facts of a particular case where the trader has a legitimate expectation that reasons would be given. [104]

The Rule Against Bias

It is elementary to the rules of natural justice that the deciding body is to be free from 'bias'. The rule determines who is qualified to decide the matter in question. Bias might arise in a number of ways. The decision-maker may have a personal interest in the outcome of the decision; he or she may have overlapping roles as, for example, in the case where a prosecutor assists in the decision; or, finally, bias might arise where a body, having already determined policies preventing it from deciding a matter with complete impartiality, cannot exercise a proper discretion. [105]

A hall-mark of the rule against bias is that appearance counts for more than the reality: Lord Atkin's injunction that "justice should not only be done, but should manifestly and undoubtedly be seen to be done" [106] is familiar to all. The application of the rule is not always self-evident: judges and administrators may sometimes be remotely connected with the matter in issue without there being

---

[102] [1991] P.L, 340.
[103] [1993] The Times, Oct 6th.
[104] *Infra*. See above pp. 303-306 and below pp. 336-337.
[105] See, eg, *Bromley LBC v. GLC* [1983] 1 AC 768.
[106] *R v Sussex Justices ex p McCarthy* [1924] 1 KB 256, 259.

any real likelihood or even suspicion of impropriety or favouritism. The task of the courts is to strike the difficult balance of preserving the integrity and impartiality of the administrative process without overturning *bona fide* administrative decisions on the "flimsiest pretexts of bias". [107]

It is trite law that a person who has a direct financial interest in the outcome, no matter how small, will be disqualified from deciding a particular matter regardless of whether there was any likelihood of bias. [108] Statutory recognition of this principle is enshrined in s.94 of the Local Government Act 1972 which makes it an offence for any member of a local authority to take part in or vote on any contract or other matter in which he or she has a pecuniary interest whether this is direct or indirect. [109]

Disqualification also arises *de cursu* if actual bias on the part of the decision maker is established. Naturally that will arise only rarely. In cases other than those involving actual bias, or a pecuniary interest, there has been some difference of opinion as to whether the decision should be invalid where there is a " a real likelihood of bias" or a "real suspicion of bias". The "real likelihood" test was accepted by Blackburn J in *R v. Rand* [110] but support for the "reasonable suspicion test" derives from the classical judgment of Lord Hewart C.J in *R v. Sussex Justices, ex p McCarthy,* [111] and it has found recent support. [112]

The question is not merely of academic interest because, depending on how each test is actually interpreted, [113] the outcome can differ according to which test is applied. If there is a need to establish a probability of bias fewer cases are likely to succeed

---

[107] *R v. Camborne Justices ex p Pearce* [1955] 1 QB 41 at 52.
[108] *Dimes v. Grand Junction Canal Co. Proprietors* (1852) 3 HLC 759; *R v. Rand* (1866) LR 1 QB 230; *R v. Gough* [1993] 2 All ER 724, 730.
[109] But if he or she so acts whilst disqualified the actions will not be invalidated: s.82.
[110] (1866) LR 1 QB 230, 275; also *Frome United Breweries Co v. Bath Justices* [1926] AC 586 esp 590, 615, 618; *R v. Essex Justices ex p Perkins* [1927] 2 KB 475, 488 (reasonable likelihood); *R v. Camborne Justices ex p Pearce* [1955] 1 QB 41, esp 51.
[111] [1924] 1 KB 256, 259.
[112] See, eg, *per* Ackner L.J. *R v. Liverpool City Justices ex p Topping* [1983] 1 WLR 119, 123, apparently approved in *R v. Board of Visitors of Frankland Prison ex p Lewis* [1986] 2 WLR 132 and applied in *R v. Ely Justices ex p Burgess* [1992] The Times, August 21st.
[113] *R v. Gough* [1993] 2 All ER 724.

than if the need is to establish merely that a reasonable person might suspect bias.

There have also been suggestions that a variable standard is appropriate favouring the reasonable suspicion test if a body exercised a judicial function . [114] Any further development of this reasoning has, however, been curtailed by the decision of the House of Lords in *R v. Gough* [115] in which their lordships favoured a single test for all cases of apparent bias based on the "real likelihood" test which, it was stated, should prevent a decision-maker from acting where there is a "real danger of bias". A decision in which there was no danger that the alleged bias caused injustice should not be quashed. [116]

Further the court decided that it would be unnecessary to require a court to look at the matter through the eyes of the reasonable man because the court itself personifies the reasonable man.

Mixed Functions

Bias may arise an individual who has been active in the prosecution of a matter subsequently participates in the adjudication process. This occurred in a well-known market case, *R v. Barnsley Metropolitan Borough Council ex p Hook* [117] where a market trader who had been charged with a minor offence was banned for life from trading in the market by the market manager. Subsequently the trader was allowed a hearing before members of the council's sub committee with the market manager in attendance. The manager was also present at a further appeal. As Scarman LJ. emphasised, because the trader was appealing against the loss of his livelihood, the subject matter of the proceedings made it a case in which the authority should scrupulously have observed the principles of fairness. The ban was quashed because this was very

---

[114] *Steeples v. Derbyshire CC* ,(decided 1981) [1985] 1 WLR 256, 287-88.

[115] [1993] 2 All ER 724.

[116] *Ibid.* Delivering the judgement in which all concurred. Lord Goff seemed, however, to be referring only to judicial bodies (p.73); cf Lord Woolf (p.740). Even if this is so, however, administrative bodies are still subject to the real likelihood test after *Steeples v. Derbyshire, supra* (114).

[117] [1976] 3 All 452.

much the kind of case in which the prosecutor should not have taken part in the adjudication. [118]

Personal Opinion

If an administrator has formed an opinion or has a view on a matter before it falls to be decided, this need not disqualify him from deciding the question. It is different where he has in fact pre-judged the issue. For example, a magistrate who belongs to an active temperance society is not disqualified from deciding licensing matters merely because he holds strong opinions on the evils of alcohol. [119] This is because administrators and judges are inevitably going to hold opinions on a wide range of matters. What is required of them is that they decide a matter with impartiality. If, however, it can be established that a decision maker was probably influenced by his beliefs, the decision will be set aside. This occurred where a magistrate, who belonged to the Order of Rechabites- an active temperance society- voted to refuse a liquor licence and subsequently revealed that he would have been a "traitor" to the Rechabites if he had voted in favour of the licence.[120]

Policy Preferences

As the Committee on Ministers' Powers [121] noted, administrators committed to the public service may have a "zeal...which can scarcely fail to bias them unconsciously". Whether this will result in invalidity depends upon the circumstances of the case. The legal consequences of espousing a prior political commitment are, however, more appropriately considered in the chapter concerning "retention of discretion". [122]

---

[118] See especially Scarman LJ *ibid.* at p.460.

[119] *R v. Halifax ex p Robinson* (1912)) 76 JP 233; *R v. Nailsworth Licensing Justices ex p Bird* [1953] 1 WLR 1046.

[120] *R v. Halifax ex p Robinson, ibid.*

[121] Cmnd 4060 (1932) at p. 78.

[122] Ch. 18.

322   *The Law of Street Trading*

Necessity

If the decision maker whose impartiality is questioned is the only person or body statutorily empowered to act, what would otherwise constitute bias will not disqualify. [123]

Waiver

There is some authority that an objection should be taken that the proceedings are unfair as soon as the individual affected by them becomes aware of the defect. If he does not do so, he may be deemed to have waived his right to object. [124] If correct, it is therefore inappropriate to remain silent on the issue in the hope of a favourable outcome, ostensibly reserving the right to mount a subsequent challenge if the outcome proves to be unfavourable. However, there is some doubt whether this rule continues to be applied strictly. [125] And it appears to be inconsistent with the fundamental principle that a breach of the rules of natural justice renders a decision void. [126]

---

[123] Eg, *Dimes v. Grand Junction Canal Co Proprietors*, (1852) 3 HLC 759 *The Judges v, A-G for Saskatchewan* (1937) 53 TLR 464.

[124] *R v. Nailsworth Licensing Justices ex p Bird* [1953] 1 WLR 1046.

[125] *R v. Barnsley MBC ex p Hook* [1976] 1 WLR 1052 where the trader might have objected to the presence of the market manager at any stage in the appellate process. The possibility of waiver does not seem, however to have been argued.

[126] *Ridge v Baldwin* [1964] AC 40.

CHAPTER 17

ABUSE OF DISCRETION

In licensing matters, and in street trading in particular, Parliament often confers wide discretionary powers upon administrators. Two examples from the Street trading code illustrate the kind of power conferred. Paragraph 2 of Schedule 4 states that " A district council may by resolution designate any street in their district as "a prohibited street, a licence street or a consent street." Para 7 (2) states that, subject to the limitations in a sub paragraph (3), the council may grant a street trading consent if they think fit. Power is ostensibly drafted in subjective terms in so far as the council seems to be unimpeded in the exercise of its discretion. This is a case, however, where the appearance masks the reality.

Subjectivity

The above examples are illustrative of cases where statute seems to make the subjective judgment of an authority the only pre-condition to an exercise of the power. This form of drafting might be thought to make the honest belief of the authority the only relevant consideration; proof that it has such a belief would then be sufficient to exclude review. In fact, this is another occasion when the process of statutory interpretation is coloured by judicial policy: the literal approach is conspicuously abandoned. The effect is that such formulations are treated as if drafted objectively, and the decisions of local authorities are amenable to review on the principles that will shortly be considered. The reason for this is that uncontrolled exercise of discretionary power contradicts the constitutional principle of the Rule of Law. All power has legal limits; the task of the courts is to identify and to enforce them. [1]

Traditionally this is done out of obedience to Parliament which cannot have intended to confer almost absolute power. As Wade states,[2] in principle, the same limits should apply regardless of how subjective the language used in the drafting.[3] The rules governing the use of discretionary power will now be considered in more detail.

The Limits Implied by the Courts

The Use of Power for an Improper Purpose

A statutory power may only be employed for the purposes laid down in the relevant statute. These purposes may be expressed within the statute or implied from its general scope and intent. It is well-established that any thing done which is incidental to an express power will not be treated as *ultra vires* unless expressly prohibited.[4] The existence of implied powers can be recognised in statute. Under s.111(1) of the Local Government Act 1972, a local authority has power to do anything which is "calculated to facilitate, or is conducive or incidental to, the discharge of any of their functions." This confers implied power to act in furtherance of its *intra vires* functions.[5] An authority's "functions" embrace all of its the powers and duties. [6]

In searching for the purpose for which a power was conferred, the statute must be examined as a whole. The application of this principle is not always straightforward. An important and recent example in which a local authority erred was *R v, Manchester City Council ex p King.*[7] Here the authority increased the fees for street

---

[1] Eg, *Sydney Municipal Council v. Campbell* [1925] AC 338.

[2] Wade, *Administrative Law*, 6th edition, 1988, pp. 445 *et seq.*

[3] See also Lord Wilberforce in *Secretary of State for Education and Science v. Tameside MBC* [1977] AC 1014, at p.1047.

[4] Eg, *Per* Lord Selborne LC in *A-G v. Great Eastern Rly Co.* (1880) 5 App Cas 473, 481.

[5] Eg, *Hazell v. Hammersmith and Fulham LBC* [1991] 1 All ER 545.

[6] *Ibid*, p 554.

[7] (1991) 89 LGR 996, considered below.

trading licences issued under the Local Government (Miscellaneous Provisions) Act 1982 by an amount in excess of 1000%. It will be recalled that they had been guided by commercial considerations and sought to impose the maximum charges that the market would bear. The court held that the council had purported to achieve an improper purpose. On its true construction, the 1982 Act was concerned with the regulation and control of street trading. It enabled local authorities to charge reasonable fees having regard to the costs of administering the scheme and prosecuting offenders. The power to licence was not an income-producing asset but simply a regulatory power.

Unreasonableness

Introduction
Lord Greene's exposition of reasonableness in *Associated Provincial Picture Houses Ltd v. Wednesbury Corporation*[8] has become classical. It is often referred to as the "*Wednesbury*" test or formula in which he stated:

"It is true that discretion must be exercised reasonably. Now what does this mean? Lawyers..often use the word "unreasonable" in a rather comprehensive sense. It has frequently been used ...as a general description of things that must not be done. For instance, a person entrusted with a discretion must...direct himself properly in law. He must call his own attention to the matters which he is bound to consider. He must exclude from his consideration matters which are irrelevant to what he has to consider. If he does not obey those rules, he may truly be said... to be acting unreasonably. Similarly, there may be something so absurd that no sensible person could ever dream that it lay within the powers of the authority..."

This formulation embraces two strands, each of which has radically different consequences. First, if the decision-maker takes into account irrelevant matters or fails to address relevant ones, he or she is acting unlawfully. This strand of reasonableness examines the decision-making process. It is, as Lord Brightman indicated, [9] a

---

[8] [1948] 1 KB 223, 229.
[9] *Chief Constable of North Wales Police v. Evans* [1982] 1 WLR 1155 at p. 1174.

process of review based on the manner in which the final decision was reached. Review under this category does not control the outcome. This means that where the decision is quashed the decision-maker is at liberty to re-consider the matter and to reach the same decision provided that in doing so he directs his mind to the relevant questions etc. The second limb is more far-reaching. If the court decides that the decision is "irrational", in other words "so absurd that no sensible person could ever dream that it lay within the powers of the authority", the court is controlling the outcome of decision. The decision, or course of action resolved upon, is an illegitimate one; it is outside the power of the decision-maker and can never be adopted.

Relevancy/Irrelevancy

Identifying which considerations are relevant to a particular decision depends upon the construction of the statute in question. Often the ambit of relevancy is implied from its scope and intendment, although the courts clearly execise a creative role in this field.[10] If a consideration is relevant, the administrator must normally asddress his or her mind to it. It need not, be decisive of the matter in issue where there are other competing considerations.[11]

It has been argued that unless a decision maker is expressly required to take into account a particular consideration, he can only 'impliedly' be required to take it into account if it is one which no reasonable body would fail to consider. This is incorrect. A relevant consideration is mandatory in the sense that the administrator is bound to consider it. [12] Yet a failure to do so will not invariably lead the court to quash the decision. [13] Where the factor wrongly omitted is "insignificant" the court is unlikely to grant relief.[14] But the court's discretion to refuse relief is not confined merely to cases where the error is trivial.[15]

---

[10] Eg, *Roberts v. Hopwood* [1925] AC 578.

[11] *Cumings v. Birkenhead Corporation* [1972] Ch 12.

[12] Per Hodgson J in *R v. Secretary of State for the Environment ex p Bolton Metropolitan BC* [1991] JPL 32.(Decision appealed but appeal dismissed on other grounds).

[13] See Hodgson J *ibid* at p. 35.

[14] *Hanks v. Minister of Housing and Local Government* [1963] 1 QB 999, 1020.

[15] *Supra* n (13).

A well-known example of how the courts define the ambit of relevancy is *Roberts v. Hopwood* [16] which is perhaps one of several decisions which take judicial control to its very limits. Poplar Borough Council, elected on a socialist manifesto, resolved to become a "model employer". In a period of deflation it did not reduce its wages but continued to pay men and women equally £4 per week. The relevant statute gave it power to pay its employees "such wages as..(it) ..may think fit." [17] There was no express statutory restriction on the factors which should guide them in setting wages.

The District Auditor considered the payments to be excessive and disallowed a proportion of the expenditure in so far as it related to the excess. Councillors were surcharged, and this was eventually upheld in the House of Lords because the wage rates were unlawful in so far as they exceeded the market rate. Lord Sumner observed that the council had failed to be guided by ordinary economic considerations and had been influenced by such irrelevant considerations as its socialist principles. When it is recalled that the statute *ex facie* merely empowered the council to pay such wages as it thought fit this result powerfully demonstrates how far-reaching are the judicially implied limitations on administrative powers.

Although the courts often profess to identify relevant considerations by a process of statutory interpretation, [18] in many cases searching for legislative intention is, for most practical purposes, fruitless: indeed such expression would probably be inimical to the purpose of conferring wide discretionary powers. As *Roberts v. Hopwood* demonstrates, the judicial process is far more creative; relevancy is determined by judicial perceptions as much as legislative directions and can give rise to considerable uncertainty both for administrators and those affected by the decision because it is clearly difficult to predict in advance what considerations the court will regard as relevant.

This problem is compounded by doctrinal uncertainties. For example, in *Roberts* the authority erred by giving insufficient weight to market forces notwithstanding its election promises.

---

[16] [1925] AC 578.

[17] Metropolitan Management Act 1855, s.62.

[18] E.g., *Congreve v. Home Office* [1976] QB 629.

Other judicial decisions have, however, emphasised the weight and importance of respecting local democracy. [19] and some sympathy can be felt for the decision-maker who on the facts of *Roberts* might have felt that breaching an election promise was "more" relevant and had a greater bearing on the wage setting process than merely embracing the wages policy of other employers. [20] This reveals the confusion in judicial values.

The real difficulty for administrators is that policy considerations conflict: in *Roberts* the interests of the local ratepayers were in conflict with local authority employees. The administrator gave greater weight to the latter, and the court to the former. The decision was one based on policy. This could not have been identified from the statutory context in which Parliament had offered no directions to administrators. [21]

Similar problems of interpretation and lack of certainty can, of course, be seen in the leading street trading decision in *Ex p King*. [22] But this decision, in contrast to that in *Roberts*, rejects commercial considerations ostensibly to reflect the different purposes of the legislation.

The difficulty for administrators faced with the appearance of unfettered discretionary power is to identify the kinds of limits the courts will imply *before* proceedings are actually commenced. *Roberts* and *Ex p King* demonstrate that the indeterminacy both of principle and outcome in judicial review makes this task a difficult one.

Mixed Motives
Difficult questions arise where a decision is be based upon a mixture of relevant and irrelevant considerations, or where the authority has acted for a plurality of purposes, some of which fall entirely within its powers and others do not. In such circumstances, is the decision liable to be set aside?

---

[19] Eg, *Kruse v. Johnson* [1898] 2 QB 91.

[20] There is also an argument that to shadow the wages policy of other employers would have been an unlawful surrender of discretion! *Infra* Ch. 18.

[21] See also decisions such as *Bromley LBC v GLC* [1983]1 AC 768; *Wheeler v. Leicester City Council* [1985] 1 AC 1054.

[22] (1991) 89 LGR 996.

Professor Evans [23] aptly described the topic of plurality of powers as a "legal porcupine which bristles with difficulties as soon as it is touched." In the past, the courts have adopted a number of approaches to resolving this issue, some of which are mutually inconsistent. [24] A detailed analysis lies beyond the scope of the present work, but it may be noted that, of these, the most orthodox was probably the "dominant purpose" approach which legitimated action undertaken for multiple objectives if the dominant purpose or objective fell with the statutory power. Accordingly, where an authority exercised a statutory power to construct public conveniences, and did so with an entrance on each side of the street so that the facility could be used as a sub-way, the court held that it had acted within its powers because "(i)n order to make out a case of bad faith it must be shewn that the corporation constructed this subway as a means of crossing the street under colour and pretence of providing public conveniences which were not really wanted at that particular place." [25] This demonstrates that if the authority has used its powers for the proper object, it is immaterial that a subsidiary object has been obtained.

The more modern approach is to examine whether the decision is vitiated by irrelevant considerations.[26] Under this approach, if the irrelevant consideration (i.e. the improper purpose) has materially influenced the authority's decision, the decision is a nullity. If the influence of an irrelevant factor is established, it does not appear to be necessary to prove that it was the sole or even the dominant influence; it seems enough to prove that its influence was substantial.[27] If this influence has not been "substantial", the court will normally not interfere.[28]

If the lawful and unlawful considerations are separate, as, for example, where separate reasons are given for a decision, some of which are, and others of which are not, lawful, the court may not

---

[23] "de Smith's Judicial Review of Administrative Action 4th edit (1980) pp 329.
[24] *Ibid.*
[25] *Per* Lord Macnaghten, *Westminster Corporation v. LNWR Co.* [1905] AC 426, 432.
[26] See Megaw J in *Hanks v. Mininster of Housing and Local Government* [1963] 1 QB 999, 1020, followed in *R v. Inner London Education Authority ex p. Westminster City Council* [1986] 1 WLR 28, Glidewell J. esp at p 49.
[27] Forbes J in *R v. Rochdale Metropolitan Borough Council ex p Cromer Ring Mill Ltd.* [1982] 3 All ER 761, 769-70, approving a passage in de Smith *loc cit.*
[28] See Megaw J in *Hanks, supra* n (26).

intervene if the body could have reached the same decision relying solely on the lawful reasons. [29] If, however, the relevant and irrelevant considerations are inextricably mixed up, the court will strike down the decision. Accordingly, the decision of a local authority to boycott Shell products as a protest against links the company had with South Africa was unlawful because, although it was partly motivated by a desire to promote race relations, (a lawful objective) it was tainted by a desire to put pressure on Shell to withdraw from South Africa. The wish to alter Shell's policy was inextricably bound up with the desire to promote race relations and thus the boycott was *ultra vires*.[30]

"Wednesbury" Unreasonableness
We are here concerned with an "irrational" decision, or one which unreasonable in the *Wednesbury* sense. This is one which the decision-maker has no power to make, and it can never be lawful regardless of the propriety of the procedures followed in making it. It is the substance of the decision which is impugned, not the manner in which it was reached. This doctrine denies authority to the administrator to reach decisions which are deemed to be "unreasonable"; and a decision may be unreasonable even though the administrator directed his mind to all relevant matters and has disregarded irrelevant ones. It may therefore fulfil Lord Diplock's "legality" requirement and yet be unlawful.

This is a developing area of law and the challenge it presents is to identify why a decision is unreasonable in the relevant sense. The oft-advanced principle is that the decision must be so unreasonable that no reasonable person could reach it. [31] Yet this disguises the real process and motivation of judicial review. As Jowell and Lester argue, [32] review often occurs where a decision is "coldly rational".[33] The tests for unreasonableness offer little practical certainty for administrators. The difficulty for them is to know when a court will intervene. Some commentators have,

---

[29] See May L.J. in *R v. Broadcasting Complaints Commission, ex p. Owen* [1985] QB 1153 at p 1177.
[30] *R v. London Borough of Lewisham ex p Shell UK Ltd.* [1988] 1 All ER 938.
[31] *Secretary of State for Education and Science v. Tameside MBC* [1977] AC 1014, 1074.
[32] [1987] PL 368.
[33] *Ibid.* p. 372.

however, identified in decisions condemned as unreasonable a series of separate grounds for substantive review which the *Wednesbury* principles merely camouflage. [34] Whilst there is some force in this, even the proponents admit that at least a residuary category of unreasonablenes (and therefore of uncertainty) is inevitable.

Because the doctrine places much power in the hands of the judges there have been repeated warnings that it should be used with delicacy. In *R v. Secretary of State for Trade and Industry ex p Lonrho* Lord Keith of Kinkel stated: " The judgments of the Divisional Court illustrate the danger of judges wrongly though unconsciously substituting their own views for the views of the decision-maker who alone is charged and authorised by Parliament to exercise a discretion. The question is not whether the Secretary of State came to a correct solution or to a conclusion which meets with the approval of the Divisional Court but whether the discretion was properly exercised." [35] Similar fears were expressed in *R v. Secretary of State for the Home Department ex p Brind* [36] and produced circumspection in introducing into English law a doctrine of proportionality lest that invite judges into weighing the merits of the decision. [37] Whether the judges have always been cognisant of these restraints can be judged in the following discussion. [38]

Despite these kinds of exhortation for restraint, the courts have sometimes been highly interventionist in this field; their activity is not merely confined to cases in which the decision is so "outrageous in its defiance of logic or of accepted moral standards" that no sensible person could have reached it.[39] *Wheeler v. Leicester City Council* [40] provides an important illustration of the

---

[34] *Ibid.* p. 368.

[35] [1989] 1 WLR 525, 535.

[36] [1991] 1 All ER 721.

[37] See in particular Lord Ackner at p735,and Lord Lowry at p739. Note also *Nalgo v. Secretary of State for the Environment* [1992] The Times, December 2nd.

[38] Some sign of a more cautious approach can be seen in *Nottinghamshire County Council v. Secretary of State for the Environment* [1986] AC 240,247 where Lord Scarman was also concerned to show caution in interfering in the substance of administrative decision making. He thought that challenge was only possible where the decison maker had taken leave of his senses.

[39] *Council of Civil Service Unions v. Minister of Civil Service* [1985] 2 AC 374, 410.

[40] [1985] 1 AC 1054. Noted (1985) 44 CLJ 333,Turpin.

scope of this power. Here Leicester City Council prevented a rugby club from using a recreation ground owned by the Council. The ban was imposed in the purported exercise of its statutory duty to promote race relations, [41] because the Council was unhappy with the Club's attitude to a proposed tour of South Africa in which three of its members were members of the touring side. It was also important that the Council was committed to a policy of good race relations and had resolved that there should be no sporting links with South Africa in accordance with the Gleneagles Agreement. It had a significant Asian and Afro-Caribbean population living in its area. The object of the ban was to signal its dissatisfaction with the Club.

The application to have the ban quashed failed both at first instance and before the Court of Appeal. The House of Lords unanimously reversed the decision of the Court of Appeal. Here the Council were condemned for forcing the club to accept their own policy and because it was prepared to use sanctions to achieve this end. The club was being punished although it had done nothing wrong and could not be obliged to accept views dictated by a public authority.

The decision underscores the willingness of the Courts to control the outcome of the decision-making process. As Peiris argues [42] such an approach seems to offer few concession to administrators confronted with contentious issues of public policy. An authority bound by a duty to promote race relations might reasonably have felt that it would act unlawfully if it took no action in the matter. Their lordships response is highly expansive of the supervisory role of the courts.

Presumptions of Ultra Vires Action
Decisions may be condemned as unreasonable or "irrational" where they offend values which the judges regard as important. It is important for the administrator to understand what these values are, and there are signs that some separate *prima facie* grounds for substantive review have been established. In employing these, the courts presume that a decision maker has no authority to disregard these values in the absence of a clear and unambiguous statutory

---

[41] Race Relations Act 1976, s.71.
[42] [1987] CLJ at pp. 80-81.

intention. This creates a *de facto* presumption that certain policies are illegitimate. The values upheld by the courts are thus bestowed with an almost constitutional significance.

Discrimination

An example of *prima facie* unreasonable action arises where the decision-maker purports to burden one section of society at the expense of another. Unless there is clear statutory authority for doing so the decision may be *ultra vires*. [43]

The Non Business-like Spending of Public Money: The Legality of Subsidy

In the absence of express and unequivocal statutory language, public money must be spent according to sound business principles and not employed for "philanthropic" purposes. [44] A local authority cannot discriminate between different classes of the population.

The presumptive sanctity of business principles in regulating public expenditure can be seen in *Bromley London Borough Council v. Greater London Council* [45] where the GLC was held to have acted unlawfully in issuing a precept to all London boroughs to levy an additional rate so that fares on London transport could be reduced. The court held that the fiduciary duty owed to the ratepayers required the pursuit of sound business principles in operating the public transport system. By incurring a deficit in running the system, the GLC had unlawfully burdened the ratepayers in order to benefit public transport users. [46] The decision evinces a strong judicial preference for arguments based on the sanctity of private property.

As Hutchinson suggests, by confining the scope of the legitimate action of the GLC to business principles the courts "confirming a very clear vision of society" [47] as well as disregarding the mandate

---

[43] *Bromley LBC v. GLC* [1983] 1 AC 768; *Kruse v. Johnson* [1898] 2 QB 91. See further below.

[44] *Roberts v. Hopwood* [1925] AC 578.

[45] *Supra* n (43).

[46] Cf *R v. London Transport ex p GLC* [1983] QB 484.

[47] [1986] 48 MLR at 308.

of local electorate. The decision clearly penetrates the sphere of elected decision-makers in formulating public policy, and demonstrates the activism of the courts in controlling the outcome of administrative decision-making.

A similar refusal to countenance decision-making having discriminatory effects can be seen in *Prescott v. Birmingham* [48] where a subsidised transport scheme was again condemned for burdening ratepayers in violation of accepted business principles in the absence of clear statutory authority to do so. There was no power to confer the "gift of free travel" on "benevolent or philanthropic grounds.." [49]

These decisions suggest that any local authority minded to do so must exercise caution in using economic concessions to subsidise street trading from local taxes. This may, however, be subject to the *caveat* that the regulation of street trading arising in a different legal context in which commercial considerations need not always be supreme. [50] Nevertheless, if these principles do apply, it is probably unlawful to make no charge for street trading licenses and consents since the costs of administering street trading would then be borne by the taxpayer. Whilst this so, it need not follow that a uniform charge must be made to all since it is consistent with business principles to impose differential charges according to the profitability of the trade. [51]

The legality of concessions which are made on grounds other than economic ones may depend upon their extent and purpose. In the *Prescott* case, Jenkins L.J. stated that travel concessions for children would probably be lawful because they were customarily adopted by transport undertakings and could probably be justified on business principles anyway.[52] This argument did not apply to concessions for the blind but could be "classed as a minor act of

---

[48] [1955] 1 Ch. 210.
[49] *Per* Jenkins L.J, *ibid.* at p.235.
[50] Eg *R v. Manchester City Council ex p King* (1991) 89 LGR 696.
[51] And there may be an analogy with with the local authority's ackwnowleged power to charge differential rents to their tenants: *Smith v. Cardiff Corporation No.2* [1955] Ch 159. There was held to be no obligation to subsidise affluent tenants by charging low rents. Similar considerations may apply to rent or stallage where a trader's business is highly profitable.
[52] *Supra.* n (48) at p. 236. This presumably because fare paying adults would be encouraged to use the 'buses.

elementary charity to which no reasonable ratepayer would be likely to object." [53] In an *obiter dictum* in *Ex p King* [54] Roche J. considered that a local authority administering the street trading code would not be bound to recover in the license fees all the costs of the scheme. It would be lawful to recover "such part of the cost of operating the scheme as they consider reasonable". These views seem to leave open some scope for concessionary regulation.[55]

The Sanctity of Private Property

The presumptive sanctity of interests rooted in private property has long influenced review on the grounds of irrationality. It can be seen in two well-known planning decisions [56] which have wider implications. In *R v. Hillingdon ex p Royco Homes,* [57] planning permission for development was granted subject to conditions that the house to which it related should be occupied by persons on the local authority's homeless persons' register. It was held that the conditions were invalid on the grounds of fundamental inconsistency with the rights of private ownership. They were also conditions which no reasonable planning authority could impose. The authority was essentially attempting to shift its statutory responsibilities onto a private developer. The principle is of general application and might apply in the street trading context to prevent, for example, a local authority granting a licence on condition that a trader assume some public burden such as removing refuse at his own expense caused by street traders other than himself.

---

[53] *Ibid.*

[54] *Supra* n (50).

[55] See also *R v. London Transport Executive ex p Greater London Council* [1983] QB 484 This was a sequel to the GLC case (noted above) where it was explained that the requirement to run public transport along business principles did not mean that fare revenue had to be maximised according to to ordinary commercial principles of profit and loss. If an efficient, economic and integrated transport system inevitably involved increased losses these could lawfully be incurred.

[56] *Hall v. Shoreham UDC* [1964] 1 WLR 240; *R v. Hillingdon ex p Royco Homes* [1974] QB 720.

[57] [1974] QB 720.

Administrative Inconsistency

In cases of administrative inconsistency the courts have sometimes turned to the emerging jurisprudence on legitimate expectations and "fairness" to prevent an authority from resiling from its promises. The law is in a rapid state of development and the tensions between these emerging trends, the shrinking of the concept of estoppel in public law, and other rules preventing an authority from fettering its discretion have yet to be satisfactorily resolved.

The point has, however, been reached where inconsistent dealings may vitiate a decision, either because a legitimate expectation has been breached, or because the administrator has violated the *Wednesbury* principles or both.

(i) Legitimate expectation

The doctrine of legitimate expectations evolved from the principles of natural justice and, as originally conceived, served to extend process rights. [58] The courts have since recognised legitimate expectations where the expectation is not so much a that a procedure will be followed before a decision is reached [59] but that there will be a particular outcome in the decision making process. For example, in *R v. Secretary of State for the Home Department ex p Khan* [60] a Home Office circular indicated that the Secretary of State would exercise his discretion if certain criteria were met. The Home Secretary subsequently chose to apply different criteria . It was held that the applicant had a legitimate expectation that the published criteria would be followed.[61]

It seems, however, that if an undertaking does have substantive effects, the public body can resile from it if there is some overriding public interest in so doing.[62] This is the essence of Parker LJ's dictum in *Ex p Khan*: the " Secretary of State is..at liberty to change the policy but in my view, *vis a vis* the recipient of such a letter, a new policy can only be implemented after such recipient has been given a full and serious consideration whether

---

[58] Eg, *Schmidt v. Secretary of State for Home Affairs* [1969] 2 Ch 149.
[59] *A-G for Hong Kong v. Ng Yuen Shiu* [1983] 2 AC 629.
[60] [1984] 1 WLR 1337.
[61] See also *R v. Secretary of State for the Home Dept. ex p Ruddock* [1987] 1 WLR 1482; *R v. Watford Borough Council ex p. Incorporated West Herts Golf Club* [1990] 1 EGLR 263.
[62] *HTV v. Price Commission* [1976] ICR 170.

there is some overriding interest which justifies a departure" from it. [63] This suggests that a legitimate expectation does not always guarantee substantive protection: the administrator will be free to depart from the expectation where the public interest so dictates. Naturally such an approach is fraught with uncertainty. There are signs that the courts are becoming more sensitive to arguments about fettering administrative discretion. [64] Legitimate expectations are increasingly protected by conferring process rather than substantive rights. This permits administrators to make necessary changes in policy provided that these changes are fairy carried out. In *R v. Torbay ex p Cleasby* [65] a local authority's licensing system, expected to endure at least until 1992, was lawfully altered in 1988, causing the applicant to suffer serious loss. Prior consultations had taken place with all affected by the change. It was held that the applicant could not, in the absence of any legal right, restrain the council from altering its policies where a fair procedure had been followed. In other words, if she had a legitimate expectation at all, it did not go beyond giving her procedural rights which the local authority had honoured. [66]

(ii) Inconsistent Dealings and the Wednesbury Principles
There is a significant overlap between the emerging doctrine of legitimate expectation and the *Wednesbury* principles because a body whose decision is quashed for breaching a promise or undertaking might be held to have failed to take into account a relevant consideration, or to have acted unreasonably or unfairly.

In *R v. Inland Revenue Commissioners ex p Preston* [67] the House of Lords considered that where the conduct of a public body is

---

[63] *Supra* n (60) at p. 1346.
[64] *R v. Secretary of State for Health ex p United States Tobacco International.* [1992] The Indep, Jan 4th.
[65] [1991] COD 142.
[66] See also *R v. Secretary of State for Trade ex p Vardy* [1992] The Times, Dec 30th where British Coal were held to be at liberty to withdraw the modified colliery review procedure provided it was replaced by an alternative. Legitimate expectations should not fossilise adminstrative policies. The trend is further illustrated in *R v. Criminal Injuries Compensation Bd ex p P* [1993] The Independent, April 29th. Where it was held that if what is claimed is a privilege and not a right the only legitimate expectation is that the cases will be treated according to current policy.
[67] [1985] AC 835.

equivalent to a breach of contract or a "breach of representation", its conduct could be so unreasonable as to invalidate the decision. Such conduct would constitute an abuse of power and so be unfair to the individual. For review to be available, the undertaking or statement relied on should be consistent with the statutory duty of the public body and "clear, unambiguous and devoid of relevant qualification." This means that no legitimate expectation could arise from an *ultra vires* concession made by a body with a duty to enforce a regulatory structure. [68] If, however, there is no breach of statutory duty and the authority cannot resile from its undertaking without substantial unfairness to the individual, it may act *ultra vires* if it purports to do so.

Further refinements occurred in the *MFK Underwriting Agencies Ltd* case, [69] where the court sought to control the operation of this doctrine to achieve safeguards for the public body, and yet do justice to the individual. Whilst it upheld the principle that a promise by a public body in relation to its future actions can generate a legitimate expectation that the promise will be honoured, casual or informal undertakings given by junior staff would not normally be binding. Thus the manner in which the undertaking was given would be an important issue.

It was held that if a policy or undertaking were published in a formal manner, it would be binding on any case falling within that published policy. If the undertaking were of a less formal nature it would be necessary to show that the representee behaved openly in relation to the public body [70] because it was important that the body should know of the reliance the individual was proposing to make on the statement. It should know the precisely what undertaking the individual sought. This information would enable the authority to know whether it was appropriate to make any undertaking at all and, if so, at what level the problem should be considered. [71] This would allow senior staff to decide whether an

---

[68] An extreme example might arise if a local authority undertook to allow a person under 17 years to street trade. This is prohibited by para 3 (4) of the street trading code.

[69] [1990] 1 All ER 90.

[70] A concept evocative of Equity.

[71] See especially Bingham L.J. at p. 410.

undertaking was appropriate and, if necessary, allow them not to give one if flexibility was to be preserved.

These *caveats* suggest that mere casual remarks by less senior staff will not necessarily generate a legitimate expectation and so not become binding.[72] Internal practices should therefore be structured to require junior staff to refer the matter to more senior personnel where the matter can be fully appraised. As Mowbray suggests, the citizen can then know that the undertaking he receives is a considered one and he can justifiably rely on it.

It was again stressed that any undertaking must not conflict with the statutory duty of the administrative authority. This could, however, give rise to difficulties in its application. Judicial creativity may enable the courts to exploit tensions in the inter-relationship of the powers and duties of a public authority and so possibly to widen its statutory competence. For example, counsel in the *MFK Underwriting Agencies Ltd* case had argued that the Revenue's undertaking which diminished the tax liability of the applicants could not be binding because the statutory duty of the Revenue was to collect the taxes levied by Parliament. It had no dispensing power and so any purported undertaking fell outside its powers and conflicted with its statutory authority. The court succeeded in "expanding" the scope of the legitimate action of the Revenue by holding that it did have a a power to give assurances and advice to taxpayers in order to encourage co-operation between the public and the Revenue. Undertakings such as that given did not necessarily conflict with its statutory duty to collect taxes.

Proportionality and Wednesbury Unreasonableness
As will by now be apparent, Administrative law continues to grow at a rapid pace. The rate of change has generated speculation as to whether a doctrine of "proportionality" should be developed as a separate head of judicial review. If it were, administrative action might be invalidated simply because it was excessive or disproportionate to the problem it sought to address.

In the *GCHQ* case, Lord Diplock ventured the possibility that "proportionality, recognised in some continental jurisdictions," might well be developed as part of our law. [73] In this, Lord Diplock

---

[72] Mowbray (1990) LQR at p. 570.
[73] *Council of Civil Service Unions v. Minister of Civil Service* [1985] 2 AC 374, 410.

was recognising that the seed germs of such a doctrine already lay in the soil of the common law and that these seeds were possibly about to sprout. In one of the famous market trader cases, *R v. Barnsley Metropolitan Borough Council ex p Hook* [74] it will be recalled that the trader was banned for life from the market for having committed the minor offence of urinating in a side street after the market and public lavatories were closed. The ban was quashed on the grounds of bias because the market manager who had "prosecuted" the case had also participated in deciding the outcome. Lord Denning MR also held, however, that the court could intervene because of the excessive severity of the punishment. Sir John Pennycuick was also prepared partly to rest his decision upon that ground, although Scarman L.J. expressly confined his reasons for quashing the ban to the breach of the rules of natural justice.

The state of the law concerning proportionality was considered by the House of Lords in *R v. Secretary of State for the Home Department, ex p Brind*.[75] In general it was unwilling to expand review beyond the scope of the existing Wednesbury principles. These already outlaw a decision which suffered from a "total lack of proportionality" because such a decision would be one which no reasonable decision-maker could make. To go further and allow an attack based on "proportionality" would be a "wrongful usurpation of power" [76] blurring the distinction between appeal and review by entangling the courts in the merits of decisions.[77]

Nevertheless there were indications that the door has not finally been closed. Lord Roskill (with whom Lord Bridge agreed) left open the possibility of a future developments based on proportionality, but thought that the doctrine would not have been appropriate on the facts of *Brind* anyway.

Many cases which could be attacked on "proportionality" grounds may alternatively be vulnerable on existing grounds of review. As already noted, some such cases will be irrational because the steps taken were so excessive that no reasonable administrator could have acted similarly. Moreover, a

---

[74] [1976] 3 All ER 452.
[75] [1991] AC 696, noted Lewis (1991) CLJ 211.
[76] *Ibid., per* Lord Ackner at p.757.
[77] *Ibid* at pp 758 and 767.

"proportionality" case may well involve a failure to address relevant matters, or the consideration of irrelevant ones.

CHAPTER 18

RETENTION OF DISCRETIONARY POWER

The Rule Against Delegation

It is a cardinal principle of administrative law that a power must be exercised by the authority upon whom it is conferred. To hold otherwise would defeat the intention of Parliament in entrusting that body with the power in question. This means that power is normally inalienable; for example, it cannot normally be delegated to another body or individual unless there is a specific statutory authority to do so. This meant that the dismissal of a dock worker was ineffective because a Board which had the power to dismiss had exceeded its powers by delegating the matter to a disciplinary committee.[1]

Permissible Delegation

Delegation is, however, a necessary and inevitable process and exceptions to the general rule have been recognised by statute. The Local Government Act 1972, s.101 allows local authorities (subject to certain exceptions) to allow for the discharge of their functions by committees, sub-committees or officers of the authority, or by any other local authority. By such delegation, committees may have one of two types of power to reach a decision. In some cases, the decision becomes effective as soon as it is reached by the committee. In others, a decision may not be effective until confirmed by the authority. If a committee is authorised to act in either of the above

---

[1] *Vine v. National Dock Labour Board* [1957] AC 488.

senses, it may delegate power to a sub-committee or to an officer[2] unless the local authority directs to the contrary.

Two or more local authorities may discharge their functions jointly, for example through joint committees or even through an officer of one of the authorities. [3] Under s.101 there is, however, no power to delegate to a member of the authority. [4] This rule cannot be evaded by creating single member committees. [5] It is, however, common for standing orders to provide that power may be delegated to an official acting in consultation with a member.[6] This is acceptable provided that the donee of the power- the official- exercises his discretion and does not act on the dictation of the member concerned.[7]

Similarly, an official may lawfully be required to obtain the approval of a member before acting because he or she has already exercised a judgment and reached a provisional view on the matter before consulting the member. [8]

A list of powers delegated to officers must be published by local authorities. [9]

Unlawful Delegation

In the absence of express statutory authority, any purported delegation is normally unlawful. The rapidly developing doctrines of "fairness" and "legitimate expectation" may, however, qualify this rule so that, in some circumstances, a citizen may be able to treat as binding a representation or undertaking made by an unauthorised body. [10] In the absence of such special circumstances the purported delegation will normally result in invalidity.

---

[2] Section 101 (2).

[3] Section 101 (5).

[4] *R v. Secretary of State for Education and Science ex p Birmingham City Council* (1984) 83 LGR 79.

[5] *R v. Secretary of State for the Environment ex p Hillingdon BC* [1986] 1 WLR 867.

[6] Normally the chairman of a committee or sub-committee.

[7] *R v. Port Talbot BC ex p Jones* [1988] 2 All ER 207.

[8] *Fraser v. Secretary of State for the Environment* (1987) 56 P & CR 386.

[9] Section 100G.

[10] *Supra*. Note *Robertson v. Minister of Pensions.* [1949] 1 KB 227.

If there has been unlawful delegation, there will normally be no possibility of ratifying what has been done.[11]

Other Cases of Surrendering Discretion

Dictated Policy

The general prohibition on delegation also prevents the authorised body from allowing another to dictate the manner in which the power is exercised. Dictation would, in substance, transfer the power to the unauthorised body.

The rule does not prevent consultation by the decision maker provided he or she retains the ultimate power of decision. A minister erred where he adopted a policy of refusing permission to develop land for gravel extraction on good agricultural land if the application was opposed by the Minister of Agriculture. Such a policy transferred the decision-making power to the latter Minister.[12]

Loyalty to party policy poses interesting questions. A member is entitled to attach weight to party loyalty but should not blindly follow party policy. In *R v. Waltham Forest LBC ex p Baxter* Lord Donoldson MR stated that a member's duty is:

"..to make up his own mind on how to vote, giving such weight as he thinks appropriate to the views of other councillors and to the policy of the group of which he is a member. It is only if he abdicates his personal responsibility that questions can arise as to the validity of his vote. The distinction between giving great weight to the views of colleagues and to party policy, on the one hand, and voting blindly in support of party policy may on occasion be a fine one, but it is nevertheless very real..." [13]

---

[11] *Barnard v. National Dock Labour Board* [1953] 2 QB 18 at 40. Note the scope of ratification on public law is uncertain. It may have some role: *Stoke on Trent City Council v. B & Q (Retail) Ltd.* [1984] AC 754 where the defective decision of the environmental health sub-committee to commence proceedings under s.222 of the Local Government Act 1972 was properly ratified by the policy committee after proceedings had been commenced.

[12] *Lavender & Sons Ltd v. Minister of Housing and Local Government* [1970] 1 WLR 1231.

[13] [1988] 1 QB 419, 427.

A member would act unlawfully, for example, where he or she resolves to adopt the party-line to the exclusion of all other considerations, [14] or if the member felt bound, contrary to his assessment of the merits, to support a proposal merely because it was enshrined in the manifesto upon which he was elected. [15] But there is nothing to prevent the member from supporting the majority if he or she has considered all the available options.

Accordingly, discretion was not surrendered where members of a political group who were privately opposed to a rate increase (but who suffered defeat on this point by the majority of the group at a private meeting) supported the increase as group policy at a full council meeting. [16]

Lawful Adherence to Policy

There are obvious tensions between the prohibition on fettering discretion on the one hand and the promotion of administrative consistency on the other. The purpose of the former is to require a body to make an informed choice between options. It is the failure to choose between those options according to their respective merits which is unlawful, and an over rigid adherence to policy can cause problems. Nevertheless, the formulation of policy and adherence to it promotes consistency and ensures that like cases are treated alike. The distinction can cause confusion.

Judicial review may be available where administrators act inconsistently. [17] They must normally be careful to ensure that the formulation and pursuit of policy is structured so as to permit of exceptions. They must navigate a narrow and treacherous channel permitting the application of policy but not at the expense of the merits of individual cases which may be so overwhelming as to demand an exceptional treatment.

The general rule thus prevents inflexible adherence to policy which ousts a proper consideration of the merits. A breach of the rule may arise, for example, where a party is elected having made certain promises in its manifesto and regards these as irrevocable once in office regardless of the weight of other competing

---

[14] *Ibid.* at p 427, per Stocker LJ.
[15] *Bromley LBC v. GLC* [1983] 1 AC 768.
[16] *R v. Waltham Forest LBC ex p Baxter* [1988] 1 QB 419.
[17] *Supra* p. 336 *et seq.*

arguments. The GLC fell foul of this principle in *Bromley LBC v. GLC* [18] where the authority regarded itself bound to the policy announced in their election campaign of providing significant subsidies for public transport in London. In doing so they erred in law since they ought to have exercised a discretion in the matter. This required them properly to evaluate the issues some of which only became apparent to them on assuming office. Such decisions demonstrate that, whilst there is no objection to having a policy, each case must be considered on its merits. Consistency cannot be pursued regardless of merit. [19]

A street trading licensing authority erred in law by an over rigid adherence to policy in *Perilly v. Tower Hamlets LBC.* [20] The authority had granted street trading licences on a "first come, first served" basis regardless of the merits of competing applications. Lord Denning MR pithily reminded the authority of its obligations:

"There must be.. a discretion in the (authority) to decide between applications according to the merits." [21]

Exceptions to the Rule
There may, however, be circumstances in which the rules are applied less rigorously. The courts seem prepared to relax the requirement that each application be considered individually on its merits where there are very significant numbers of applications for a limited resources, whether these be grants of financial assistance or licences. Here the courts have stated that it would be pointless for all individual applications to be considered where they were bound as a result of the decision-maker's policy decision to fail.[22] "Representations could of course be made that the policy should be changed." [23] Lord Reid once stated, [24] "..a Ministry or large authority may have had to deal already with a multitude of

---

[18] *Supra* n. (15). Note also *Roberts v. Hopwood* [1925] AC 578.
[19] *R v. Flintshire CC Licensing Committtee ex p Barratt* [1957] 1 QB 350.
[20] (1972) 70 LGR 474.
[21] *Ibid.* at p 480.
[22] See Lord Dilhorne in *British Oxygen Co Ltd v. Minister of Technology* [1971] AC 610 at 631.
[23] *Ibid.*
[24] *Ibid.* at p. 625.

similar applications and then they will almost certainly have evolved a policy...There can be no objection to that, provided the authority is always willing to listen to anyone with something new to say."

Much will depend upon the circumstances of each case. Whether this more relaxed approach will apply in the context of street trading depends in large degree upon the number of applications received for licences. Normally these are probably not received in sufficiently large numbers to excuse the licensing authority from considering each on its merits.[25] There may, of course, be exceptions.

Fettering Discretion by Contract or Undertaking

A Conflict of Interests

Problems arise where an administrative body seeks to exercise a discretionary power which conflicts with an existing obligation. This may arise from a contract, or an undertaking given by the authority to an individual. The existence of such an obligation may compromise a proper evaluation of the options which would otherwise have been available to the authority. How are the two sets of obligations to be reconciled? On the one hand, the beneficiary of the undertaking, or party to the contract, may *prima facie* be entitled to expect that the undertaking will be honoured, or the contract performed. On the other, the administrator should be free to act in the public interest according to the circumstances which prevail at the time the decision falls to be made.

Clearly all contracts and undertakings are a limitation on the freedom of action of a public body. Not all can be struck down, but where is the line to be drawn?

---

[25] See *Perilly v. Tower Hamlets, supra* n.(20).

The Test for Validity

The courts will normally interfere where there is an incompatibility between the purposes of the statutory power and the contract or undertaking. [26] If a contract or undertaking is incompatible in this sense it is void; the authority has no power to conclude it.

An administrative authority cannot divest itself of a discretion by concluding a contract or offering an undertaking. [27] It cannot renounce completely its freedom of action. There may be cases, however, where some limitations on the way its exercises its discretion are not incompatible with its statutory function. For example, in *Birkdale Electricity Supply Co, v. Southport Corporation* [28] a statutory electricity company resolved not charge higher prices than a neighbouring company. This was attacked as a fetter on its discretion to charge, yet it was upheld since it was clearly entitled to fix its prices according to business needs and the competition offered by other suppliers. An agreement such as this was justifiable since it would offer commercial certainty and thereby attract business.

By analogy with the *Birkdale* case, a licensing authority which voluntarily undertook not to charge fees for street trading licences in excess of those in neighbouring districts, might not act unlawfully. It could be argued that such an undertaking could attract street traders into its area in order to provide a comprehensive range of goods to the public. But the position is likely, however, to be more complex because one licensing authority is not normally in competition with another, and, further, licensing authorities are confined to setting fees in relation to the costs of administering the licensing scheme, and these need not be the same from one authority to another.[29]

It is possible, however, that if such an undertaking were offered it may give rise to a legitimate expectation in individual traders that the undertaking would not be revoked, at least

---

[26] What follows should be read subject to the recent developments concerning the doctrine of legitimate expectation, *supra* p. 303 *et seq*: p. 336..

[27] *Ayr Harbour Trustees v. Oswald* (1883) 8 App Cas 623.

[28] [1926] AC 355.

[29] *R v. Manchester City Council ex p King* (1991) 89 LGR 696.

without inviting those affected to submit representations in accordance with the principles of fairness discussed above. [30]

The Grant of Trading Licences

It seems that a licensing authority could not normally enter contracts and so bind itself to grant street trading licences. [31] This would, however, be subject to the caveat that an undertaking creating a legitimate expectation might then be binding at least until consultation had taken place.

Valid Restrictions on Power

There are cases where public bodies must be able to bind themselves in order to carry out their functions. In *Stourcliff Estates Co. Ltd. v. Bournemouth Corporation* [32] the court held that where a local authority had concluded a restrictive covenant, it was valid and enforceable against the authority. The corporation had acquired land for a public park and had entered a restrictive covenant with the vendor preventing the construction of buildings on the land. Subsequently, in the purported exercise of a statutory discretionary power the authority sought to build public conveniences in the park. It argued that it was at liberty to depart from the terms of the restrictive covenant since it was *ultra vires*. The plaintiff, however, obtained an injunction restraining them from doing so. The court decided that the covenant was binding because it was consistent with the statutory powers. As Buckley LJ. stated [33] the power to place urinals in the park did not necessarily require them to do so and the prohibition on erecting buildings did not prevent the land being used for the primary purpose for which it was acquired.

It must also be remembered that there is a distinction between exercising a statutory power in such a way which limits an authority's future action- such as where a lease is granted- and the

---

[30] Above pp. 336-7, see *R v. Liverpool City Council ex p Liverpool Taxi Fleet Operators' Assoc.* [1972] 2 QB 299.

[31] *Stringer v. Minister of Housing and Local Govenment* [1970] 1 WLR 1281.

[32] [1910] 2 Ch 12.

[33] *Ibid.* at p. 22.

case where the authority agrees in advance how its statutory power will be exercised. The former is a valid "fetter" because, having exercised a power to grant a lease, the authority has inherently fettered its future action in relation to the property in question. [34]

Fettering Discretion by Estoppel

The doctrine of estoppel used to be invoked where a public official offered misleading advice, and the individual who relied on it suffered loss when that advice conflicted with the public body's subsequent decision. It was also relevant where an individual relied on an assurance that a public body had power which it did not in law possess. The question in such cases was whether a public body could depart from the advice or undertaking given notwithstanding the injustice to the individual. Arguments against binding public authorities emphasised the importance of a public body retaining its freedom to exercise its discretionary powers for the public benefit. There was also the problem that providing justice to the individual might entail injuring the interests of others not before the court. [35]

The cases on estoppel conflict, but the scope of the doctrine has been narrowed leaving public authorities a greater freedom to act in the public interest. Parallel developments in the doctrine of legitimate expectation must not, however, be ignored. [36]

Estoppel in Public Law

No doubt aware that the *ultra vires* doctrine would be undermined, if the contrary were possible, the courts have held that estoppel cannot give an authority power which it does not in law possess. [37]

---

[34] *Dowty Boulton Paul Ltd. v. Wolverhampton Corporation* [1971] 1 WLR 204, esp p.210.

[35] Eg, in in a development control case such as *Lever Finance Ltd. v. Westminster LBC* [1971] 1 QB 222 neighbouring landowners in particular and the public generally might be prejudiced.

[36] *Supra* p. 303 *et seq*; p. 336.

[37] *Rhyl UDC v. Rhyl Amusements Ltd.* [1959] 1 WLR 465; cf *Robertson v. Minister of Pensions* [1949] 1 KB 227.

By similar reasoning, a public authority cannot be prevented from
performing its statutory duties by an undertaking to the contrary; to
hold otherwise would mean that the statute in question would be
disapplied from the facts of the individual case. [38]

Estoppel was often raised to bind the authority to advice given
by an official because the courts were willing to give considerable
weight to the interests of the individual affected. This can be seen
in *Robertson v. Minister of Pensions* [39] where Denning J (as he then
was) emphasised that, by assuming authority in a matter, a
government official entitles an individual to rely on that
authority. The citizen does not know and cannot be expected to know
the limits of the official's powers. Representations made in the
course of such assumed authority were thus capable of binding the
authority. Similarly, in *Lever Finance v. Westminster
Corporation* [40] Lord Denning MR stated that a representation or
advice might give rise to an implied delegation binding the
authority. "If an officer acting within the scope of his ostensible
authority makes a representation on which another acts, then a
public authority may be bound by it. A private individual is
entitled to expect that all necesary resolutions have been
passed." [41]

That final sentence was held to be a mere *obiter dictum* and was
criticised as being too wide by Megaw L.J. in *Western Fish Products
Ltd v. Penwith District Council.* [42] In this case, the Court of Appeal
re-asserted more orthodox decisions and re-affirmed the general
principle that a statutory discretion cannot be restricted by
estoppel. An estoppel could only arise in cases where an authority
impliedly delegated some of its power to its officers. Any decision
made in the exercise of this authority cannot be revoked.
Representations made by an official exercising the power devolved
to him thus bind the authority.

The person relying on the representation of a public official
must also adduce some evidence for his belief that the officer was

---

[38] *Maritime Electric Co. Ltd v. General Dairies Ltd.* [1937] 1 WLR 465.
[39] [1949] 1 KB 227.
[40] *Supra.* n. (35).
[41] See also Denning LJ's view in *Howell v. Falmouth Boat Construction Co* [1950] 2KB 16,
26. The case was appealed to the House of Lords.
[42] (1978) 38 P & CR 7.

able to bind the public authority employing him. His official status alone, however senior, is not enough. For example, the representee in *Lever Finance* would have been aware of the widespread practice of delegating the approval of minor amendments to planning permissions to planning officers and this would reasonably have lead him to believe that the planning officer was able to bind the planning authority.

Secondly, an authority may waive certain procedural requirements; if it does so, it may be estopped from relying on non-compliance to justify altering its position. Even this exception was, however, subject to the *caveat* that much will turn on the construction of the statutory provisions setting out what the required procedure is to be.

The doctrine of estoppel now seems to have only a restricted role in Administrative law. The limitations on the doctrine can be seen in *Rootkin v. Kent County Council* [43] where a local authority, having awarded a bus pass to a child who was thought to live more than three miles from her school, were held to be entitled to withdraw the pass when it was later discovered that she in fact lived within the relevant distance. It was decided that a statutory discretion "must be exercised freely and cannot be thwarted by estoppel." [44] The conclusion rightly to be drawn following this is that "estoppel appears to operate only at the periphery of judicial review." [45] At least this is so if the doctrine is treated as a separate head of review.

Recent Developments

Whilst the doctrine of estoppel will not normally prevent a public authority from departing from an informal undertaking or representation, the problem for administrators is that the courts have begun to weave other skeins to tilt the balance more favourably towards the individual. Rather than re-asserting estoppel as an independent ground for intervention, emphasis is now placed upon the consistency and overall fairness of the decision within the broader category of "irrationality", or *Wednesbury* unreasonableness. In some cases, as we have seen, inconsistent

---

[43] [1981] 1 WLR 1186.
[44] Eveleigh LJ. at p. 1197.
[45] DGT Williams (1981) 40 CLJ 198.

dealings may give rise to a finding that no reasonable authority could have departed from the prior advice or undertaking; to do so would thus violate the *Wednesbury* principles. [46] The rapidly developing area of "legitimate expectations" can also confer rights on individuals who have received representations from officials, although the emerging jurisprudence does not apparently seek to bind public bodies to representations casually made by junior officials. [47]

Where the representation seeks to guarantee some procedural safeguard to the individual or class of individual, the public authority may not reach a decision without having first observed those procedures. [48] Once the required procedures have been observed, the authority is normally free to exercise its discretion.

The principles on relevancy may also come into play where a public body wishes to depart from unofficial advice; in doing so it may, in some cases be accused of failing to give due weight to a relevant consideration. Much will depend upon the facts of each individual case.

The law on official representations is thus in a state of development for, paradoxically, whilst the courts have curtailed the scope of estoppel in public law, the problem of injustice to the individual has not been adequately resolved, and the courts have sought to address this by expanding other legal concepts. The precise inter-relationship of these concepts has yet to be comprehensively explored. Until it is, the administrator should be cautious in offering advice.

---

[46] Note, eg, *Ex p Preston* [1985] AC 835.
[47] Note discussion, *supra*. 0000
[48] See e.g. *A-G for Hong Kong v. Ng Yuen Shiu* [1983] 2 AC 629.

CHAPTER 19

STANDING

Introduction

A street trader confronted with an abuse of a power by a public body may wish to take legal proceedings by way of judicial review to have the decision quashed and the matter re-considered according to law. Similarly, he or she may wish to take action against rivals who seek an unlawful competitive advantage, or who perhaps benefit from the *ultra vires* grant of a trading licence. It is, however, a cardinal principle of English law that an individual cannot invoke the assistance of the courts unless he has standing, or *"locus standi"* to do so.

This means that a street trader cannot contemplate proceedings merely because there has been a breach of the law, whether by a public authority or a private citizen; there is no "citizen's action" in English law. For example, in *Gouriet v. Union of Post Office Workers* [1] a trade union proposed to breach the criminal law by imposing a "boycott" of mail to South Africa. The plaintiff came to the court merely as a private citizen to prevent it from interfering with the mail. [2] Since Gouriet had no personal interest at stake in the proceedings, and had no special concern with the matter, he was not a competent plaintiff. The general interest in securing the due observation of the law was not sufficient.

The *Gouriet* decision demonstrates that private citizens can enforce their own private legal rights but only those with a sufficient interest may enforce public rights. This is not so where proceedings are brought by the Attorney-General who always has

---

[1] [1978] AC 435.

[2] Mr. Gouriet went to court in his own name after having unsuccesfully having asked the A-G to lend his *fiat* to the proceedings.

locus standi. Similarly, local authorities are given limited statutory powers to enforce public rights. An individual lacking standing may request one of these bodies to intervene in an appropriate case.

Enforcement by Institutions

(i) The Attorney-General

A person without "standing" may be able to bring "relator" proceedings with the consent or "fiat" of the Attorney-General, or he may ask the Attorney to intervene "*ex officio*". In either case, the Attorney-General has a discretion whether or not to allow proceedings to be brought and this discretion cannot, it seems, be challenged in the courts. [3]

Ex officio proceedings are now rarely brought; and "relator" proceedings seem only to be brought in a small number of cases because the standing rules are now more liberal. [3a] In a relator action, the proceedings are brought in *name* of the Attorney, but the individual relator has the day to day management of the litigation and will be responsible for the costs. He could not, however, settle or compromise the action without the Attorney-General's consent.

(ii) Local Authorities [4]

Because local authorities have important public duties it is desirable that they should be able to take proceedings in their own name without recourse to the Attorney-General. The Local Government Act 1972, s.222 now provides:

"When a local authority consider it expedient for the promotion or protection of the interests of the inhabitants of their

---

[3] *Gouriet v. UPW* [1978] AC 435. Cf Hough, "*Judicial Review where the Attorney General refuses to act*". [1988] *Legal Studies* 189. Note also that courts seem to be increasingly willing to review the exercise of prerogative powers of which the A-G's discretionary power to enforce a public right is but an example: *R v. Home Secretary of State for the Home Department ex p Bentley* [1993] The Times 379.

[3a] See Hough "*Local Authorities as Guardians of the Public Interest*". [1992] PL 130, 135.

[4] See generally Hough *op cit.*

area......they may prosecute, defend or appear in any legal proceedings, and in the case of civil proceedings, may institute them in their own name."

As we shall see, this power is often used by a local authority to seek an injunction to restrain certain criminal conduct, such as illegal street trading, where the fines imposed for such conduct will be an inadequate deterrent. But the provision is more widely available, although its precise meaning is far from clear. If read literally, the section seems to permit proceedings to be taken where the consequences of the action are beneficial for the local community. Despite this, the courts construe the section more narrowly. A local authority may only rely on s.222 if the matter in issue is one "generally associated" with the local authority's jurisdiction. [5] Although this is somewhat ill-defined, cases in which the section has been successfully employed seem to have fallen within this model; in contrast, where a local authority has attempted to use the power step outside what might be perceived as its traditional role, it has been held to have acted *ultra vires* .[6]

When the *Stoke-on Trent City Council v. B & Q (Retail) Ltd.* case was before the Court of Appeal, [7] Ackner L.J. offered some illustrations of the boundaries of the s.222 power. He stated that it cannot be used to control criminal conduct such as, for example, obscenity occurring in a local theatre, or the sale of pornography from a newsagent's shop. It could, however, be used to prevent illegal Sunday retail trading. [8] The distinction between these kinds of cases seems somewhat tenuous but is based upon the perception of a local authority's traditional role. [9] This is not an attractive distinction because, whether the matter concerns the control of pornography or the control of Sunday trading, the local community may be supposed to drive a benefit, and this satisfies the only stated condition to the operation of s.222.

---

[5] See submissions of *amicus curiae* to the Court of Appeal in the *Stoke-on-Trent* case [1984] 1 Ch 1 at 9, which were apparently approved by Lord Templeman in the House of Lords [1984] 1 AC 754, 774.

[6] *R v. Secretary of State for Social Services ex p CPAG and GLC* [1984] The Times, 16th Aug where the GLC was seeking to challenge a DHSS policy in not reviewing welfare claims.

[7] [1984] 1 Ch 1.

[8] *Ibid.* at p. 26.

[9] *Ibid.*

A further limitation on the local authority's power is that
s.222 cannot be employed to benefit "persons who are inhabitants of
the (local authority's) area. There "must be some general interest
common to the inhabitants taken as a whole." [10] Strictly applied,
this distinction would almost make s.222 a dead-letter since any
proceedings would be bound to have an adverse impact on *some* local
interests. Further, the *dictum* is misleading because the courts
qualify it in practise. For example, the enforcement of the law is
perhaps one matter in which a community of interest may exist, but
such an activity does not fall within s.222 because it benefits the
population of the country as a whole rather than the locality in
question. "A more localised interest must be found." [11]

These limitations demonstrate that local authorities should be
cautious in employing s.222 in areas of law enforcement activity
which have not been seen as their preserve. Nevertheless, most
street trading matters typify *par excellence* a field of regulatory
activity for which local authorities have had a long established
responsibility. [12]

Injunctions
Where the fine or other penalty is inadequate to prevent repeated
or continuing breaches of the criminal law, local authorities acting
in their enforcement role, may wish to seek an injunction to restrain
the offender.

It was settled by the House of Lords in *Stoke-on Trent v. B & Q
(Retail) Ltd* [13] that local authorities do have standing to seek an
injunction in their own name without recourse to the Attorney-
General. Before calling in aid the civil law it will normally be
necessary first to have used the criminal law in an endeavour to
restrain the offender. [14] Nevertheless, an application may be made
even before criminal proceedings have been concluded if it can be
shown that the offender was 'deliberately and flagrantly flouting

---

[10] Oliver L.J. at [1984] 1 Ch 1, 33.
[11] *Ibid.*
[12] Eg, *Westminster CC v. Freeman* (1985) 135 NLJ 1232.
[13] [1984] AC 754.
[14] *Ibid.* at p. 776.

the law'. [15] Repeated commission of the offence following prosecution and conviction would normally supply the evidence that the offender was doing so. As Millett J. subsequently held in *Wychavon DC v. Midlands Enterprises (Special Events) Ltd.*, [16] the key question is whether the court is satisfied that the defendant's unlawful operations will continue unless they are effectively restrained by injunction and that nothing short of this remedy will be sufficient to restrain them. [17] It must also be shown that the offender would have no defence to a prosecution if one were instituted. It is noteworthy that in the *Wychavon* case no prior prosecution had been instituted. [18]

The power to seek an injunction has proved to be useful in the street trading context. Examples of its use include proceedings to restrain unlicensed street trading. In *Westminster City Council v. Freeman* [19] unlicensed traders persistently traded in Oxford Street notwithstanding fines imposed by local magistrates. Because the fines had no deterrent effect, the local authority was held to be entitled to seek an injunction to prevent further trading and had *locus standi* to do so under s.222.

Section 222 may also allow a local authority to obtain an injunction to restrain the holding of a Sunday market in breach of planning controls. In *North Shropshire DC v. Edwin H Edwards etc.*[20] there had been persistent breaches of the planning permission granted by the General Development Order, and disobedience to an enforcement notice; and although a fine had been imposed, it was in sufficient to deter subsequent breaches.

Local authorities have also been able to rely on s.222 to restrain repeated breaches of the prohibition on Sunday trading, [21] to control noise pollution [22] and to restrain a public nuisance. [23]

---

[15] The House of Lords in the *Stoke-on-Trent* case approving the dictum of Bridge L.J. in *Stafford BC v. Elkenford Ltd.* [1977] 1 WLR 324, 330.

[16] [1988] 1 CMLR 397.

[17] This was approved in *City of London Corporation v. Bovis Construction Ltd.* [1992] 3 All ER 697.

[18] An injunction was obtained without recourse to a prior prosecution in *Runnymede BC v. Ball* [1986] 1 WLR 353.

[19] (1985) 135 NLJ 1232.

[20] [1991] JPL 958.

[21] *Stoke-on Trent City Council v. B & Q (Retail) Ltd.* [1984] AC 754.

[22] *City of London Corporation v. Bovis Construction* [1992] 3 All ER 697.

Judicial Review

In its decision to bring proceedings under s.222 a local authority is subject to judicial review. [24] This means that the authority must direct itself properly and act reasonably in the *Wednesbury* sense[25] in reaching its decision. It must formally take into account all relevant considerations and exclude irrelevant ones. [26]

Individual Standing

(i) Standing to Apply for Judicial Review

The law of standing for judicial review is in a confused state. This is unlikely to be resolved until the courts identify the purpose served by the standing rules. A judiciary sympathetic to private law influences justifies intervention in the administrative process in order to redress individual grievances. In its extreme form this approach allows the court to grant a remedy only to protect an individual whose rights have been affected. [27] One argument often advanced in support of this approach is that it excluded "busybodies" from interfering in matters which do not concern them.[28]

On the other hand, if the purpose of judicial review is simply to restrain administrative bodies from exceeding their powers, the courts will intervene on proof of illegality. The identity of the applicant for judicial review under this model is of marginal importance because the key issue is whether the public authority

---

[23] *Gillingham BC v. Medway (Chatham) Dock Co. Ltd.* (1993) 91 LGR 160, although the claim was unsuccessful on the merits.

[24] *Stoke-on Trent supra* n (13) especially at p. 775.

[25] *Associated Provincial Picture Houses v. Wednesbury Corpn.* [1948] 1 KB 223.

[26] An informal consideration of the issues may suffice if the court is satisfied that a formal consideration would have made no difference to the decision to invoke the power: *Gillingham BC v. Medway (Chatham) Dock Co. Ltd* (1993) 91 LGR 160.

[27] Eg, *Gouriet v. UPW* [1978] AC 435.

[28] A recent example is *R v. Legal Aid Board, ex p Bateman* [1992] The Times, March 4th. Another argument is that a citizen's action opens the floodgates and the courts would be inundated with claims: see, for an early statement, *Iveson v. Moore* (1699) 1 Ld Raym. 486. Recently, this line of reasoning has been extended so that an applicant who was not a "busybody" but whose application was "quixotic" might be denied standing: *R v. Legal Aid Board ex p Bateman* , *ibid.*

has exceeded its powers. Proponents of this latter view suggest that there should be a right for every citizen to challenge administrative action.

Whilst the courts have, at times, favoured the first view, there has never been a settled body of law which would favour "open access" as a matter of general principle.[29] It does not follow, however, that a member of the public who does not seek to vindicate any private right or interest can never bring proceedings.

"A sufficient interest"
To have standing, the applicant for judicial review must have "a sufficient interest in the matter to which the application relates."[30] An application for judicial review cannot be made without the leave of the court at which stage the sufficiency of the applicant's interest will be assessed so that any hopeless case can be filtered out. Standing may also be disputed at the full hearing.[31]

The "sufficient interest" formula is a fluid test which has given the courts something of an open canvas. This was deliberate: the courts were to be permitted to fashion more satisfactory standing rules than had previously existed. [32] It is now recognised that they have had only a partial success. [33]

The courts have employed the "sufficient interest" formula to extend standing beyond those whose rights have been infringed so as to include others who have otherwise been adversely affected. "Busybodies" meddling in matters which are not perceived as their concern are always excluded, however; and there have been inconsistencies where administrative decisions affect the public at large, or where a citizen or group of citizens steps forward to challenge it.

The leading decision on standing is that of the House of Lords in *R v. IRC ex p National Federation of Self Employed and Small*

[29] Note especially the views of Lords Scarman and Diplock in *R v. Inland Revenue Commissioners ex p National Federation of Self-Employed and Small businesses Ltd.* [1982] AC 617, 644, 644, 654.
[30] Supreme Court Act 1981, s.31.
[31] *R v. Inland Revenue Commissioners ex p National Federation of Self-Employed and Small businesses Ltd.* [1982] AC 617.
[32] (1976) Cmnd 6407.
[33] Consultation Paper no.126, HMSO, (1993).

Businesses Ltd. [34] (the *Fleet St. Casuals* case) and this demonstrates the weakness of the public interest litigant. Here a pressure group representing small businessmen challenged an alleged tax amnesty given to casual workers on Fleet Street. The Inland Revenue had agreed that it would not investigate tax evaded by these workers prior to 1977 provided they submitted returns for subsequent years. The applicants alleged that this was unlawful because the Revenue had, in substance, agreed to abdicate its primary responsibility for the collection of tax.

The House of Lords denied the applicant standing because, on an analysis of the substantive issues and a proper construction of the relevant legislation, the members of the Federation did not have a sufficient interest in the amount of tax paid by third parties. [35] This was a confidential matter, and the public interest dictated that this confidentiality should be maintained. Therefore, as Lord Wilberforce observed: "an aggregate of individuals each of whom has no interest cannot of itself have an interest." [36]

At the level of principle, their lordships stressed that an examination of the legal and factual context, and in particular the statute under which the public body derived its powers, would be necessary to see whether an applicant for judicial review had a sufficient interest in raising the matter before the court. Concern with the enforcement of the law is not enough.

However, their lordships seemed anxious not to rule out the possibility of a citizen's action in some, perhaps extreme, cases. Most agreed that serious unlawful conduct by the defendant would be capable of affording standing for the benefit of an applicant who would otherwise lack it. This means that the courts are not closed to the public spirited citizen or trade association seeking to vindicate the public interest in appropriate cases. [37]

Decisions on standing subsequent to *Fleet St Casuals* reveal some inconsistencies particularly where the decision impugned affects

---

[34] Supra n. (31).

[35] The claim also failed on the merits because the Inland Revenue Commissioners were acting within the scope of their management powers when they reached the impugned agreement with Fleet St. workers.

[36] [1982] AC 617 at p. 633; see also Schiemann J in *R v. Secretary of State for the Environment ex p Rose Theatre Trust Co.* [1990] 1 All ER 754.

[37] [1982] AC 617, 633, 647, 662.

the public at large an no one individual in particular. Here the courts ostensibly examine the challenger's interest in or relationship to the subject matter of the case, but this does lead to uncertainty since perceptions of what constitutes a cognisable interest or relationship inevitably differ. Nevertheless, a member of the press was permitted to act as a guardian of the public interest in challenging a policy of local magistrates not to reveal their identities. [38] In *R v. IBA ex p Whitehouse* [39] a TV licence holder was granted standing to allege that the IBA had failed in its duty to maintain broadcasting standards. It is, however, difficult to see here how the interest of one such individual differed from many other members of the public. [40] A note of dissonance was struck in *Holmes v. Checkland* [41] where a citizen was unable to challenge a decision of the BBC to broadcast coverage of a snooker championship sponsored by a cigarette company. He was not a competent plaintiff because he had suffered no greater harm than other members of the public generally. This seems to mark a contrast with *Ex p Whitehouse* and *Ex p Leigh*. [42]

In the important *Rose Theatre* case, [43] which marks a more restrictive approach to standing, Schiemann J. held that a group of objectors, including expert archaeologists, who came together from a wide variety of backgrounds to save the remains of the Rose Theatre did not have standing to challenge the decision of the Secretary of State not to schedule the site. On the proper construction of the statute in question, they were not "beneficiaries" of any legislative intention to give them access to court. Such an approach suggests that challenges by individuals or groups in the public interest are unlikely to succeed unless there is some evidence that the statute under which the body acted intended to confer the necessary status upon them as challengers. Since statutes are often

---

[38] *R v. Felixstowe Justices ex p Leigh* [1987] 2 WLR 380; see also *R v. Clerkenwell Magistrate's Court, ex p Telegraph plc* [1993] 2 All ER 183 where news media was recognised as guardians of public interest in open justice.

[39] [1984] Times,14th April.

[40] For another generous approach to the standing issue see *R v. London Borough of Lambeth ex p Sharp* (1986) 55 P & CR 233, esp 240, Woolf J.

[41] [1987] The Times, 15th April.

[42] *Supra.*

[43] *R v. Secretary of State for the Environment ex p Rose Theatre Trust Co. Ltd.* [1990] 1 All ER 754.

silent on the question of who should have standing, this is an unwelcome development.

Street Trading Cases
Despite inconsistencies, the above decisions reveal that a street trader will normally have standing to challenge a unlawful decision affecting street trading licensing matters. This would follow *a fortiori* where the trader's livelihood was at stake. For example, the refusal of a street trading consent has been amenable to judicial review at the instance of street traders concerned. [44] But there may be other cases, such as planning or other matters, where standing is less clear. [44a]

The courts have also been sympathetic to applications by traders seeking to challenge the legality of the grant of a street trading licence to a rival. [45] Even in matters concerning the assessment of a rival's tax liability, a matter normally confidential to the taxpayer, and one in which a third party *prima facie* has no sufficient interest, it has been held that *locus standi* can arise [46]

A member of the public having no connection with street trading and not in any way adversely affected by the decision impugned will not normally be qualified to bring proceedings, especially after the *Rose Theatre* case. [47] But there may be exceptions benefiting, for example, journalists acting in the public interest. [47a]

Associations Challenging Administrative Action
An important issue is whether groups representing traders will be able seek judicial review on behalf of their members. Often individual traders will lack the resources to do so in their own

---

[44] *R v. Bristol City Council ex p Pearce* (1985) 83 LGR 711.
[44a] For example, it is not certain that traders in one district could challenge the decision of a local authority to acquire a market in another district unless the decision prejudiced them.
[45] *R v. Thames Magistrates' Court ex p Greenbaum* (1957) 55 LGR 129.
[46] *R v. A-G ex p ICI plc* [1987] 1 CMLR 588.
[47] *Supra* n (43).
[47a] *Supra* n. (38).

name so that representation by trade associations will be a significant safeguard against any abuse of power.[48]

Associations may represent their members if they have a sufficient interest in their own right. [49] It will be important to ask whether their members, if applying in their individual capacity, would have had standing [50] by virtue of having been adversely affected by the decision challenged, and whether the association stands in a sufficiently proximate relationship to those individuals. [51] The *Fleet St.* case also suggests that an association otherwise lacking standing may nevertheless proceed if the matter is sufficiently grave. [52] Pressure groups and similar bodies fare less well where their members are unaffected by the decision in question.[53]

If the standing of the association is in doubt, an application should be brought by an individual whose standing is not. The association may support a "test" case, or proceedings could be initiated member or officer in his own name with the association's support. For example, in *R v. Manchester City Council ex p King* [54] Mr King, representing the Manchester Street Traders' Association, brought a successful application to challenge the increase in licence fees. It is possible to bring such an application by way of representative proceedings under RSC Ord 15 r. 12. [55]

---

[48] See Cane [1990] PL 307.

[49] *Rose Theatre* case, *supra* n (43).

[50] *Fleet St. Casuals* case, *supra* n. (31); *Rose Theatre* case, *supra* n. (43).

[51] *R v. Chief Adjudication Officer ex p Bland* The Times Feb 6th 1985.

[52] *Supra.* Examples of pressure group standing include *R v. Hammersmith & Fulham BC ex p People Before Profit Ltd.* [1981] JPL 869; *Covent Garden Community Association v. GLC* [1981] JPL 869; (Decided before *Fleet St.*) More generally see *R v. Chief Adjudication Officer ex p Bland,* The Times Feb 6th 1985; also *RCN v. DHSS* [1981] AC 800.

[53] *Fleet St. Casuals* , *supra* n (31); also *R v. Poole BC ex p BeeBee* [1991] C.O.D. 264.

[54] (1991) 89 LGR 696.

[55] E.g., *Ashby v. Secretary of State* (1979) 40 P & CR 362.

Standing Where there is a Legitimate Expectation/Duty to Act Fairly

The existence of a legitimate expectation can establish the requisite standing. This was recognised by Lord Scarman In *Ex p Findlay* [56] where he stated,

"A legitimate expectation can provide a sufficient interest to enable one who cannot point to the existence of a substantive right to apply for judicial review." [57]

Even if a legitimate expectation cannot be established, a duty to act fairly may be still be found to have existed on the facts, and a breach of this duty can confer standing. Breach of the duty to act fairly may thus provide the substantive grounds for the challenge and the standing in those to whom the duty was owed.[58]

Cases Outside Judicial Review

Standing may also be at issue where an individual wishes to enforce a public duty outside the judicial review procedure. An example of this might arise where a trader wishes to have criminal conduct restrained by means of an injunction. In the street trading context the most appropriate course would normally be to apply to a responsible authority, such as a district council, and request that it take action. If it improperly fails to do, it may itself be subject to judicial review.

If the authority does fail to act, it seems that the individual trader could only institute proceedings in his own name without recourse to the Attorney-General if a private legal right of his own was infringed or where he had suffered "particular damage". [59] What constitutes "particular damage" is considered below.

---

[56] [1985] AC 318, at p. 338.
[57] See *supra* for a discussion of legitimate expectation.
[58] *R v. Great Yarmouth BC ex p Botton Bros Arcades Ltd.* [1988] JPL 18.
[59] *Gouriet v. UPW* [1978] AC 435.

Statutory Appeals: A "Person Aggrieved"

As we have seen, standing to bring an appeal under a statutory framework is often limited to a "person aggrieved ". [60] These words cannot be understood in their literal sense because legitimate and reasonable administrative decisions can generate an acute sense of grievance in those adversely affected by them. A "grievance" must assume a special meaning, its ordinary meaning being circumscribed by the dictates of law and policy.

In a case in which a district council revokes a licence, or refuses either to grant or to renew a licence, the trader directly affected will normally be a "person aggrieved". [61] The question which is still not satisfactorily resolved concerns the extent to which other individuals can be "aggrieved" by a licensing decision. For example, can a competitor, or even a member of the public ever be aggrieved by a decision to award a licence to a particular trader? To answer these questions it is necessary to survey the principles which govern this area.

The starting point is the statutory context which is always paramount. [62] Nevertheless, in order to prevent arbitrariness, and to unify the judicial approach, the courts have established more general principles.

A decision long influential was that of *In re Sidebotham* in which James L.J. stated:

"The words "person aggrieved" do not really mean a man who is disappointed of a benefit which he might have receive if some other order had been made. A "person aggrieved" must be a man who has suffered a legal grievance, a man against whom a decision has been pronounced which has wrongfully deprived him of something or wrongfully affected his title to something." [63]

---

[60] Eg para 6 (5) of the street trading code: Local Government (Miscellaneous Provisions) Act 1982, Sch 4.

[61] Eg, *R v. Southwark Crown Court ex p Watts* [1992] C.O.D 140 where Mr Watts, who had his application for renewal refused after holding a series of annual trading licences, was a "person aggrieved" by the decision and so able to appeal to the local magistrates.

[62] *R v. London Quarter Sessions* [1951] KB 508, 511, *per* Lord Goddard C.J.

[63] (1880) 14 Ch.D 458, 465.

James L.J's test was frequently followed [64] and produced some strange results. For example, in *R v. Keepers of the Peace and Justices of the County of London* [65] it was held that, because a prosecutor's private rights in a criminal appeal were not at issue, he could not be "a person aggrieved".

Such reasoning had important consequences in the context of administering the street trading system. Applying James L.J's test in *R v. London Quarter Session ex p Westminster Corporation* [66] it was held that a licensing authority could not be a "person aggrieved". Accordingly, where a licensing authority had cancelled street trading licences and there had been a successful appeal by the traders concerned to the metropolitan magistrate, no appeal against this lay to the quarter sessions because the council was not "aggrieved" by the magistrate's decision. It was also held that such a local authority was not a "person" within the meaning of the relevant statute.[67]

These matters were re-considered by the Court of Appeal in *Cook v. Southend BC.* [68] which held that the courts had adopted an unduly restrictive approach to who is a person aggrieved. Subject to a contrary statutory intention, the following guidelines would apply:

(i)   a body corporate is as capable of suffering a cognisable grievance as an individual. This removes any doubt as to whether such a body is a "person".

(ii)   Any person who has a decision against him, particularly in adversarial proceedings, will be a person aggrieved for the purposes of appealing against that decision unless the decision amounts to an acquittal of a purely criminal offence. This disposes of *Ex p Westminster Corporation*. For good measure Woolf L.J added: "..the fact that the decision against which a person wishes

---

[64] Eg, *Ex p Official Receiver* (1887) 19 QBD 174.

[65] *R v. Keepers of the Peace and Justices of the City of London* (1890) 25 QBD 357.

[66] [1951] 2 KB 508.

[67] See also *R v. Southwark Crown Court ex p Watts* (1989) 88 LGR 86.

[68] [1990] 1 All ER 243.

to appeal reverses a decision which was originally taken by that person does not prevent that person being a person aggrieved." [69]

After *Cook* a local licensing authority is a competent plaintiff to pursue a statutory appeal to the Crown Court if its original decision is quashed by magistrates.

The question remains whether other individuals are able to use the appeal structure as "persons aggrieved."

Cook endorsed a more liberal trend towards the statutory formula which had not firmly rooted. [70] Earlier decisions had abandoned the requirement that the appellant be affected in his legal rights. For example, in *A G for the Gambia v. N'Jie* [71] the Privy Council held that the Crown was a "person aggrieved" by the decision to restore a barrister's name to the professional list even though its rights were not at issue. In bringing the approach to standing for statutory remedies in line with what was then the test for judicial review- a matter which the Court of Appeal in *Cook* also regarded as important- Lord Denning MR held that a person aggrieved should merely be someone with a "genuine grievance". [72] This approach was followed and applied in *Maurice v. LCC*.[73]

Surprisingly, there are now signs that the courts are prepared to construe the "person aggrieved" formula more widely than that of the "sufficient interest" test which governs judicial review. In the planning context, for example, it now seems clear that anyone who has appeared at a planning inquiry may be a "person aggrieved" against the resulting decision by the Secretary of State.[74]. This is significant when it is recalled that anyone with a relevant contribution may appear at a planning inquiry and this even includes individuals concerned about places far away from where they live. [75]

---

[69] *Ibid.* at p. 246.

[70] Eg, *R v. Southwark Crown Court ex p Watts, supra* n (61).

[71] [1961] AC 617.

[72] Note his approach in cases of judicial review: *R v. Paddington Valuation Officer ex p Peachey Property Corporation Ltd.* [1966] 1 QB 380 at p. 400.

[73] [1964] 2 WLR 715.

[74] Eg *Hildenborough Village Preservation Association v. Secretary of State and Hall Aggregates.* [1978] PL 708.

[75] *R v. Hammersmith and Fulham BC ex p People Before Profit* (1981) JPL at 869-70.

Such a wide interpretation has enabled pressure groups who have appeared at a planning inquiry to qualify as "persons aggrieved" [76] in circumstances in which they may not have had standing to seek judicial review after the decision in then *Rose Theatre* case. [77]

Although, of course, these decisions arise in an entirely different legal context from that in street trading cases, it may be that they indicate that wider access rules may enable a wide range of individuals to have a legitimate concern in street trading matters.

It must not be forgotten, however, that who is "aggrieved" depends on the statute in question which is always paramount. There are instances where the relevant statute does limit who is deemed to be "aggrieved". For example, under para 6 (5) of the street trading code, which governs appeals against council decisions in a range of matters such as the revocation of licences or the refusal of a council to grant or renew a licence, appeals are limited to the trader directly affected. This is because the appeal right arises where certain grounds of refusal are specified. The "grounds" in question relate only to the trader concerned.

There are similar restrictions under the London Local Authorities Act 1990, s.30 where the appellant must be a person aggrieved by a decision of the borough reached on specified grounds which only apply to individual applicants/traders. This does not apply, however, in the case of a person aggrieved by a resolution prohibiting ice cream sales in prohibited streets.

Standing may extend beyond traders affected by the decision under the City of London (Various Powers) Act 1987 where s. 11 confers a right of appeal on any person aggrieved by the refusal of the Corporation to grant or renew a street trading licence. [78] Since the appeal does not arise on certain limited grounds relevant only to individual traders it could be argued that standing extends more widely.

---

[76] *Save Britain's Heritage v. Secretary of State* [1991] 2 All ER 10; *Bath Society v. Secretary of State* [1992] 1 All ER 28.

[77] *R v. Secretary of State for the Environment ex p Rose Theatre Trust Co. Ltd* [1990] 1 All EDR 754.

[78] Or any person aggrieved by the revocation or variation of a licence or any prescription within it.

The "person aggrieved" formula is not confined to appeals against the decisions of local authorities under the various licensing regimes. A "person aggrieved" is also entitled to complain to the magistrates about a statutory nuisance [79] and the formula also controls who is entitled to challenge the decision of the Secretary of State in a planning appeal. [80]

Standing to Enforce the Right of Passage on the Highway

Street trading can constitute an obstruction of the highway. If so, it is an interference with the public's right of passage. Most often the authorities will resort to a prosecution under s.137 of the Highway Act 1980. [81] The same obstruction may, however, give rise to a civil action in public nuisance. Who is entitled to restrain street trading where a public nuisance occurs? There may be a number of possible plaintiffs: a local authority may wish to restrain the public nuisance for the sake of highway users; a neighbouring trader may be concerned at the obstruction of access to his premises; highway users themselves may be inconvenienced by the obstruction; the owners of neighbouring property may be concerned about other effects of street trading, including perhaps the gathering of crowds and the consequent noise. Are these competent to bring an action in public nuisance?

Standing rules *prima facie* remove from every citizen the right to take civil proceedings in respect of public nuisance. As we have seen, the right to pass along the highway is a right vested in the public and not in any individual member of the public. The Attorney General has traditionally been the guardian of public rights and he has a discretion whether or not to take proceedings.[82]

A local authority acting under s.222 of the Local Government Act 1972 could also be a competent plaintiff. Such a body does not require the consent of the Attorney General in order to take proceedings for public nuisance. [83] In practice, local authorities

---

[79] Environmental Protection Act 1990, s.82.

[80] Town and Country Planning Act 1990, s.288.

[81] Discussed Ch. 1

[82] *Supra.* p. 356.

[83] *Gravesham BC and Port of London Authority v. BRB* [1978] Ch 379.

may wish to resort to civil proceedings where the imposition of a criminal penalty has not proved to be a deterrent. [84]

An individual will have standing if the public nuisance of which he complains also interferes with some private right of his own, or where it causes him to suffer "particular damage". [85] These limitations conflict with the notion that nuisance serves to protect the public's right of passage along the highway since the right of action is removed unless an individual shows loss in his private capacity. If no individual suffering such loss steps forward, the public's right is not protected. It can thus be seen that the law provides a remedy for private injury and not public wrong.

Interference with Rights
Interference with the public right of passage will rarely impinge upon the private legal rights of others. It may do so, however, if a right of access to property is blocked, [86] or where, in an extreme case, the placing of a stall outside a property interferes with a legal right to light entering at its windows. [87]

"Particular damage"
The requirement that a plaintiff who has not suffered the infringement of a legal right must show "particular (sometimes referred to as "special") damage" is of considerable antiquity. The rule was created by the courts as an emanation of judicial policy to avoid numerous plaintiffs bringing proceedings in respect of a single tortious act. [88] An obstruction of the highway might affect many hundreds if not thousands of individuals. As an oft-cited *dictum* makes clear: "if one man may have an action, for the same reason a hundred thousand may." [89] The "particular damage" rule therefore emphasises the need for the plaintiff to have suffered uniquely in order to distinguish him from all other members of the public to avoid overwhelming the judicial process. Whilst the courts have

---

[84] E.g., *Westminster City Council v. Freeman* (1985) NLJ 1232.

[85] *Boyce v. Paddington* [1903] 1 Ch 109.

[86] Even if no legal right were infringed, the person directly affected would have suffered "particular damage" and thereby have standing, *infra*.

[87] *Boyce v. Paddington supra* n (85).

[88] It is now thought to originate in *Williams' Case* (1535) YB 27 Hen. 8 Mich p. 10.

[89] *Iveson v. Moore* 1 Ld Raym 486, 492.

generally been consistent in their requirement for "particular damage" to be shown, there has been considerable debate as to its meaning.

Whether there remains a need for this filtering mechanism is open to doubt. The prospect of a "hundred thousand" individuals troubling the courts and clogging the lists seems somewhat fanciful in modern times. Individuals do not normally trifle with the courts; costs alone are a sufficient barrier to deter all but the most genuine of claims.

Despite these objections, the particular damage rule remains. As Brett J. observed in the leading case of *Benjamin v. Storr* ,[90] a plaintiff must be able to show "a particular damage to himself beyond that which is suffered by the rest of the public. It is not enough to show that he suffers the same inconvenience in the use of the highway as other people do........The injury to the individual must be direct and not a mere consequential injury. ......Further the injury must be shown to be of a substantial character not fleeting or evanescent."

The requirement of uniqueness can be seen in the insistence that the damage inflicted be "beyond that suffered by the rest of the public".

Categories of Particular Damage"

(i) Physical injury
Because personal injury is normally direct, it usually confers the necessary quality of uniqueness upon the plaintiff. [91]

Only rarely, will the operations of street traders cause physical injury by virtue of any obstruction of the highway. But such injuries remain possible where the trading, perhaps from mobile vans and similar vehicles, occurs on or beside dangerous or heavily used highways.

(ii) Pecuniary loss
Pecuniary loss may also give rise to "particular damage". In cases of pecuniary loss, however, the plaintiff may not be the only individual who suffers loss of this kind. The courts have sometimes

---

[90] (1874) LR 9 CP 400, 406.

[91] *Greasley v. Codling* (1824) 2 Bing 263, 365; *Wall v. Morrisey* [1969] IR 10.

been willing to find the necessary uniqueness in the plaintiff's claim in the extent to which he or she suffers. Thus pecuniary loss suffered to a greater extent than other members of the public may suffice. [92] This, as we shall see, causes difficulties when the rule is applied. How much "additional" expense needs to have been incurred? Is the question relative? For example, should the infliction of a small burden on an impecunious individual be as important as a larger burden born by a wealthy organisation?

An obstruction forcing highways users to divert and take an alternative route may cause loss of trade to proprietors of business affected. Such might occur if an unlawful street fair largely blocks a right of way. The case-law on this point is not altogether free from doubt, but the emerging view is that this is capable of constituting "particular damage". In *Wilkes v. Hungerford Market Co Ltd.* [93] an unlawful obstruction on the highway diverted passers-by causing a book seller to suffer a loss of trade. The court held that this was a "peculiar and private" damage sufficient to maintain an action.

Lord Denman expressed some reservations about allowing a shop keeper to sue in cases where all other keepers in a street suffered loss in their businesses as a result of the diversion of passers-by. Yet, if sustained, this objection would produce the unsatisfactory result that an obstruction could be actionable if it affected only one shop keeper, but if it affected a larger number and became a more serious problem, the right of civil action would be lost.

Despite its consistency with such venerable authority as *Iveson v. Moore*, [94] the status of the decision in *Wilkes* has been doubted following *obiter* remarks made in the House of Lords in *Ricket v. Metropolitan Railway Co.* [95] Subsequently some judges thought that *Wilkes* had been overruled by *Ricket*, [96] but it seems that this was not so. *Wilkes* is supported by the classical authority of *Benjamin v. Storr* [97] which accepts the principle that damage to

---

[92] *Gravesham BC etc v. BRB supra* n. (83).
[93] (1835) 2 Bing (NC) 28.
[94] 1 Ld Raym 486.
[95] (1867) LR 2 HL 175, 188, 189.
[96] See eg Willes J in *Becket v. Metropolitan Rly.* (1867) LR 3 CP 82.
[97] (1874) LR 9 CP 400.

trade can constitute particular damage. [98] It is likely that *Wilkes* is still good law. Thus where the plaintiff has property near a highway which has been unlawfully obstructed by street trading and he is thereby put to greater expense in the conduct of his business or suffers a diminution in business, he is probably to be regarded as having suffered "particular damage" sufficient to maintain an action for damages. [99]

This proposition finds modern support in *Gravesham BC and the Port of London Authority v. British Railways Board* [100] where one of the plaintiffs was held to have suffered "particular damage" because the alleged public nuisance caused it to suffer significant but non-recurring expenditure.

The decision is a lenient one because other members of the public affected were also put to significant expense which might, in time, have exceeded that of the plaintiff. In other words, the court seemed to take a relaxed approach to the need to establish uniqueness of damage. [101]

Interference with business can also occur where the plaintiff is put to expense to avoid pollution. For example, in *Benjamin v. Storr* [102] the defendant auctioneers loaded and unloaded horse drawn vans outside the plaintiff's coffee shop in a narrow street throughout the day thereby obstructing access to the shop and blocking natural light forcing the plaintiff to burn artificial light all day. The stench of the horses also made the premises "incommodious and uncomfortable". The losses, and, in particular, the expenditure of burning gas for lighting, were held to be direct and sufficient to constitute "particular damage".

In other cases, occupiers of premises have been able to maintain an action for the obstruction of their access. Such occurred in *Barber*

---

[98] See also Greer LJ in Bundy, *Clark and Co. Ltd v. London and N. Eastern Rly Co.* [1931] 2 KB 334, 353-4, 362; Lord Hanworth MR in *Harper v. G N Haden & Sons Ltd.* [1933] Ch 298, 306; Slade J in the *Gravesham* case [1978] Ch at 379, 398. The matter is discussed by Kodilinye (1986) 6 Legal Studies 182.

[99] The *Gravesham* case is a recent example of this, *supra* n. (83).

[100] [1978] Ch 379.

[101] See also *Birmingham & Midland Motor Omnibus Co. Ltd. v. Worcestershire CC* [1967] 1 WLR 409 where standing was conferred in circumstances in which similar objections would apply.

[102] *Supra* n (97).

v. Penley, [103] in which a theatre queue unreasonably obstructed the doors of the plaintiff's lodging house at a time when potential customers would be looking for lodgings, thus causing her to lose trade. *Lyons, Sons & Co v. Gulliver* [104] is to similar effect where the action was brought by a neighbouring shopkeeper whose access was obstructed. In the former case, North J held that whilst a theatre queue could be a public nuisance, it could also be a private one. [105] In cases where the nuisance is private, the "particular damage" rule has no application.

(iii) Delay and Inconvenience

The orthodox view seems to be that an individual who is merely inconvenienced by an obstruction is not a competent plaintiff. He cannot maintain an action since his inconvenience is likely to have been shared by other members of the public who, like him, have been compelled to make a detour. [106]

The courts have shown occasional discontent with the orthodox approach. *Smith v. Wilson* [107] provides an example of this. Here the removal of a bridge and the erection of a fence forced the plaintiff, an elderly local farmer, to take a longer route to market each week. Occasionally, the plaintiff hired a car to enable him to make the journey. The majority of the court decided that, although the damage pleaded in his case was "slighter" than the courts had previously admitted, the loss of time, inconvenience and hire charges were sufficient. Nevertheless there was at least some evidence of pecuniary loss.

Gibson J. stated: "The objection founded upon the necessity of peculiar injury is an artificial one. The object of suing is not to onerate the defendant with damages but to get the way restored. There is little danger nowadays of the multiplicity of actions which two centuries ago seems to have alarmed the judges". [108]

---

[103] [1893] 2 Ch 447.

[104] [1914] 1 Ch 631.

[105] See also *Dwyer v. Mansfield* [1946] KB 437, although the claim failed.

[106] See *Winterbottom v. Lord Derby* (1867) LR 2 Ex. 316; cf *Smith v. Wilson* [1903] 2 IR 45 where the court was not persuaded that, in modern times, there remained a need to filter actions by means of the particular damage rule. See also *Birmingham & Midland Motor Omnibus Co. Ltd. v. Worcestershire CC* [1967] 1 WLR 409.

[107] [1903] 2 IR 45.

[108] *Ibid.* at 75-6.

(iv) Reduction in Property Values

Unlawful street trading which constitutes a public nuisance becomes actionable by an owner of land whose property suffers a reduction in value because the access to that property is prevented or restricted.[109] The case-law on this point is mainly concerned with statutory compensation schemes, [110] but the principles are analogous since it was held in *Becket v. Midland Railway Company* [111] that particular damage must be shown to qualify under one of these schemes. Here, the plaintiff was able to bring a claim for damages after the defendant had so constructed an embankment that it interfered with access and light to his premises to such an extent that the property sustained a permanent reduction in its value.

The Canadian decision in *Culp v. Township of East York* [112] suggests that a claim in damages can be brought even if access to the property is unaffected provided enjoyment of the land is impaired as a result of a public nuisance on the highway. In this case the claim was made in respect of increased noise after the local authorities unlawfully positioned traffic lights outside the plaintiff's property having omitted to secure the necessary approval.

The decision is significant because, not only was access unaffected, but the court decided that damages could be awarded for inconvenience and loss of enjoyment of the property even if there was no evidence of any permanent reduction in the value of the land. [113] If this properly represents English law, it is arguable that, for example, an *ultra vires* designation of a street for street trading purposes which results in trading which materially interferes with the enjoyment of adjacent property might permit a claim in damages for nuisance.

There is authority that the only cognisable loss is loss to the value of the land. Compensation could not be claimed for loss which was personal to the owner or related to some use of the land. Such

---

[109] For a discussion, see Kodilinye (1986) 6 Legal Studies 182.

[110] Lands Clauses Consolidation Act 1845; Railway Clauses Consolidation Act 1845.

[111] (1867) LR 3 CP 82.

[112] (1956) 6 DLR 2d 417.

[113] This was so because the lights would either be removed or the necessary approval acquired.

an approach prevented "particular damage" arising where the street trading interfered with the occupation of the premises or the trade carried on inside them. [114] However, these propositions derive originally from *Ricket* and, as we have seen, may not now be authoritative if *Wilkes* is now regarded as good law.

Conclusion

At the level of principle, the requirement to show "particular damage" is a restraint designed to limit the enforcement of the public's right of free passage on the highway to cases where limited cognisable private interests have been affected. Its existence demonstrates the absence of a judicially recognised communitarian interest in keeping those highways unobstructed.

At a more practical level the requirement was introduced as a creature of judicial policy for the particular purpose of avoiding the choking of the courts by a multiplicity of actions. This threat has, in modern times, virtually disappeared and the rule is obsolete. It, however, remains so firmly entrenched in the law that it is likely that the intervention of Parliament would be necessary to remove it.

---

[114] Eg *Argyle Motors v. Birkenhead Corporation* [1974] 1 All ER 201.

CHAPTER 20

COMPENSATION FOR ABUSE
OF REGULATORY POWERS

If a licensing authority abuses its powers, the primary remedies are available by way of appeal and review. Judicial review in particular provides the means by which the invalid decision can be declared void, and the trader treated according to law. A licence wrongfully refused may subsequently be granted, or a condition improperly included in a licence can be quashed. In each case, however, the trader may well have suffered a loss of profits, even a loss of livelihood, until the administrative illegality is cured. The question now to be considered concerns the very limited circumstances in which, under English law, compensation for such loss may be available. The problem, as we shall see, is that there is no general right to damages for maladministration.

Liability in Tort

A public authority may sue and be sued in tort. The ordinary principles of the law of tort apply to public bodies although there are restrictions which exclude liability in certain cases. As so often in the law relating to street trading, the applicable law is difficult to state with any certainty. Many cases will raise issues on the "edge of developments of the law".[1] The courts have acknowledged that the whole question of compensation for administrative "wrong doing" is unsatisfactory.[2] Complex questions surround such issues as whether a duty of care is owed by a public authority to take

---

[1] *Per* Schiemann J, *R v. Knowsley MBC ex p. Maguire* (1992) 90 LGR 653, 655.
[2] *Ibid.*

reasonable care in the exercise of its statutory functions. Can an individual suffering loss as a result of the negligent exercise or failure to exercise a statutory power claim damages in respect of that loss? In what circumstances is purely economic loss recoverable?

It is proposed briefly to consider some of the salient principles of civil liability of public bodies as there may be cases in which cognisable loss is sustained, whether it be of a physical character, or falling within one of the recognised categories of recoverable economic loss.

Statutory Authority

A public authority may be empowered to take action which, in the absence of statutory authority for it, would be tortious. It may for example seize a trader's stall if it is not removed to a place of storage. [3]

The public authority is under no liability where the allegedly tortious act or omission is expressly or impliedly authorised by statute. In straightforward cases, the scope of the power will be clear from the statute. Occasionally this is not so, and the courts will be confronted with a power of somewhat indeterminate scope. In *Metropolitan Asylum District Managers v. Hill* [4] the public authority were liable for the nuisance caused by a smallpox hospital built near residential property. Although the authority had a statutory power to build, the statute did not specify the actual site for the hospital. Had it been shown that the hospital was erected in place authorised by the statute, its proximity to residential property would have given rise to an implied defence to an action for nuisance. But the Act specified no site, and there was no evidence that Parliament had intended the hospital to be built at the expense of private rights. The authority should have exercised its powers lawfully by choosing a more appropriate site.

This decision may have interesting consequences for street trading licensing authorities. The authorities may designate streets for street trading purposes, and, of course, the actual sites chosen are a matter for them. It is arguable that they could be

---

[3] E.g., London Local Authorities Act 1990, s. 35.
[4] (1881) 6 App Cas 193.

liable for some of the nuisance effects caused by street trading if the site chosen were inappropriate, for example if the street were one in a residential area.

It is, however, possible that a distinction could be drawn between some kinds of nuisance and others. The authority might not be responsible for all of them. The reason for this is that in the *Asylum* case the nuisance was the inevitable and inherent consequence of the proximity of the smallpox hospital. Since street trading is not inherently a nuisance of itself, [5] the presence of a nuisance depends on the manner in which trading is carried out. The authority may not be responsible for all of the actions of the traders. If this is correct it might relieve the authority of liability for nuisances caused by noise and other pollution. The nuisance caused by obstruction of the highway is a different matter. If, for example, this causes loss, liability may arise by analogy with the *Asylum* case.

Public authorities are bound to act within the four corners of the power conferred in order to legitimate what would otherwise be *prima facie* tortious. The authority can become liable if it attempts to achieve a lawful purpose but does not exercise due care in doing so. The classical dictum on this point is that of Lord Blackburn in *Geddis v. Proprietors of Bann Reservoir.*[6]

"...it is now thoroughly well established that no action will lie for doing that which the legislature has authorised, if it be done without negligence, although it does occasion damage to anyone; but an action does lie for doing that which the legislature has authorised, if it be done negligently."

Statutory authority thus extends only to carrying out activities with reasonable care.

Jenkins L.J subsequently considered that questions falling to be decided would be these:

"first, was the act which occasioned the injury complained of authorised by the statute?; secondly, did the statute contemplate that the exercise of the powers conferred would or might cause injury to others?; thirdly, if so, was the injury complained of an injury of a kind contemplated by the statute?; and, fourthly, did

---

[5] Except in so far as it may obstruct the highway.
[6] 3 App Cas 430, 455.

the statute provide for compensation in respect " of the injury in respect of which the claim is made. [7]

The defence of statutory authority is not necessarily available even where the works giving rise to the nuisance are authorised on a specific site. The authority may still be under a duty to minimise the harmful consequences of its actions. [8]

Negligence

Although public bodies are subject to the ordinary principles of the law of negligence, the street trader will encounter significant difficulties in claiming damages as a result of the negligent exercise of a licensing power. First, the possibility of liability is removed from some types of decision. Decision-making powers are conferred upon administrators by virtue of their expertise. There must be an area of decision-making or policy in which they may make decisions without the court assessing the reasonableness of their actions. The courts, as we have seen, are not suited to weighing the merits of competing policy arguments. This means that certain decision-making is unlikely to give rise to an action for negligence. [9] This lifts the possibility of liability for decisions which it is inappropriate for the courts to examine. Where what is at issue is not so much the issue of policy, but negligence in the manner in which the public authority is actually performing its activities there is no reason to withhold liability. Thus a distinction is drawn between "policy" and "operational" matters.

In the present context, a policy-type question might be, for example, how many resources could be devoted to policing the street trading system. How refuse is collected after a street market would be an "operational" issue. Lord Wilberforce indicated that the more operational a power or duty may be the more readily a duty of care would exist so that the negligent performance of an operational matter would more readily give rise to liability. Liability may still arise even in the case of a "policy" question if the authority's

[7] *Marriage v. E Norfolk Rivers Catchment Board* [1950] 1 KB 284 at p. 306.

[8] *Manchester Corporation v. Farnworth* [1930] AC 171.

[9] *Dorset Yacht Co. v. Home Office* [1970] AC 1004; *Anns v. Merton LBC* [1978] AC 728; *Lonrho plc v. Tebbit* [1991] 4 All ER 973.

decision is *ultra vires* as well as in breach of a duty of care owed in private law.[10]

The dichotomy thus forged between policy and operational matters has been criticised as difficult to apply [11] and described as "fine and confusing" in *Rowling v. Takaro Properties.*[12] Controversy also surrounds its present validity as a tool of analysis since *Anns* was overruled in *Murphy v. Brentwood District Council.*[13] Their lordships judgments however did not address the policy/operational dichotomy. It was relied upon in *Lonrho v. Tebbit,*[14] but its validity is nevertheless open to some doubt.

If the dichotomy survives, the key to identifying a "policy matter" is its non-justiciability.[15] It concerns the weighing of competing public interests, perhaps of a political, economic or financial character.[16] The distinguishing feature of a political decision is that it involves considerations of "expense, political viability, and competing demands of governmental projects."[17] It seems clear, however, that without qualification, this principle does not fully explain the case-law, for decisions taken on the grounds of cost (ostensibly therefore policy matters) have been held to be negligent.[18] There are, however authorities which are consistent with this analysis of policy. These are cases such as *Anns* itself where the decision of how many houses to inspect would have been one for the authority.[19]

If a matter falls within the "policy" immunity, the courts cannot examine the reasonableness of the authority's actions because the matter is not an appropriate one for the courts to assess. Does it make any difference where the authority reaches its policy

---

[10] *Per* Lord Wilberforce in *Anns v. Merton LBC* [1978] AC 728 at p. 758.

[11] Bowman and Bailey (1986) CLJ 430.

[12] Quilliam J [1986] 1 NZLR 22,35.

[13] [1991] AC 398.

[14] [1991] 4 All ER 973.

[15] See Bowman and Bailey *loc. cit.*

[16] *Per* Browne Wilkinson V-C,in *Lonrho v. Tebbit supra* (14) at p 981.

[17] See *Takaro Properties, supra* n 12.

[18] Eg *Refell v. Surrey County Council* [1964] 1 WLR 358.

[19] See also *Rigby v. Chief Constable of Northamptonshire* [1985] 2 All ER 985 where the decision of the Chief Constable to use an inflammable type of CS gas in preference to another type which carried the risk of personal injury was a matter for him which could not be impugned. It was not, on the facts, negligent anyway.

by taking into account an irrelevant matter and so acts *ultra vires*? Consider the case where a local licensing authority negligently disregards the principles enunciated in *Ex p King* [20] and charges a commercial rate for its street trading licences. A trader who cannot afford these fees is denied his livelihood at least until the licensing authority's decision is quashed.

The orthodox view [21] appears to be that liability should not be imposed in such cases. The reason for this is that the policy questions affecting the level of fees are a matter for the local authority and not for the courts. It does not become an appropriate matter simply because the authority has acted *ultra vires*. This argument emphasises that the immunity focuses on whether the matter is suitable for judicial resolution, not whether the authority is acting in pursuit of a valid discretion.

The matter is not uncontroversial. Counter arguments would focus on the point that a policy decision which is *ultra vires* and negligent is not authorised. It may also be unreasonable in the *Wednesbury* sense and thus one in which the courts would be prepared to examine its rationality. Further, the taking into account of an irrelevant consideration, or the failure to take proper account of the state of the law governing the exercise of the power, could be seen as a failure at the operational level! [22]

Different issues may arise where what is alleged is the negligent failure to exercise a power to grant a licence. This may not involve policy questions but rather how policy is applied. An argument in favour of imposing liability could draw upon the general public law duty properly to consider whether to exercise a power. [23] This is because a public body is under a duty to give proper consideration as to whether its powers should be exercised. This could be seen to be an operational matter. [24]

---

[20] (1991) 89 LGR 696.

[21] See Craig, *Administrative Law*, 2nd edition, (1989) pp. 455-457, and Arrowsmith, *Civil Liability and Public Authorities*, at p. 176.

[22] See Arrowsmith, *loc. cit.* pp 176-7.

[23] *Anns v. Merton LBC* [1978] AC 728.

[24] *Ibid*. See also *Lonrho v. Tebbit* [1991] 4 All ER 973.

Liability under English Law is, however, only exceptionally imposed for negligent omissions. [25] Although the possibility of a wider basis of liability was apparently signalled by the decision in *Anns v. Merton LBC* [26] judicial retrenchment has characterised recent decisions. [27]

Whilst these matters do not appear to have been satisfactorily resolved, the balance of authority suggests that the courts are not in favour of imposing liability. In *R v. Knowsley MBC ex p Maguire* [28] taxi drivers who had unlawfully been denied licences but who were subsequently granted them, sought damages *inter alia* on the ground that the local authority had been negligent in misconstruing their powers. Significantly, Schiemann J held that negligence had not been established on the facts. He nevertheless emphasised that not every misconstruction of a statute could properly be described as negligent. There had to be something more. This clearly demonstrates that even if liability could be imposed as a matter of principle, the plaintiff may face significant difficulties in establishing negligence.

Since the authority had not been negligent, Schiemann J found it unnecessary to consider the whether, as a matter of principle, the local authority owed a duty of care to the applicants not to be negligent in their construction of the statute. The answer, he concluded, was "not self-evident". [29] Even if the duty of care existed in principle, it might be difficult to establish that the authority failed to exercise reasonable care in construing its powers. As we have seen, the task of understanding the scope of statutory discretionary powers is often a matter of considerable complexity: merely establishing that an irrelevant consideration affected the decision would not necessarily establish a lack of reasonable care on the part of the decision-maker.

---

[25] Where a special relationship exists. See W Rogers, Winfield and Jolowicz on Tort, 13th edition 1989, pp 91-96.

[26] [1978] AC 728.

[27] See, eg, *Hill v. Chief Constable of West Yorkshire* [1988] 2 All ER 238, and *Kun Yeu v. A-G for Hong Kong* [1988] AC 175 where the Privy Council appeared unwilling to impose liability for omissions in the absence of a special relationship.

[28] (1992) 90 LGR 653.

[29] *Ibid.* ap 661. Other decisons also seem inconclusive. See *Dunlop v. Woolahra Municipal Council* [1982] AC 158; *Rowling v. Takaro Properties* [1988] AC 473.

Even if arguments favouring liability were sympathetically received, the practical impact in the street trading context might be limited. A trader complaining of a negligent misconstruction of a statute resulting in a failure to grant him a licence would have to establish as a matter of evidence that the licensing authority would have granted him the licence had it acted lawfully. The discretionary nature of licensing powers makes this inherently difficult. More generally, the loss sustained-loss of profits - would generally be economic loss. This is normally s irrecoverable in the absence of a "proximate relationship". The courts are now hesitant to expand the categories of such relationships beyond the few which have already been recognised. [30]

A duty to avoid causing economic loss by negligent misstatement was, however, established in *Hedley Byrne v. Heller*.[31] This means that compensation may be recovered for negligent official advice where the necessary special relationship exits. [32] The local government ombudsman may be able to gain compensation if maladministration is established. [33]

The restriction on recovery for economic loss places a severe restriction on the recovery of damages for the negligent exercise of a licensing function. There are persuasive arguments that this is unjust. [34] Licences are fundamental to the pursuit by street traders of their livelihoods and these important interests deserve better protection in law. It is paradoxical that a trader may recover for damage negligently caused to his stall even if this includes an element for lost profits, but he cannot recover where his licence to trade is negligently withheld and his livelihood curtailed.

Breach of Statutory Duty

Street traders seeking compensation for abuse of regulatory power may in some cases be able to pursue a claim for damages for breach

---

[30] Eg, *Murphy v. Brentwood DC* [1990] 2 All ER 908.

[31] [1964] AC 465.

[32] Note, however, the recent restrictive approach in *Caparo Industries v. Dickman* [1990] 2 AC 605.

[33] See *infra* and note Mowbray [1990] PL 68.

[34] See Justice/ All Souls Review "Administrative Justice; some necessary reforms (1988) para 11.33.

of statutory duty. The caveat must immediately be entered, however, that it remains unclear whether such an action lies for a failure to confer a commercial benefit. In *Booth & Co (International) v. National Enterprise Board* [35] Forbes J. stated that even if individuals became eligible for a benefit by fulfilling statutory criteria, so that a public body had a duty to confer that benefit, the individuals concerned might not have a right enforceable by action for a breach of that duty. If correct, [36] it could have far-reaching implications for traders denied licences. There is, however, an argument that this should not apply where, as in the case of street trading licences, the authority has a duty to grant a licence where the applicant fulfils certain conditions. [37] An authoritative ruling on this point is awaited. [38]

If a statutory *duty* is imposed upon a public authority, any person who suffers loss as a result of a breach of that duty may sometimes be able to seek damages. It is not necessary to prove that the public authority was negligent; and limitations on the recovery of economic loss do not normally apply, although much will turn upon the interpretation of the statute in question. [39] For an action to succeed, it has to be shown that the enactment was intended to confer a right of action on the class of individuals to which the plaintiff belongs. [40]

The doctrine is traditionally parasitic upon the imposition of a statutory *duty*. An attempt, to extend it to statutory *powers* recently occurred in *R v. Knowsley MBC ex p Maguire* [41] where it was alleged that a public authority is under a *duty* not to misconstrue

---

[35] [1978] 3 All ER 624.

[36] This was stated only in the context of an interlocutory hearing on an application to strike out the plaintiff's claim.

[37] See *infra* pp. 389-390.

[38] The point was not argued in *R v. Knowsley MBC ex p Maguire* (1992) 90 LGR 653. If Forbes J's dictum had been advanced successfully it could have been fatal to this element of the plaintiff's claim.

[39] *Cutler v. Wandsworth Stadium Ltd.* [1949] AC 398; *Read v. Croydon Corporation* [1938] 4 All ER 631; *R v. Knowsley MBC ex p Maguire* (1992) 90 LGR 653 where no objection was raised to a claim by taxi drivers for damages for lost profits after licences were refused. On the point concerning economic loss cf *Merlin v. British Nuclear Fuels plc* [1990] 3 WLR 383 where the question turned on the particular construction of the Nuclear Installations Act 1965.

[40] The taxi-drivers failed on this point in *Ex p Maguire supra* n. (38).

[41] *Supra* n. (38).

the ambit of its statutory *powers*. The point was left open, although Schiemann J remarked that it was not "self-evident" that such a duty could be imposed. [42]

Also fundamental is the nature and scope of the duty imposed. This can determine whether a public body is actually in breach. Sometimes the obligations imposed are absolute; [43] but if this were the general rule it would often place an unreasonable burden on public authorities. [44] If an absolute obligation is imposed, for example, on a trader to sell food complying with safety standards, if the burden became intolerable, the courts reason that he or she can cease trading. A public body cannot divest itself of its responsibilities in this way, and so is less likely to be subjected to absolute obligations where even the utmost skill and diligence may not be sufficient to discharge the duty. The duty may simply require that the public authority exercise reasonable care to achieve the object of the legislation. In *Read v. Croydon Corpn.*, [45] for example, a duty to provide "pure and wholesome water" was held to require only that reasonable care and skill in then provision of the water supply.

This may be important in the street trading context particularly in relation to the prohibition on Sunday trading. The local authority is under a duty to enforce the Shops Act 1950, but this has not been seen as absolute: the expense of so doing may sometimes be relevant in determining whether proceedings should be brought. [46] Further, the authority has a discretion in the manner in which the objective to be achieved, the duty is unlikely to be absolute; for example, the duty to enforce the Shops Act 1950 need not require proceedings to be taken where other means of enforcement would be equally effective.

Whether an action is possible will depend upon the construction of the statute under which the duty is imposed. This process is not straightforward. Statutes do not often expressly state that a right to damages is conferred and so the courts will have to undertake a complex inquiry to determine whether such an intention can be

---

[42] *Ibid* at p. 661.

[43] For example, see the duties imposed under the Food Safety Act 1990.

[44] *Hammond v. St Pancras Vestry* (1874) LR 9 CP 316, 322, per Brett J.

[45] [1938] 4 All ER 631,esp 650-651.

[46] *Stoke-on-Trent City Council v. B & Q (Retail) Ltd.* [1984] AC 754, 769.

implied in the statute and the circumstances of its enactment. [47]
This burden on the courts is a matter about which judicial concern
has been expressed, but with little effect. [48]

Not every breach of statutory duty which causes an individual
to suffer loss is actionable. Restrictions on liability may derive
from the words of the statute, its purpose, and the availability of
other remedies. As already indicated, a key issue will be whether
there is a definable class of individuals intended to benefit from
the duty, and whether Parliament intended a private right of
action to be conferred. [49]

A damages remedy is presumed to have been intended where no
other remedy is available. Accordingly, where a statute imposes a
penalty for non-compliance with the duty, there is a weak
presumption this is the exclusive remedy: no action in damages will
normally lie. [50] The presumption is capable of being overridden [51]
as it was in *Read v. Croydon Corporation.* [52]

The tests are not straightforward in their application and so do
not by themselves afford certainty of outcome. Regrettably, they
often need to be interpreted through the medium of the court
making litigation more likely. [53]

Breach of a Duty to Confer a Licence

Under the statutory licensing schemes there is a duty to grant a
licence once the authority has made a determination that the
trader fulfils certain conditions. [54] The trader cannot seek damages

---

[47] See in particular *Merlin v. British Nuclear Fuels Ltd., supra* n. (39).

[48] *Cutler v. Wandsworth Stadium Ltd.* [1949] AC 398, 410, *per* Lord du Parq.

[49] *Hague v. Deputy Governor of Parkhurst Prison* [1991] 3 All ER 733 HL; *West Wiltshire DC v. Garland* [1993] The Times, March 4th.

[50] *Doe v. Bridges* (1831) 1 7 Ad 847, 849; see also *Pasmore v. Oswaldtwistle Urban Council* [1898] AC 387, 394 and *Lonrho v. Shell Petroleum (No.2)* [1982] AC 173.

[51] *Ibid.* [1982] AC 173, 185.

[52] [1938] 4 All ER 631 where the Waterworks Clauses Act 1847 provided a penalty for breach of statutory duty, but on the true construction of the Act this did not exclude a damages remedy.

[53] See Schiemann J in *R v. Knowsley MBC ex p Maguire supra* n. (38); also *Cutler v. Wandsworth Stadium Ltd.* [1949] AC 398.

[54] Para 3 (5) of the street trading code (sch. 4 of the Local Government (Miscellaneous Provisions) Act 1982) in which the licensing authority has a duty to grant the application for a licence unless one or more grounds specified in sub-paragraph (6) are established. Similar rules apply to the grant of licences in the City:

for breach of statutory duty until the authority has decided that he has satisfied the necessary conditions. As Lord Bridge stated in *Cocks v. Thanet DC,* [55] this is because to grant damages before the determination as to eligibility was made would, in effect, mean that the court was substituting its view for that of the authority. The applicant could only be said to have suffered loss once a determination had been made and the licence not conferred. A challenge to the authority's decision, or its failure to decide, can only be made by way of judicial review. [56] After reaching such a determination, if the licence is not granted an action will lie in private law. [57] Damages may not, however, be recoverable for the loss sustained in the period until the challenge by way of judicial review is brought. [58]

A further difficulty likely to be encountered by street traders seeking compensation is that regulatory enactments are intended to confer benefits on the public at large and not street traders. [59] Further, appeal rights are often conferred against the refusal of a licence or the imposition of conditions within it, and this also suggests that a remedy damages was not intended to be conferred. Finally an authoritative ruling is awaited on the question whether an action in damages will lie for a failure to confer a commercial benefit such as a trading licence.

Misfeasance in a Public Office

Public law powers are to be exercised in the public interest. If any power is used for purpose known to be outside the authority's jurisdiction it may give rise to a remedy in damages. As Nourse L.J stated in *Jones v. Swansea City Council,* [60] "The assumption of honour and disinterest on which the tort of misfeasance in a public office are deeply rooted in the polity of a free society."

City of London (Various Powers) Act 1987,s 8; and also the London boroughs: London Local Authorities Act 1990, s.25.

[55] [1983] 2 AC 286, 294.

[56] *Cocks v. Thanet DC ibid.*

[57] Arrowsmith, *Civil Liability and Public Authorities,* at p. 199; *Cocks v.Thanet DC* [1983] 2 AC 286.

[58] *Ibid.*

[59] This was contributory to the failure of the claim in *Ex p. Maguire, supra* n. (38).

[60] [1990] 1 WLR 54, 85.

The tort of misfeasance in a public office has been described as "well-established" [61] although there have been few cases in which its elements have been considered. It is an important tort, however, because it is free from limitations on the recovery of economic loss. [62]

Personal liability is also imposed on administrators and the local authority employer may not always be vicariously liable. [63] Vicarious liability applies to unauthorised acts which are connected with authorised acts and which are "modes" of doing these acts. If the unauthorised act is not a "mode" of doing the authorised act and is essentially independent, vicariously liability does not apply. [64] This seems to mean that malice in the exercise of public duties does not take an administrator outside the scope of his employment provided the malice occurs in the course of a decision which he was employed to make.[65]

The juridical nature of the power abused seems not to matter: whether the power originates in private law, such as a power under a contract, or under a statute, its abuse may be actionable. [66] This is a matter of considerable importance in the present context where the regulation of street trading relies on powers rooted in private law as well as public law. A local authority maliciously abusing its powers as the owner of a franchise market, for example, may be liable for damages for misfeasance even though the power abused originates in private law. [67] If correct, this means that nature of the office and not the power exercised which is important.

---

[61] Per Lord Diplock in *Dunlop v. Woollahra Municipal Council* [1982] AC 158, 173.

[62] *Bourgoin SA v. Ministry of Agriculture Fisheries and Food* [1986] QB 716 and also *Roncarelli v. Duplessis* (1959) 16 DLR (2d) 689 where lost profits were recovered.

[63] *Racz v. Home Office* [1992] The Times December, 17th.

[64] *Ibid.*

[65] Atiyah, *Vicarious Liability in the Law of Torts* (1967).

[66] *Jones v. Swansea City Council* [1990] 1 WLR 54 CA. The point was left open in the House of Lords but with an indication that the decision of the Court of Appeal on this point represents good law: see [1990] 1 WLR 1453,1458.

[67] It should be noted that the exercise of some kinds of power is not within the scope of the tort. In *Calveley v. Chief Constable of Merseyside* [1989 AC 1228, the making of a report was held not to be a "relevant exercise of authority". What constitutes a "relevant exercise of authority" is not clear.

What Conduct Suffices for Liability?
In the *Dunlop* case it was held that *ultra vires* administrative action is not by itself misfeasance in a public office. [68] A mere error of judgement in construing the ambit of a statutory power is not actionable. The defendant must be shown to have acted with malice, that is, for reasons of personal dislike or otherwise with an intention to injure the plaintiff. Alternatively, if malice is not present, the tort may be committed where the defendant acted unlawfully with knowledge that his conduct was unlawful and that his act would injure the plaintiff. [69]

A licensing power was used with an intention to injure the plaintiff in the important Canadian decision in *Roncarelli v. Duplessis* [70] where the plaintiff's liquor licence was revoked on the instructions of the Premier of Quebec because he was a prominent Jehovah's Witness who had annoyed the administration by furnishing bail for other Jehovah's Witnesses who had distributed pamphlets. The revocation here was not to further any object or purpose of the licensing legislation, but for a wholly extraneous purpose, and the administration was liable in damages for it. Rand J stated:

"Malice in the proper sense is simply acting for a reason and purpose knowingly foreign to the administration...(This was) a breach of an implied public statutory duty toward the appellant; it was a gross abuse of legal power expressly intended to punish him for an act wholly irrelevant to the statute, a punishment which inflicted on him, as it was intended to do, the destruction of his economic life...." [71]

The tort is also committed where the decision-maker knows that he has no power to reach the decision with the knowledge that it would injure the plaintiff. In *Bourgoin SA,* [72] French turkey

---

[68] *Dunlop v. Woollahra Municipal Council* [1982] AC 158.
[69] Wade *Administrative Law*, 6th edition, 1988, at pp 777 *et seq.*, esp. p 782, and this was recently upheld in *Bourgoin SA v. Ministry of Agriculture Fisheries and Food*. [1986] QB 716.
[70] (1959) 16 DLR (2d) 689.
[71] *Ibid.* at p 706.
[72] *Supra* n. (69).

producers, who required a licence in order to import turkeys into the UK, had their licence revoked ostensibly on public health grounds. The true reason for the revocation was the protection of home producers contrary to the Treaty of Rome. The French producers sought damages for misfeasance. The British government denied liability on the grounds that its purpose had not been to injure the plaintiffs. The Court of Appeal held that it would be sufficient to show that the government had acted in the knowledge that it had no power to revoke the licence.

Two areas of uncertainty remain. First, it is not clear whether actual foresight of injury is required. It may be sufficient to establish that the official ought to have known his actions would cause the plaintiff loss, although this has yet to be judicially determined. Further, much will turn on whether actual knowledge of a lack of legal competence is required. In principle, liability may be imposed where the official was reckless as to the scope of his powers; but there may be difficulty in extending liability to cover cases of negligence. In the *Dunlop* case [73] it will be recalled that "mere inadvertence" was insufficient. The imposition of liability in these circumstances might also undermine the restrictions on the recovery of economic loss in negligence cases.

The tort is of particular importance in the context of street trading. A "malicious" misuse of a statutory licensing power has been held to be actionable. [74] It seems that a local authority which revokes a street trading licence or consent for reasons which it knows to fall outside the scope and purpose of the licensing regime may thus find itself liable in damages to the trader. Any purported exercise of power in the knowledge that it lies beyond the authority of the licensing body is potentially actionable.

In an application case, damages could only be recovered where the trader can establish that, had the power not been used maliciously, he would have been granted a licence. Where this cannot be done, the trader has suffered no substantial loss. [75] A possible solution in such a case would be for the trader to take proceedings to compel the licensing authority to re-consider its

---

[73] *Supra* n. (68).

[74] *David v. Abdul Cader* [1963] 1 WLR 834 and, of course, in *Roncarelli v. Duplessis, supra* n. (70).

[75] See eg, *David v. Abdul Cader ibid.*

decision since this may result in the award of a licence. A claim might then be possible for the loss sustained in the intervening period in which no trading was possible. Alternatively, the applicant might show that the statutory criteria for the award of a licence were fulfilled in his case and that in those circumstances the licensing authority, directing itself properly, would have granted him a licence. [76]

Misfeasance is a potentially useful means of recovering compensation for certain abuses of licensing powers in the context of street trading. This is especially the case since the tort is not encumbered by the limitations on the recovery of economic loss which so limit the possibility of an action in negligence. It will be recalled that in both *Roncarelli* and *Bourgoin*, damages claims were admissible for lost profits.

Compensation for Lawful Administrative Action

Street traders may frequently suffer loss as a result of the lawful revocation of a licence or the terms on which trading is permitted. Such decisions are taken in the interest of the public. Revocation may be required, for example, because an increase in the volume of traffic means that the stall constitutes an unacceptable obstruction of the highway. [77] In such circumstances there may be no question of liability arising in tort; indeed, as we have seen, even if the action were tainted by irrelevant considerations and *ultra vires*, there would not necessarily be any liability in negligence, or for misfeasance in a public office.

If the inability to continue to pursue his livelihood were attributable to the fault of the individual trader the absence of compensation might be more acceptable. [78] The principle denying compensation is not so persuasive when the livelihood is removed where the interests of the public require it and the trader is not at

---

[76] See, for example, para 3 (5) of the street trading code in which the licensing authority has a duty to grant the application for a licence unless one or more grounds specified in sub-paragraph (6) are established.

[77] See, eg, para 5 (1) of Schedule 4 of the Local Government (Miscellaneous Provisions) Act 1982 permitting the revocation of a street trading licence on this ground.

[78] See para 5 (1) (b) of Sched 4 of the 1982 Act.

fault. The consequence is that the risk of altered circumstances is born by the trader concerned. Traders are extremely vulnerable to such matters as the increase in traffic in the streets in which they trade. It is something which they cannot possibly guard against, yet it may, in extreme cases, result in a loss of livelihood.

It has been argued [79] that risk of governmental activity should be shared by the community at large since the community is the beneficiary of such action. Acquiring the benefits of any revocation of a licence should entail bearing the burden of it. The idea of extending compensation to individuals affected by lawful governmental activity is not a novel one. It is already seen as appropriate in some circumstances to grant compensation as, for example, in where land is subject to compulsory purchase.

Arrowsmith argues that the rules of interpretation of statutes could theoretically be moulded so as to imply a right to compensation in no-fault revocation cases. [80] The courts already presume that Parliament did not intend (in the absence of clear words) a power to be exercised so as to impose the burden of providing a public benefit upon a private individual [81] and similar creativity could give rise to a right to compensation. Such an approach is, however, most unlikely in the foreseeable future. It would, in effect, pre-suppose that the street trader has a cognisable right to pursue his activities. This, as has been demonstrated, is inconsistent with the long history of judicial decisions in this field. Moreover if compensation were to be granted it would be on the basis of the restricted category of economic loss which is not normally recoverable even where negligence is established. The problem of defining coherent principles governing the scope of liability has lead commentators to reject the creation of an judicially implied duty to compensate. [82] If it is to be made available within specific regimes this is more appropriately a matter for the legislature.

---

[79] Hogg, *"Liability of the Crown"*, (1989) pp115-6; Arrowsmith *loc. cit.* p.240.

[80] *Loc. cit.*

[81] Eg, *Hall & Co. Ltd. v. Shoreham-by-Sea UDC* [1964] 1 WLR 240.

[82] Hogg *loc. cit.* p 117; Arrowsmith, *loc. cit.* p. 246.

CHAPTER 21

THE LOCAL GOVERNMENT OMBUDSMAN

Where maladministration has occurred, a complaint to a local government ombudsman will often provide a cheaper and more accessible remedy than pursuing litigation. Such a course may also provide a means of obtaining compensation for maladministration causing economic loss which could not have been recovered in an action for negligence.

The ombudsman's jurisdiction is, however limited: he cannot normally interfere in matters which are more appropriately resolved in the courts. There are signs that, in the case of complaints which might be raised by way of judicial review, the ombudsman should *prima facie* decline to intervene.

A further limitation is that there is no mechanism for compelling local authorities to act upon his recommendations. In most cases [1] where maladministration is established, local authorities do accept his recommendations. If they do not, the complainant has no right of appeal. But authorities which believe that they have been unjustly treated in the ombudsman's report seem willing to challenge it by way of judicial review. [2]

Jurisdiction
Whether the ombudsman has jurisdiction is determined by four criteria. First, the body against which the complaint is made must be one within his remit. Second, the matter must of the kind he is permitted to investigate. Third, the complainant must have

---

[1] 95%: Bailey, Jones and Mowbray, *Cases and Materials on Administrative Law*, at p. 184.
[2] *Infra.*

sustained injustice as a result of the alleged maladministation, and finally the matter must not be one more suited to judicial resolution.

(i) Relevant Bodies

Local government ombudsmen may investigate written complaints concerning the bodies falling within their jurisidiction. By s.25 of the Local Government Act 1974, local authorities are included within the ombudsman's jurisdiction. This brings the decisions of both members of the authority, its officers as well as the decisions any other body to whom a local authority has delegated its functions within the ombudsman's remit.[3] This means that in practice many street trading matters are dealt with by bodies subject to the scrutiny of the ombudsman. The complaint may now be made direct to the ombudsman by the complainant or on his or her behalf. [4]

The complaint must normally be made within twelve months from the date the complainant first had notice of the matter giving rise to the complaint, although later claims may be considered if the ombudsman considers it reasonable to do so. In *R v. Local Commissioner etc. ex p Bradford Metropolitan City Council*, Lord Denning MR considered that a complainant's the general lack of knowledge about the existence the ombudsman and the procedure for making complaints could constitute a reasonable ground for entertaining a late complaint.[5] Such an excuse may become less reasonable as time passes and the public generally become more aware of their existence.

(ii) The Subject Matter of Investigations

The complaint may be made " by or on behalf of any member of the public who claims to have sustained injustice in consequence of maladministration." [6] Crucial to this is what constitutes "maladministration." The Act offers no definition, although Schedule 5 removes certain matters from the ombudsman's remit.

---

[3] Section 25 (4).
[4] Local Government Act 1988 sched 3 para 5.
[5] [1979] 1 QB 287, 310.
[6] Local Government Act 1974, s.26 (1).

For example, no investigation can be conducted into the commencement or conduct of legal proceedings, nor generally into contractual or commercial transactions. Personnel matters such as recruitment and pay are also excluded.

"Maladministration"

Ombudsmen are to investigate maladministration, not to provide a forum in which policy decisions reached in the exercise of discretionary powers are disputed. They have no authority to usurp this policy making role since the local authority is ultimately responsible to the local electorate for its policies. The manner in which those policies are implemented is a different matter. Where injustice is caused to the individual at this "operational" level there is no reason to withhold redress. The immunity for policy matters is reflected in the scheme of the legislation. Section 34 (3) prevents the ombudsman from questioning "the merits of a decision taken without maladministration by an authority in the exercise of a discretion vested in that authority."

Much therefore turns on the meaning of maladministration. Crossman offered a "catalogue" of examples of maladministration: "bias, neglect, inattention, delay, incompetence, ineptitude, perversity, turpitude, arbitrariness".[7] Approving this list, Lord Denning MR explained that these matters indicate that administration and maladministration are concerned with the manner in which a decision is reached or discretion exercised. Eveleigh LJ described the jurisdiction as one concerned with "faulty administration" or "inefficient or improper management of (public) affairs". [8] Excluded from investigation are the merits of the decision itself. The ombudsman is not concerned normally with whether a decision taken in the exercise of discretionary powers is right or wrong.

The boundary between a "policy" issue and "maladministration" seems to echo the distinction between "policy" and "operational " matters introduced in *Anns v. London*

---

[7] HC Debs. 5th series vol. 735, col 51, Oct 18th 1966, approved by Lord Denning MR in *R v. Local Commissioner for Administration for the North and East Area of England, ex p. Bradford Metropolitan City Council* [1979] QB 287, 311, 314, 319.

[8] *Ex p Bradford, supra* at p. 314.

Borough of Merton. [9] The indeterminacy of these concepts makes the dichotomy difficult to operate as can be seen in *R v. Local Commissioner for Administration for the South ex p Eastleigh BC.*[10] where the policy/ operation distinction was crucial to the decision. Here a complaint was made that a local authority had been guilty of maladministration in allegedly failing to conduct proper inspections of a sewer. The council's policy limited inspection to four of the nine stages of construction to save costs. The tests actually carried out on the sewer were not adequate to identify the relevant defects.   The ombudsman found (i) that "good administration dictates that the council carry out inspections" in respect of all stages, although he added that the council could legitimately decide to inspect on fewer occasions; and (ii) that the sewer had not been fully or properly inspected because no test had been conducted which would have been likely to reveal its defects. The council realised that the ombudsman's report would expose them to the risk of a finding of maladministration whenever it failed to inspect at the nine stages of construction. This would require an expensive change in the council's policy.   The council argued, inter alia, that the report failed to respect the immunity of policy under s.34 (3) of the 1974 Act.   Nolan J, in the Divisional Court agreed that the ombudsman had trespassed into the forbidden zone of discretionary policy.

In the Court of Appeal Lord Donaldson MR acknowledged that the choice of test was a matter for the authority and they might have substituted an equivalent test in place of the ball test. Maladministration lay in the inadequacy of the chosen test which was not capable of detecting the defect. [11]

Parker L.J. also thought that there had been maladministration because the tests chosen were not designed to ensure that the sewer had been constructed according to the Regulations. However, the ombudsman's statement that good administration required inspection at all stages of construction had been an improper one. [12]

---

[9] [1978] AC 728.
[10] [1988] 1 QB 855.
[11] *Ibid.*At p. 864.
[12] *Ibid* at p. 864.

Taylor L.J. decided that the number and occasions of the inspections was a matter for the council as was a decision as to the type of inspection employed. The ombudsman had trespassed into the policy zone by expressing a view as to what test should be adopted. Maladministration, in his opinion, could only occur where a particular test had been required by the council and it had not been carried out.[13]

There was also confusion about the policy/operation distinction at a more general level. Lord Donaldson MR stated "Administration and maladministration have nothing to do with the nature, quality or reasonableness of the (policy) decision itself." [14] This suggests that any consideration of the merits of a policy decision is *ultra vires*.

The better view is probably that of Parker L.J. whose judgment is more faithful to the words of s.34 (3):

"The terms of s. 34 (3) do not preclude the ombudsman from questioning the merits of all discretionary policy decisions, but only those taken without maladministration." [15]

Commentators have argued that this decision enables some policy questions to be questioned where the manner in which the policy is formulated is tainted. This would leave only the substance of policy within the immunity. There is, for example, some force in Jones' argument [16] that maladministration may be found on grounds closely analogous to those of the *Wednesbury* principles. A policy which is tainted by irrelevancy or improper purposes may on this view be condemned as maladministration. More controversially, a decision which is so unreasonable that it is perverse should not be immune from the ombudsman's jurisdiction. This seems sensible although it would enable the merits of policy to be questioned. The argument that this should be permitted is that the ombudsman is used as a sensible alternative to litigation and it would be undesirable if the principles operating under these two remedial

---

[13] *Ibid.* at p.870.
[14] *Ibid* at p. 863.
[15] *Ibid* at p.868.
[16] [1988] PL 608; 615-616.

structures were significantly to diverge. [17]   On the other hand it may be that, after *Ex p Croydon* [18] the courts may regard this type of issue as a matter more appropriate for judicial review than for the ombudsman, and may quash his report if he investigates. [19]

(iii) Injustice

The complaint is only admissible if the complainant has sustained injustice in consequence of the maladministration. The use of the term "injustice" avoids narrow and technical distinctions about such concepts as "loss" (and in particular the non-recoverability of economic loss). Yet there remains the problem of causation; the maladministration must have caused the injustice to be suffered.

This was a problem in *Ex p Eastleigh*. [20] Here the ombudsman had found that even if final inspection had properly taken place it was not certain that the defect would have been discovered so he recommended that the council contribute only a portion of the costs of the repairs. By majority the Court of Appeal held that the ombudsman had erred in so doing. The complainant could only be said to have suffered injustice if the failure properly to inspect was the reason why the defect had not been discovered. The maladministration must therefore be shown to be the effective cause of the "injustice" sustained by the street trader. In most cases, however, this should present little difficulty.

(iv) Legal Redress

A further limitation on the ombudsman's powers is found in s.26 (6) of the 1974 Act which provides that an investigation shall not be conducted where the complainant has a remedy which he may pursue (or has pursued) in the courts unless it is not reasonable to

---

[17] Jones *loc. cit.* at 617; Bradley [1980] CLJ 304, 332.

[18] *R v. Local Commissioner for Local Administration ex p Croydon London Borough Council* [1989] 1 All ER 1033.

[19] Discussed *infra*. This is so unless the proviso in s.26 (6) is applied. The tenor of remarks by Woolf LJ in *Ex p Croydon* suggests that the ombudsman should be cautious in subjecting a local authority to investigation in a matter which could be raised by way of judicial review because the latter procedure has safeguards for public bodies not found under the ombudsman regime.

[20] *Supra* n. (10).

expect that person to resort to that remedy (or have resorted to it). The provision precludes investigations which might "trespass" on the jurisdiction of the courts. [21]

A complaint of maladministration may raise issues which give rise to no cause of action. [22] In such a case the ombudsman has an exclusive jurisdiction. In other matters, maladministration may also embrace issues which would enable to the complainant to pursue a judicial remedy. S. 26 (6) clearly recognises this but enables the ombudsman to act where the proviso in the sub-section is applied. In such a case, the ombudsman's jurisdiction is *prima facie* co-exists with that of the courts. There are also cases in which the exclusive remedy lies in the courts and therefore the ombudsman will have to decline to investigate. The question is when this is so. When do the courts enjoy an exclusive competence?

The Effect of s.26 (6)
It is clear that s. 26 (6) operates as a threshold requirement so that the ombudsman who recognises that a matter is more suited to judicial resolution should decline to intervene at the outset, unless the proviso can be applied. Section 26 (6) may also come into effect once an investigation has commenced. If it becomes apparent during the investigation that the courts are the more appropriate forum for adjudicating the complaint, the ombudsman should consider exercising his discretion [23] to discontinue an investigation which has already been commenced; and it may be necessary for him to do so unless the proviso may be applied. One factor which he is entitled to consider in this process is the stage the investigation has reached. [24]

Non-Intervention
The ombudsman should decline to act where a judicial remedy exists *regardless of whether* any proceedings brought would be

---

[21] *Per* Lord Denning MR in *Ex p Bradford* [1979] 1 QB at p.310.
[22] Eg, where there is no duty of care: *Murphy v. Brentwood DC* [1991] 1 AC 398.
[23] Under s. 26 (10).
[24] *Ex p Croydon, supra* n. (18).

successful. [25] The ombudsman is only entitled to ask whether the court is the appropriate forum.[26]

The effect of the proviso is, however, that even if there is a judicial remedy available, it need not provide the sole remedy. The ombudsman may still investigate if it is not reasonable for the complainant to institute proceedings. In *Ex p Croydon*, Woolf L.J considered that where there is a tribunal or court which is "specifically designed" to deal with an issue that body *prima facie* should have an exclusive jurisdiction. The ombudsman should not investigate such a matter. [27]

In street trading cases, for example, in a dispute over whether a licence was properly refused, and where there is a right of appeal to the magistrates' court, [28] it seems that this appeal should normally be exercised rather than a complaint made to the ombudsman. This is because the magistrates' court would perhaps be regarded as "specifically designed" to deal with this matter since the jurisdiction is expressly conferred upon it by the statute concerned and by virtue of its long association with trying such matters. The ombudsman might intervene if, in exceptional circumstances, other factors made it unreasonable for the complainant to exercise the right of appeal, however.

In cases where the complainant is essentially raising a matter which could be raised by way of judicial review, Woolf L.J thought it particularly important that the ombudsman should not intervene. This is because the judicial review mechanism incorporates important safeguards for public bodies which are not present in the ombudsman regime. It is considered to be contrary to public policy for these safeguards to be circumvented by recourse to the ombudsman in a matter which was appropriate for proceedings by way of judicial review. [29]

---

[25] *R v. Local Commissioner for Local Administration ex p Croydon London Borough Council* [1989] 1 All ER 1033.)

[26] See esp. Woolf L.J. at p. 1044.

[27] *Ibid.* at p.1045.

[28] See, eg, para 6 of the code.

[29] [1989] 1 All ER 1033, 1045 and note *O'Reilly v. Mackman* [1983] 2 AC 437.

Conclusion

The ombudsman regime is undoubtedly an important and influential means of obtaining redress against maladministration by local authorities. One important study has concluded that "the impact of the Local Ombudsman upon local government has been impressive, both in relation to securing redress for complainants and in improving procedures." [30] It will almost always be preferable for the aggrieved street trader to ask the ombudsman to investigate a case in which he has jurisdiction than to initiate proceedings in the courts. As we have seen, in some cases the ombudsman will decline to intervene if it is reasonable for a judicial remedy to be sought. However, nothing prevents the street trader from initiating a complaint to the ombudsman; it is for him to decide whether he may investigate. The street trader should not pre-empt that decision by commencing legal proceedings unless there are special reasons for doing so.

---

[30] Lewis, Seneviratne, Cracknell, *Complaints Procedures in Local Government,*University of Sheffield, 1987, at p.59.

406

The considerations quoted undoubtedly an important and influential means of obtaining redress against maladministration by local authorities. One important study has concluded that the impact of the Local... in patterns of... government... be important both in relation to securing redress for complainants and in improving procedures. ...

BIBLIOGRAPHY

Alder, *Development Control*, London: Sweet & Maxwell Ltd., 2nd edit., 1989.

Arrowsmith, *Civil Liability and Public Authorities*, Winteringham: Earlsgate Press, 1992.

Bailey, *Cross on Local Government Law*, London: Sweet & Maxwell Ltd.

Bailey, Jones and Mowbray, *Cases and Materials on Administrative Law*, London: Sweet & Maxwell Ltd., 2nd edit., 1992.

Bellamy & Child, *Common Market Law of Competition*, London: Sweet & Maxwell Ltd., 3rd edit., 1987.

Butterworths' Law of Food and Drugs, London, 1993.

Cross (editor) *Encyclopedia of Local Government Law*, London: Sweet & Maxwell Ltd., 1980.

Cousins and Anthony, *Pease and Chitty's Law of Markets and Fairs*, Croydon: Charles Knight, 1984

Craig *Administrative Law*, London: Sweet & Maxwell Ltd., 2nd edit., 1989.

Fleming, *The Law of Torts*, Sydney: Law Book Co., 8th edit, 1992.

Goyder, *EC Competition Law*, Oxford: Oxford University Press, 3rd edit, 1993.

Green, Hartley and Usher, *The Legal Foundations of the Single European Market*, Oxford: Oxford University Press, 1991.

Hill and Redman's Law of Landlord and Tenant Vol 1, London: Butterworth, 18th edit., 1993.

Justice/All Souls Review "Administrative Justice; some necessary reforms, Oxford: Clarendon Press,1988.

Lewis, Seneviratne, Cracknell, *Complaints Procedures in Local Government*, University of Sheffield, 1987.

Megarry & Thompson, *Megarry's Manual of Real Property*, London: Sweet & Maxwell Ltd. 7th edit, 1993.

Morgan, *Retailers and the Local Authority*, London: Sweet & Maxwell Ltd., 1989.

Rogers, *Winfield and Jolowicz on Tort*, London: Sweet & Maxwell Ltd., 13th edition, 1989.

Sauvain, *Highway Law*, London: Sweet & Maxwell Ltd. 1989.

Snell, *Equity*, London: Sweet & Maxwell Ltd., 29th edit, 1990.

Wade, *Administrative Law*, Oxford: Oxford University Press, 6th edit., 1988.

Whish *Competition Law*, London: Butterworth, 3rd edit., 1993.

INDEX

Appeals
        see licences
Articles.. 101-102, 108, 178, 222, 250
Assistants.. 81, 241-242, 257

Attorney General.................... 70, 163, 168, 169, 355, 356, 358, 366
Auction sales
        not rival markets.. 89
Barrows.. 265, 267
Bias
        rule against.. 318-322
        test for.. 319-320
        mixed functions.. 320-321
        personal prejudice... 321
        necessity... 322
        waiver.. 322
British Railways Board.. 192
By-laws
        challenging.. 57-57-60
        children and young persons.................................... 49-50
        City, street trading in.. 257
        commons... 52
        esplanades..52
        food.. 50
        good rule and government.....................................54
        markets... 53
        nuisances, to suppress.......................................35, 52
        photographers.. 257
        pleasure fairs...51
        pleasure grounds.. 51
        street collections... 54
        travellers.. 52-3
        validity of... 54-57
        walkways.. 50-51